A Most Gallant Resistance:

The Struggle for Control of the Delaware River, 1775-1778

By
James R. Mc Intyre

In Memory of a Brother: David R. Mc Intyre 1955-2021

A Most Gallant Resistance: The Struggle for Control of the Delaware River, 1775-1778
Cover from
This edition published in 2022

Winged Hussar is an imprint of

Winged Hussar Publishing, LLC
1525 Hulse Rd, Unit 1
Point Pleasant, NJ 08742

Bibliographical References and Index
1. History. 2. American Revolution. 3. Delaware Campaign

Contents

Acknowledgments   6

List of Abbreviations   8

Introduction   9

Chapter 1-Defending Philadelphia   17

Chapter 2-Independence and First Tests   53

Chapter 3-Setting the Stage   78

Chapter 4-The Contest for the Delaware Round One:
Jockeying for Position   115

Chapter 5-The Contest for the Delaware Round Two:
The Battle of Red Bank   149

Chapter 6-Tightening the Noose- Preparations for
the Siege of Fort Mifflin   190

Chapter 7-The Siege of Fort Mifflin   225

Chapter 8-The Evacuation of the Forts and the
End of the Navy   254

Conclusion   301

Bibliography   312

Index   334

McIntyre has given us a thoughtful, deeply researched, and revealing inquiry into the ferocious fighting to take and to defend Forts Mifflin and Mercer on the Delaware River in the fall of 1777. He convincingly treats the struggle for the forts as a campaign unto itself, with the stakes never higher for both sides. A patriot success would have been disastrous for Sir William Howe's army in Philadelphia - perhaps even dooming it. A must-read, McIntyre's new volume is a genuine contribution to our understanding of a key chapter in the War for Independence. - Mark Edward Lender

Acknowledgments

In developing a study of this scope and depth, one accrues a myriad of debts. Some of these obligations are professional, some personal, some are intellectual and some emotional. Likewise, there are some that overlap into several categories. They are too numerous to count, so to anyone whom I miss below, my sincerest apologies.

On the intellectual side, there are those at the various repositories I have visited along the way, including the David Library of the American Revolution, the Historical Society of Pennsylvania, the Library Company of Philadelphia, the Museum of the American Revolution, the Philadelphia Maritime Museum, the Gloucester Historical Society, the Delaware Historical Society, the Society of the Cincinnati Library in Washington, D.C. and the Newbury Library in Chicago. In addition, there were the historical sites, including, Fort Mifflin on the Delaware, Redbank Battlefield, Valley Forge National Historic Park, and Cliveden Estate in Germantown, Pennsylvania.

In the realm of personal intellectual debts, I first have to thank the late Russell F. Weigley, Professor Emeritus from Temple University, a true mentor and gentleman. On a more practical level, this book would not have been possible were it not for Sue Yach, the Inter-Library Loan representative at Moraine Valley. She has filled some very obscure requests and provided me with the necessary research materials to make this work possible. Likewise, there was Dr. Katrin Marx Jaskulshi of the Hessische Staatsarchiv in Marburg, Germany who aided me in securing the permission to use the map of the attack on Fort Red Bank.

At my second-home the United States Naval War College, colleagues Stan D.M. Carpenter, K.J. Delamer and Andrew Zwilling were outstanding in their support for this project. Likewise, I owe my thanks to the various seminars and lectures given for this august institution in which I laid out the case for the significance of the contest for control the Delaware. I am grateful for the sometimes-challenging questions students posed in the course of these sessions as well. Collectively, they prevented me from going too far afield. The same can be said of Alexander Burns a rising star of a military historian, who has been interested in the project since I began writing. Alex has often posed insight questions which made me reconsider certain points the campaign. In addition, I must thank Michael C. Harris, who read the entire manuscript and of-fered very valuable commentary. This is a much better book as a result of his efforts. Finally, there was Daniel Popek, who generously shared some of the materials he collected for his outstanding regimental his-tory on the Rhode Island Continentals. This greatly enhanced my un-derstanding of the role played by the Rhode Island troops at both Forts Mercer and Mifflin.

Certainly, there are personal debts that are both intellectual and emotional. At the top of this category must surely be the late Dorothy "Dori" McDunn of the Fort Mifflin on the Delaware Historic site in Pennsylvania. She took a chance on a young, bookish and introverted historian and gave him the chance to be a docent at the site. This was an invaluable experience both personally and professionally, and it set in motion the circumstances that led to the book before you.

Likewise, one of my former students, Victoria Stewart, alerted me to the existence of Gregory M. Browne's MA Thesis, which helped a great deal in the early stages of the research. Conor Robison, a former student, and a truly gifted writer and historian in his own right, often posed questions about the operations on the Delaware River that forced me to rethink certain ideas on the conduct of the campaign as well.

Then there are the purely personal debts. First among these must be my late brother, David Mc Intyre who started the ball rolling by taking me to many of the Revolutionary War sites in and around Phila-delphia. It seems to have paid off. Likewise, to my mother, Florence Mc Intyre, who always encouraged and never discouraged my interests in history and my desire to study it professionally. I only wish both of you were here to see this project come to completion.

Finally, to my family, wife Catherine, daughters, Jessica and Tara, and son Nathanael, who have endured numerous trips to Forts Mifflin and Mercer historical sites, and watched their father drift off as he looked out on the river trying to visualize events that happened over two centuries ago. Thank you for your love, patience and forbearance. This work never would have come to fruition without all of you.

List of Abbreviations

JCC	*Journal of the Continental Congress*
JSAHR	*Journal of the Society for Army Historical Research*
JMH	*Journal of Military History*
LoD	*Letters of the Delegates to the Continental Congress*
MPNB	*Minutes of the Pennsylvania Naval Board*
NDAR	*Naval Documents of the American Revolution*
PA Arch	*Pennsylvania Archives*
PMHB	*Pennsylvania Magazine of History and Biography*
Washington, Rev. War	*Writings of George Washington, Revolutionary War Series*

Introduction

Most histories of the American War of Independence discuss what are usually regarded as the two major campaigns in 1777. Either they describe the invasion from Canada led by General John Burgoyne which resulted in his subsequent defeat and the surrender of his force at Saratoga, New York, or they focus on William Howe's Philadelphia Campaign. Often left out of these discussions, or treated only in passing, is the reduction of the Delaware River defenses. The struggle for control of the river engaged much of the resources and attention of Washington and Howe through the latter months of 1777. The following work proceeds from the premise that the fighting on the Delaware has been grossly under-appreciated by historians of the War of Independence. As a noted historian of the fighting, John W. Jackson asserted in 1973, "the Delaware engagements have been dismissed as unimportant except for a few studies by local historians."[1] In his solid but dated narrative of the War of Independence, the eminent historian Don Higginbotham paid scant attention to the fighting in and along the Delaware. Much the same is true of Robert Middlekauff's *Glorious Cause*. In his *Battles of the Revolutionary War, 1775-1781*, historian W.J. Wood does not address the fighting on the river at all.[2] Unfortunately, Jackson's assessment remains valid to the present. Indeed, most recent works which have focused on the Philadelphia campaign have generally neglected its final stages along the river.[3]

To an extent, this neglect is understandable. The common perception is that Gates' victory at Saratoga stood as the essential turning point in the war, though some have recently challenged this perception.[4]

Upon closer examination, however, as the following pages will show, the struggle for control of the Delaware encompasses a significant effort all its own, and one which contemporaries - both in the Philadelphia area and beyond, kept under close observation. It will assert that the continuing determination of the rebels to deny control of the river to the British sent a message to the French as significant in its own way as the victory at Saratoga.

Beyond the idea that the contest for control of the Delaware deserves greater attention than most historians have accorded it, several other lessons emerge from a close study of the fighting in the river and along its banks. First and foremost, the fighting along the banks of the Delaware offers a case study in what can be termed early modern joint operations, or "military actions conducted by joint forces and those Service forces employed in specified command relationships with each other, which of themselves do not establish joint forces." [5] Simply, the Delaware River campaign offers a prime example of the coordination of the land and sea forces in pursuit of a common goal. Certainly, there were other examples, however, the relatively confined parameters of the struggle for control of the river make this an excellent example.[6] By the time of the American War of Independence, the British possessed significant experience in this realm, to the extent that they had even "written the book" on the conduct of such operations.[7] The British skill in joint operations, in turn, makes the ability of the Americans to hold out as long as they did all the more impressive.

Secondly, the American defense of the Delaware River forts and the obstacles they protected stood as one portion of a much larger war effort against the Crown forces operating in Pennsylvania. All these exertions, however, lay under the control of one overall commander, George Washington. At the same time, Washington, while not directly involved, committed vital military assets to block Gen. John Burgoyne's invasion of New York as well. Thus, an investigation of this campaign permits an examination of the Commander-in-Chief's methods of balancing the competing claims for resources between two distant theaters. All of this serves as excellent material for an examination of the George Washington's leadership style.

Lastly, the Delaware River campaign allows for an examination the combination of land and maritime military assets conducted on an inland waterway, what is referred to today as a 'brown water' operation.[8] What the following study will show is that while these operations are often overlooked by historians, they often possess a great deal of significance for understanding the final outcome of a campaign.[9]

In order to examine the defense of the Delaware in the requisite depth to mine its lessons, it is first necessary to place this fighting within to context of the overall plans for the defense of Philadelphia. This is the task of the first chapter. It highlights the importance of Philadelphia to the colonial economy and political leadership of the American Revolution.[10] In addition, it details the previous attempts of successive colonial and revolutionary governments to develop defenses on the Delaware River to protect the city. The initial efforts of both the national and state governments to develop maritime defenses will receive particular attention.

Chapter two continues the story of the evolution of the Delaware River defenses through the beginning of 1776. In addition, it described the first clashes between the nascent Pennsylvania State Navy and Royal Navy warships in the Delaware Bay. The weaknesses in the river defenses exposed by these clashes and the efforts of Pennsylvania leadership to strengthen them are examined as well. Within the preceding context, the chapter highlights the obstacles posed in the development of the river defenses by competing calls for the resources of Pennsylvania. It thus underscores the competing demands placed on the state by the local and Continental establishments, during which the latter tended to win out.

Chapter three sets the stage by situating the fighting for control of the Delaware River in the broader context of larger Philadelphia Campaign of 1777. The evolution of Gen. William Howe's plans for the campaign will receive attention, as will the composition of the opposing forces. The maneuvers of the campaign beginning with the landing of the British forces at the Head of Elk in Maryland through the British capture of Philadelphia and the battle of Germantown will be discussed. The status and role of the Delaware defenses at various junctures during the fighting on land will be addressed where relevant. Finally, the importance of cooperation between the land and maritime forces of both belligerents will be discussed.

Chapter four, in turn, examines the shifting focus of the campaign in the aftermath of the battle of Germantown. It examines how the commanders on both sides conceived of the river in their planning for subsequent operations. Likewise, the growing importance of control of the Delaware River for the successful British occupation of Philadelphia will receive attention. In addition, the chapter examines the heightened emphasis on the preparation of the river defenses as the operational focus shifted to the Delaware. It examines the initial British efforts in the Delaware Bay and the development of their plans to open the river. The first steps in the British opening of the river, including the capture of Billingsport, New Jersey and attempts to shift the chevaux de frise are discussed. The role of the Pennsylvania State Navy, a matter of some controversy is examined in this chapter as well. While many historians have either lauded or derided the efforts of this force in defense of Philadelphia, few have taken the time to objectively assess its capabilities in relation to it mission. Lastly, the chapter highlights the importance of cooperation between land and maritime forces for achieving the objectives of both sides.

The fifth chapter, then, focuses on the successful American defense of Fort Mercer. The development and implementation of the Hessian plan for the attack, such as it was, is addressed. The employment the land and naval forces of both sides in connection with the assault on the post and its successful defense receive detailed analysis in connection with the concept of joint operations, specifically those of the fort's defenders and the Pennsylvania Navy. The Hessian commander Col. Count Carl Emil von Donop's attack, the reasons for its failure, and its effects on the morale of both sides will receive examination. In addition, the loss of the Royal Navy vessels HMS *Augusta* and HMS *Merlin* will be highlighted.

Following the repulse at Fort Mercer, the Howe brothers once again shifted the focus of their plans. They now determined on an all-out assault on Fort Mifflin to destroy the post and all the ships and crews of the Royal Navy to remove the sunken obstructions in the river. The preparations for this showdown on both sides are examined thoroughly in chapter six. It underscores the effect that adverse weather conditions could exert on operations as well.

The "joint" aspect of both British and American forces in their duel for control of the Delaware River features prominently in chapter seven which focuses on the siege and defense of Fort Island, later named Fort Mifflin. On the British side, this consisted in the use of shore batteries as well as ships of the Royal Navy in order to batter the fort into submission, while the American defenders of the fort routinely called upon the ships of the Pennsylvania Navy for assistance. The level of cooperation between the land and maritime services of the opponents is highlighted, especially with regards as to its effect on the overall outcome of the attack on Fort Mifflin.

Late on the night of November 16, 1777, the last defenders of Fort Mifflin abandoned the works, after setting fire to the few pieces of equipment that remained serviceable. With the fort in the Delaware abandoned, the works at Red Bank no longer served a purpose, and Gen. Charles Cornwallis's advance northward from Billingsport placed the garrison at Fort Mercer in jeopardy. As a result, this work was abandoned as well, with the magazine detonated to prevent the munitions there from falling into British hands. These events form the core of the eighth chapter, as do the efforts of the remaining ships of the Pennsylvania Navy to escape up the Delaware River above the city of Philadelphia.

Finally, the conclusion addresses the campaign for control of the Delaware in connection with the larger 1777 Campaigns in both the Delaware and Hudson River Valleys. The areas of joint operations are highlighted in the discussion. It argues that William Howe, while successful in his objective of taking Philadelphia, failed to destroy Washington's Army. His partial success was not enough to overturn the stunning defeat of Burgoyne's force in the Hudson Valley, or St. Leger's force being turned back at Fort Stanwix. Therefore, there was nothing the British possessed that could restrain the French ministry from advocating involvement in the war on the American side. Further, it will point out just how adept the American political leadership were at exploiting these successes and using them as propaganda to sway the court at Versailles.

At the same time, the work highlights the manner in which what are today characterized as joint operations actually possess a fairly long history. A close examination of the fighting along the Delaware River in 1777 reveals that the British Army and Navy possessed a fairly advanced conception of how to conduct these types of operations. In addition, it will demonstrate that the Americans quickly developed their own understanding of how such actions should be conducted. One aspect that will emerge from the analysis is the degree to which cooperation between commanders, often times on a very personal level, stands as a key element in the relative success or failure of these operations.

Likewise, a close examination of the fighting on the Delaware River in 1777 supports the notion that the campaign on the Delaware River should be recognized as constituting a campaign within a campaign. Due to the numbers engaged, the ferocity of the fighting, the contest for control of the Delaware prevented either belligerent from launching any other significant operations during October and November 1777.

Before proceeding, a few caveats to the reader are in order. As noted above, most accounts of the Philadelphia Campaign of 1777 place the great land battles of Brandywine and Germantown at center stage, perhaps describing the fighting in the river in a few pages here and there. The current narrative juxtaposes that approach by placing the river and the fighting that occurred there as the focal point. While the land battles are discussed, their coverage is consciously general in nature. Those interested in gaining a more thorough knowledge of the battles of Brandywine, Germantown and Paoli are directed to the bibliography and the end notes for a list of relevant works.

Secondly, major players in the Delaware River campaign are identified and their biographies given when they are first mentioned. The biographies of lesser figures are contained in the end-notes to facilitate the flow of the narrative.

Lastly, a note on spelling. The eighteenth century was a time of creative spelling. Thus, the reader will see chevaux-de-frise, chevaux de frize, and chevaux de fries. I have decided to use chevaux de fries in the main text. At the same time, I have generally left the original spellings as they were from all primary accounts so as to preserve the authenticity of the source. The only exceptions being when these interfered with clarity.

CHAPTER NOTES

[1]John W. Jackson *The Pennsylvania Navy, 1775-1781: The Defense of the Delaware* (New Brunswick, NJ: Rutgers University Press, 1974), p. vii.

[2]See Don Higginbotham, *The War of American Independence: Military Attitudes, Policies and Practice, 1763-1789* (Boston: Northeastern University Press, 1983), Robert Middlekauf, *The Glorious Cause: The American Revolution, 1763-1789*(New York: Oxford University Press, 1982) and W.J. Wood, Battles of the American Revolutionary War, 1775-1781 (New York: DeCapo Press, 1995), pp. 92-114.

[3] These works include Gregory T. Edgar, *The Philadelphia Campaign 1777-1778* (Westminster, MD: Heritage Books, 2004), Thomas McGuire, *The Philadelphia Campaign.* 2 vols. (Mechanicsburg, PA: Stackpole Books, 2006-7) and Stephen R. Taaffe, *The Philadelphia Campaign, 1777-1778.* (Lawrence: University of Kansas Press, 2003).

[4] See Theodore Corbett, *No Turning Point: The Saratoga Campaign in Perspective* (Norman: University of Oklahoma Press, 2012).

[5]Joint Chiefs of Staff, JP3-0 *Incorporating Change*, 17 January 2017 – 22 October 2018 (Washington, DC: United States Department of Defense, 2017), p. 1-1.

[6] For an overview of amphibious operations requiring cooperation between land and naval forces, see Jeremy Black, *Combined Operations: A Global History of Amphibious and Airborne Warfare* (Lanham, MD: Rowman and Littlefield, 2018). For additional materials specifically related to the British experience in amphibious warfare during the eighteenth century, see Richard Harding, *Amphibious Warfare in the Eighteenth Century: The British Expedition to the West Indies, 1740-1742* (Suffolk, UK: The Boydell Press, 1991); David Syrett, "The British Landing at Havana: An Example of an Eighteenth Century Combined Operation." *The Mariner's Mirror.* 55, (1969): 325-332, and "The Methodology of British Amphibious Operations during the Seven Years' War" in *The Mariner's Mirror.* 58, (1972): 269-280.

[7]Thomas More Molyneux, *Conjunct Expeditions, or Expeditions that have been Carried on Jointly by the Fleet and Army: with a Commentary on Littoral Warfare* (London: R and J. Dodsley, 1759).

[8] They are given the name brown water operations in order to differentiate them from fighting between ships on the high seas, which are termed blue water operations.

[9] The key naval theorists who first wrote on this period overlook these sorts of operations complete. See Sir Julian Corbett, *England in the Seven Years' War: A Study in Combined Strategy* (London: Longmans, Green, and Company, 1907) and Alfred Thayer Mahan, *The Influence of Sea Power upon History, 1660-1783* (Boston: Little, Brown and Company, 1890).

[10] The terms American Revolution will be used throughout to refer to the political developments surrounding the break of the North American colonies from British rule. By the same token, War of Independence will be used when referring to the military operations around achieving or suppressing the independence movement.

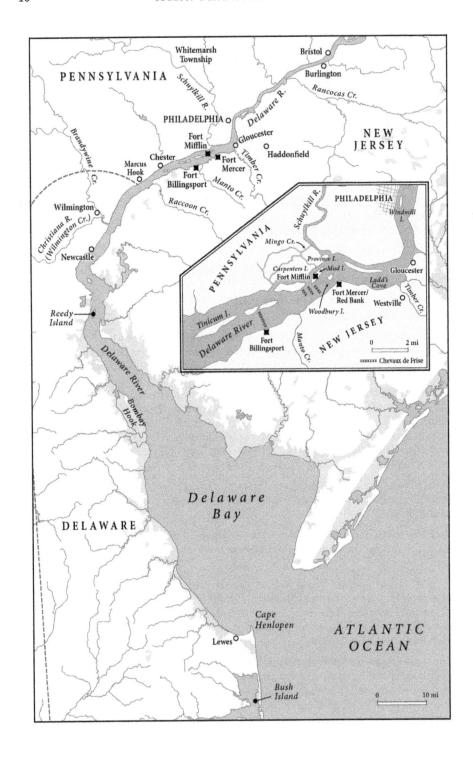

Chapter One
Defending Philadelphia

"Rivers throughout history, have been
vital arteries of transportation, economics and
communication."[1]

No one living in North America in 1775 would have doubt-
ed the importance of Philadelphia to the economic life of Britain's
North American colonies. The city possessed a major port, situated
well inland and therefore protected from the storms that often rav-
aged the Atlantic coast. The location offered protection from surprise incursions by attackers as well. Due to its central location and
the enlightened policies of its first proprietor, William Penn, the city
grew quickly into the most populous of the coastal urban centers. By
the time the British invaded the Delaware Valley in force in 1777,
the city included some 5,000 dwellings and 3,000 other buildings,
with the population standing somewhere between 30 and 40,000,
making it the fourth largest in the British Empire.[2] In addition,
the city boasted nearly three miles of waterfront with nearly one
hundred docks and wharves, the latter being constructed mainly of
wooden frames filled with stone jutting out into the Delaware River.
These facilities could service roughly a thousand vessels per year. In
order to protect these vessels and their cargoes, the city maintained
a police force and several fire companies. The wealth generated by
the port helped to support a thriving cultural and intellectual community as well. [3]

The city proper encompassed an area eight blocks west of the
Delaware River. If the suburbs of Northern Liberties and South-
wark were included, that area expanded to fourteen blocks. Beyond
the urbanized area there were sprawling farms and a scattering of
country houses.[4]

The same factors that combined to make Philadelphia such
a thriving center of economic life made it an appealing target for
potential enemies as well. Philadelphians were not ignorant of the
possible dangers they faced and took measure to look to their own
security. Through much of the first half of the eighteenth century
however, the efforts at colonial defense were blocked by the paci-
fist Quaker proprietors. The following pages will survey the devel-

opment of the river defenses of Philadelphia from the end of the French and Indian War (Seven Years' War in Europe) through the first year of the American War of Independence.[5]

Even with the political interference of the Quakers a more aggressive-minded group, the Philadelphia Associators, had succeeded in creating some defenses, such as a battery along the waterfront south of the Gloria Dei (Old Swede's) Church, which was erected during the War of the Austrian Succession or King George's War (1740-1748).[6]

Fig. 1 Manuscript Map of Delaware River by Loyalist George Spencer from Huntington Library. It shows the locations of the various key points along the Delaware River south of Philadelphia. Property of the Huntington Library.

By the late 1760s, however, the battery had fallen into disrepair. It was clear that should any significant maritime assault be launched on the city additional defenses would be necessary.[7]

In 1770 then Governor John Penn, realizing the vulnerability of the port of Philadelphia, asked General Thomas Gage, commander of British forces in North America, for assistance in strengthening the city's defenses. In reply to Penn's entreaty, Gage dispatched Captain John Montresor (1736-1799) of the Royal Corps of Engineers.[8]

Montresor was born in Gibraltar to a military family and traveled with his father James to North America in 1754. The younger Montresor served as an ensign in the 48th Foot in Brad-dock's disastrous march to the Monongahela in 1755, where he was slightly wounded, and was present at the reduction of Louisburg later in the war. Near the end of the French and Indian War, he car-ried important messages from Gen. James Murray to Col. Thomas Gage. Montresor took part in the suppression of Pontiac's Rebellion and performed an important survey of the route from the Kenne-bec River in what is now Maine to the St. Lawrence. An annotated journal of the last expedition would later serve as the main intelli-gence from which Benedict Arnold planned his march to Canada.[9] During the early 1770s, he worked on fortifications and barracks in New York City, the Great Lakes region, the Bahamas and Boston as well as in Philadelphia. Ironically, Montresor would later be the engineer tasked with the reduction of the fort he was now being commissioned to construct.[10] As will be explained below, however, Montresor did not have any direct input into the fort constructed on the Delaware, so the notion that he later destroyed the work of his own hands is in reality the creation of popular local legend.

Captain John Montresor arrived in Philadelphia on April 21, 1771. He immediately went to meet with Governor Penn. On arriv-ing, however Montresor was informed by the Governor's Secretary that the governor was out for the day.[11] Clearly, the engineer's visit did not start off on the right foot, and the situation quickly deterio-rated further. The following day, Montresor returned to the Gover-nor's office. As he recorded the scene in his journal,

> *This morning being nearly elapsed, waited on the Secretary, who shewed me a sketch of that part of the River where Mud Island is situated, being as their opinion the proposed spot for fortifying...the whole without scale, compass, or remark, together with some bearings or distances.*[12]

Such a rankly amateurish presentation clearly upset the engineer's professional sensibilities. He was further aggravated when the secretary informed him that the governor had in fact determined that the Committee would meet the following day at the state house, all without personal introduction or explanation.[13] These delays constituted grave breaches of etiquette among gentle-men whose behavior was governed by such conventions.

Two days later, Montresor met with the governor and his Board of Commissioners, who were charged with overseeing the project. At this meeting, Penn again produced a sketch of a low-lying area south of the city known as Mud Island and suggested that a defensive work be located there. Montresor studied the site and made a careful reconnaissance of the surrounding waterways, islands, and shoreline. As a result of this study, he developed a series of six possible defensive configurations for the city. The first plan Montresor pre-

Fig 2. Captain John Montresor (Jonathan Singleton Copley).

sented consisted of a star-shaped redoubt to be situated on Mud Island. When completed, it would mount thirty-two cannon, four mortars, and two royal howitzers and would require a garrison of 400 men.[14] This was the engineer's preferred choice, however, it came with an important complication. Much of Mud Island lay below water level and was therefore prone to flooding. In order to construct a solid fortification on the site, piles would have to be constructed before a foundation was laid, thus incurring substantial additional expense. Still, the practice was in keeping with the accepted standards of the day.[15] Montresor's final estimate of the cost of the fortification as he envisioned it came to 40,000 £, an unacceptable amount to political leadership of Pennsylvania.[16]

There ensued a period of wrangling between the political leaders of the colony and Capt. Montresor. The Board of Commissioners accused Montresor of devising a design that was more ornate than necessary. Their suggestion made the engineer indignant. For his part, Montresor refused to make any alterations in the designs he originally submitted to the colonial leadership. In the end, the Pennsylvania Assembly appropriated £15,000 for the purchase of Mud Island and the construction of a much smaller fortification there without the necessary, but expensive, stabilizing piles. Montresor traced the lines of the fortification himself on June 4, 1762, shortly before leaving for his return to New York City.[17] Work at the site would commence under the direction of a Lt. Myers of the 60th Regiment. Still, decisions concerning certain aspects of the design of the fort were postponed indefinitely. In the end, all that resulted from the efforts was a single stone wall facing south along the Delaware. The works on Fort Island remained only partially constructed, and what did exist lacked the pilings Montresor so ardently advocated.[18] He therefore should not be credited or blamed for the works on Mud Island as they existed by the British invasion in 1777. One contemporary described the results of the initial work on the island as "ill-situated and constructed."[19]

Ill-situated and constructed was precisely how the river defenses stood in Philadelphia as the political conflict between Great Britain and her North American colonies intensified once again in the early 1770s. There had already been a series of Parliamentary attempts to exert greater control of over the colonies and to integrate them into the British imperial system. These actions, which included such legislation as the Sugar Act, Stamp Act, and the Townshend Duties, as well as disputes over quartering of British troops in the colonies only resulted in waves of colonial protest and economic warfare in the form of nonimportation of British manufactures.[20]

The Tea Act of 1773, designed to save the financially troubled British East India Company, instead ignited a fresh wave of violent protests. At the forefront of these activities were the Sons of Liberty. In Boston, their actions peaked on the night of December 16, 1773, when members of the group dumped forty-five tons worth of tea, valued at the modern equivalent of $1,000,000, into the harbor. But, as they were reminded at the time, someone would have to pay the fiddler for the frolic.[21] The bill for the Tea Party arrived in the form of the Coercive or Intolerable Acts. These essentially placed Boston under martial law with a military governor, General Thomas Gage, commander of British forces in North America, replacing the former civilian royal governor, Thomas Hutchinson.

Ironically, the laws that were intended to make an example of Boston and break the back of colonial resistance to ministerial policy produced the exact opposite effect. The colonies united as never before, calling a Continental Congress to meet and develop policies for united political and possibly military action against the Crown. Likewise, up and down the east coast of North America the major ports began to prepare their defenses, no longer against French or

Spanish incursions, but against ministerial troops. While Philadelphians certainly took part in the resistance to ministerial policy and opposition to the Coercive Acts, they simultaneously struggled with major internal dissent.

The discord derived from an internal struggle for political control of the colony. The contest pitted the traditional elites against a newly rising group of merchants and artisans. These local clashes were severe enough to work their way into national politics. For instance, when the First Continental Congress convened in Philadelphia in September 1774, there was some competition over where the group would hold their meetings. Conservative leader Joseph Galloway offered the Pennsylvania State House, (later Independence Hall) while many of the more radical members of the local resistance, drawn from the city's artisans and mechanics offered Carpenter's Hall.[22] The Congressional delegates chose the latter, hoping to win over popular support within the city. The preceding gives some sense of the conflicts going on in Philadelphia simultaneously with the larger conflict between colonies and the metropole.[23] The internal power struggles of Pennsylvania are often lost within the larger imperial contest taking place within colonies.

On the larger stage, British Gen. Thomas Gage arrived in Boston on May 13, 1774 to oversee the implementation of the Coercive or Intolerable Acts. Less than twelve months after assuming his post in Boston, protests had transformed into outright rebellion. On April 19, 1775, with the skirmishes at Lexington and Concord, the political conflict between Great Britain and the colonies exploded into open warfare.[24] As a result, when the Second Continental Congress convened in Philadelphia on May 10, 1775, they became, by default, the governing body of a rebellion against the British Crown. Philadelphia, then, quickly emerged as the political center of the rebellion, and its defense from maritime attack quickly became an issue of supreme importance. Both the Pennsylvania government and the Continental Congress took a role in developing defenses for the city. At times, their efforts complimented one another, while at others they seemed to work at cross-purposes.

In response to the news of the fighting in Massachusetts, the local Committee of Correspondence in Philadelphia called for the arming of the city and its surrounding counties in order to defend against a possible incursion such as the one attempted to the North.[25] The more radical members of the Pennsylvania Assembly pushed the governor of the colony, John Penn, aside, essentially disregarding his authority. In his place, the members of the legislature created the Pennsylvania Committee of Safety, on June 30, 1775, to act as the executive for the colony. The Committee included many prominent Philadelphians such as Benjamin Franklin, Robert Morris, Owen Biddle and Anthony Wayne. Altogether, it was composed of some twenty-five members, though if necessary seven could serve as a quorum to conduct business. The Committee met for the first time on July 3. As testament to the importance of the maritime defense of the city, the second resolve the body passed, after the one creating itself, tasked it with defending against "Armed Ships or Vessels" sailing up the Delaware River.[26]

On a suggestion from the Continental Congress, the Committee of Safety began to investigate the defenses of Philadelphia. The Committee of Safety formed a sub-committee of seven to make a thorough examination of the river approaches to Philadelphia as well as the numerous islands in the Delaware River.[27] The survey was performed on July 6 with a view towards determining the best means of defending the city against maritime attack. Accompanying the members of the Committee of Safety on their tour of the river was one Lewis Nicola, former British officer turned Pennsylvania merchant, who possessed some experience in military engineering.[28]

The group performed the survey and reported their findings to the full Committee. Nicola was the chief author of the report, which opened apologetically concerning the potential for controlling the maritime approaches, "I am sorry to say any effectual defense thereof, so as to protect this city from an insult by water, appears to me very difficult, tho' not impossible..."[29] The gentleman's concern was cost, he feared "the expense of doing it to good purpose will be thought too heavy."[30] Nicola's concerns were not unfounded given the fate of Montresor's proposals a decade earlier. Rather than advocate for fixed defenses, the inspectors instead advocated for the construction of a number of shallow-draft vessels that could patrol the river approaches to Philadelphia and augment the shore batteries already existent or under construction.[31] As a result of the report, two of the members who conducted the survey, Capt. Robert Whyte and Owen Biddle, were designated "to be a Committee for the Construction of Boats & Machines for the defense of the River."[32] It was recommended to them by the Committee of Safety to employ Joseph Wharton, Joseph Marsh, Emanuel Eyres, Jacob Miller, Thomas David and Joseph Govett to assist them in their endeavors. Many of these men played significant roles in the development of the river defenses over the following two years.[33]

The river defenses were not Pennsylvania's responsibility alone. On July 15 they dispatched several members, including Daniel Roberdeau and Samuel Morris to make contact with local leaders in New Jersey and determine if they would "assist this Province in Defense of the River, and in what manner."[34] The full Committee received the reply from the leaders of southern New Jersey on July 17, when their representatives reported that the people they had met with "seem willing to give every assistance in their power," and "will immediately furnish some Loggs for building the Machines for the Obstruction of Navigation." [35] In addition, the people of south Jersey proposed "to man one or two of the Boats for the Defense of the River."[36]

As alluded to above, one method of preventing the British from gaining access to Philadelphia via the Delaware River would be to place obstacles in the river so as to hinder navigation. A number of designs were submitted to the committee by local inhabitants.[37] Several designs were submitted by one A.R. Donaldson of Philadelphia on July 11, 1775 under the cover sheet addressed to the Committee which stated that the "City and Libertys might be saved from a sudden attack by watter" if his plans were accepted.[38] One of Donaldson's plans called for a "string of combustible flats that extended from Mud Island to the main channel."[39] Likewise, the Committee resolved on July 13 to give its thanks to one Ebenezer Robinson for a plan he submitted for "stopping the Channel of the river Delaware."[40] The details of the plan were not included in the minutes.

Eventually, the Committee adopted obstacles known as chevaux de frise or Frisian horses.[41] As utilized in the Delaware River, these were an adaptation of anti-cavalry obstacles long employed in Europe. In the land warfare version, these were essentially wooden stakes mounted on a central column and placed in front of the infantry to ward off a cavalry charge. In their maritime version, they consisted of much larger stakes, twenty feet tall or better in some instances, and tipped with iron sheathing that tapered to a point. These beams were then attached to a large wooden box so that they pointed downstream. The box would be floated out to a designated spot in the river and there filled with between twenty and forty tons of stone. Once submerged, the obstacles would be essentially undetectable since the tips of the beams then were to be no more than six feet below the surface of the river. They would, however, be capable of ripping the hull out of any unsuspecting ship unfortunate enough to attempt to sail over them. [42]

In order for the chevaux de frise to fulfill their purpose, they each had to be constructed with the beams of a different height in order to sink below the surface of the river at different depths. In essence, each chevaux de frise was constructed specifically to fit a predetermined site in the river. This would allow them to remain hidden from the eyes of any lookouts until it was too late to change the direction of the incoming vessel.

Fig 3. Chevaux de Frise from Harte 1946.

A recent example discovered in the Delaware River gives some idea of the dimensions of the beams. The particular chevaux de frise stood at 28 feet, 8 inches in length and 13.6 inches in diameter at the widest point. The spear was simply a tree trunk which had the branches and bark removed. The spike affixed to the narrow end was composed of a triangular piece of iron which was attached to the log's end by four iron langets (bands), three of which were still intact on the discovery of the piece. The langets, in turn, were fastened to the trunk and point by nails.[43]

Some of the wooden boxes could be much larger. The remains of one, on display at Fort Mercer on the New Jersey side of the Delaware possessed squared logs up to 63 feet in length. N.R. Ewan believed that these formed the outside of the frames for the chevaux de frise and were probably laid lengthwise.[44]

Fig 4. Example of a chevaux de frise with approaching ship.
Property of Independence Seaport Museum.

The first mention of these obstructions appears in the Pennsylvania Council of Safety minutes for August 5, 1775. While the credit for devising these obstacles is usually awarded to Benjamin Franklin, they were in fact the work of Robert Smith, a Philadelphia architect and carpenter, also a member of the Committee of Safety. Smith had previously presented a model of his obstacle to the Committee of Safety on July 24.[45] His design was "simple, solid and efficacious" in the words of one historian of the river defenses.[46]

In addition to inventing the chevaux de frise, Smith developed a machine for lowering the stones into the hopper of each frame, allowing them to be sunk in the river. Since he proposed the chevaux de frise, the Committee further tasked Smith with overseeing their construction and placement. The Committee sought his advice on the merits of a rival plan for obstructions submitted by Govett and Guion as well.[47]

Once the Committee of Safety approved Smith's design, work commenced on the obstructions. Fort Island became the hub of activity on the Pennsylvania side of the river, while several other contractors established their operations along the shore near the town of Gloucester in New Jersey. Various purveyors provided finished wood, logs, scantling, and chains, while others piloted barges that carried these materials to the assembly points.

Placement of the chevaux de frise stood as a major concern for the Committee as well. In order for them to serve as an effective obstruction to river traffic, the chevaux de frise had to be placed so as to deny any but authorized vessels access to Philadelphia. Therefore, on July 29, the members Committee of Safety examined the river and decided, in combination with members of the Gloucester County Committee, that they were "entirely satisfied with the propriety of fixing the frames opposite the upper end of Hog Island, in preference to Billingsport."[48] By August 24, 1775, Robert Smith could report to the Council of Safety that seventeen frames were ready to be positioned in the river. Constructed on shore, the wooden boxes were towed into place in the river. The positioning of the frames was a labor-intensive task which demanded a great deal of skill. Smith made this point quite clear in a letter he wrote to the Committee,

> *I am now ready to raise A Number of frames. But the depth of the water opisite [sic] to where we have framed them is Not to bear them off we must go lower down, The water is deeper but we have not room enough on the beach to raise them. I wo'd therefore propose that A Number of Labourers be set to work at A Gully that has been made in the Bank by the rains that has fallen from time to time, to enlarge this Gap that we may have room to lay the floors at a sufficient distance from the water till we can erect the upper works in order to add weight that the tide may not carry them off before we have finish'd the frame.*[49]

Once in position, the chevaux de frise were initially lowered to the bottom of the river using anchors.[50] After they were positioned, Smith's machine filled the wooden crib with ballast to ensure the obstacle remained in place. In September, the first row of chevaux de frise was positioned off Mud Island to the south of Philadelphia. This row of obstacles would eventually total forty-three frames of varying sizes. In addition to the sunken obstacles, the defenders constructed a heavy chain that was stretched across the river between the two piers of Mud Island Fort.[51]

Developing obstructions for the river constituted only a portion of the Committee of Safety's responsibilities. While the Delaware River formed an important part of their purview, it was only a part, its duties encompassed the entire defense of Pennsylvania. As a result, the Committee's other responsibilities often distracted its members from consistent efforts on the river defenses. For example, through much of August, the Committee busied itself with organizing the state naval forces, as well as responding to the requests of other colonies for aid. Later in the month, and through September the body returned to the issues of maritime defense. On September 1, for instance, the Committee focused its attention first on the armed boats and determined that the manning for these should be between thirty and fifty men. In addition, they set the rates of pay for the officers and crewmen of the Pennsylvania Navy, as well as their allowances for provisions.[52]

The Committee then turned their attention to the river pilots. These were men who guided larger vessels up the Delaware to the port of Philadelphia, Chester, or Newcastle. As such, they possessed an intimate knowledge of the river and its hazards. Such information held obvious value for both sides. Therefore, keeping them on the side of the Committee stood as a concern of great importance. As a result, the Committee warned them to "use their utmost endeavours to avoid going aboard or being taken on Board British ships of war."[53] The Committee further expressed the opinion that the pilots should put up their boats for the winter on or before September 20, and avoid waterways as well as places on land where they could be seized by agents from British warships on station in the Delaware Bay.[54] Finally it stated that anyone who refused to lay up his boat by the aforementioned date, or put himself in a position to be taken by the British, or would voluntarily agree to serve on one of their ships, would be "deemed an Enemy to American Liberty."[55]

This level of concern on the part of the Committee derived from fear of the British taking one of the river pilots prisoner. This fear is expressed time and again in the above resolves. The key to the success of the chevaux de frise, as well as the other defensive precautions initiated by the Committee lay in protecting the city from invasion while still allowing trade to continue. It was necessary to allow the state and Continental-commissioned privateers to leave for the sea as well. Thus, the Delaware had to remain open, but on a selective basis.

This interpretation is supported by the resolution of the Committee dated September 20, 1775, in which they permitted the pilot Daniel Murphy to guide the brigantine *Nancy*, under a Captain Douglass down the river, provided he avoid "going or being taken on board any Man-of-War, or other British armed Vessell." The Committee provided the same instructions to pilot John Lambert when he petitioned them for permission to guide the ship *Peace and Plenty* two days later.[56]

At the same time, the committeemen continued to see to the colony's other defensive needs. For instance, on September 23, they interviewed a Mr. Samuel Slade, recently arrived from England, concerning his interest in the river defenses. Upon questioning him, and following up on his references, the Committee determined that he "had no bad intentions" in making his inquiries. Still, they did make a "Charge to him that he inform this Board when he intends to leave this Province."[57]

The day after the group questioned Slade as to his intentions, the Committee conducted much the same interview with no less a figure than the famous ranger leader, Robert Rogers. Rogers had recently returned from England, where he had attempted to gain some remuneration expenses he incurred during the French and Indian War. The famed ranger leader sought to remain neutral at this time and look to his own financial interests. Since Rogers held a commission as major in the British army, he was released on parole.[58]

The preceding gives some idea of the broad scope of responsibilities the Committee of Safety took on in the early period of its existence. As will be seen, it later created subcommittees to address particular issues. Clearly the attention of the members of the Committee of Safety was stretched thin in addressing the numerous issues of local defense simultaneously. The dispersal of the Committee of Safety's efforts is further evidenced by their activities concerning the construction of a state navy for Pennsylvania.

At the same time that the Committee of Safety worked to close off the river approaches to Philadelphia to all but friendly shipping, they worked to construct a navy for the active defense of the river. Two means were to be used to procure the ships for the fleet. One was to purchase vessels already constructed, while the other involved commissioning local shipwrights to construct warships for the fleet. Accordingly, requests were made for local shipbuilders to submit designs to the Committee. Two local builders, John Warton and Emanuel Eyre submitted similar plans for small row galleys to guard the river approaches to the city. The committee apparently approved both men's designs, and construction began on the galleys.[59]

The basic design for these vessels comprised a keel measuring between forty-seven and fifty feet in length, with a beam of thirteen feet and a depth of four-and-one-half feet. They were pointed at both bow and stern. The ships were to be completely decked with the oarsmen working on deck and spaces for storage and quartering below. Each ship was to mount a canon in the bow. By the end of July 1775, the first eleven such craft had been built.[60]

At times, members of the Committee were present for the launching of some of craft, such as on July 26 when they attended the launching of the galley *Bull Dog*, the first galley completed. Following the launching, members boarded the galley and sailed down to Gloucester, New Jersey to hold a meeting.[61] The ride to Gloucester served several purposes. On one level, it marked a celebration of a milestone in the Committee's efforts at maritime defense. Simultaneously, it advertised their success to the people on both sides of the river as a reinforcement of the Committee's ability to achieve results and see to the security of the region.

Supplementing the galleys, but smaller than them, were the guard boats. These were thirty-five feet in length and flat-bottomed.[62] They had ten to twelve oars and a single lateen sail. Their armament consisted of a single two, three, or four-pounder canon and several swivels. The crews were provided with small arms as well. Since the ships only had a single deck, the men had to sleep on deck under awnings. Each boat was issued a small iron pot for cooking as well. The standard crew for the guard boats was fourteen including officers and sailors, though they often sailed with far less than a full complement.[63]

In all, some twenty-one guard boats were constructed, with the duty of patrolling the many creeks and inlets along the banks of the river.[64] In doing so they would prevent intelligence and supplies from being passed by Loyalists to British ships in the Delaware Bay. They would likewise help to assure that only those vessels given permission by the Pennsylvania government were allowed to navigate the river.

Complementing the galleys and guard boats as an offensive weapon were a number of fire rafts. These were small vessels, loaded with combustibles. The rafts varied in size, but in general were some thirty-five feet in length, and about thirteen feet wide. Railings surrounded the combustibles which were stored under sail cloth, to protect against accidental ignition and so they remained dry. On the bow of each raft were a set of iron prongs designed to grasp onto the intended target and hold the fire raft to its victim. Forty-eight fire rafts were deployed in groups of six rafts linked together, known as chains. Each chain had a guard boat or galley assigned it. The guard boat or galley's role consisted in maneuvering the chain into action against its intended target.[65] The ship would also remove any crew from the fire rafts once they had set the combustibles alight. In addition to the fire rafts, the Committee of Safety purchased eight larger vessels to serve as fire ships. These craft were provided with cargoes of combustibles as well. The fire ships maneuvered themselves into position under their own sails, and therefore possessed larger crews than the fire rafts.[66]

On command, these would be ignited and released to float down the Delaware River on the tide. It was hoped that by timing their movement properly, they would explode and shower any vessels targeted with bits of flaming debris. The falling debris would, it was hoped, ignite fires on the enemy craft. The most dangerous activity for the crews on the fire ships was the actual igniting of their cargo. This was a hazardous job that could often inspire panic, leading to premature ignitions as well as evacuations. Such actions would, in turn, cause the vessel to explode too far from its intended target to inflict any damage. By the same token, the various fire vessels of the Pennsylvania Navy served a valuable purpose in that their mere existence acted as a deterrent and made the British less likely to risk ships in any attempt to force their way up the Delaware. Fire was the great fear on board a wooden hulled sailing ship. For any British commander brazen enough to test his luck against the fire rafts and fire ships, and possibly succeed in running their gauntlet, there remained the river obstructions. The Committee selected Philadelphia merchant Capt. John Hazelwood to oversee the construction of the fire rafts.

Little biographical information survives relating to John Hazelwood. He was born in England in 1726 and emigrated to the North America sometime in the 1740s. He commanded merchant vessels based in Philadelphia beginning in the 1750s and continued to do so until the outbreak of fighting between Britain and the colonies. Called into service along with other prominent merchants, Hazelwood could claim substantial sailing experience, though he possessed little, if any, combat experience.[67] Hazelwood supervised the construction of at least forty-eight of these vessels, and became quite proficient in their construction, so much so that he was dispatched to New York to advise the leadership in that city on how to develop obstructions for the North River.[68]

Hazelwood would eventually become Commodore of the Pennsylvania Navy. First to fulfill this role, however, was one Thomas Read. Born around 1740, Read was the youngest of four brothers who hailed from Delaware. He possessed substantial experience as a ships' master in the Atlantic and West Indies trade, though nothing that would single him out as particularly fitted for this position of high responsibility.[69] He was nominated for the post on October 23, 1775 and recommended for it to the Assembly by the Committee of Safety on the same day.[70] While the Committee filled his and other important command positions, work continued on the Delaware River defenses. As the summer of 1775 waned, the Committee worked to complete the underwater obstructions blocking navigation in the river.

In October, the Committee determined to buy three hulks and sink these "in the most convenient places for the Defense of the River."[71] Robert Wharton and Colonel Roberdeau were to oversee the purchase of the vessels, while Samuel Morris and Robert White were to "fix upon the *properest* [sic] places for sinking them."[72] If all these actions were not enough, the Committee of Safety supervised the selection of officers for the ships and forts as well. For instance, on August 1, 1775, they appointed Nicholas Biddle to command the *Franklin*, Captain John Hamilton to command of the *Congress*, Captain Henry Dougherty to command the *Washington*, and Allen Moore to command the *Experiment*.[73]

Choosing the designs for the ships, recruiting crew, and selecting officers were not the only tasks that occupied the Committee. They had to arm the vessels and provide small arms for the crews as well. Cannon were procured both through purchase, when possible, and by the provision of contracts to local manufacturers. The provision of small arms for the crews of the vessels proved a more difficult challenge to meet. As noted by the Committee of Safety on September 30, it proved "impracticable either to purchase or, have made, any fire arms in proper time for our Defense."[74] The Committee, therefore, settled on the expedient of asking the members of the local defense force, the Philadelphia Associators, with arms in their possession to deliver them to the Commissary, Robert Towers.[75] It is worth noting that the arms contracts for the fleet as well as the

Continental Navy and Army helped to spur further industrialization in Pennsylvania.[76]

Various other expedients were tried to provide the crews with firearms in addition to purchase and manufacture. An October 3, resolution provides for the use of pistols and carbines for the men, "provided they are suitable for that purpose."[77] Thus, the Committee of Safety moved away from providing only muskets to arming the men of the galleys and guard boats with whatever guns they could acquire.

As the initial efforts of the Committee of Safety began to lead to the raising of both land and maritime forces, it quickly became apparent that the day-to-day control of the troops, ships, construction of the chevaux de fries, and other tasks would need to be delegated to others. As a result, the Committee appointed several trusted individuals or formed sub-committees to oversee various aspects of their defensive measures.

On September 16, 1775, John Ross, a local merchant applied for and received the post of muster master of the officers and men serving aboard the ships of the Pennsylvania Navy. One factor that seemed to support his application for the job was the fact that he volunteered to work without pay.[78] Several days later, on the 23rd, the Committee approved Edward Chamberlain to take on the position of Master-at-Arms and Armourer for the armed boats at the rate of fourteen dollars a month.[79] A few weeks later, on October 6, they appointed one John Maxwell Nesbitt as paymaster for the Pennsylvania Fleet, with a description of the duties his office entailed.[80] He oversaw the pay of the crews of all ships in the growing Pennsylvania Navy from the galleys to the fire ships and guard boats.

In all, twenty-one of these latter vessels were constructed in 1775. Their primary duty consisted in patrolling the many creeks and inlets along the banks of the Delaware to interdict smuggling activity. Over time, the duties of guard boats expanded to include protecting the fire rafts, as well as observing the traffic on the river. In fulfilling their duties, these vessels rarely went far from the shore for fear of swamping.[81]

Complementing the sunken obstructions, and the various ships of the Pennsylvania Navy, several sets of fortifications were planned along both the New Jersey and Pennsylvania sides of the river. The fortifications were to be situated so as to defend the sunken obstacles in the river. The premise was that should the British come up the Delaware River in force and begin to try to remove the chevaux de frise, the forts and small vessels of the state navy could take their vessels under fire. In this capacity, the combination of the forts and sunken obstacles would act as a sort of deterrent in that any British ship commander would have to weigh the odds of his being able to get through the obstructions while under fire. The other option would be to launch a combined assault to clear the fortifications and then remove the obstructions in the river. The British possessed a significant body of experience in these latter sorts of operations.[82]

It should be kept in mind, however, that there were differing views on the role any fortifications on Mud Island, and later the other locations, should play. While the members of the Committee of Safety who possessed maritime experience viewed the works on Mud Island as serving as a naval station and supply depot, the Continental Congress saw them as a defensive point for guarding the river approaches to Philadelphia. As a result of these differing perceptions of the function of the fort, various approaches were employed in the construction taking place on Mud Island.[83]

For Whyte and Biddle, the fort already begun on Mud Island during the 1760s would serve as a key position in the river defense, and work was to be resumed there.[84] It is clear that from the outset, the members of the Committee of Safety planned to incorporate the already existing works at Mud Island into their overall network of defenses. These, however, were in a state of significant disarray. For instance, at the Mud Island works, there were no platforms constructed for mounting the artillery. In addition, the cooking facilities for the garrison were rudimentary, and there were no fireplaces to keep the barracks warm.[85] Further complicating matters was the fact that the members of the Committee possessed no knowledge of military engineering. They therefore deferred to the advice offered by various Pennsylvania militia officers. These men understood the art of constructing blockhouses on the frontier strong enough to withstand an attack by Native Americans, but not how to construct a fort capable of withstanding a European foe equipped with heavy artillery.[86]

As a result, the fortifications on Mud Island remained rudimentary at best. For instance, after visiting Mud Island on October 15, a delegation of the Committee of Safety authorized the construction of a lean-to against the only stone wall of the fort then constructed as a shelter for the garrison.[87] These were temporary structures constructed of materials close to hand such as tree branches, fence rails, straw, sod and so forth. While they could offer some protection against the sun or light rain, they were understood by contemporaries as only very temporary shelters.[88] At this time, the post possessed no garrison as yet as none had been raised. Until a garrison was recruited and dispatched to the fort, the lean-to would serve as barracks for the galley crews of the Pennsylvania Navy.[89] The Committee further directed that fireplaces be constructed in the barracks on Mud Island for the relief of the eventual garrison as well as the crews of the ships.[90] The Committee followed through on these resolutions on October 23, when they instructed that a Captain Long be ordered to buy a quantity of boards and send them to Fort Island "for the purpose of building a leantoo [sic] shed against the inside of the Fort Wall, sufficient to cover two or three hundred Men in bad weather." [91]

Further efforts were made to improve the post on Fort Island during the fall of 1775, such as when Commissary Robert Townes sent six 18-pounder cannons to the fort as well as stores. In addition, it was directed that a "forge for heating shot be erected." [92] This would allow the gunners to heat the round-shot so that when it hit an enemy warship it could set it afire. The same directive ordered that a company be raised to man the guns. The company was to consist of two officers, a captain and a private, a drummer and fifer, and twenty-five men. The men were to serve an enlistment of twelve months, unless discharged prior to that date by the Committee or the Assembly. If the men in the artillery company were discharged prior to their full term of enlistment, they were to receive a month's wages over and above what they earned to date. The task of executing these directives fell to Robert Whyte and Samuel Morris.[93]

On October 27, the Committee of Safety appointed Thomas Proctor as Captain of the artillery company to be "raised and employed at Fort Island."[94] Proctor was the son of Irish immigrants who came to Philadelphia, probably sometime in the 1750s. He had taken up the trade of carpenter, and on December 31, 1766, married Mary Fox. Soon after receiving his commission, Proctor began raising his company, and by December he had approximately 90 men serving under him stationed at Fort Island.[95] This was the origin of the Fourth Continental Artillery.[96]

On November 6, the Committee ordered the Barrack Master, Robert Towers, to provide Proctor and his men with six cannons, equipped with carriages, as well as all the other equipment necessary to handle the guns.[97] This created a problem as the guns sent to Mud Island in response to the Committee of Safety's order were sent without carriages, and so could not be mounted to defend the fort. This would remain the case until February of 1776. At this point one Thomas Nevil was contracted to construct carriages for the guns and mount them in the Fort Island battery.[98] In addition, the Committee ordered the construction of a raised earthen causeway to create a dry connection between Mud Island and an old ferry wharf. The wharf linked Mud and Province Islands. During this period, the commander at Fort Island, Thomas Proctor housed his artillery company at the Pest House on Province Island as the barracks on Mud Island remained incomplete.[99] Following on these initial efforts, the weather precluded any significant activity at Mud Island through the winter of 1775-76.[100]

As efforts progressed in the construction on Mud Island, it grew increasingly apparent that there existed severe design flaws in the works. For instance, the main battery was situated south of the stone wall that was a part of the original construction. As a result, canon shot that flew over the battery could ricochet off the wall and wreak havoc among the gunners.[101]

Thomas Proctor ordered his men to assist the workmen at Mud Island in their work on the fortification. He petitioned the Committee of Safety for better winter quarters as well. The lean-tos constructed on Mud Island were unsuitable for the cooler autumn nights, and so would be useless when the winter cold arrived. Quartering the men would remain a significant problem throughout much of the autumn of 1775. The Committee responded to Proctor's requests by ordering the barracks on the island repaired and supplies of wood and blankets for his men. Unfortunately, the Barracks Master, one Joseph Fox, could not procure the necessary supplies of bedding and so substituted straw for the captain and his men.[102]

On October 15, several members of the Committee of Safety journeyed to Mud Island to see for themselves the situation of the troops stationed there. They noted particularly a lack of fireplaces, which made it difficult for the men to prepare food and keep warm as the seasons changed. It was then ordered that fireplaces or a forge be installed on the island.[103]

Two days later, on October 17, a Mr. Gray and a Mr. Doherty waited on the Provincial Commissioners, "who gave their hearty consent to the Board's erecting any works on the Province Island that they may think proper and necessary for the defense of this Province."[104] Samuel Morris, Jr. toured the works and reported to the Committee of Safety in early November that Fort Island was "an improper place for erecting a shed for defending the People from the inclemency of the weather."[105] In response to the report, the Committee resolved that Robert White join Morris in selecting any structures already on the island, and repair them for the use of the garrison. They were to build any additional buildings they deemed necessary as well. They were, further, to employ enough men to throw up a bank and construct a pier at the north end of the island. The purpose of the pier was for "sending with more speed any succors that there may be occasion for at the Island from the main."[106]

One aspect of constructing and garrisoning the fort that the Committee did not have concern itself with at this juncture was manpower. They received an offer on November 2 from a Capt. William Davis, offering his service and that of a number of men he recruited to act as volunteers on Fort Island. Davis and his men received the thanks of the Board, who went on to recommend "to the said Gentlemen to qualify themselves in such Exercise of the Great Guns, as will be useful in the department in which they offer to serve;" The Committee added, "this Board do Resolve to Call upon them to act as Volunteers, under the officer appointed by this Board, Whenever the Public Service shall require."[107] The offer of these men to serve without pay in the defense of their home state should be seen as a manifestation of what Charles Royster described as the *rage militaire*.[108]

In late November, the Committee ordered Colonel John Bull's Pennsylvania militia battalion to the fort as well. This move significantly expanded the number of men stationed on the island, and further exacerbated the already difficult housing situation. On November 25, Francis Proctor was appointed a Lieutenant and assigned to his kinsman's artillery company.[109] Soon thereafter, an incident occurred between Bull and the Proctors. The Committee investigated and found the Proctor's guilty of conduct unbecoming an officer. They were ordered to apologize. At first, they refused, and were dismissed from the service. After a few days' consideration, they returned and apologized, and Thomas Proctor was reinstated as commander of Fort Island's garrison.[110]

The preceding highlights one of the difficulties encountered in garrisoning the forts as well as supplying crews for the ships. Issues of discipline and pay were rife, not only among the enlisted men, but among officers as well. In many ways, these local difficulties mirrored the challenges Washington faced as he worked to mold civilians into soldiers in the newly formed Continental Army.[111]

The Committee of Safety faced additional problems as well, which often distracted them from the task of constructing the defensive network in and along the Delaware River. For instance, on November 11, 1775, the Committee of Safety heard the case of John

Saunders,

> *Pilot, being a Person who, by the Regulations*
> *of this Board, ought not to bring a Vessel higher up the*
> *River Delaware than the Town of Chester having wan-*
> *tonly in defiance of this Board, brought a Ship through*
> *the Chivaux de Frize to the great danger of damaging*
> *the said Ship and hazard of this Province.[112]*

Upon review of the facts in the case, the Board resolved that "the said John Saunders be committed to the Common Goal of this County, and there to be kept in safe in Custody, during the pleasure of this Board."[113]

As the Committee were making efforts to reinforce Fort Island, they received word from a Dr. Duffield, whom they had sent to view the Pest House on Province Island that it was fit to accommodate some forty sick men.[114] Thus another piece was added to the puzzle of the river defenses of Philadelphia.

Several historians have noted that the defensive plans set in motion by the Committee of Safety over the course of the summer of 1775 constituted a defensive system or network.[115] There is much truth in this assessment as none of the constituent parts would be truly effective on their own. The chevaux de frise posed a significant obstruction to any ships making their way up the river, however, they could be moved to clear a channel, unless guarded by fortifications. Likewise, it might be possible for ships to send crews up to survey the obstructions and remain outside the range of the land fortifications, thus the importance of the various vessels of the Pennsylvania navy. Finally, the fire ships bolstered the capabilities of the forts to inflict damage on any would-be intruders. One of the last significant acts of the Committee in 1775 involved the creation of a series of alarm posts set to run from the Delaware Bay to Philadelphia.[116]

The Committee delegated the establishment of these posts to one Henry Fisher. Fisher constructed a series of thirteen posts, each manned by a single look-out equipped with a signal cannon and a small boat. As a back-up, Fisher established a series of post-riders that made possible the transmission of a message from Lewes, Delaware near Cape Henlopen, to Philadelphia within twenty-one hours. [117] Thus, he linked the various components together with a system which could give both the forts and Pennsylvania Navy time to prepare themselves to defend against a British maritime incursion.

As autumn came to the Delaware Valley, the efforts of the Committee began to bear late summer fruit. A number of ships had been constructed. Likewise, the members of the Committee agreed upon the form for the river obstructions and had begun their construction and placement. They further succeeded in having seventeen of the chevaux de frise constructed and sunk in the river. Each frame cost £100, so the total cost was £1700.[118] The Committee appointed Owen Biddle, Robert Whyte, and George Clymer to examine the most effectual way of connecting the chevaux de frise by chains and to procure the chains necessary for that purpose.[119]

The fortifications at Mud Island were being worked on as well. Still, some residents of the region, such as Richard Riley, held concerns about how much of the area would be defended. Writing to George Gray from Marcus Hook on September 13, he noted that the "Province boats will shortly be finished and their Station appointed."[120] He continued, "If it is to be above the Shiver de frees's, I apprehend they will be a partial defense, which ought not to be, as every person within the Province is Intitled [sic] to a Provincial protection."[121] Finally, Riley voiced the very real concern for security no doubt felt by many in the region, "If they are stationed at the Fort, Chester and Marcus hook may be reduced to ashes before any relief can be obtained..."[122]

At the same time, ideas for additional defenses continued to be submitted to the Committee, such as the one described in a letter by one John Belton to the Committee on September 4. Belton described a device he had developed, and previously submitted plans for, which would essentially fire cannons into ships from underwater.[123] Belton was nothing if not persistent, as he followed up with the Committee again on September 11, this time offering to bring his device into the service of the cause in return for a bounty of "twenty pounds upon every gun, which said Ship or Ships doth carry..." referring to the ships he intended to either sink or burn with his device.[124] There are no records to indicate that the Committee followed up on this idea. There did occur a brief hiatus while members of the Committee of Safety stood for election.

The members of the Committee of Safety were returned on October 20, 1775, with Benjamin Franklin as its president and Robert Morris as vice president.[125] The group would continue to direct the military apparatus of Pennsylvania into 1776.[126] The Committee soon returned to the river defenses and appointed David Rittenhouse as engineer to the Board on October 27.[127] Likewise, on

October 27, they appointed Mr. Towers to test all the muskets that were to be used by the city and province.[128]

In 1776, a new constitution would drastically alter the political organization of the state. In the first year of its existence, however, the Pennsylvania Committee of Safety made enormous strides in placing the colony on a defensive footing.

While the winter weather slowed work on the fortifications in the Delaware, work continued on the ships for Pennsylvania's small river navy. On November 3, 1775 they advanced the opinion that further measures for the defense of Philadelphia were necessary. They therefore instructed Clymer, Howell, and Nixon to enquire into the prospects for immediately purchasing a vessel for the service of the province. It was to mount twenty eighteen-pounders. Failing that, they were to determine how quickly and at what cost such a ship could be constructed.[129] The sub-committee returned its initial finding four days later, determining that a ship of this type, "Exclusive of Guns and the necessary Ammunition, Seamen's' Wages, and Provisions," would cost "the Sum of Nine thousand pounds."[130] This sum contributed still further the major spending the Committee undertook in establishing defenses for Philadelphia.

An extract from an anonymous letter of another Philadelphian, dated December 6, 1775, noted the accomplishments of the Committee with a certain sense of pride. The author observed, "we look on ourselves quite safe here." Surveying the military projects, they noted, "Our frigates, and our fort, which is a regular one, on Mud Island....Our ballast vessels and Chevaux de Frise, at the narrows and flats, will be very sufficient to defeat any ship that may attempt to annoy us."[131] While they certainly overstated the works on Mud Island, it is clear that the Committee had accomplished a great deal.

They laid the foundations for an impressive network of defenses from the Delaware Bay up to the confluence of the Delaware and Schuylkill Rivers. It is noteworthy as well, that these efforts came at the same time that they were overturning one government in favor of another. Likewise, the Committee often provided material support for initiatives from the Continental Congress. The new leaders of Pennsylvania were not only looking to their own defense, but they were coordinating military activities with the new national government, raising troops and dispatching them to fight with the Continental Army.

As a result of these competing demands on its attention, not all of the efforts called for by the Committee of Safety were put into action seamlessly. There were often miscommunications, for example, on November 28, 1775, the Committee wrote to Henry Fisher to inform him that some of the River Pilots claimed they had not been informed that they should proceed no further north than Chester and wait for the pilots assigned to guide ships through the chevaux de frise to guide any vessels entering Philadelphia on the remainder of their journey. They called on Fisher to "immediately acquaint all your Pilots of the above regulation."[132] Even under the best of circumstances, organizations encounter such communications breakdowns.

Still, the Committee of Safety in cooperation with the Continental Congress succeeded to a large extent in developing a mutually reinforcing defense in depth for Philadelphia. The Delaware River defenses truly constituted a network, as the forts were sited in order to guard the chevaux de frise. Likewise, the guard boats of the Pennsylvania Navy protected the chevaux de frise in the middle of the river, out of the range of the cannon of the forts. These vessels could retire under the guns of the forts for protection as well. By the same token, it seems that the members of the Committee were often in the position of responding to events as they occurred. One example of such reactive behavior is set out above where members of the Committee determined, on November 16, that it was necessary to add an additional tier of chevaux de frise to the river defenses. They therefore instructed Samuel Morris and Robert White to provide logs and plank to build this third tier.[133] Certainly this accounts for the haphazard nature of the defenses as they were developed in 1775.

Samuel Morris, Jr. and Robert Whyte, the two men previously charged with purchasing logs for the construction of the chevaux de frise were ordered to purchase enough logs to construct a total of three tiers of them. [134] The Committee further resolved that a third tier be "sunk above those already sunk near to Fort Island."[135] Further, they authorized the pair to "contract for and engage a sufficient number of Logs sufficient for three tier of them."[136] Finally, they ordered that "one more tier of Chivaux de Frize be sunk above those already sunk near Fort Island."[137] It was determined "for the further security of this province," to place two tier of chevaux de frise "In the Channel opposite or near to Marcus Hook."[138] Thus, the defenses around the fort were to be doubled.

The Committee further ordered that Reed, Miles and Whyte act as a sub-committee and go to Fort Island and consider what additional defenses should be established on either it or Province

Island for the security of the Fort and the passage through the chevaux de frise.[139]

During much of the month of December, the attention of the members of the Committee of Safety turned from the Delaware River to focus on land forces to be raised for the defense of the colony. In addition, the Continental Congress requested that the Committee raise additional troops and supplies for Washington's army outside Boston. The leaders did their best to comply with these requests and raise the men and material. At the same time, such efforts, again, proved to be a distraction from work on the local defenses.

While the committee took the Christmas holiday off, they returned to the business of defending the province on the 26th and ordered one Lt. Symmonds to assume command of the Artillery Company and move to Liberty Island. He was to remain at the post, guarding the battery and stores gathered there until further orders.[140]

Among the last acts of the Committee for 1775 was to appoint Capt. John Hazelwood to command of ten of the fire rafts. In addition, they engaged Hazelwood as superintendent of the entire fleet of fire rafts. The Committee made this decision on December 28, 1775.[141] That same day, the Committee resolved to construct a floating battery. Completion of the battery was placed in the hands of Samuel Howell, Robert Whyte and George Clymer who were likewise to ensure that the vessel was armed and supplied as necessary.[142]

Lastly, the board reinstated Thomas Proctor as commander of the artillery company at Fort Island, after he made apologies to Capt. Williams and Lieutenant Watson at the post, as previously required by the Committee.[143]

Finally, it is further worth noting that the Committee of Safety's efforts did not go unnoticed by the British. The November 9-11 issue of the *London Evening Post* contained a letter from Philadelphia which described how the Philadelphians possessed "A number of galliots and floating batteries, mounting from 18 to 32 pounders, carrying two lateen sails, and from 16 to 32 oars each." It likewise detailed how a boom was laid across the harbor and how "our magazines are filled with military stores - great quantities are daily arriving; and every preparation is making here for a vigorous campaign."[144] All of this was quite impressive for a group which had only recently come to power in the colony. It is important to keep in mind, however, that the activities of the Committee came about during a period in which Philadelphia was generally not threatened by the British military. This period of relative safety would not endure permanently. War soon placed additional demands on the military resources of Pennsylvania, and the colonial leadership had to choose between local defense and support of the overall war effort. National concerns won out.

By the same token, there existed real deficiencies in the Pennsylvanians efforts to date. One clear shortcoming lay in the lack of trained military engineers. This was a defect they sought to fix however, as a letter from Benjamin Franklin to an acquaintance Alexander Dumas, then in the Hague, written December 12, 1775, demonstrates:

> *We are in great Want of good Engineers, and wish you could engage and send us two able ones in time for next Campaign; one acquainted with Field Service, Sieges, &c. the other with fortifying Sea Ports.*[145]

Notice that Franklin explicitly requested an engineer versed in the defense of seaports. Someone possessing those qualification would find ample work in the rebellious colonies as all boasted ports and their defenses all required improvement. It is not clear whether Dumas ever referred any to Franklin. Many foreign engineers, as well as those claiming to knowledge in this branch, would come to Pennsylvania and work on the Philadelphia defenses. As will be shown below, at times they made valuable contributions to the defense of the City of Brotherly Love, while at others they merely spawned distracting controversies.

CHAPTER NOTES

[1]R. Blake Dunnavent, "Muddy Waters: A History of the United States in Riverine Warfare and the Emergence of a Tactical Doctrine, 1775-1789." (Texas Tech University: Phd Diss., 1998), p. 1

[2] These figures are taken from Thomas J. McGuire, *The Philadelphia Campaign*, vol.1 *The Battle of Brandywine and the Fall of Philadelphia.* (Mechanicsburg, PA: Stackpole Books 2006), p. 124-5.

[3] Information concerning the port facilities, police and fire departments of Philadelphia is drawn from George W. Geib, "A History of Philadelphia, 1776-1789." (PhD. Dissertation, University of Wisconsin, 1969), 38-9. Concerning Philadelphia's role as a cultural and scientific center of the colonies, see John W. Jackson, *Fort Mercer, Guardian of the Delaware* (Gloucester, NJ: Gloucester County Cultural and Heritage Commission, 1986), p. 5.

[4]McGuire, *Philadelphia Campaign*, vol. 1, 125. See also Aaron Sullivan, *The Disaffected: Britain's Occupation of Philadelphia During the American Revolution* (Philadelphia: University of Pennsylvania Press, 2019), p. 13.

[5]The French and Indian War is referred to as well as the Seven Years' War, and the Great War for Empire. This account will use the denominations Great War of Empire and French and Indian War interchangeable to refer to the North American theater of the conflict in order to avoid monotony.

[6]Joseph Seymour, *The Pennsylvania Associators, 1747-1777* (Yardley, PA: Westholme Publishing, 2012), p. 51.

[7]There were earlier attempts at providing Philadelphia with some defenses. Among the most successful of these was the formation of a group known as the Pennsylvania Associators. They constructed a battery in Philadelphia at Wiccacoe just south of Old Swedes Church during King George's War. These developments as well as the entire history of the Pennsylvania Associators are covered very thoroughly in Seymour, *Pennsylvania Associators,* 30-60. On the disrepair of the battery, see Gregory M. Browne, "Fort Mercer and Fort Mifflin: The Battle for the Delaware River and the Importance of American Riverine Defenses during Washington's Siege of Philadelphia." (MA Thesis: Western Illinois University, 1996), p. 27.

[8]Fortification was considered something of an art form in the eighteenth century. In its current form, the development of fortifications had begun during the Italians Wars of the late fifteenth and sixteenth centuries. This period is seen as marking a major transition due to the greater use of artillery in the reduction of fortresses and the development of the *trace italienne* style of fortification. It had reached its peak by the end of the seventeenth century during the wars of Louis XIV. Due to the influence of Louis XIV's military engineer, Sebastien de le Pestre de Vauban, the French were seen as the best military engineers in Europe, and most of the significant works on fortification were in French. By the same token, there were several significant works available in English by John Muller. Concerning the development of fortifications since the Middle Ages, see Christopher Duffy, *Siege Warfare: the Fortress in the Early Modern World, 1494-1660* (London: Routledge, 1979) and *Fire and Stone: The Science of Fortress Warfare 1660-1860* (London: Peters Fraser & Dunlop, 1975). The works of John Muller include: *A treatise containing the elementary part of fortification : regular and irregular : with remarks on the constructions of the most celebrated authors particularly of Marshal de Vauban*

and *Baron Coehorn* (London: J. Nourse, 1746); *A treatise of artillery : containing I. General constructions of brass and iron guns used by sea and land ... To which is prefixed an introduction, with a theory of powder applied to fire-arms. The second edition, with large additions, alterations, and corrections* (London: John Millan, 1768) and *The attack and defence of forthfied places. In three parts. : Containing I. The operations of an attack, from the beginning to the end. II. The defence of every part of a fortification. III. A treatise on mines. For the use of the Royal Military Academy, at Woolwich. By John Muller, professor of fortification and artillery, and Military preceptor to His Royal Highness William, Duke of Gloucester* (London: T. and J. Egerton, Whitehall, 1791).

[9] Biographical information on Montressor is from Mark M. Boatner, III *Encyclopedia of the American Revolution* (Mechanicsburg, PA: Stackpole Books, 1994), p. 729. See also Francis L.D. Goodrich, "John Montresor, 1736-1799, Engineer and Cartographer." in *Michigan Alumnus Quarterly Review*. 64 (1988): 124-129 and Ira D. Gruber, *Books and the British Army in the Age of the American Revolution* (Chapel Hill: University of North Carolina Press, 2014), pp. 103-5.

[10] It is often alleged that Montresor later destroyed the fort he built. A close review of the evidence debunks this interpretation, as he merely submitted a plan, which the Pennsylvania colonial government essentially rejected.

[11] John Montressor, *The Montressor Journals*. G. D. Scull, ed. (New York: Collections of the New York Historical Society, 1881), p. 414.

[12] Ibid, p.415.

[13] Ibid.

[14] Scull, *Montresor Journals*, p. 416.

[15] Christopher Duffy, *Fire and Stone*, p. 40.

[16] Browne, "Fort Mercer and Fort Mifflin," p. 28.

[17] Scull, *Montresor Journals*, p. 417.

[18] Browne, Thesis, pp. 27-8.

[19] Phillipe Trouson du Coudray, "A Definitive Project Upon the Defense of Philadelphia in the Present State of Affairs." Worthington C. Ford, ed. *The Defenses of Philadelphia* (Brooklyn, NY: Historical Printing Club, 1897), p. 16.

[20] The most recent discussion of Quartering, and one which sheds substantial new light on the issue is John Gilbert McCurdy *Quarters: The Accommodation of the British Army and the Coming of the American Revolution* (Ithaca: Cornell University Press, 2019).

[21] The preceding is a paraphrase of the words of British Admiral John Montagu, Commander-in-Chief on the North American Station. The actual quote reads, "Well, boys, you've had a fine, pleasant evening for your Indian caper, haven't you? But mind, you have got to pay the fiddler yet." Admiral John Montagu, quoted in Christopher Hibbert, *Redcoat and Rebels: The American Revolution through British Eyes* (New York: W.W. Norton and Company, 1990), p. 21.

[22] Joseph Galloway (c. 1731-1803) was a prominent Pennsylvania lawyer and vice-president of the American Philosophical Society. He was a close friend of Benjamin Franklin. Politically, he worked to advance the interests of the Pennsylvania colony and the merchant elites. He therefore supported the end of the Proprietary government in the colony and its replacement with a Royal government. He also

devised what was known as Galloway's Plan on Union. This would have solved the dispute between Great Britain and the colonies by granting the latter what would essentially be dominion status within the Empire. While the plan was at first well-received in Congress, it was ultimately rejected by a single vote. The growing radicalism of Pennsylvania politics forced Galloway to give up his offices and retreat to his country estate. He joined William Howe on his advance into New Jersey in December of 1776, and eventually served as the head of the civil government in Philadelphia during the British occupation in 1777-78. When the British evacuated the city in spring 1778, Galloway left with them and eventually journey to England where he died in 1803. See Boatner, *Encyclopedia*, p. 409.

[23] On this point, see Agnes Hunt, *The Provincial Committees of Safety of the American Revolution* (New York: Haskell House Publishers, 1968). Internet: http://www. committee.org/PCOSindex.htm. Last accessed, September 3, 2021.

[24] A great recent study of these developments is Walter R. Borneman *American Spring: Lexington, Concord, and the Road to Revolution* (New York: Little, Brown and Company, 2014).

[25] Jeffrey M. Dorwart, *Fort Mifflin of Philadelphia: An Illustrated History* (Philadelphia: University of Pennsylvania Press, 1998), p. 18.

[26] Notes of the Council of Safety, June 30, 1775 quoted in Samuel Hazard, ed. *Pennsylvania Archives*. Colonial Records Series, vol. 10, (Harrisburg: T. Fenn, 1853), 279. Hereinafter *PA Archives*. The full Committee of Safety consisted of: John Dickinson, George Gray, Henry Wynkoop, Anthony Wayne, Benjamin Bartholomew, George Ross, Michael Swoope, John Montgomery, Edward Biddle, William Edmunds, Bernard Daugherty, Samuel Hunter, William Thompson, Thomas Willing, Benajmins Franklin, Daniel Roberdeau, John Cadwalader, Andrew Allen, Owen Biddle, Francis Johnson, Richard Reiley, Samuel Morris, jr., Robert Morris, Thomas Wharton, and Robert White. Clearly, the membership included many who would be prominent figures in the War of Independence and the founding of the nation. On the membership, see *PA* Archives, Colonial Records, vol. 10, p. 280. On the role of the Committee, see Agnes Hunt, *Committee of Safety of the American Revolution*. Internet: http://www.committee.org/PCOSindex.htm. Last accessed, September 3, 2021.

[27] The sub-committee was composed of Luke Morris, Oswell Eve, John Wharton, Thomas Penrose, Major Nichols, Thomas Hanson, and Peter Reeve. See Minutes of the Pennsylvania committee of Safety, July 4, 1775, quoted in *Naval Documents of the American Revolution*. vol. 1, p. 815. *Naval Documents of the American Revolution* hereinafter *NDAR*.

[28] Lewis Nicola was the son of Huguenot immigrants to Ireland. He purchased a commission as ensign in the British army in 1740. Through the 1740s he served in a number of Irish garrison towns, including Galway, Londonderry, Dublin and Cork. He did see brief service on the continent in the War of Austrian Succession in Flanders in 1745. On the conclusion of hostilities he returned to Ireland and made his home at Kinsale for the next twenty-one years. The deteriorating economic situation in Ireland of the mid-1760s determined Nicola and his second wife, Jane Bishop, to emigrate to America. They came to Philadelphia and Lewis opened a store, which quickly brought some financial success. Likewise, he quickly became immersed in Philadelphia society and politics, being admitted to the American Society for Promoting Useful Knowledge. Politically, Nicola joined the Whig faction in his adopted home and began to work along with them to improve the city's defenses. For additional biographical data on Nicola, see Lewis Nicola, *A Treatise of*

Military Exercise. James R. Mc Intyre, ed. (West Chester, OH: The Nafziger Collection, 2009), pp. viii-xii.

[29] Lewis Nicola to the Pennsylvania Committee of Safety, July 6, 1775, quoted in *PA Archives*, Ser.1, vol. 4, p. 635.

[30] Ibid.

[31] Ibid, pp. 635-6

[32] Minutes of the Pennsylvania Committee of Safety, July 6, 1775 quoted in *NDAR*, vol. 1, pp. 830-31 See also John W. Jackson, *The Delaware Bay and River Defenses of Philadelphia, 1775-1777.* (Philadelphia: Philadelphia Maritime Museum, 1977), p. 5. See also Browne, "Mercer and Mifflin," p. 30.

[33] Robert Smith to Council of Safety quoted in Charl Peterson, *Robert Smith, Architect, Builder, Patriot (1722-1777).* (Philadelphia: The Athenaeum of Philadelphia, 2000), p. 156.

[34] Minutes of the Council of Safety, July 15, 1775, quoted in *PA Arch.*, Colonial Records, volume 10, p. 287.

[35] Notes of the Council of Safety, July 17, 1775, quoted in Ibid, p. 287.

[36] Ibid.

[37] William S. Stryker, *The Forts on the Delaware in the Revolutionary War.* (Trenton, NJ: John L.Murphy Publishing Co., 1901), p. 4.

[38] A.R. Donaldson to the Committee of Safety, July 11, 1775 quoted in William H. Egle, *PA Archives* Series 2, vol.10 (Harrisburg, PA: E.K. Meyers, State Printers, 1887), p. 803.

[39] Dorwart, *Fort Mifflin*, p. 19.

[40] Minutes of the Pennsylvania Committee of Safety, July 13, 1775, quoted in *NDAR.* vol. 1, p. 880.

[41] Alternate spellings include *chevaux de freis, chevaux de frize,* and *chevaux de frees.* The eighteenth century was a time of creating spelling. For the purposes of the current work, the standard spelling will be *chevaux de frise,* as this tends to be utilized in much subsequent secondary literature. The singular for this is *cheval de frise*

[42] Jackson, *Delaware Defenses*, p. 5

[43] Nicole Witting and Lawrence Babits "A Mnemonic Artifact: A 1777 Cheval de Frise from the Delaware River Battlefield." Online source: https://www.academia.edu/9354605/A_Mnemonic_Artifact_A_1777_Cheval_de_Frise_from_the_Delaware_River_Battlefield Last accessed, September 3, 2021.

[44] N.R. Ewan, "Chevaux-de-frize," p. 1.

[45] Peterson, *Robert Smith*, p. 154.

[46] Browne, "Fort Mercer and Fort Mifflin," p. 36.

[47] Ibid. Stewart credits Franklin with devising the chevaux de frise as he was known to have procured a pike during the period in which the Committee was reviewing different submissions for river defenses. See Frank H. Stewart, *History of the Battle of Red Bank with Events Prior and Subsequent thereto.* (Woodbury, NJ: Board of Freeholders of Gloucester County, 1927), p.6. The confusion on the actual invention of the chevaux-de -rise, as noted by Jackson, *River Defenses*, stems from

a request made by Franklin the previous day for some models of pikes. See Notes of Committee of Safety, *PA Arch. Col. Rec.*, vol. 10, p.298. The assumption being that these pikes were to serve as models for the poles attached to the frames on the chevaux de-frise. Sometime later, however, Franklin produced a version of pike that was intended for the use of the crews of the ships in the Pennsylvania Navy. See Notes of Committee of Safety, *PA Arch. Col. Rec.*, vol. 10, . On the Committee's request for Smith to look over rival plans for obstructing the Delaware, see Joseph S. Harris, "Robert Smith." in *PMHB*, 4,1 (1880): 82.

[48] Minutes of the Pennsylvania Committee of Safety, July 29, 1775, quoted in *NDAR*, vol. 1, 1004.

[49] Robert Smith to the Committee of Safety, quoted in Peterson, *Robert Smith*, p. 158.

[50] Browne, "Mercer and Mifflin," 36.

[51] Jackson, *Delaware Bay*, p. 6. On the positioning of the chevaux de frise off Mud Island, see Browne, "Mercer and Mifflin," p. 38.

[52] Minutes of the Pennsylvania Committee of Safety for September 1, 1775, quoted in *PA Arch, Col. Rec.* vol. 10, p. 329.

[53] Minutes of the Pennsylvania Committee of Safety for September 16, 1775, quoted in *PA Arch, Col. Rec.* vol. 10, p. 336.

[54] Ibid.

[55] Ibid, pp. 336-37

[56] Minutes of the Pennsylvania Committee of Safety for September 20, and 22, 1775, quoted in Ibid, pp. 340-1.

[57] Minutes of the Pennsylvania committee of Safety, September 22, 1775, quoted in *PA Arch Col. Rec.* vol. 10, p. 342. For background on why Rogers was in Philadelphia at this time, see John Ross, *War on the Run*,

[58] Minutes of the Pennsylvania committee of Safety, September 22, 1775, quoted in *PA Arch Col. Rec.* vol. 10, 343.

[59] Notes of Committee of Safety, July 31, 1775, quoted in *PA Arch, Col. Rec*, vol. 10, p. 296. Models of ships were routinely submitted to purchasing agents prior to the final agreement to build so that they buyer would be to see what they were purchasing.

[60] Ibid, p. 31.

[61] Browne, "Mercer and Mifflin," p. 33.

[62] Isidor Paul Strittmatter, *The Importance of the Campaign in the Delaware...* (Philadelphia: The Medical Club of Philadelphia, 1932), 6 asserts that the two craft were actually the same type and that the half-galley was the English designation for guard boats, however, this is not borne out by the subsequent research.

[63] Browne, "Mercer and Mifflin," p. 33.

[64] Ibid.

[65] Ibid, p. 34.

[66] Browne, "Mercer and Mifflin," p. 34.

[67] As noted, biographical information on Hazelwood is sparse. See Josiah G. Leach "Commodore John Hazel wood, Commander of the Pennsylvania Navy in the Revo-

lution." in Pennsylvania Magazine of History and Biography. 26, 1 (1902): 1. Pennsylvania Magazine of History and Biography hereinafter *PMHB*.

[68]Browne, "Mercer and Mifflin," pp. 33-34.

[69] Biographical information on Thomas Read derived from Boatner, *Encyclopedia*, p. 922.

[70]Minutes of the Pennsylvania Committee of Safety, October 23, 1775, quoted in *PA Arch. Col. Rec.* vol. 10, p. 379.

[71] Minutes of the Committee of Safety, October 15, 1775, quoted in *PA Arch. Col. Rec.* vol. 10, p. 368.

[72] Ibid.

[73] Minutes of the Committee of Safety, August 1, 1775, quoted in *PA Arch. Col. Rec.* vol. 10, p.296.

[74] Minutes of the Committee of Safety, September 30, 1775, quoted in Ibid, p. 350.

[75]Ibid. The resolution includes the injunction that Colonels Cadwallader, Dickinson, and Roberdeau provide a list of men in their respective Associator battalions to Towers so that he could make inquiries to the men directly for their arms.

[76] On this point, see Robert F. Smith, *Manufacturing Independence: Industrial Innovation in the American Revolution* (Yardley, PA: Westholme Press, 2016).

[77]Minutes of the Committee of Safety, October 3, 1775, *PA Arch. Col. Rec.* vol. 10, p. 354.

[78] Minutes of the Committee of Safety, September 16, 1775, quoted in Ibid, p. 338.

[79]Minutes of the Committee of Safety, September 23, 1775, quoted in Ibid, p. 343.

[80] Ibid, p. 356.

[81]Browne, "Mercer and Mifflin," p. 33

[82]Consider Molyneux's *Conjunct Expeditions* already noted in the introduction, as well as the fine amphibious operations conducted at Quebec (1759) and Havana (1762). On the former, see David Syrett, "Methodology of British Amphibious Operations" *The Mariner's Mirror*, pp. 269-280.

[83] Dorwart, *Fort Mifflin*, p. 21.

[84]Browne, "Mifflin and Mercer," pp. 30-31.

[85]Ibid, p. 46.

[86]Ibid.

[87] Ibid.

[88] Thomas J. McGuire, *The Philadelphia Campaign*, vol. 1, *Brandywine and the Fall of Philadelphia*. (Mechanicsburg, PA: Stackpole Books, 2007), p. 135.

[89] Dorwart, *Fort Mifflin*, p. 21.

[90]Pennsylvania Committee of Safety, October 16, 1775 quoted in *PA Arch. Col. Rec.* vol. 10, pp. 367-8.

[91] Pennsylvania Committee of Safety, October 23, 1775 quoted in Ibid, p. 378.

[92] Ibid, p. 402.

[93] Ibid, p. 368.

[94] Pennsylvania Committee of Safety, October 23, 1775 quoted in Ibid, pp. 382-3.

[95] Benjamin M. Nead, "A Sketch of General Thomas Proctor, with Some Account of the First Pennsylvania Artillery in the Revolution." in *PMHB* 4,4 (1880): 454-5.

[96] Major William C. Pruett, "A History of the Organizational Development of the Continental Artillery during the American Revolution." (MA Thesis: Command and General Staff College, Fort Leavenworth, KS, 2011), p. 112.

[97] Notes of the Pennsylvania Committee of Safety, November 6, 1775, quoted in *PA Arch. Col. Rec.* vol. x, p. 394.

[98] Dorwart, *Fort Mifflin*, p. 21.

[99] Ibid.

[100] Ibid.

[101] Ibid, pp. 21-2.

[102] Browne, "Mifflin and Mercer," p. 47.

[103] Pennsylvania Committee of Safety, October 15, 1775, quoted in *PA Arch. Col. Rec.* vol. 10, p. 367.

[104] Pennsylvania Committee of Safety, October 17, 1775, quoted in Ibid, p. 371.

[105] Pennsylvania Committee of Safety, November 2, 1775, quoted in Ibid, p. 388.

[106] Ibid.

[107] Ibid, pp. 383-4.

[108] The *rage militaire* is a concept developed by Royster to explain the American passion for the rebellion against Great Britain in 1775, as well as a fixation on all things martial. See Charles Royster, *A Revolutionary People at War: The Continental Army and the American Character, 1775-1783* (Chapel Hill, NC: University of North Carolina Press, 1979), pp. 25-53.

[109] Most accounts list Francis Proctor as Thomas Proctor's brother. Pruett, however, lists him as Thomas Proctor's father, who was born in Longford County, Ireland, in the early eighteenth century, and enlisted when substantially older than most recruits, even officers. He was eventually removed form his son's company. See Jackson, *Pennsylvania Navy*, p. 42, and Jackson, *Fort Mifflin*, p. 7. See also Pruett, "Continental Artillery," pp. 111-12.

[110] Pennsylvania Committee of Safety, November 2, 1775, quoted in *PA Arch. Col. Rec.* vol. 10, p. 388.

[111] There is a substantial literature on the Continental Army. Among the more useful works for understanding how it became a disciplined fighting force include: Caroline Cox, *A Proper Sense of Honor Service and Sacrifice in George Washington's Army* (Chapel Hill: UNC Press, 2004); James Kirby Martin, and Mark Edward Lender, *A Respectable Army: The Military Origins of the Republic, 1763-1789* (Wheeling, IL: Harlan Davidson, Inc. 1982); Charles P. Neimeyer, *The Revolutionary War* (Westport, CT: Greenwood Press, 2007). For understanding the problems of discipline, some very useful anecdotes are contained in John A. Nagy, *Rebellion in the Ranks Mutinies of the American Revolution* (Yardley, PA: Westholme Publishing, 2008). See also an unpublished paper James R. Mc Intyre, "Oh, What a Tangled Web We Weave, When First We Practice to Recruit." April 19, 2008. 75th Annual Meeting of the Society for Military History, Ogden, Utah. Finally, for un-

derstanding the relationship of the Continental Army to larger colonial culture, see Charles Royster, *A Revolutionary People at War The Continental Army and American Character, 1775-1783*. (Chapel Hill: University of North Carolina Press, 1979).

[112] Committee of Public Safety, November 11, 1775 quoted in *PA Arch.*, vol. x, p. 402.

[113] Ibid.

[114] Notes of the Committee of Safety, November 2, 1775, quoted in *PA Arch. Col. Rec.* vol. 10, p. 390.

[115] This point is made repeatedly by Jackson in his publications concerning the river defenses. See also, Brown, "Mifflin and Mercer," p. 46

[116] Browne, "Mifflin and Mercer," p. 48.

[117] Ibid.

[118] Notes of the Committee of Safety, September 29, 1775, quoted in *PA Arch. Col. Rec.* vol. 10, p. 350.

[119] Notes of the Committee of Safety, November 8, 1775, quoted in *PA Arch. Col. Rec.* vol. x, p. 399.

[120] Richard Riley to George Grey, September 13, 1775 quoted in *PA Arch.* Ser. 2, vol. 1, p. 550.

[121] Ibid.

[122] Ibid.

[123] John Belton to the Committee of Safety, September 4, 1775 in *NDAR* vol. 2, pp. 13-16.

[124] John Belton to the Committee of Safety, September 11, 1775, quoted in Ibid, p. 79.

[125] Minutes of the Committee of Safety, October 20, 1775, quoted in *PA Arch. Col. Rec.* vol. x, p. 374.

[126] Hunt,

[127] Minutes of the Pennsylvania Committee of Safety, October 27, 1775, quoted in *PA Arch. Col. Rec.* vol. 10, p. 383.

[128] Ibid.

[129] Minutes of the Committee of Safety, November 3, 1775, quoted in *PA Arch. Col. Rec.* vol. 1, p. 390.

[130] Ibid, p. 397.

[131] Extract of a Letter from Philadelphia, December 6, 1775, December 6, 1775? quoted in *NDAR*, volume 2, pp. 1307-08.

[132] Letter from the Pennsylvania Committee of Safety to Henry Fisher, November 28, 1775, quoted in Ibid, p. 1184.

[133] Minutes of the Pennsylvania Committee of Safety, November 3, 1775, quoted in *PA Arch. Col. Rec.* vol. 10, p. 390.

[134] Minutes of the Pennsylvania Committee of Safety, November 16, 1775, quoted in Ibid, p. 404.

[135] Ibid.

[136] Ibid, November 16, 1775, p. 404.

[137] Ibid.

[138] Ibid.

[139] Minutes of the Pennsylvania Committee of Safety, December 19, 1775, quoted in *PA Arch. Col. Rec.* vol. x,p. 432

[140] Ibid, December 26, 1775, quoted in Ibid, 437.

[141] Ibid, December 28, 1775, quoted in Ibid, 437.

[142] Ibid.

[143] Ibid.

[144] Extract of Letter from Philadelphia, September 9, 1775 reprinted in *London Evening Post*, November 9-11, 1775 quoted in *NDAR*, vol. 2, p. 60.
[145]Extract from a letter, Benjamin Franklin to Frederick Dumas, December 12, 1775, quoted in *NDAR*, vol 3, p.74.

Chapter Two

Independence and First Tests

The members of the Pennsylvania Committee of Safety made great strides in constructing a comprehensive network of river defenses in 1775. These initial steps are all the more impressive as they were taken while they were wresting control of the colony from the former government. Still, the Committee and its supporters possessed some advantages, first and foremost stood the fact that they were not under attack by the British, nor was there even the imminent threat of attack during the early stages of their efforts. Throughout 1775, the war remained confined to the northern theater. The siege of Boston continued until March of 1776. Likewise, there occurred the failed strike into Canada under Benedict Arnold and Richard Montgomery. Meanwhile, Philadelphia remained a safe haven in the early stages of the colonial revolt. These conditions changed drastically in 1776.

First and foremost, the nature of the conflict changed, when, on July 4, 1776, the Continental Congress officially severed their political bond with Great Britain. This act altered the nature of the war from a revolt against Crown policy to a war of national liberation. Simultaneously, it opened up the Americans to the possibility of gaining foreign aid against Great Britain, and potentially widening the dimensions of the war substantially. Interestingly, the following day, two representatives of the Continental Congress, George Clymer and Michael Hillegas, purchased ninety-six acres of land at Billingsport in New Jersey to begin the construction of a fortification to cover the lower set of chevaux de frise. The acquisition of this plot stood the first land purchased by the national government following independence.[1]

Even before these momentous events began to unfold, the Committee of Safety continued their labors in erecting defenses for the Delaware River. The members of the Committee made several trips down to Fort Island between December 1775 and February 1776 in order to determine what further measures were necessary for the defense of Philadelphia from a maritime assault.[2]

January of 1776 saw considerable efforts made towards the completion of the land forces raised by Pennsylvania in the previous year. For instance, the Committee of Public Safety appointed chaplains to the various units and filled a number of officers' billets. In addition, the members devised a method for inspecting surgeon candidates for the state's nascent formations.[3] The acquisition of a sufficient and reliable supply of gunpowder continued to stand as a major challenge for the Committee, and a number of efforts were made to meet the demands of the coming campaign. These efforts included both attempts to procure gunpowder from foreign sources, and the stimulation of domestic manufacture.[4] In addition, the Committee sought to honor requests made by the Continental Congress for supplies of various kinds, as well as troops.[5]

Through all of the above efforts, it may appear that the defense of the Delaware River fell into the background. It did to some extent. The lack of effort expended on the river defenses stemmed, to some degree, from the simple fact of the season. In January the river froze. Consequently, the chances of a maritime assault on the city were nonexistent. Still, there were positive developments in the maritime defenses of Philadelphia over the winter of 1775-76. One such stride came in the form of greater cooperation between the various governments based in the city.

The Pennsylvania Committee of Safety and the Continental Congress began to work more closely late in 1775 and the partnership continued into 1776. Their combined efforts are evidenced by the request by the Continental Congress, received on New Years' Day, 1776 for three of the Pennsylvania pilots to conduct vessels belonging to Congress down to Reedy Island. The Committee of Safety complied with the request the same day, informing one Capt. Dougherty that he was to order "such a number of men from on Board the armed Boats under your command, as may be necessary to navigate the vessels belonging to the Congress down to Reedy Island."[6]

The Committee enacted some additional measures concerning the river defenses as well. For instance, Thomas Proctor, once again in favor with the Committee of Safety, was ordered to assume command of the artillery company stationed on Fort Island on January 9, 1776.[7] Several days later, on January 13, Andrew Caldwell "having applied to take the command of the fleet in the Service of this Province, and consented thereto," was appointed to the command of the Pennsylvania Fleet.[8] As will be seen, his would be a tempestuous tenure. Likewise, the Committee resolved to appoint a second in command for the fleet as well.[9]

A major concern of the Committee of Safety centered on locating and recruiting enough soldiers and sailors to man the impressive defensive system they were developing. The body took several steps to address these manpower needs. First, on January 15, they ordered John Ross to provide a complete return of the men then serving on board the armed boats.[10] Then, on January 19th the Committee directed that four hundred "Sea men and Lands men immediately be recruited for the service of the armed boats and other Naval equipments..."[11] In addition, the Committee resolved on the same day to send three of its members, David Rittenhouse, Robert Smith, and John McNeal, to Liberty Island in order to determine what works should be developed for the protection of the city at that site.[12] The three men were empowered to not only survey the site and determine what works would be most efficacious for its defense, but to oversee the construction of whatever works they devised as well.

The crews of the fleet discussed above were not the only ones to receive reinforcements. On January 25, Captain Proctor was directed by the Committee "to enlist seventy Volunteers, who are to be instructed principally in the use and management of Artillery..."[13]

Lastly, late in January 1776, the Committee of Safety took an additional step towards stiffening the river defenses. They appointed Samuel Morris, along with Rittenhouse, McNeal, and a Capt. Joy to "Survey the Jersey Shore from Billingsport to Newtown Creek, to determine what posts it may be necessary to fortify against the attempts of an Enemy who may endeavor to land."[14] They were to complete the survey and provide a report of their findings, including an estimate of expenses of any proposed fortifications within a week.[15]

The four men made their report to the Committee on February 2. In the report, the group first presented their methodology for making the measurements. Next, they provided an overview of the area they surveyed to the Committee. The men then suggested that neither Billingsport nor Red Bank would serve as appropriate places to erect defenses, as they were too far from the chevaux de frise, and from the works on Fort Island, to lend sufficient support. Likewise, they noted that "if a fort were built at either of these places, the Enemy could land above or below it, without any difficulty, (unless a superior army could be collected before, on the spot to oppose them,) and oblige our people to spike their Cannon and quit the fort."[16] The members of the sub-committee then submitted their own idea for the defense of the river along the New Jersey side.

Instead of a static defense along the Jersey side of the river, the group suggested that the colonies instead employ a number of 12- or 18-pounder cannon "mounted on strong traveling carriages, and previous to the enemy's approach to raise Breastworks at the most convenient places, from whence those Guns, thus mounted, and well ply'd with Star and Cross Barr'd Shot, &c., will annoy the enemy much;"[17] Thus, they proposed a more mobile defense composed of several less permanent works that could be occupied or left abandoned as circumstances dictated. Such a configuration would allow for less investment of time, effort and manpower, as troops could be shuffled around to different locations along with the guns. The Committee accepted the report of the four men; however, no actions were taken that day.

On February 20, the Committee once again returned to the river defenses. They enacted a series of resolves designed to complete the work initiated the previous year at Fort Island in the Delaware. For instance, on that day, Jacob Myers was appointed "Armourer to the armed Boats and Vessels, and to be employed at Fort Island."[18] They followed up this resolve with one calling on Owen Biddle and Capt. Whyte to "order a Smith's shop and forge to be erected on Fort Island, and to furnish the same with the proper Smith's tools." [19] These men were to form a committee, an additional duty of which was to "see that the necessaries wanting at Fort Island for the use of the Battery, and for Capt. Procter's Company, not mention'd in the above the Revolves be supplied." Clearly, the last point constituted a catch-all to empower the men sent to Fort Island to address needs as they were discovered. This can be seen as an indication of the growing sense of confidence felt by the Committee both in itself and its individual members, as they no longer felt the need for reports prior to taking action on issues necessary for the defense of the city.

Housing the troops already stationed at the fortifications remained problematic. The shortage of adequate barracks on Fort Island led to the following resolution on the part of the Committee of Safety, "That Captain Procter make use of seven Rooms in the Pest house on Province Island for quartering part of the Artillery Company." [20] Given that the Pest House served as a quarantine area for incoming visitors to the city to be held in while it was determined that they were not carrying any disease into Philadelphia, this move was likely not very popular with the men under Proctor's command. Still, they would at least have a roof over their heads, and in February, that would certainly preserve their health better than living in the tents and lean-tos which workers constructed at Fort Island the previous year.

Looking to the training of the artillery company stationed on Fort Island, the Committee further authorized that Capt. Procter "have the use of as many firelocks as he may have occasion for, and a 6-pound canon to exercise the men under his command, and that Robert Towers be directed to deliver the same." [21]

The growing confidence of the Committee of Safety is further evidenced in a resolve of February 29th, when they organized James Biddle, George Clymer, and Owen Biddle into a subcommittee and entrusted them with broad powers "to carry into execution everything necessary towards compleating [sic] the Fortifications on Fort Island, Barracks excepted, and to employ suitable persons to accomplish the same."[22] The preceding likewise demonstrates that the members of the Committee by now possessed a clearer sense of priorities for the work on Fort Island. The completion of the fortifications was to take precedence over the work on the barracks. This may reflect a growing concern that the British would launch an attack on the city sooner rather than later and that the defenses had to be brought up to a greater state of readiness to prepare for this eventuality. In addition, the Committee of Safety authorized Procter to procure a flag staff for the fort, "with a Flagg of the United Colonies."[23] The preceding stands as one of the first mentions of a national standard on record.

In the spring of 1776, the Committee of Safety determined to construct another row of chevaux de frise further south in the Delaware. Since the lower row of obstructions, moving up the river, was to be located off of Billingsport in New Jersey, it was decided to construct a fort there. Initially, the man entrusted with the project was one Robert Smith, the same man who already contributed so much work on the development of chevaux de frise. A number of obstacles prevented Smith from giving the works his full attention.

On the same day, the Committee ordered Cmdre. Caldwell and Capt. Procter to "fix upon proper Signals for the Fleet, Merchantmen & Battery, and that the same be communicated to the Pilots employed in Navigating Vessels through the Chevaux de Frise."[24] The Committee were attempting to delegate the task of devising a uniform system for guiding the movement of ships through the obstacles. Finally, the Committee ordered Robert Towers to "put up 50 rounds of Cartridge, with different kinds of Shot, for each of the six 18-pound Canon on the Battery at Fort Island."[25]

As usual, the Committee's attention was not focused entirely on the fortifications, they attended to all matters relating to the defense of the colony concurrently. This included a resolution, dated March 6, calling on a Capt. Brown to "Raise fifty able bodied Men for the Marine service of this Province." [26] Thus, the birth of the Pennsylvania State Marines. That same day, the Committee ordered a survey made of the region between Reedy Point and an area referred to as the Pea Patch.[27] The execution of this resolve was turned over to the Commodore, who was to send a pilot and two "discreet and capable officers" in two armed boats to Reedy Point to determine the "sound the narrowest part of the Channel there and to take an accurate survey of the depth & breadth of the said Channel, with the various soundings across the same, for the information of this Board." [28] Two days later, on March 8, it was represented to the Committee that pilot boats could be "employed to more advantage in sounding the Channel at Reedy Point than the Armed Boats," and it was therefore resolved to do so.[29]

The Committee worked to achieve a more formal organization in their defensive network as well. Their efforts in this direction are evidenced in a resolution of March 9, 1776, in which the Committee called upon Capt. William Richards, Capt. Nathaniel Falconer, and Capt. Thomas Reed to be empowered to "fix signals for giving alarm at cape Henlopen, and at such other places on either side of the Bay and River Delaware as they shall judge proper..."[30] The three officers were further authorized to "engage for Men and Horses to be in readiness to convey intelligence by Land and to do everything necessary to effect the said service." The men were authorized to call on the Committee for any funds necessary to put their orders into execution as well. [31] These measures were a step towards adding a vital aspect to the river defenses, a communications network that could forward information and intelligence on any enemy incursion from the Delaware Bay northwards to the city of Philadelphia and alert all the posts in between. The network these men developed would not wait long for its initial tests under fire. Following these actions, the Committee's attention focused for several days on the land forces of Pennsylvania.

Soon, however, the Committee returned to the business of the river defenses. On March 13 they ordered that Arthur Donaldson "be employed to launch the Chevaux-de-Frise built at Gloucester, and that he be fully authorized to procure anything for the purpose..."[32] In addition, he was authorized to hire men to aid him in the work at the best rate he could obtain and draw on the Committee for his expenses.[33] Next, the Committee resolved to employ John Coburn "to take the Chevaux-de-Frise, when launched at Gloucester, and sink them in their proper places near Fort Island..."[34] Coburn was permitted to procure materials and manpower necessary to achieve his mission as well.[35] Finally, the Committee resolved that

"Capt. Rice be applied to, to assist in taking down the Chevaux-de-Frise, and that he attend this Board to-morrow Morning."[36] It seems apparent from the last point that the Committee of Safety wanted one of their members to oversee the work and report upon its progress. The Committee further resolved for five additional small guard boats be built for use in the river.[37]

Finding adequate manpower for the Philadelphia defenses continued to pose a significant problem for the leadership. On March 15, the Committee ordered the Commodore to send "such Officers as he shall think proper to recruit Seamen and able-bodied Landsmen for the Naval Service of this Province..."[38] That same day, the Committee furthered the work of its members in creating a system of signals by resolving that the Commissary deliver to Capts. Richards, Falconer, and Reed the necessary materials for "fixing Signals, such as Guns, Ammunition, and Implements, as they shall require for the service." [39]

The following day, the Committee returned to the chevaux de frise. Now that the ice on the river began to give way, it became possible to take on the task of moving the large frames for the chevaux de frise into place and sinking them so as to block the Delaware to hostile shipping. Accordingly, on March 16 the Committee of Safety resolved that "Captain Rice be employed to take the Chevaux de Frise, when launched at Gloucester, and sink them in their proper places near Fort Island; and that he be authorized to procure anything for the purpose, hire persons under him, on the best and cheapest terms, and that he draw on this Board for the Expense."[40] The Committee followed up the preceding order with a resolution on March 16, that Cmdre. Caldwell "give directions to the Officers of the Boats for the Chevaux-de-Frise now sunk at Fort Island, to be examined, and make report of their situation to this Board, by Tuesday Next."[41] The Committee seemingly sought to determine if any of the frames had shifted due to the freezing and thawing of the Delaware.

On March 20, the Committee drew an order for £300 Pennsylvania currency in order to pay for Nathaniel Falconer for the materials and his work in setting the signals "in the Bay and River Delaware."[42] At the same time, the Committee added one Capt. Leeson Simmons to the Committee for fixing signals in the bay and river.[43] Soon, the defensive system the Committee labored so intensely to create received its first test.

On March 25, the frigate, *HMS Roebuck* under the command of Capt. Andrew Snape-Hamond entered the Delaware Capes. The ship searched for American vessels to capture as prizes. The authorities in Philadelphia reacted quickly ordering the Pennsylvania Navy boats to prepare for action. At the same time, Capt. John Barry of the Continental brig *Lexington* proceeded southward down the Delaware to engage the British vessel. As he approached the *Roebuck*, Barry realized that she was more than a match for his own vessel. He prudently clung to the coast, staying out of the range of the frigate's guns, until he could make for open sea and search for British prizes.[44]

While no engagement materialized between the British and American forces in the Delaware on this occasion, the overall significance of the event was not lost on the local authorities. The Delaware defenses were going to be tested, and this test would likely occur sooner rather than later. The Pennsylvania authorities did not have long to wait.

The incursion likewise made it clear to the Committee of Safety that their efforts to date had not yielded the comprehensive defensive network they had hoped to build. So much is evidenced by the fact that on March 25, the body created a subcommittee composed of David Rittenhouse, John McNeal, Col. Samuel Miles, Owen Biddle and George Clymer. The men were tasked with fixing "upon proper places upon the Delaware River for erecting fortifications." Up to this point, the chief fortification on the river was at Fort Island. The members of the Committee of Safety clearly believed that that post alone would not be sufficient to block an attack by a determined foe and therefore sought to expand the defensive network already under construction.

As a part of their renewed focus on the Delaware defenses, the members of the Committee of Safety determined to block off some sections of the river completely. On March 30, the Committee appointed three gentlemen, Mr. Howell, Mr. Nixon, and Capt. Whyte, to compose a committee to "look out for two Vessels most proper for sinking in the passage between the Chevaux-de-Frise and make Report of their proceedings to this Board."[45] In addition to searching for ships to sink in order to close off the channel between the chevaux de frise, the Committee determined to construct a boom and chain across the river, to be held between two piers. In order to set the chain across the river, the Committee requested Robert Morris to "purchase a sufficient Number of Logs for building two Piers, for fixing the Boom to for obstructing the Navigation." Further, they instructed Morris and Capt. Whyte to contract with someone to build the piers.[46]

As a means to provide warning against incursions by British vessels, three members of the Committee; Nixon, Mease, and Roberdeau were "desired to look out for a small vessel, proper to fit out as a cruiser in the Bay of Delaware against the Ministerial armed Tenders now obstructing the Commerce of this Province, and that they make Report of their proceedings as soon as possible to this Board."[47]

The Committee sought to tighten their control over traffic in the river as well. On April 13, they directed that either the Commodore of the Fleet or the Commanding Officer at Fort Island ensure that outbound vessels not carrying a permit be directed not to pass the chevaux de frise. They further instructed the same officers to prevent inbound vessels from passing without a permit from this Board.[48]

It seems that the new awareness of the urgency of improving the river defenses pushed the Committee of Safety to focus their efforts to a greater degree. In order to quickly stiffen the defenses, the main committee formed a series of sub-committees tasked with addressing specific deficiencies in those fortifications. These included such bodies as a Canon Committee, tasked with procuring canons for the defenses. This group consisted of George Clymer, Owen Biddle, Samuel Howell, David Rittenhouse, and Jonathan Cadwalader. The Committee of Safety likewise formed a Fire Raft Committee, on which Howell and Biddle also served, along with the latter's brother James. This committee saw to the needs of the Fire Rafts stationed in the Delaware. Other committees included a Ship Committee, a Committee for Providing Pikes and Entrenching Tools, a Chevaux de Frise Committee, and a Fort Island Committee, among others. All told, the Committee of Safety generated nineteen sub-committees. [49]

Clearly, there existed a significant amount of overlap in the membership of the committees. It is unclear if this was done intentionally, in order to foster coordination of efforts between the various panels or if it were done simply out of a lack of adequate members. Likewise, it is unclear if the creation of these committees actually succeeded in making the work of developing the river defenses flow more smoothly. Still, at least some of the sub-committees began to address their tasks almost immediately. More importantly, they started to produce results. One of these was the Committee for Further Defenses, composed of George Clymer, David Rittenhouse, Owen Biddle, Samuel Miles, and John McNeal. On April 19, they reported to the Committee of Safety their recommendation for the construction of a "Floating Battery of a similar, or nearly similar Construction with the one now in service..."[50] The larger Committee took up this recommendation and resolved to construct the additional floating battery. In the process, they created yet another sub-committee, on Floating Batteries, composed of Howell, Clymer, and Whyte, to oversee the construction.[51] All these efforts would soon be put to the test.

On April 28, 1776, one of Henry Fisher's express riders carried news to Philadelphia of the sighting another British ship. The HMS *Roebuck* had returned, and this time she had run aground near Wilmington while in pursuit of the Continental warship *Wasp*.

Upon receiving news of the *Roebuck's* predicament reached the Committee of Safety, they ordered that the eight galleys stationed at Fort Island be readied for service and dispatched down the river to engage the enemy vessel. The Pennsylvania Navy's armed vessel *Montgomery* and the Continental Navy ship *Reprisal* received orders to make ready and follow the galleys as soon as possible to provide extra firepower. To obtain the manpower necessary for the excursion, the Committee of Safety ordered Captain Reed to "make up his Compliment of Seamen out of the Floating Battery, and to take a detachment of Capt. Procter's artillery." In a testament to the support for the sailors, many citizens came out to assist in loading supplies, arms, and munitions aboard the latter vessels despite a driving rain.[52]

The eight galleys left Fort Island early on April 29. As the *Montgomery* and *Reprisal* made their way down past the upper row of chevaux de frise, they encountered the smaller vessels returning from their cruise into the lower Delaware. The *Roebuck* managed to free herself and was therefore more than a match for the firepower of the small vessels.

The Committee of Safety, understandably puzzled with the lack of an engagement, sent James Mease and Samuel Morris down to meet with the Commodore and determine whether the ships should return, and if the *Roebuck* had left the Delaware Bay.[53] This second incursion by a British vessel into the Delaware Bay, inconclusive as it was, heightened the awareness of the members of the Committee of Safety to the very real dangers of a British maritime assault on the city and its shipping.

One action taken by the Committee in the days following this alarm was to task Howell and Mease to constitute a sub-committee to determine "if two of the armed Boats can be fitted out, in order to go down to the Bay of Delaware, to be there station'd for the protection of the commerce of this Province." They were further directed that "if they find that it is practicable to fit or alter two for that purpose, that they employ proper persons to carry the same into execution."[54] A sub-committee tasked with implementing this decision and composed of Col. Nixon and Capt. Whyte was created the next day.[55]

On May 6, the Committee received a new report via express that the *Roebuck* and *Liverpool*, as well as several smaller vessels, had returned to the Delaware Bay. The messenger believed the destination of the force was Philadelphia. The garrison on Fort Island prepared themselves for battle, as did the vessels of the Pennsylvania Navy.[56] The defenses brought to bear on this occasion were quite impressive, and included the *Montgomery*, as well as thirteen row galleys. Further, the Committee ordered the floating battery manned for action and positioned by the upper row of chevaux de fries. They dispatched the fire ships and two chains of fire rafts to Fort Island as well. Finally, three Continental vessels, the *Reprisal*, *Lexington*, and *Hornet* prepared to offer support to the Pennsylvania ships.[57] Orders were then issued from the Committee of Safety calling on the "Commanding officer of the Fleet & Artillery Company at Fort Island, to call every Boat & Soldiers to their stations, & each to prepare for immediate action."[58]

The Committee further sent Nixon and Whyte to the Fort Island as advisers to the commanders on the scene.[59] Likewise, they ordered all the officers and men of the boats then in Philadelphia down the river to Fort Island.[60] Finally, the Committee ordered Capt. John Hazelwood to "send down the Fire Vessels & 2 Chains of Fire Rafts, & to dispose of them in the most convenient situations, near Fort Island."[61] The colony was preparing itself to repel a full scale attack, and with good reason.

An express from Port Penn received on the night of May 6 indicated that:

> *two Ships of War, a Top Sail Schooner & three smaller Vessels supposed to be tenders, were in sight of Port Penn, half past 11 O'Clock on Monday last, the Board, in consequence thereof, gave orders to Capt. Reed to order down the thirteen armed boats under the command of the Senior Officer, with directions to proceed down the River, when they must concert the best method to attack, take, sink, destroy, or drive off the said Vessels if possible, but to be careful in exposing*

> *any of the Boats to Capture or destruction, and to send*
> *down the Fire Sloop Commanded by Captain Gamble,*
> *one other officer & 4 or 6 Men, with some bedding and*
> *other necessaries; also a six or four oard [sic] Boat; &*
> *to acquaint the Officers and Men in the Fire Sloop,*
> *that for their encouragement in performing any Essen-*
> *tial Service, this Board reward them handsomely.*[62]

In addition, the Committee called a special meeting same evening at 5:15 P.M to respond to the growing crisis. The members present determined to dispatch four of their number down to the fort to make certain that the orders of the committee were carried out. The men selected were to travel to the fort on the *Province*, with "full and ample powers to enforce such orders as have already been Issued, or may Issue from this Board..."[63]

It seems the Committee were not completely confident in the commanders of the fort or the Pennsylvania Navy, as demonstrated by the following,

> *That the said Committee, in Conjunction with*
> *the Commanding Officer be fully authorized to Issue*
> *such further orders to the Fleet as they may think nec-*
> *essary, in Consequence of any further information they*
> *may not receive respecting the motions of the Enemy.*[64]

They further ordered that the sub-committee sent to Fort Island retain two row boats to remain in motion between the works and the Pest House, in order to maintain a speedy flow of intelligence. In keeping with this injunction, they further authorized Owen Biddle to commission two men with horses to maintain an express between the city and Province Island for the duration of the alarm.[65]

Over the course of the next several days, the attention of the Committee of Safety, and much of the populace of Philadelphia were taken up by the happenings in the river. On May 5, two ships entered the Delaware Bay and sailed to the vicinity of Wilmington. Unbeknownst to the Americans, they were only coming into the bay in order to fill her water casks.[66] The ships were the *Roebuck*, the British frigate under the command of Capt. Hamond, accompanied by another vessel, the *Liverpool*.

As events unfolded, they were covered in the local press. For instance, on May 7, the *Pennsylvania Evening Post* reported

> *Yesterday morning an express arrived from the capes, informing the Committee of Safety that the men of war were coming up the river, and between ten and eleven the alarm guns were fired; and at ten o'clock last night another express came from Reedy-Island, which said that at half after eleven o'clock two men of war with several tenders and prizes were in sight, but no further advices were received by the Committee when this paper went to press, at half past four o'clock this afternoon.[67]*

Since the first ships to come in contact with the *Roebuck* were the pilot boats stationed at Chester, they took aboard Miles Pennington and twenty-six of his Pennsylvania State Marines and made their way downriver to engage the British ship.[68]

The British squadron entered the Delaware Bay and anchored off Bombay Hook.[69] Hammond dispatched foraging parties ashore in search of supplies and fresh water. The British vessels encountered two shallops as well. These were small vessels, about thirty feet in length, initially developed in the seventeenth century. They were propelled by oars but had a mast and one or two sails as well. They were utilized for coastal sailing. One of these was most likely the *Black Duck,* as it was the only shallop listed with the Pennsylvania Navy.

Hamond dispatched boats from the *Roebuck* to capture these vessels, which they did. At this point Henry Fisher, the lookout posted at Lewes, sent his first dispatch rider to Philadelphia. In the interim, the Chester County militia under the command of Col. Samuel Miles were called out and attempted to capture the landing party. Miles stationed his men at Marcus Hook anticipation of further developments. Hamond recalled his men from shore, narrowly escaping Miles and his militia. Following these contacts, Hamond anchored the *Roebuck* south of Reedy Island, near Morris Lister's Creek.[70]

Early on the morning of May 7, while Hamond and Capt. Henry Bellew, the commander of the *Liverpool* stood awaiting the arrival of the brig *Betsy* as well as several other auxiliary ships. Some of these attempted to capture the Continental schooner *Wasp*, captained by Charles Alexander. This ship managed to escape up the Christiana River where she was later joined by a small schooner.[71] Another small schooner

Fig. 5. Image of a shallop from the 17th century. This is the same general design as the vessels that made their way down the Delaware. *Source: Wooden Ship Magazine, Internet: PILGRIM SHALLOP II | WoodenBoat Magazine Last accessed 10/10/21.*

beached itself while trying to evade capture by the British warships. The *Liverpool* and *Roebuck* dispatched boats to refloat the vessel and take it as a prize. The British flotilla stood off Wilmington, Delaware for the night.

South of Reedy Island is where they were discovered by Capt. Henry Dougherty with thirteen galleys and a fire sloop from the Pennsylvania Navy on May 8. His ships left their anchorage off Fort Island at 6 AM, slipped through the lower chevaux de frise and headed downriver to engage the British interlopers. Two other vessels, the provincial ship *Montgomery* and the floating battery *Arnold* were directed to remain above the chevaux de frise and form a secondary line of defense should one become necessary.[72]

Late morning fog hung over the Delaware Bay as the galleys from the Pennsylvania Navy made their way downriver. This dispersed between noon and one in the afternoon, the breeze died down as well. Lookouts in the masts of the British ships called below as they sighted the American galleys passing down the river towards them. As the American vessels approached, many of the British officers aboard the small force displayed a smug contempt for the American interceptors. Their view was not shared by Hamond, an experienced officer. He ordered the decks cleared for battle.[73]

Fig 6. The Continental schooner Wasp, one of the first eight vessels authorized by the Continental Congress. *Source: Public Domain. Internet: USS-Wasp1775 - USS Wasp (1775) - Wikipedia. Last accessed 10/10/21.*

Cannons boomed and muzzles flashed, sending heavy iron balls hurtling through the air. When these projectiles connected with their intended targets, they splintered heavy timbers hurling deadly bits of shrapnel in all directions. These splinters could be quite deadly or lead to amputations in any unfortunate sailor they wounded in the limbs. Further, the iron balls bored holes in the wooden vessels allowing the waters of the Delaware easy access. If the contest between the two forces was decided simply by number and weight of cannons, the British ships would undoubtedly take the laurels. Both the *Liverpool* and the *Roebuck* could fire broadside which surely would annihilate the small galleys coming at them. The smaller galleys of Pennsylvania Navy possessed their own advantages. Maneuverability encompassed one of their assets. They could change course much faster than the larger Royal Nay frigates. In addition, they could quickly duck up one of the streams that dotted both shores of the river, where their larger opponents could not follow.

While the Pennsylvania galleys seized the initiative and opened fire first, they did so while still roughly a mile distant. At such extreme range, their initial volleys constituted mere wasted shots, a fact that would lead to recriminations later. As the contest opened, crowds of people began to gather along the shore in the hopes of getting a view of the ensuing engagement.

As the Americans closed, the *Roebuck* and the *Liverpool* maneuvered themselves into position to meet the attack. Still in the process of maneuvering, the *Roebuck* gave what fire she could from her stern chasers. The two vessels turned so that the *Roebuck's* bow faced eastward while the *Liverpool's* faced westward across the river. [74] Now the British vessels would be able to fire their full weight of broadsides.

Once the Liverpool and Roebuck attained their positions, they moved upriver on a slight breeze, exchanging fire with the ships of the Pennsylvania Navy. The two sides exchanged fire for over two hours.

In the midst of the battle, Capt. Alexander, the commander of the *Wasp*, attempted to capture the brig *Betsy*. At a point when the attention of the British ships seemed entirely focused on the galleys, he quickly sailed out of Wilmington Creek in the *Wasp* to the *Betsy* to board and capture her. With his prize under control, Alexander then returned to the safety of Wilmington Creek. [75]

At roughly four o'clock in the afternoon, the galleys broke off their attack on the British ships and returned upriver. The reason for their abandoning the attack lay in the fact that they had completely expended their limited supplies of shot and powder. Dougherty, therefore, decided to replenish his supplies and return the next morning and renew the engagement. [76]

Damage and casualties from the clash were light on both sides. The Pennsylvania galley *Camden* was hit once, and had a crewman killed. The *Roebuck* incurred some damage to her rigging and received a few holes in her side. More importantly, as the engagement broke off the *Roebuck* ran aground on the Jersey side of the river. [77] Unaware of the reason for the galley's departure, Hamond dispatched boats from both the *Roebuck* and the *Liverpool* to act as pickets should Capt. Henry Dougherty's ships return. As the tide ebbed, the ship heeled so far that Hamond ordered her gunports closed to prevent flooding. His action rendered the *Roebuck* defenseless should the Americans return and attack in the night. [78]

Fortunately for Hamond and his crew, no such attack occurred. Dougherty encountered difficulties all his own. First and foremost, among these stood replenishing the ammunition racks in his galleys. While the Committee of Safety expended significant efforts to secure the vital shot and powder, according to commodore Thomas Read, (Dougherty's superior) many of the cartridges fell apart when handled.[79]

A contingent of Continental sailors under John Barry from the *Lexington* further exacerbated these woes. While Barry's sailors would make a welcomed addition to the manpower of the Pennsylvania Navy in the crisis, they were accompanied by numerous volunteers who, while full of patriotic ardor, knew nothing of the mariner's trade.[80]

Read managed to overcome these difficulties and rearm the ships for a new attack on the British interlopers. Likewise, the crews of the *Roebuck* and *Liverpool*, working through a tense and sleepless night, managed to free the former from the sandbar. Both forces prepared for a renewed confrontation.

A thick fog obscured the dawn on May 9, and it was not until after 8 o'clock that Hamond espied the galleys of Dougherty's squadron about two miles upriver from his position. Hamond ordered the *Roebuck* and *Liverpool* to close with the galleys. The galley crews, now more accustomed to their craft and with some combat experience, reacted much more dexterously in maneuvering their craft around the larger British frigates.[81]

As the *Liverpool* and the *Roebuck* closed, Hamond noticed he was drawing only six inches clearance over a shoal. Fearing a repeat of the previous night's anxieties and the very real possibility that the Americans would take advantage of his distress today, he ordered a withdrawal downriver. Hamond planned to continue replenishing his fresh water, the main intent of his incursion from the outset.

At four in the afternoon, Hamond was amazed to see the galleys once more bearing down on his ships. Again, Hamond found himself in a predicament as his ships were caught in some narrows which drastically restricted their ability to maneuver. He ordered his ships downriver once again to provide more room to receive the brazen American assault.

The galley crews, having faced the British successfully the day before, took courage and came within three-quarters of a mile of the British ships before they opened fire. At such close range, their shots proved much more effective than the previous day.

The fight in the river raged for nearly four hours, and once again attracted numerous onlookers on both shores. With light fading and the ammunition once again running out on the galleys, Dougherty again ordered his ships to break off. The galleys came away with minimal damage and had only a few wounded. The *Roebuck*, on the other hand, sustained substantial damage. The ship's carpenters reported taking "forty of the row-galley's ball out." In addition, "the rigging, sails and spars...were often struck damaged, and cut."[82] After the two forces separated, the British anchored off Reedy Island, while the Americans positioned themselves near Newcastle.[83] Clearly, The British took the worst in the second confrontation.

The two sides maintained a wary distance from one another for the next three days, while the British crews made repairs to their ships and continued filling their water casks. In their first tests under fire, the galleys and their crews demonstrated remarkable courage and adaptation. While they gave a lackluster performance on the first day, they quickly improved as both cohesive crews and at showing courage under fire. However, much of this was missed at the time. As John W. Jackson observed, "...when the smoke cleared much had been learned about the most effective ways to use the galleys."[84] He later expanded on this verdict, noting "If used under the proper conditions, and in the narrow confines of the upper river, they could be an effective force in defending the city."[85] Unfortunately, much of this knowledge lay obscured in the short-term amidst clouds of controversy.

The more significant short-term aspect of the confrontation lay in the aftermath on the American side. Criticisms quickly began to circulate that the Pennsylvania ships had not been aggressive enough and had essentially thrown away their shot. The accusations and debates continued long after the war. At least one historian alleged that the officers of the Pennsylvania Navy turned the blame on the Committee of Safety. The ship commanders perceived that the military failure supported the notion that the Committee was too conservative. Many of the officers of the fleet hailed from the more radical faction of Pennsylvania politics and sought to move towards declaring independence. [86]

For their part, the members of the Committee took away the valuable lessons from the British incursion into the Delaware Bay. To some extent, the defensive network the Pennsylvania leadership worked so hard erect over the previous year demonstrated at least a level of effectiveness. The alarm guns sounded, and the express riders communicated intelligence of the incursion promptly. The ships of the fleet responded well and sailed down the river to engage the enemy. Many Philadelphians demonstrated their support by helping to load the guard boats as well.

At the same time, the incursion revealed the limits of the military capabilities of the fleet in stark relief. The Committee perceived the need for additional firepower both on the banks and in the river itself. To the latter end, the Committee determined, on May 13, to fortify some part of the Jersey shore as further defense of the obstacles placed in the river.[87] On the same day, the body authorized payment to those who had aided in the sinking of the chevaux de frise and directed the purchase of a vessel for housing the crews of the fire rafts stationed in the Delaware as well.[88]

The following day, some of the gentlemen of Philadelphia presented the Committee with an offer to "form themselves into Companys [sic] of Volunteers, and whenever called upon in defense of this River, to enter into actual service on Board any Armed Boat that shall be provided for them by this Committee under their own officers."[89] Such an offer, while appealing on the surface, presented the members of the Committee with a delicate situation. On the one hand, such a ready reserve, with its attendant motivation, could be very useful in addressing the endemic manpower problems of the fleet. At the same time, the autonomy of wanting to serve under the own officers brought with it the concern that these men might work outside the larger naval command structure. The Committee deferred action on the matter.

Two days later, one Thomas Cuthbert and John Britton were authorized to "purchase four Old Flats for Hulks for covering the Gondolas at the Chevaux de Frize..."[90] The idea seemed to be that the hulks, ships with all their sails and hardware removed, would serve as floating gunnery platforms to add additional firepower to protect the gondolas. Cuthbert and Britton were further sanctioned to draw on the Board for the cost of the hulks.[91]

The Committee of Safety took another significant measure when they appointed John Reed to serve as Clerk, Commissary, and Barrack Master at Fort Island. The action served further regularize the efforts they already initiated following the British incursion.[92]

On May 24, the Committee resolved to have Wharton and Morris direct the fitting out of four flats to serve as hulks and provide cover for the crews of the armed boats by Fort Mifflin.[93] For the next several days, additional efforts at raising and equipping the land forces of the state occupied much of the Committee's time. On May 27, they addressed a memorial to the Pennsylvania House,

*That about the beginning of this Month, this
Committee being advised that two of the King's Ships
which for some time before, near Cape Henlopen, in-
fested the trade of this Colony, had alter'd their stations there, and were proceeding up the River Delaware, they Issued orders to the officers of the armed
Boats or Gondolas to stop their Progress, that in the
engagement that succeeded it, some are of opinion that
it was in the power of the Gondolas to have taken or destroyed the Roebuck of 44 Guns, one of the said Ships;
but this was not done, and she return'd down the River
to her former station. In a Variety of Opinions respecting the causes of the miscarriage, the Commanders of
the Boats have, in a publication, attributed it to the
Misconduct of this Committee, in not furnishing them
with sufficient quantities of ammunition, by this accu-
sation the Committee have been in some Measure, rendered parties. Request your Honorable House will take
the premises into consideration and promote such an
inquiry as shall satisfy the public where the blame &
Misconduct is justly chargeable. And whatever shall
be the determination respecting them, they will cheer-
fully acquiesce in it.*[94]

The members of the Committee were requesting an official
hearing. The men likely initiated this action in order to calm the
storm of recriminations and counter-charges that began swirling
following the British incursion into the river.

On July 2, the Continental Congress, meeting at the State
House, took the monumental step of voting in favor of declaring independence from Great Britain. The declaration was made public
two days later. From that moment, Patriot military fortunes crumbled. After witnessing the evacuation of Boston by British forces,
now under the command of Lieutenant-General William Howe and
his brother Admiral Sir Richard, the new commanders of British
land and naval forces in North America respectively, the Americans
witnessed a series of victories which seemed to cement the righ-
teousness of their cause. On February 27, a rising of Loyalist forces
in North Carolina collapsed in fighting at Moore's Creek Bridge.
Likewise, on June 28 an attempt by a British force to break into
the harbor at Charleston, South Carolina was repulsed with heavy

losses.[95]

Once the Crown forces departed Boston, Washington began funneling troops southward to New York City. The Continental Army commander in chief rightly guessed that this would be the next target for the British. This stood as a logical strategic assessment. New York boasted an excellent harbor capable of serving as a main base for the Royal Navy forces in American waters. Add to this its central location on the North American coast and the appeal to Admiral Sir Richard is obvious. The city offered access to the inland waterways as well. The North (Hudson) River offered a point of entry to the interior as far as Albany.

In addition, there were rumors of significant Loyalist sentiment in New York, something that Boston certainly lacked. Those who sided with the Crown could serve as an important force in re-establishing Royal control, and potentially serve as a reservoir of manpower to compliment the regulars and Hessian subsidy troops being dispatched from Europe.[96]

Ironically, the same day that the Continental Congress voted on Independence, Crown forces landed on Staten Island. Their arrival eventually led to the battles of Long Island (August 27), Harlem Heights (September 16) White Plains (October 28) and the assault on Fort Washington. All of the preceding engagements, save Harlem Heights, were clear American defeats. The string of defeats generated flagging morale in the ranks of the Continental Army. This, combined with the one-year enlistments led to much of the American army melting away as they retreated out of New York state and across New Jersey in November of 1776.

To his credit, Washington learned from his mistakes and adopted what many referred to as the Fabian Strategy. Under this approach, he would husband the Continental Army, fighting only small engagements when there existed a clear chance of victory, all the time wearing down the numbers of his adversary.[97] Only twice did he part from this approach between the fall of 1776 and September 1777, and this was when the times called for a major risk and a win to restore sinking morale and bring in desperately needed recruits for the coming campaign.

CHAPTER NOTES

[1] Jackson, *Pennsylvania Navy*, pp. 59-60.

[2] Browne, "Fort Mercer and Fort Mifflin," p.48.

[3] Notes of the Pennsylvania Committee of Safety, January-February 1776,

[4] Currently, the most complete work detailing the effort of Pennsylvania to develop the industrial capacity necessary to support the war effort is Smith, *Manufacturing Independence*.

[5] See *Col. Rec. of PA*, vol.10, pp. 400-451.

[6] Notes of the Pennsylvania Committee of Safety, January 1, 1776, quoted in Ibid, pp. 441-2.

[7] Notes of the Pennsylvania Committee of Safety, January 9, 1776, quoted in Ibid, p. 452

[8] Notes of the Pennsylvania Committee of Safety, January 13, 1776, quoted in Ibid, p. 456.

[9] Ibid.

[10] Minutes of the Pennsylvania Committee of Safety, January 15, 1776, quoted in Ibid, p. 457

[11] Minutes of the Pennsylvania Committee of Safety, January 19, 1776, quoted in Ibid, p. 462.

[12] Notes of the Pennsylvania Committee of Safety, January 19, 1776, quoted in Ibid, p. 462.

[13] Interestingly, the men raised under this order agreed to serve both on land and on the ships in the river, as the defense of the province might require. Essentially, they were to act as a sort of amphibious reserve. Minutes of the Pennsylvania Committee of Safety, January 25, 1776, in Ibid, p. 468.

[14] Minutes of the Pennsylvania Committee of Safety, January 22, 1776, quoted in Ibid, p. 465.

[15] Ibid.

[16] Minutes of the Pennsylvania Committee of Safety, February 2, 1776, quoted in Ibid, pp. 474-75. In describing the outcomes of fortifying these positions, these men were remarkably prophetic, as will be seen.

[17] Ibid, p. 475. The different types of shot mentioned were developed for different purposes. Bar shot looks like and is the ancestor of modern barbells. It was used on the sails and rigging of shipping to tear through them. It could wreak havoc with both personnel and structures as well.

[18] Minutes of the Pennsylvania Committee of Safety, February 20, 1776, in Ibid, p. 490.

[19] Ibid.

[20] Minutes of the Pennsylvania Committee of Safety, February 24, 1776, in Ibid, p. 494.

[21] Ibid.

[22] Minutes of the Pennsylvania Committee of Safety, February 29, 1776, in Ibid, p. 494.

[23] Ibid.

[24] Ibid.

[25] Ibid.

[26] Minutes of the Pennsylvania Committee of Safety, March 6, 1776, in Ibid, p. 505.

[27] Ibid, p. 506.

[28] Ibid.

[29] Minutes of the Pennsylvania Committee of Safety, March 8, 1776, in Ibid, p. 508.

[30] Minutes of the Pennsylvania Committee of Safety, March 9, 1776, in Ibid, p. 510.

[31] Ibid.

[32] Minutes of the Pennsylvania Committee of Safety, March 13, 1776, in Ibid, 513.

[33] Ibid.

[34] Ibid.

[35] Ibid.

[36] Ibid.

[37] Ibid, p. 514.

[38] Minutes of the Pennsylvania Committee of Safety, March 15, 1776, in Ibid, p. 515.

[39] Ibid.

[40] Minutes of the Pennsylvania Committee of Safety, March 16, 1776, in Ibid, p. 516.

[41] Ibid, p. 519.

[42] Minutes of the Pennsylvania Committee of Safety, March 20, 1776, in Ibid, p. 521.

[43] Ibid.

[44] Jackson, *Pennsylvania Navy*, pp. 36-37.

[45] Minutes of the Pennsylvania Committee of Safety, March 30, 1776, in *PA Arch*, Colonial Records Series, vol. 10, p. 530.

[46] Ibid.

[47] Minutes of the Pennsylvania Committee of Safety, April 2, 1776, quoted in Ibid, p. 534.

[48] Minutes of the Pennsylvania Committee of Safety, April 13, 1776, quoted in Ibid, p. 540.

[49] For the different committees formed and their membership, see Minutes of the Pennsylvania Committee of Safety, April 16, 1776, quoted in pp. 543-44. On the number of sub-committees created, see Jackson, *Pennsylvania Navy*, p. 39.

[50] Minutes of the Pennsylvania Committee of Safety, April 19, 1776, in Ibid. For the composition of the Committee for further defenses, see *PA Arch*, Col. Rec. Ser. 2, vol. 10, p. 544.

[51] Ibid, p. 547.

[52] Notes of the Committee of Safety for April 29, 1776, quoted in Ibid, p. 552.

[53] Ibid.

[54] Minutes of the Pennsylvania Committee of Safety, May 1, 1776, quoted in Ibid, p. 553.

[55] Minutes of the Pennsylvania Committee of Safety, May 2, 1776, quoted in Ibid, p. 554.

[56] Browne, "Fort Mercer and Fort Mifflin," pp. 49-50.

[57] Ibid. p. 50.

[58] Minutes of Pennsylvania Committee of Safety, May 6, 1776 in *Col. Rec. of PA*, vol. 10, p. 557.

[59] Ibid.

[60] Ibid.

[61] Ibid.

[62] Minutes of Pennsylvania Committee of Safety, May 7, 1776, quoted in Ibid, pp. 557.-8.

[63] Ibid, p. 559.

[64] Ibid.

[65] Ibid.

[66] Browne, "Fort Mercer and Fort Mifflin," 49. See also, Jackson, *Delaware Defenses*, p. 9.

[67] Pennsylvania evening Post for Tuesday, May 7, 1776 in *NDAR*, vol. 4, p. 1443

[68] Browne, "Fort Mercer and Fort Mifflin," p. 51.

[69] This site is now part of a wildlife preserve of the same name in eastern Kent County, Delaware.

[70] Browne, Fort mercer and Fort Mifflin," p. 52.

[71] Jackson, *Pennsylvania Navy*, p. 44. See also, Browne, "Fort Mercer and Fort Mifflin," p. 53. At this time the Christiania River was also known as Wilmington Creek.

[72] Ibid, pp. 51-2.

[73] Browne, "Fort Mercer and Fort Mifflin," p. 53.

[74] Ibid, p. 54.

[75] Ibid.

[76] Ibid, pp. 54-55.

[77] Ibid.

[78] Ibid, p. 55.

[79] Thomas Read report to Pennsylvania Committee of Safety, quoted in Jackson, *Pennsylvania Navy*, p. 48.

[80] Ibid, pp. 48-9.

[81] Ibid, p. 49.

[82] "Depositions of William Barry and John Emmes," in *Pennsylvania Evening Post*, June 29, 1776.

[83] Browne, "Fort Mercer and Fort Mifflin," p. 57.

[84] Jackson, *Pennsylvania Navy*, p. 53.

[85] Ibid, p. 57.

[86] Hunt, *Provincial Committees of Safety*, p. 89.

[87] Minutes of Pennsylvania Committee of Safety, May 16, 1776, *PA Arch*, vol. 10, p. 569.

[88] Ibid, p. 570.

[89] Ibid, p. 569.

[90] Minutes of Pennsylvania Committee of Safety, May 16, 1776, p. 572.

[91] Ibid.

[92] Browne, "Fort Mercer and Fort Mifflin," p. 57.

[93] Minutes of Pennsylvania Committee of Safety, May 24, 1776, quoted in *PA Arch*, vol. 10, p. 579.

[94] Minutes of Pennsylvania Committee of Safety, May 27, 1776, quoted in *PA Arch*, vol. 10, p. 582.

[95] Concerning the first British attempt on Charleston, see Dan L. Morrill, *Southern Campaigns of the American Revolution* (Point Pleasant, SC: Nautical and Aviation Publishing Company, 2003), pp. 15-26 On Moore's Creek, see Hugh F. Rankin, "The Moore's Creek Bridge Campaign." *North Carolina Historical Review*. 30 (1953): 23-60.

[96] The key works on the various contingents raised in the Holy Roman Empire are Rodney Atwood, *The Hessians: Mercenaries from Hessen-Kassel in the American Revolution* (Cambridge: Cambridge University Press, 1980). See also

[97] Donald Stoker and Michael W. Jones "Colonial Military Strategy," in *Strategy in the American War of Independence*. Donald Stoker, Kenneth J. Hagan and Michael T. McMasters, eds. (London: Routledge, 2010), pp. 9-16.

Chapter Three
Setting the Stage

The battles of Trenton, Assunkpink Creek (sometimes referred to as second Trenton) and Princeton, the ten crucial days as they are sometimes known, saved the Revolution.[1] While the numbers engaged were small, even by the standards of the War of Independence, their propaganda value to the American cause was immense. At the same time, they served to undermine the morale of the Crown forces. Captain Johann Ewald (1744-1813) of the Second Company Hessen Cassel Jäger Corps left this stark description of the change in the initiative of operations,

> *Thus had the times changed! The Americans had constantly run before us. Four weeks ago we had expected to end the war with the capture of Philadelphia, and now we had to render Washington the honor of thinking about our defense.[2]*

Ewald entered the service of Hessen-Cassel at the age of 16. He was therefore able to gain some experience in the latter stages of the Seven Years' War. In 1770, he lost an eye as a result of a duel. Even prior to his service in America, Ewald demonstrated a keen military mind, publishing a book on military tactics in 1774. He was promoted to captain of the Second Jäger Company in 1776 and dispatched with his unit to North America as part of the Hessen-Cassel contingent of the German contract troops to serve the king of England in North America. He arrived in New Rochelle, New York on October 22, 1776, and was in action against American riflemen the next day. Ewald took part in the remaining phases of the 1776 campaign. In addition, he took part in the Philadelphia campaign of 1777, winning a medal for his conduct during the battle of Brandywine. He kept a diary of his experiences in the War of Independence, which serves as a valuable commentary on the Hessian experience of the war. In the years after the American War of Independence Ewald wrote and published a number of works on the use of light troops, and finally ended up as a General in the Danish Army. [3]

At the same time, these battles drove home the need for the leadership of Pennsylvania to redouble their efforts with local defense as well. This work would continue in 1777 and reached a new level of intensity in the summer as the threat of a British invasion of the region manifested. Still, some of the personnel who began this work changed. A major loss came to the Patriot side early in the new year.

On February 11, 1777, Robert Smith, the man who had done so much to begin the defenses along and in the Delaware River, died. The last work the Committee of Safety, now the Council of Safety, entrusted to him was the construction of the fort at Billingsport. For a variety of reasons, including the threat posed by the British march into New Jersey in late 1776, Smith failed to give the works his full attention. He did receive some aid beginning in October of 1776. On August 30, 1776, a Polish immigrant, Thaddeus Kosciuszko (1746-1817) presented a memorial to Congress, which was promptly referred to the Board of War. Kosciuszko was the scion of the Polish nobility, forced out of his homeland for his opposition to Russian domination of Poland and his failed attempt to elope with a noblewoman of a higher station. He did, however, possess training as a military engineer, which he received in France. The Board of War returned with a report on the young Pole's credentials on October 18, at which time Congress resolved to accept him as an engineer in the service of the United States.[4] He made some modifications, especially to Billingsport. In addition, Kosciuszko initiated work on a post at Red Bank, which would eventually become Fort Mercer.[5] However, as a trained engineer, his services were in high demand, and he was often reassigned. The work on the post fell back on Smith. The Council quickly replaced Smith with Col. John Bull of the militia. Bull was determined to complete the work which Smith had started.[6]

Bull was a Pennsylvania militia officer and not a military engineer by training, exemplifying Franklin's concern, noted at the end of the first chapter, over the lack of trained military engineers in the state. While Bull clearly possessed some knowledge of frontier fortification, he was not versed in the art of fortification in any formal sense. As a result, he tended to lay out works that were too large for the manpower and artillery available to garrison them. Such was the case with Billingsport.[7] Most contemporaries believed that to adequately man the fort at Billingsport would require a garrison of between 1,000 and 1,500 men. Anything less than this number, and the fort would become more of a liability than an asset. As a result, several reductions in the size of Billingsport would be made over the course of the spring and summer. In addition to the issue of resources to adequately garrison the post, Bull focused all of the armaments of Billingsport towards the River. The possibility of an assault from the landward side seemed not to have occurred to him.[8]

The fort Bull laid out covered three and one-half acres and included bastions at each of its four corners. Its earthen walls were seven and a half feet high, and nine feet deep, an eighteen-foot-wide moat surrounded the entire fortress. The armament for the fort as Bull wanted it constructed would consist of four nine-pounder and one twelve pounder cannon.[9] As one historian noted, "The fort he laid out was extensive, if not grandiose."[10]

Later in the spring, Bull received reassignment to Red Bank to begin construction on a new fortification there. He arrived at the location, adjoining the Whitall Farm on April 16 with some Pennsylvania militia and began working on the new post. From the beginning of his efforts to construct the post, the Pennsylvania militia served as a constant irritant. A number of the men brought their wives along with them. In addition, numerous camp followers attached themselves to both the officers and the men. Most of those in this second category were the "offscourings of Philadelphia's waterfront tippling houses and brothels."[11] Such a situation could not help but lead to problems of discipline and a consequent drop in morale. Finally, on May 7, 1777, in an attempt to bring the situation under some semblance of control, Bull issued the following orders:

> *The Officers are to take Care of the men & see that they keep themselves clean and to prevent their being sick. It is with the greatest Reluctancy that I perceive that great numbers of them and officer are Disabled and unfit for Duty with that Vile and uncleanly [sic] Disorder Called the Clap as it is a Disorder that they bring upon themselves for if they would not Roger any they would not take it--Therefore am Determined to lay the fine of 3 £ upon the Captains as I Perceive they are very subject to that Disorder. As for the Subalterns I Perceive they are not Subject to that Disorder I therefore order a Gill of Rum to be given them on the 1st Day of May 1777 Gratis.[12]*

Those enlisted who continued to be stricken with the preventable disorder were to receive 50 lashes. It is unclear whether Bull's orders achieved their desired effect.[13] Not only were women of ill-repute a source of frustration for Bull, but liquor sales at the fort also created their own disciplinary problems. Therefore, in early June the colonel took the draconian action of having all sutlers selling liquor confined to the guardhouse at the fort and their supplies confiscated.[14]

Other disciplinary factors interfered with the work on the post at Red Bank as well. The men often engaged in two practices which could quite easily alienate their neighbors, an important consideration in a civil war. One of these fell under the heading of disrespect for private property. To get wood for cooking and other uses, the men often felled fruit trees or stole fencing. The other area encompassed simple hygiene and decorum. While latrines were dug at the site, many of the men simply relieved themselves wherever and whenever they felt the need. This practice not only offended those living near the fort but could lead to outbreaks of disease as well.[15] As John W. Jackson aptly summarizes, "Dissipation combined with insubordination frequently found the men unfit to work on the ramparts."[16]

John Bull was not the only person employed in stiffening the river defenses. Second in command of the Pennsylvania Navy, Capt. John Hazelwood, ordered a redoubt and barracks constructed at Tinicum Island, near the mouth of Darby Creek. It contained a four-gun battery that would guard the back channel along the Pennsylvania side of the Delaware. He ordered an additional redoubt constructed on Bush Island (Woodbury Island) which sat a few hundred yards off Red Bank. It held two eighteen pounder guns facing downriver.

Even with all of the difficulties he encountered, Bull completed work on the post at Red Bank by June 1, 1777. Fourteen days later, the bulk of his troops, save for a small garrison to guard the post, were ordered to march to Gloucester. The detachment which remained guarding the fort at Red Bank consisted of a captain, a lieutenant, an ensign, three sergeants, one drummer, a fifer, and fifty privates. In order to create the above contingent, each of the ten companies previously engaged in constructing the fort furnished five of their men. Shortly after its completion, the post began to be referred to as Fort Mercer, for Gen. Hugh Mercer, who had fallen in the fighting at Princeton earlier in the year.[17]

Meanwhile the British and American armies spent much of the spring and early summer of 1777 sparring in northern New Jersey. The Continentals and New Jersey militia regularly engaged British forces out foraging from New York City. This gave the newly recruited Continentals the opportunity to gain practical experience against their opponents, at the same time, Washington refused all

of William Howe's attempts to draw his forces into a major battlefield confrontation. Some see Washington's approach as a more
developed version of what is usually termed Washington's Fabian
Strategy.[18]

While Howe and Washington sparred in Northern New Jersey, the Continental Congress, alerted to the build-up of shipping
in New York harbor, prepared for an amphibious assault. Thus, the
Delaware river defenses once more became the center of their attention. In the late spring of 1777, the Continental Congress appointed a committee to evaluate the defenses along the Delaware
river. Philippe Charles Trouson du Coudray, a recently arrived yet
controversial French officer served as the chief military engineer on
the committee.[19] Accompanying du Coudray on this reconnaissance
of the forts was General Thomas Mifflin.

Du Coudray's report on the committee's inspection, which
various historians have placed in June and July 1777 was defini-
tively dated to June 21 by John W. Jackson.[20] His report is worth
examining in some detail as it and the conclusions drawn by du
Coudray significantly altered, for a time, the organization of the river defenses.[21]

General du Coudray found the fort at Billingsport well situated as it covered the river at its narrowest point. Still, he believed
the work poorly executed. He asserted that the work would have to
be rebuilt with an emphasis on defending the chevaux de frise in
the river. At the same time, he noted that the changes he suggested
"would require at least four or five Months."[22] Even then, Du Coudray qualified his assessment, stating that a great number of men
would need to be employed in the project for it to be well constructed as the soil was "the most unfavorable that can be met with."[23]
Finally, concerning Billingsport, Du Coudray noted that even if the
Americans altered the fort in accordance with his suggestion, re-
modeled works would require a garrison of some 2,000 troops to
adequately man it.[24]

Du Coudray continued, listing a number of improvements
he perceived as essential in order to make Billingsport defensible
against British assault. For instance, he observed that thirty to
forty canons, facing outwards to the river, would provide sufficient
cover for the chevaux-de-frise. Likewise, du Coudray wanted to construct a demi-lune of half-moon battery on the Pennsylvania shore
opposite Billingsport in order to provide a cross-fire between the two
posts. He further noted that "To defend the Chain of Chevaux de
frise which bars the iver opposite to the Fort, all dependence for the

present must be on the Floating-Batteries and Gondolas which are ready, or which can soon be so."[25]

Moving on to Fort Mifflin, Du Coudray first observed, "The Fort is badly situated; the Battery which forms its principal object is improperly directed, which renders Half the Guns useless."[26] The French engineer further noted the poor construction of the embrasures and the fact that some of the works were so poorly constructed that they were already beginning to crumble. He summarized the state of Fort Mifflin, stating "This Fort cannot prevent the Passage of the Enemy, and when they have passed, it can be of no use; consequently, it can answer no valuable Purpose."[27]

Of all the forts guarding the Delaware River, du Coudray found Fort Mercer to be the best constructed, "this Fort is better conceived, directed, and executed than either of those above mentioned." [28] By the same token, he deemed it poorly situated. Its location made the fort too distant to support Fort Mifflin or to cover the chevaux de frise. Du Coudray's solution to the problem of defending the river was to focus all efforts on the first line of chevaux de frise. At Billingsport, observing that "it is better to make a respectable stand in one place than to defend two in an indifferent manner."[29]

De Coudray sought to construct an entrenched battery at Point of the Island, the narrowest point in that area of the river, and use that as the linchpin of the defenses as opposed to Billingsport. In addition, he would use the gallies and floating batteries as a means to supplement the firepower of the entrenched battery. He suggested moving the cannon from Fort Mercer to Billingsport but not to abandon the former location entirely, due to political considerations.[30] Had du Coudray's directions for improving the defenses been acted on, they may have created a more solid defense of the river. By the same token, they would have stripped the second row of defenses of their capabilities to a dangerous degree. Two factors militated against his directions being enacted. The first was time, there simply would not be enough time to add the additional defenses in order to meet with his specifications. Manpower constituted the second issue, the workers necessary to make the alterations he called for were not available, and all the troops were needed with the army to defend against General Howe's invasion of the region.

The Americans had constructed, albeit fitfully, a defense in depth that could, if properly manned and maintained, exact a heavy toll on any force attempting to push its way up the river. The key problem would be finding enough troops to maintain the river forts without so weakening the land forces that the British could launch a successful attack on Washington in the field and so cripple the Continental Army and in doing so, pin the garrisons of the forts against the Delaware.

Soon, the events once again distracted the attention of the Pennsylvania government as well as the Continental Congress away from the river defenses. Once again it was the threat of a full-fledged invasion of Pennsylvania which dominated the attention of the leadership. This time Lt. Gen. William Howe, the commander of British forces in North America commanded the invasion personally.

Howe planned for some time to take Philadelphia. The first iteration of Howe's plan for 1777 began boldly in November 1776, when all seemed to be going the British commander's way. While numerous facets of the William Howe's planning altered over the winter months of 1776-1777, one remained unchanged - the goal of taking Philadelphia. Since the war, numerous historians have questioned Howe's reasoning on this point, and devised a number of responses. In order to understand Howe's thinking concerning the capture of Philadelphia, some knowledge of his background is necessary, as is some understanding of the conduct of the war to this point.

Lieutenant General Sir William Howe, Fifth Viscount Howe (1729-1814), the commander of British land forces in North America descended from a highly placed noble family with possible connections to the Royal family. Initially educated by private tutors, he attended Eton where, at the time, gaining social connections was considered as important as education, and perhaps even more so. He entered the army at age eighteen, purchasing a lieutenant's commission. In 1750, he purchased a captaincy, and in 1757, a lieutenant-colonelcy. He served in the Seven Years' War in North America, where he led the advance guard of Wolfe's force up the cliffs outside of Quebec to the Plains of Abraham. He later took part in the defense of Quebec from French counterattack and the expedition to Montreal, as well as the sieges of Belle Île and Havana.[31]

Over the course of the Seven Years' War, William, like his older brother George Augustus grew interested in the new techniques merging European continental warfare with Native American warfare. As a result, William developed a reputation for being among the foremost experts on light infantry in the British army. He is even credited, rightly so, with introducing light companies to the British army.[32]

After the war, Sir William returned to England and took part in politics, serving as a Member of Parliament for Nottingham from 1765-1780. He also served as governor of the Isle of Wight in 1768.[33] Both his older brother Richard and William had publicly expressed displeasure over the Ministry's colonial policy, and Sir William had gone so far as to say that he would never command in North America. Still, when the king asked him directly, he acquiesced, but on the condition that he and his brother hold dual commissions as military commanders and Peace Commissioners. This arrangement, where the two men were charged with simultaneously trying to prosecute the war and find some amicable arrangement to end it has been singled out by at least one historian as a reason for William Howe's seeming restraint campaign as well. [34]

Shortly after the outbreak of fighting at Lexington and Concord, William Howe was dispatched to America, along with generals Sir Henry Clinton and John Burgoyne. These men were sent to bolster up Gen. Thomas Gage who was becoming increasingly unpopular with the ministry back in London. Sir William arrived in Boston in time to plan and take part on the attack on American positions on Breed's Hill on June 17, 1775, personally leading the main assault force three times as they eventually expelled the Americans from their earthworks. Some have credited this experience, with its attendant high casualties among the British force with generating a cautious streak in Howe that persisted throughout the remainder of his tenure in North America.[35] True, he preferred to outflank George Washington, which he did on numerous occasions, as opposed to wasting the lives of his men in bloody frontal assaults. Even so, he managed to come close to breaking the Continental Army in 1776.

William's brother Richard, Fourth Viscount Howe (1726-1790), commanded the Royal Navy forces in North America. Richard had begun his naval service under Adm. George Anson, serving on the HMS *Severn* at the age of fourteen. Anson planned to make a voyage around the world, however, the *Severn* was damaged in a storm just beyond Cape Horn. In 1742, at the age of 16, Richard Howe was in the West Indies, where he rose to the rank of acting lieutenant, with the rank being confirmed two years later. Following the death of his older brother George Augustus at Ticonderoga in 1758, Richard inherited the family title of Viscount Howe.

Through the 1760s, Richard Howe held several posts in government including the representative for Dartmouth in 1762. He served on the Admiralty Board in 1763 and 1765, as well as treasurer of the navy from 1765-1770. As of December 7, 1775, Howe

The Conference between the Brothers **HOW** to get Rich.

Fig 7. Print shows Admiral Richard Howe and General William Howe seated at a table discussing how to profit from the war in America. The Devil stands between them and answers their question, "... [H]ow shall we get rich" by saying, "How, How, continue the war." [London]: Publish'd by W. Williams Fleet Street, as the Act directs, 1777 Oct. 10. *Source: Library of Congress.*

achieved the rank of Vice Admiral. While royal connections certainly aided in Richard Howe's rapid rise through the naval ranks, he was known as an able officer and an innovator as well. He devised a number of improvements for signals and fighting instructions. In addition, he made proposals for altering the ships guns, the use of flannel cartridges, priming tubes and locks of the guns.[36] Of particular importance for the campaign currently under examination, "Howe issued what became the standard directives and signals for embarking and landing troops in hostile surroundings, together with regulations for maintaining the chain of command for army transport ships."[37] As a naval commander, he was well-respected and liked by his men. They bestowed on him the *nomme de guerre* of "Black Dick" for his dark complexion. Like his brother William, Richard Howe initially rejected the opportunity to serve in North America and agreed to do so only if he were granted the authority to act as a Peace Commissioner as well as naval commander. George III agreed to this stipulation and Richard assumed the naval command in North America on February 16, 1776.[38]

The appointment of the Howe brothers to command the land and naval forces in North America generated successful coordination of the army and navy, something rightly viewed as necessary for military success. Likewise, the brothers agreed on strategy, "They thought that the best and probably the only hope (though their opinion did fluctuate according to circumstances) of success was to conquer the Colonies piecemeal and, before moving on to the next area, set up a firm but benevolent government under military auspices until the local authorities could be organized and trusted to take over."[39]

William Howe submitted the first draft of his plan of campaign for 1777 on November 16, 1776. At this time, the British military fortunes in North America were riding high, and Howe planned a campaign designed to end the war in a year. Much of the internal logic of the plan was contingent on the idea that any British advance from Canada would be slow. In this initial iteration, the plan called for a reinforcement of some 15,000 troops. Howe would utilize 10,000 troops under him to invade Rhode Island. These would possibly move towards Boston if all went well. Another force of roughly the same size would move up the Hudson River, and rendezvous with an already expected invasion southward from Canada. Five thousand troops would remain to hold New York City. A third force composed of eight thousand troops would engage in operations in New Jersey. These efforts were designed to hold Washington in check while the other campaigns played out.[40]

If the campaigns to the north were successful, Howe planned for a campaign against Philadelphia in the autumn of 1777. If he should take their capital, and the Americans continued to resist, Howe intended to fight a winter campaign in South Carolina and Georgia. His ambitious design for operations in 1777 led some historians to see Howe's objective as the capture and occupation of various regions of the colonies, and in doing so, the suppression of the rebellion one sector at a time.[41] In essence, he would break the rebellion by seizing territory. Likewise, it has been noted that a major aspect of the plan was the move through disaffected areas with overwhelming force that would disrupt communication between the main centers of the rebellion.[42] It is interesting to note that initially, Philadelphia stood as a secondary target, and that the primary goal of his campaign was the same as Burgoyne's goal in 1777, to cut off New England from the remainder of the colonies.

Howe's letter outlining his projected campaign for 1777 arrived in England on December 31, 1776 and Secretary of State Lord

George Germain replied on January 14. Unfortunately for this plan, Germain refused to provide the called-for reinforcements.[43]   Germain seriously reduced the number of men Howe would receive for the 1777 campaign, from the requested 15,000 down to only 4,000. In one of the great mathematical subterfuges of eighteenth-century warfare, he managed to end up at the same final number of 30,000 effectives Howe had initially requested to implement his plan for the ensuing campaign. In essence, Germain counted all of the troops sent to North American the previous year, not allowing for erosion of forces through sickness, wounds and death in the fighting. The desire to keep the costs of the war down stood as the main reason behind Germain's creative mathematics.[44]

One of the historians to analyze the disparity between Howe and Germain chalks up their differing perspectives on the need for troops to competing perceptions on how the war should be conducted. For Howe, the correct approach to breaking the rebellion in North American involved defeating the rebel forces and occupying the country step by step. Germain, it seems according to this interpretation, did not see the necessity of occupation, merely defeat the Continental Army, and the local populace would rejoin the happy fold of loyal subjects of the empire.[45] He goes on to contend that "If the British commander was to have a force large enough to garrison every conquered district, caution in the field was the best policy so long as enough was done to expand steadily the area of British occupation."[46]

Still, before William's Howe's letter containing his initial plans had even reached England, the general was altering them as the strategic situation in North America developed. His first revision, contained in a letter dated December 20, 1776, deferred the planned attack on Boston until further reinforcements arrived. In addition, it had the virtue, at least in so far as Germain was concerned, of calling for only about half the troops requested in Howe's original plan. Howe altered parts of his original operational assessment as well, noting that the northern army invading south from Canada was unlikely to reach Albany before the middle of September, and its further progress would be determined based on the prevailing situation at the time.

To some extent, Howe himself seemed uncertain of just what his next move should be, and the first revision seemed a fall back on what he could hope to accomplish on a more limited scale. It rested on the notion of greater support from the Loyalists in the Philadelphia area. Some of these men and their families actually fled

Philadelphia for New York City and gained direct access to William Howe. [47]

For his part, when Germain received Howe's letter of November 30, he neither dismissed nor approved it. He did mention the idea of raids along the New England coast, and that only about 2,500 fresh troops would be available for continued operations. Again, reducing the number of reinforcements Howe could count on for the ensuing campaign.[48]

Howe submitted his next iteration of plans on April 2. He first acknowledged the receipt of Germain's reply to his November 30th letter, dated January 14, and received by Howe on March 9. Howe then went on to state that he had given up on any offensive plans concerning Rhode Island, at least for the time being.

Now his plan called for the use of some eleven thousand troops to invade Pennsylvania. 4,700 troops would be allocated to the defense of New York City and its environs. An additional 2,400 for Rhode Island, with three thousand provincial troops to serve around New York as well. The main point that set this plan apart from the December 20th plan was that this no longer called for any actions along the Hudson River. Another very significant difference was that the plan now called for the invasion of Pennsylvania by sea rather than by land.[49]

Historians have attributed several reasons for the change in invasion routes. One, it might prove faster, as Troyer Steele Anderson noted: "The overland route to Pennsylvania would have required a larger force for protecting communications than had been found necessary in any previous advance."[50] The use of the Royal Navy would alleviate the necessity of leaving so many detachments, something that already troubled William Howe.[51] In theory, at least, it would also allow for his troops to arrive in good physical condition at the main location of the action, without having to endure a long overland march. A further reason why the sea route recommended itself was that much of New Jersey had risen against the British in the aftermath of the battles of Trenton and Princeton, and Sir William had no desire to fight his way across a hostile environment, loosing troops, as well as time, throughout a campaign deep in enemy territory.

As Howe's plan of campaign focused more narrowly on Philadelphia, he seemed to want to take the city merely for its own sake. He did not see the capture of the de facto capital of the American rebels as translating into an end in itself as opposed to a decisive campaign to end the war. In fact, as the winter turned to spring, he seemed ever more disinclined to believe that the 1777 campaign would bring about an end to the war. He did still expect to be in control of New York, New Jersey and Pennsylvania by the end of the campaign season. For Anderson, Howe reverted once again to the methodical concept of the occupation and pacification of territory.[52]

Howe made many of these points initially in a letter he penned to Lord George Germain on April 2, 1777. Howe's letter crossed one from Germain in transit. Germain's was a response to Howe's letter of December 20, 1776, giving approval to the plan of campaign contained therein. Howe's letter communicating his latest revision of the campaign plan did not reach Whitehall until May 8 and lay unanswered until the 18th.[53]

From the above, it seemed that as time went on, Howe became more and more focused on simply taking Philadelphia. As his focus narrowed, it would seem to lend some credence to the point made by John W. Jackson concerning Howe's desire to tap into Loyalist support in the city.[54] Even Lord George Germain believed that there would be significant numbers of Loyalists willing to come out in active support of the king lurking in the interior of Pennsylvania. Should these men be willing to form provincial units, they may have augmented Howe's forces to the degree necessary for him to continue his methodical pacification of the colonies. To be fair, Howe was often lobbied by Loyalist representatives, the most prominent of whom was Joseph Galloway.[55]

If this was in fact Howe's plan, it does not explain several operational factors. First, Howe attempted to lure Washington into battle in northern New Jersey several times in the spring and early summer of 1777. In this case it seemed the British commander still hoped to cripple the Continental Army and force his opponent to the negotiating table. He still considered the Continental Army to be his main objective, or the center of gravity on the American side.[56] Then, he suddenly seemed to shift in his perception of the rebels' center of gravity and see Philadelphia as the key to victory. While William Howe possessed his own perception of how to defeat his opponents, he seemed to forget that in war the enemy always gets a vote as well.

Washington's approach to fighting the war went through several iterations during the early years of the conflict as well. Initially, he sought to fight Howe but usually from behind defensive works. This altered following the defeat around New York City, especially after the loss of Fort Washington. As he noted in a September 8, 1776 letter to Congress, Washington intended from that point on to fight a defensive war, "it has ever been called a war of posts; we should on all occasions avoid a general action, and never be drawn into a necessity to put anything to risqué unless compelled by a necessity which we ought never to be drawn."[57] Thus, the origins of the so-called Fabian Strategy. The concept derived its name from the Roman consul Quintus Fabius Maximus who successfully defended the republic against the Carthaginian leader Hannibal after the disastrous defeat at Cannae in 216 BCE. Fabius succeeded in wearing down his adversary by not allowing himself to be caught in an open confrontation with his stronger opponent. At the same time, he wore his opponent down by engaging detachments of his forces and maintaining pressure on him. The Fabian Strategy was one of attrition. One implication of this strategy was Washington refused allow himself to be drawn into a confrontation in which he did not stand a substantial chance of success. It should be noted that the Fabian Strategy went against Washington's natural proclivity for aggressive action. It thus represented an acceptance, albeit grudging at times, of the human material he had to work with in the Continental Army.

In Philadelphia however, there stood a target that for reasons both military and political, Washington had to defend, even if it meant breaking with the so-called Fabian Strategy. Militarily, Philadelphia served as a center for the production of war materials and their transportation to the Continental Army, as well as various state forces. In addition, it served as an important dockyard for the Continental Navy as well as numerous privateers.[58] The fact that the city served as the home of the fledgling Continental Congress lent Philadelphia a political importance as well. The possibility that Washington might be forced to give him the battle he so desired likely added to its appeal as a target for Howe. If Howe could critically damage the Continental Army in a field engagement and capture the capital of the rebel government, it was a triumph. If he could capture some or all of the delegates to Congress in the process, it might be enough to drive the rebels to the negotiating table.

Prior to commencing on a discussion of the Philadelphia Campaign of 1777, it is necessary to discuss the types of forces which fought that campaign. In addition, a brief discussion of the two contending armies will serve to highlight the strengths and weaknesses of both as they entered upon the campaign.

The infantry constituted the main component of land warfare in both Europe and North America during the eighteenth century. The predominant weapon the soldiers carried into battle were smoothbore muskets of various calibers. The British carried the Short Land, New Pattern musket of .75 caliber, also referred to as the Second Model Brown Bess.[59] As noted, this weapon was smoothbore, and so fairly inaccurate. Nevertheless, under the right conditions with massed fire, at ranges of eighty yards or less, it could do significant damage. For some time, it was assumed that British soldiers were wedded to linear tactics, such as were often used in Europe.[60] Recent studies, however, have shown convincingly that this was not the case.[61]

The infantry included several different types as well. First, there were the grenadiers. As their designation implies, these soldiers developed in the seventeenth century, and were often sent out to storm enemy works, throwing the earliest form of hand grenade into enemy defenses before charging in with the bayonet, an eighteen-inch-long spike attached to the musket. Thus, they were composed of the taller, more robust men of the regiment. By the eighteenth century, the hand grenades had fallen by the wayside, while these troops continued to find employment as the main assault force. Each regiment possessed a grenadier company; however, these were often brigaded together to form separate grenadier battalions to serve as assault troops.

Next came the regulars, or hat men. These men formed the bulk of any infantry regiment, in the British army, or any other European army of the time. In the British army they encompassed about eight companies.[62] When on the offensive, these troops moved to confront an enemy until close enough to engage in a short fire fight and then drive an opponent from the field with the bayonet. For the British army, certainly, the bayonet stood as the final arbiter of infantry combat.

Last, but certainly not least in importance, especially in North America, were the light infantry. While light troops of various types had existed since ancient times, their use fell in and out of vogue. The eighteenth century witnessed a return of these force in both Europe and North America.[63] These men specialized in skirmishing, scouting, and raiding. They employed open-order tactics and specialized in aimed fire. Tactically, the light infantry and grenadiers represented the current standard of European land warfare. Light infantry fought in open order, and could move quite quickly, especially on the flanks or when conducting patrols to gather intelligence. As noted above, William Howe was a major innovator of light infantry in the British Army. A North American equivalent to these troops were the riflemen.[64] In order to compensate for the riflemen, the British brought over troops called, "Jägers" from various German principalities they contracted with in the Holy Roman Empire, which will be discussed below. The light troops would prove very useful and effective in the fighting around Philadelphia.

After the infantry, the artillery comprised an increasingly important force in land warfare over the course of the eighteenth century. Artillery, specifically smooth-bore cannon throwing various weights and types of shot were usually parceled out between the various infantry regiments, instead of being concentrated in batteries. This was done as it was believed that sounds of the guns going off around them would bolster the infantrymen's confidence. On the battlefield, the artillery performed two functions. First, it engaged the enemy artillery in the hopes of destroying or disrupting it, counter-battery fire. Second, it would be turned against enemy infantry. It is worth pointing out that at times during the 1777 campaign, such as the battle of Brandywine, the guns were concentrated. In addition, as one scholar noted, "for a land force that wished to oppose ships at sea, artillery was the only weapon that could be effective in inflicting significant damage beyond musket range."[65] It will be seen just how much damage artillery could inflict on sea going vessels subsequently.

The guns came in a variety of calibers, distinguished by the weight of the projectiles they threw. These included 3-, 4-, 6-, and 12-pounder guns. The last stood as the largest piece usually used in the field. Likewise, a variety of different types of ammunition existed that were developed for specific uses. Solid shot could be used both for bombardment of fortifications and other structures and for anti-personnel work. In addition to the solid shot, cannons in the field often fired canister as well. This took the form of a tin filled with projectiles slightly larger than musket balls. Canister had the effect of turning the cannon into a giant shot gun and was employed solely for anti-personnel work. For fighting between and against sailing ships, bar-shot or grape shot were often utilized. The first resembled the modern barbell and was used on the masts and sails of enemy ships. Grape shot consisted in a number of smaller iron balls fastened to a wooden frame and covered by a canvas bag. The result resembled a bunch of grapes. At sea, grape shot was used in much the same manner as canister was on land. There were several other, less frequently employed, types of shot for land warfare, and numerous types that were used at sea as well.[66]

Finally, there was the mounted arm or cavalry. In Europe, there were several types of mounted and they each performed specific functions both on the march and on the battlefield.[67] North America, however, presented a very different set of tactical circumstances. There were few large fields where the cavalry could deploy on the flanks of an infantry formation to defend it from opposing cavalry or attack an enemy on the verge of collapse as it often did in Europe. Likewise, the road network remained very basic. As a result of these circumstances, the mounted troops enjoyed employment primarily as scouts gathering intelligence on enemy formations. In combat, the cavalry of both sides often engaged one another, a reason why Washington sought to create an effective mounted arm. Alternatively, troopers often fought *en dragoon*, meaning they would ride to the battlefield, dismount, and fight as infantry, then remount to withdrawal at the end of the engagement. The preceding tactical arrangement became quite prevalent in the later years of the war when the fighting shifted to the southern theater.[68]

During the 1777 campaign, the primary role of the cavalry consisted in scouting. In this regard, Washington certainly felt the lack of an effective cavalry arm during the fighting outside Philadelphia, especially at Brandywine.[69]

While both armies employed the same general types of troops, the specific composition of the competing forces contained some important differences as well. These distinctions are worth examining in that they provide insight into how the resultant campaign, including the efforts to take the river forts, developed.

The British army that fought the campaign in southeastern Pennsylvania in 1777 has traditionally been depicted as the product of Great Britain's jails and the press gangs, commanded by men who owed their station more to their aristocratic birth and wealth than to any talent or activity. Recent scholarship, however, has challenged if not completely dismissed this interpretation.[70] While the British army could certainly be under-strength and insufficiently trained in peacetime, it was a volunteer force recruited to serve for long terms, commanded by noble officers. While many officers below the rank of general could still purchase their commissions, safeguards existed which worked to prevent incompetents from attaining high rank. Likewise, recent research has demonstrated that many of the officers of the British Army held to a professional ethos under which they worked to better themselves through reading of the numerous works on military history and theory that became available during the eighteenth century. The officers and soldiers believed ardently in their cause as well.

As Matthew Spring, one of the more recent scholars of the British army in the War of Independence notes, "In fact the British officers and enlisted men commonly expressed real hostility to the rebellion."[71] They went so far as to lecture "rebel captives on the badness of their cause and the impropriety of fighting against their King."[72] During the early years of the war, there were a number of veterans of the Seven Years' War in the ranks of the battalions as well. The experience of these men helped to "season" the new recruits and bring them up to a high level of proficiency in their duties.[73]

Further, British troops were not, as is often asserted, wedded to the strict linear tactics of the day. They were well versed in fighting in open order. Spring spends substantial time in his work discussing how the British army likely fought in North America. More particular to the present study, Michael Harris, who provides the most detailed reconstruction of the Battle of Brandywine to date, notes "Gen. Howe had trained his soldiers to drop to the ground when the rebels fired upon them."[74] Harris adds concerning Howe's training of the men he commanded, "He instilled some light infantry tactics in all of his troops prior to the 1776 New York campaign, and many of the army's regiments were still following this practice."[75] It is worth recalling that William Howe, as well as his older brother George Augustus, were instrumental figures in developing the British Light Infantry during the Seven Years' War.[76]

More than British troops made up the Crown forces who took part in the 1777 campaign in Delaware Valley. Numerous German subsidy troops filled out William Howe's army. Contemporaries labeled these men mercenaries, and generations of historians on both sides of the Atlantic reinforced that description. Where American historians labeled these troops mercenaries, beginning in the nineteenth century, many German historians accused the minor princes of the Holy Roman Empire of engaging in the Soldatenhandeln.[77] This mean that they essentially rented their armies out to the great powers for money which they then spent on luxuries for their own courts. The preceding constituted a perhaps nuanced distinction.

In an important corrective, Peter H. Wilson, a respected historian of early modern Germany, notes that these treaties served a number of dynastic purposes for the princes who engaged in them. Wilson observes if a prince sought to fulfill their political and dynastic ambitions, which could include such things as territorial aggrandizement or a greater title, they needed a large army and robust treasury. If the prince in question did not possess these resources on their own, they had to find a new revenue stream to make up the difference. As he concludes, "The most important and politically significant form of such assistance was the subsidy treaty."[78] He, as well as other German-language historians argue that these men should be termed subsidierentruppen or subsidy troops, the term designating soldiers who fought, sometimes in the armies of other princes, but always to advance the policies of their home states.[79]

Thus, the soldiers who travelled to North America to augment those of Great Britain considered themselves as serving their sovereign and their state. As loyal subjects of their respective sovereigns, they viewed the rebels with a certain level of disdain. They looked down upon their American foes not just as rebels, but for their lack of discipline under fire, which the German troops tended to disparage as amateurish, especially when compared with their more studied evolutions.

The Hessian grenadiers in particular moved very precisely, but fairly slowly, a fact that will be borne out in subsequent descriptions. It is important to point out that this criticism did not hold for the Jägers. At least initially, these troops were recruited from the games-keepers of various German states, and operated effectively as light infantry, serving as a match to the American riflemen.[80]

The riflemen composed one element of the Continental army however, Washington had dispatched these troops to the northward to assist Gen. Horatio Gates in defending against the British invasion under Gen. John Burgoyne. To attempt to make up for the loss of these troops, Washington ordered the creation of the Continental Corps of Light Infantry, which will be discussed in greater detail below. The remainder of the American infantry were broken down into the Continental line, the state units and the militia.

Augmenting the Continental Army were state units and militia. State Troops were paid for and organized by the states for Continental service. These units varied in quality and quantity but were considered "line" troops. The militia were irregular volunteers that were limited to service locally. Militia were usually not as useful in standup battles as Continentals or even State Troops but were handy for scouting and skirmishing as well as maintaining local control.

The Continental army of 1777 constituted a fundamentally different force than its predecessors, it was one in a state of flux as well. During the first eighteen month of the war, Americans adamantly rejected the concept of long-term enlistments.[81] The refusal of many in the Continental Congress to accept longer enlistments stood as a part of a long-standing colonial bias, inherited from the experience of the English Civil War, against standing armies. The dismal showing of the Continentals in 1776 prompted Congress to accept that ad hoc forces would not be sufficient to win the war. As a result, the Continentals of 1777 were the first to be recruited for three years or the duration of the war. The body instigated other reforms as well. These reforms exerted a profound effect on the structure of the Continental army. As historian Robert K. Wright noted, "The decisions made in Congress during September and early October 1776 determined the basic size and nature of the Continental Army for the rest of the war."[82]

Operating in the field with the main army, Washington was unaware of the reforms being debated and approved in Congress and wrote the body a series of letters in December 1776. As his army was harried across New Jersey by the forces under Earl Charles Cornwallis, Washington impressed on the body his need for more troops. More infantry regiments and artillery as well as a solid force of cavalry topped the list of his needs.[83] There followed a period of discussions in correspondence between Washington and Congress as to the specifics of the new army. The dialogue ended when Congress voted to give Washington near dictatorial powers to take whatever actions he deemed necessary for the preservation of the army.[84] The result of these reforms emerged in a more mobile field army, which could shuffle forces rapidly from various departments to parry British thrusts. To some degree, this mobility helped to offset the British control of the seas. In addition, it possessed a firmer organization which allowed the army to recover quicker from tactical defeats than previously. Finally, the Continental army possessed cavalry as well, which provided a reconnaissance capability which it hitherto lacked; however, Washington did not initially utilize it in this way.[85]

The first tests of the newly modeled fighting force would take place in northern New Jersey. Following the defeats at Trenton and Princeton, the British were forced to evacuate most of their strong points in the state for the remainder of the winter. While there were incursions by Crown forces in order to gather forage for their horses, there were no full-scale military operations. For his part, George Washington finally settled into winter quarters behind the Wachtung Mountains near Morristown. Once in this superb defensible position, he began to implement the reforms he had previous discussed with Congress. In addition, he took the bold step of having the entire army inoculated against smallpox. As recruiting efforts replenished his ranks, Washington utilized the British foraging efforts as an opportunity to gain experience for his troops in skirmishing and interdicting their efforts.[86]

The war of posts came to an end in early June 1777 as William Howe concentrated some 15,000 troops in Brunswick, New Jersey. His goal was to draw Washington into a major field engagement and destroy his army. In doing so, he would clear away the most significant obstacle in the path of his planned thrust on Philadelphia.[87] Furthermore, he would collapse a center of gravity on the American side. Howe's plan was straightforward. He would march as if he were going to take an overland route to Philadelphia and draw Washington down from his base around Bound Brook. Then, Howe would engage him somewhere in the vicinity of Princeton, where the terrain favored such a maneuver.[88]

Fig. 8. Detail of a map showing the area of operations between Howe and Washington in the spring of 1777. Title: A New and accurate map of the present seat of war

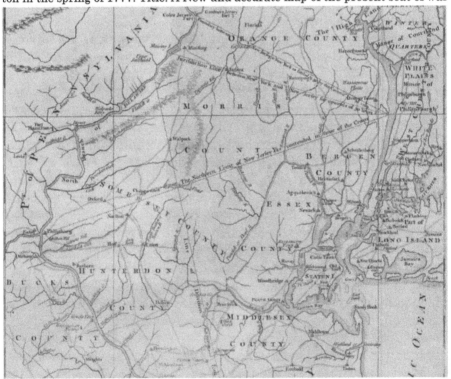

in North America, comprehending New Jersey, Philadelphia, Pensylvania, New-York, &c. London, 1777 *Source: Library of Congress.*

Initially at least, Washington possessed significant intelligence concerning Howe's movements. Based on this information, he correctly guessed the British commander's intent to move on

Philadelphia. To counter this move, Washington continued to concentrate the bulk of his main forces at Bound Brook, even calling on reinforcements from the Hudson Highlands. In addition, he dispatched one detachment, under Maj. Gen. John Sullivan, to Princeton. Washington tasked Sullivan and his troops with slowing any thrust by Howe's main army towards the American capital from that direction. For their part, Washington and his officers had determined that for the time being at least, they would continue to avoid any major engagements with Howe's forces as the Continentals remained numerically too weak to offer any significant chance of success.[89] Thus, Howe's plan was undone from the outset.

As both armies maneuvered around northern New Jersey, Washington realized that if Sullivan remained in central New Jersey with the Commander-in-Chief's force to the north, the New Hampshire Maj. Gen. could find himself in a vulnerable position. Washington therefore ordered his lieutenant to fall back on Flemington, New Jersey and collect whatever militia forces joined him in the area. Sullivan accomplished this maneuver by June 17, and the potentially dangerous situation was at an end.[90]

Seeing that his American adversary would not oblige him in coming out to fight, Howe gave up his plan and returned to Brunswick. It is notable that some see Washington's refusal to be goaded into battle as proof of his growing maturity as an army commander.[91] Now William Howe reverted to his original plan, an amphibious assault on the American capital.

Howe initiated his movements late in the campaign season of 1777, leading to much conjecture among historians. Some assert that he was waiting for a final note of permission on his plans from Lord George Germain. Others have postulated that Howe delayed because he sought to draw Washington into a decisive battle in northern New Jersey, or even that he waited so that the fodder necessary to maintain the numerous horses with his army would be green.[92]

Concerning the above speculations. Germain allowed his commanders in North America a wide latitude in determining their operations. Given the distances involved and the attendant expansion of the communication loop, there existed little alternative. The second possibility offers greater potential, since, as noted previously, Howe possessed a solid grasp of the significance of the Continental army by this point in the conflict. The last explanation seems the most far-fetched as even had he left New York in the spring, given the time in transit, he would be able to gather green forage on his arrival. Mainly, Washington's refusal to be goaded into an open confrontation in norther New Jersey finally determined Howe to attack a target his foe would have to defend. Thus, the British fleet bearing the invasion force did not clear Sandy Hook at the entrance to New York harbor until July 23. According to Lieutenant Colonel Johann Ludwig von Cochenhausen the British tsk force consisted of some 300 vessels which included six ships of the line, ten frigates and various transports and even row galleys.[93]

Howe's decision to take a seaborne rather than an overland route to Philadelphia became a determining factor in how the campaign unfolded. On the one hand, it spared the British forces a potentially long attritional campaign across New Jersey, as well as a long overland line of communication back to New York City. At the same time, it meant that the men were subject to the whims of wind and sea for a time. In addition, it made Howe's force dependent upon the Royal Navy for supply, thus they were constrained to operating within supporting distance of a port capable of docking Sir Richard's transports. The above issues aside, the fleet, left New York as noted above and cruised for several weeks along the New Jersey Coast before turning westward into the Delaware Bay.[94]

On July 29, the lead elements of the flotilla entered the Delaware Bay. Soon the Howe brothers met in conference on board the HMS *Eagle*, Admiral Howe's flagship, with the commander of the frigate HMS *Roebuck*, Capt. Andrew Snape Hamond. The *Roebuck* had been on station in the Delaware Bay for some time and had gained some intelligence of the defenses erected by the rebel government in the Delaware River. As seen previous, the *Roebuck* possessed some direct experience with the Pennsylvania Navy as well.[95]

After describing the deployment of Washington's army south of Philadelphia, Hamond stated, "That the defense of the River consisted of Row Galleys and floating [sic] Batterys which our Frigates would easily displace, and that at, and above Newcastle, no regular works had been Erected, but there were many Guns mounted in open Fleche's for the annoyance to Ships running up the River, but which would certainly be abandoned as any force landed behind them." After his report, Hamond noted that "The General then took the Admiral into the Stern Gallery for a short time, to consider, as I conjectured, upon the particular place of landing;" He continued, "to my astonishment they told me, that since there was no doubt that the Enemy was apprised of the plan of the Expedition, the General said, it confirmed him to his design of landing his army at the Head of Elk in the Chesapeake."[96] As a result, the fleet turned about and headed back out to sea.

Much debate surrounds this meeting, and Howe's subsequent decision. Hamond, after giving his report to the admiral, was not invited to the discussion between the two commanders. In his autobiography, he describes himself as perplexed by the decision as well.[97] While the discussions which transpired onboard the *Eagle* were not recorded by any of the participants at the time, several years later, Hamond was called to testify at an inquiry into William Howe's conduct of the campaign. When asked about the whole number of ships the Americans deployed in defense of the river at the time of the fleet's incursion into the Delaware Bay, he gave the following response,

> *There were two frigates at Philadelphia, not complete as to men—at Mud Island , where the fort was there was a ship called the Province ship, which mounted eighteen 18 pounders—the Delaware frigate of twenty-eight 12 pounders—two xebecks mounting each two 24 pounders in their bow, two 18 pounders in their stern, and four 9 pounders each in their waist—a brig mounting sixteen 6 pounders—two floating batteries, the one of twelve 18 pounders, the other of 10 these guns were moveable on either side—thirteen row gallies each carrying one gun, from 32 pounds to 18—thirty-six row boats, or half gallies, carrying a 6 pounder, or a 4 pounder—I believe that was all, except fire rafts of which there were twenty -five, or thirty— each composed of five stages chained together.*[98]

Hamond's testimony paints an impressive picture of the naval force arrayed against the British flotilla. Still, the captain's intelligence was incomplete. He was neither asked in the proceedings, nor did he volunteer, any information on either the manning of the American fleet or of the river forts. While Hamond may not have possessed any information of these points, if he did, it would underscore that the river defenses were nowhere near as formidable as they appeared. The reasons for this omission will be addressed in the conclusion.

Most historians agree that while Hamond gave accurate intelligence to the Howes as to the defensive network the Americans developed to that point in the Delaware, he also made them aware that in his estimation the defenses constituted a paper tiger.

Hammond was correct in his assessment of the Delaware coastal defenses at this point in the campaign. They were incomplete and undermanned at that time. In fact, some posts held barely any garrison at all. Therefore, a movement up the Delaware remained possible, with a landing, possibly at Wilmington, which would allow for a rapid move on Philadelphia. Likewise, the British could have landed their troops at Newcastle in Delaware. A smaller port, to be sure, but still a practicable landing site, and one from which Gen. William Howe could have moved on Philadelphia while a good portion of the campaign season remained open to him. Gregory Edgar asserts, "This was probably Howe's biggest blunder of the Philadelphia campaign, as it wasted further time at sea, giving his enemy time to further their preparations."[99]

William Howe left some insights into his thinking on the matter in the narrative he prepared for his defense before a Parliamentary inquiry several years later.[100] Howe's explanation as to his reasons for leaving the Delaware Bay warrant some discussion as they help to explain why the subsequent campaign unfolded as it did. By the same token, they offer some insights into the thinking of the British general. On his arrival in the Delaware Bay with his brother, Adm. Richard, William Howe noted "Several days must have been employed to surmount the difficulties of getting up the river, and I inferred from thence that I should not be able to land the troops before Gen. Washington would be in force at Wilmington, where there was also a corps."[101] Thus, the ability to move without transmitting his intentions to his opponent formed part of Howe's motivation. He went on to declare,

> *There was besides no prospect of landing above the confluence of the Delaware and Christiana-Creeks at least the preparations the enemy had made for the defense of the river, by gallies, floating batteries, fireships and fire rafts, would have made such an attempt extremely hazardous.*[102]

All of these factors were reported to Howe by Hamond. The former went on to observe how the terrain in the vicinity of the Delaware Bay stood as a factor in his decision,

> *I also had to consider the country below, where the troops must have landed, and where only the transports could have laid in security (I mean about*

> *Reedy-Island) was very marshy, and the roads upon narrow causeways intersected by creeks. I therefore agreed with the Admiral to go up the Chesapeake-Bay, a plan which had been preconcerted, in the event of a landing in the Delaware proving upon our arrival there, ineligible.*[103]

The switch to the Chesapeake landing site, therefore, stood as an agreed contingency rather than a sudden shift in the operations. It seemed to constitute a fallback plan for the Howe brothers all along. At least that was the way William Howe depicted it after the fact.

He further supported his decision by noting that if the brothers had chosen a landing site above Wilmington, they would still have had to follow the same route, "From the Head of Elk, by way of Aiken's Tavern, otherwise called Pencadder."[104] The actual landing site, then, would have made little difference.

While it could be argued that Howe's explanation was something of a justification after the fact, it does explain, logically, the sudden turn-about of the British fleet in a rational manner. Lacking any additional contemporary evidence that effectively undermines his account, Howe's words on the matter must be accepted at face value as the reason for the change in British plans.

There exist some additional possibilities that support this interpretation not mentioned in the Howe's *Narrative*. With an apparently impressive defensive network barring the river approach to Philadelphia, and a short transit behind them from New York to the Delaware Bay, the Howe bothers may have decided to risk continued good sailing weather and add to the operational deception against Washington. If the weather continued as it had been, they might make the Chesapeake in another week, and at the same time deceive Washington into believing that they intended to strike a more southern target, such as Norfolk in Virginia or even Charleston, South Carolina. If Washington took the bait, they could hope to march on Philadelphia unopposed, or with Washington furiously counter marching in a race to prevent the British commanders from taking Philadelphia and Congress.

It must quickly be pointed out, however, that this is all merely supposition without any supporting facts. Whatever the actual reason, the fleet turned about and headed back out to sea on July 31. When word of the British departure from the Delaware Bay reached Washington, it succeeded as a work of deception. The news left the American commander further confused as to his opponent's intentions.[105] In an attempt to determine his opponent's design once again, Washington ordered some of his commanders back northward on August 1. Likewise, he moved the main army slowly towards Coryell's Ferry, rationalizing that from this central location he could respond to any British moves once he possessed sound intelligence.

As for the Howe brothers, the move out to sea proved disastrous for any timely campaign. The wind died. Ships floated along the coast with soldiers, sailors and horses suffering the effects of the heat and humidity of an east coast summer. Storms exacerbated the misery felt by all on board the fighting ships and transports.

Lieutenant Carl Philipp von Feilitzsch of the Anspach-Bayreuth Jäger company added a vivid description of the weather conditions he encountered during the second leg of the voyage,

> *Storms here in America are much stronger and last longer than in Europe. A storm is therefore much more dangerous because our fleet consists of about 300 ships more or less, and when there is such weather it is usually accompanied by winds, making it difficult for the ships to sail in company.*[106]

Captain John Montresor of the British engineers noted the conditions in his journal as the fleet slowly made its way up the Chesapeake in August. On August 12 he wrote, "The heat of the Sun here feels more like an artificial than a genial heat, and the heat of this night Insupportable."[107] The following day, he observed how "The intense heat and closeness horrid, obliged now to lay on deck."[108] Finally, on August 14, he bemoaned "The heat of this day (if possible) more insupportable than yesterday, the pitch melting off the seams of the vessel."[109]

Two days later, on August 16th, the fleet finally made its way into the Chesapeake Bay. Now, however, they had to backtrack northward to find a suitable landing area. This required nearly another week, and it was not until six days later that the fleet anchored off the Head of Elk (modern Elkton) in Maryland on August 22nd. The Howe brothers took three smaller armed vessels and reconnoitered the area the following day. Returning, they announced that the landing would commence in two days.[110] The Howe brothers were setting the stage for the momentous drama that would be the

1777 campaign in the Delaware Valley.

The fighting in Pennsylvania in 1777 included the largest engagement of the war, the battle of Brandywine, fought on September 11, 1777. In brief, the campaign opened in earnest with the landing of British troops at Head of Elk in Maryland on August 25. [111] The troops came ashore in three waves, with the light troops landing first and engaging in some desultory skirmishing with local militia. The defense was purely symbolic and quickly pushed aside. The small militia force present stood no chance of denying the Crown forces the beach. They could report that they engaged the enemy, albeit briefly, and had not retired without firing a shot.

The Crown forces spent the next several days reconnoitering, searching for forage, especially for horses, and regaining their land legs. On August 28, Washington conducted a reconnaissance of the British camp from atop Iron Hill in Delaware. Meanwhile, William Howe reconnoitered in preparation for his northward march on the same day. Soon thereafter, the British moved out. Capt. Johann Ewald of the Second Company Hessen-Cassel Jäger Corps served in the vanguard. He noted in his diary that on August 29, about nine in the morning, "The army was alarmed on all sides by enemy parties. A few foot Jäger and some infantrymen were killed and wounded, since our sentries beyond the two highways could scarcely see over twenty paces in front of themselves because of the thick wood."[112] Further skirmishing followed.

On September 3, the Crown forces began to move in earnest. Washington, bereft of his corps of riflemen, whom he dispatched to support Horatio Gates in New York, formed a Corps of Light Infantry under Brig. Gen. William Maxwell. His newly formed corps confronted the advancing Crown forces in a series of skirmishes known as the Battle of Iron Hills or Cooch's Bridge. The American forces managed to slow, but not halt the British advance. Still, they did buy time for Washington to better organize his defenses.

While Washington committed to a policy of avoiding general engagements, politically, he could not sacrifice the capital without making some kind of a stand. The Continental commander in chief chose to make his stand along Brandywine Creek in southeastern Pennsylvania.

In the engagement itself, Howe dispatched Hessian Gen. von Knyphausen with one column to lock the Americans in place, while he with Gen. Cornwallis made a flanking march, essentially employing the same stratagem he utilized successfully the previous year on Long Island. Once again, Washington fell for the bait. On this occasion, however, when the Americans learned they were out-maneuvered they changed front to meet the new threat and ended by retiring from the field in relatively good order. The Continentals were growing in tactical maturity and proficiency.[113]

Following the defeat at Brandywine, Howe failed to pursue Washington for several days. During this time, he foraged further in the area of the battlefield, much to the detriment of the local residents.[114] Next there was a period of maneuvering as the British commander sought to make his way to the American capital while Washington attempted to block his opponent's march. These moves resulted in one near encounter at the so-called battle of the Clouds on September 16.[115] In an attempt to inflict some damage on Howe's forces, Washington had sent out Brig. Gen. Anthony Wayne with a column to stay on Howe's rear and look for opportunities to skirmish with him.

The plan culminated in Wayne himself being somewhat surprised by a British night attack led by Gen. Charles Grey, the engagement came to be known as the Paoli Massacre by the Americans. For their part, the British perceived it as a very successful and daring operation. Night attacks were uncommon in the eighteenth century as it was very difficult to maintain march and fire discipline. Grey and his subordinates managed both of these tasks very well, ordering his men to remove the flints form their firelocks to guard against disclosing their position on the march through random fire. For this order, Grey earned the nomme de guerre "No Flint Grey." As for the allegation of a massacre, most of the recent historians to study the engagement remark that while there were certainly instances of excess on the part of the Crown troops, there was not a premeditated plan to slaughter the Americans, nor were they caught completely off guard. The problem primarily lay in developing an organized defense and getting the troops out of the combat zone, especially when the bulk of the infantry were trapped behind the slower moving artillery wagons in the line of march. All these factors could be attributed to what the Prussian military theorist Carl von Clausewitz referred to as friction, that ephemeral quality under which "Action in war is like movement in a resistant element." [116] The only antidote Clausewitz could discern for friction was experience of the commander. Given that Wayne had only about two years' experience in significant commands, he came up lacking against his British counterparts.

After once again outflanking Washington, for the sixth time overall, Howe gained access to Philadelphia. On September 26, Earl

Charles Cornwallis led the British vanguard into Philadelphia. Accompanying Cornwallis were a number of prominent local Loyalists, including Joseph Galloway. Howe had secured the American capital. Now the question became more and more, would he be able to retain it? That question would be answered in the Delaware River. The same day, Washington moved with the army across Perkiomen Creek and arrived at Pennypacker Mills. The move brought him ten miles closer to the capital. Still, he remained a relatively safe distance from Philadelphia.

CHAPTER NOTES

[1] On the Trenton-Princeton campaign, see William M. Dwyer, *The Day is Ours! An Inside View of the Battles of Trenton and Princeton, November 1776-January 1777* 9New Brunswick, NJ: Rutgers University Press, 1983), David Hackett Fischer *Washington's Crossing* (New York: Oxford University press, 2004), William S. Stryker, *The Battles of Trenton and Princeton* (Trenton: The Old Barracks Association, 2001 reprint of 1998 orig.).

[2] Johann Ewald, *Diary of the American War.* Joseph P. Tustin, ed and trans. (New Haven, CT: Yale University Press, 1979), p. 44.

[3] For biographical information on Johann von Ewald, see Boatner, pp. 356-57. See also Ewald, Johann *Diary of the American War: A Hessian Journal, Captain Johann Ewald, Field Jäger Corps.* Joseph Tustin, trans. and ed. (New Haven, CT: Yale University Press, 1979), xvii-xxi; and James R. Mc Intyre, *Johann Ewald, Jäger Commander.* (New York: Knox Press, 2020).

[4] There are three main English-language biographies from which the information on Kosciuszko is derived: Miecislaus Haiman, *Kosciuszko in the American Revolution (*New York: The Kosciuszko Foundation, 1975); Francis Casimir Kajencki *Thaddeus Kosciuszko: Military engineer of the American Revolution* (El Paso, TX: South Polonia Press, 1998); Storozynski, Alex *The Peasant Prince: Thaddeus Kosciuszko and the Age of Revolution* (New York: St. Martin's Press, 2009).

[5] Haiman, *Kosciuszko*, pp. 9-11.

[6] Browne, "Fort Mercer and Fort Mifflin," p. 65.

[7] John W. Jackson, *Guardian of the Delaware*, p. 6.

[8] Jackson, *Delaware Bay and River Defenses*, p. 8.

[9] Ibid.

[10] Ibid.

[11] Jackson, *Guardian of the Delaware*, p. 7

[12] Bull, General Orders for May 1, 1777, quoted in Ibid, p. 7.

[13] Ibid, pp. 7-8.

[14] Ibid, p. 8.

[15] Ibid.

[16] Ibid.

[17] Ibid, p. 8.

[18] Stoker and Jones, "Colonial Military Strategy," p. 15.

[19] Jackson, *Pennsylvania Navy*, 96. Du Coudray was not solely at fault for the controversy that surrounded him. Most of the blame lay with the America agent in France, Silas Deane. In order to recruit du Coudray, Deane offered him the senior command of the American artillery. On learning of this appointment, several American general officers, including Nathanael Greene, Henry Knox and John Sullivan wrote directly to Congress threatening to resign their commissions. Washington, caught directly in the middle of this early civil-military dispute, sought to restore order and smooth over offended pride. On orders from Congress, chastised his generals. Congress initially demanded an apology form the generals. When none was

forthcoming, they wisely allowed the matter to drop. Meanwhile, the legislators mollified du Coudray with a staff appointment as Inspector General of Ordnances and Military Manufactories.

[20] Ibid, p. 98.

[21] Charles Philippe Trouson du Coudray "Observations on the Forts intended for the Defense of the Two Passages of the River Delaware, July 1777." in *PMHB* 24,3 (1900): 343-47.

[22] Ibid, p. 343.

[23] Ibid.

[24] Ibid.

[25] Ibid, p. 344.

[26] Ibid, p. 345.

[27] Ibid.

[28] Ibid.

[29] Ibid, p. 346.

[30] Ibid, pp. 346-47.

[31] Biographical information on William Howe is derived from Boatner, *Encyclopedia*, 522-526. The most recent full biographical treatment of Howe is David Smith, *William Howe and the American War of Independence*. (London: Bloomsbury, 2015). On Howe's role at Belle Île and Havana, see also Andrew Jackson O'Schaughnessy, *The Men Who Lost America: British Leadership, the American Revolution, and the Fate of Empire*. (New Haven: Yale University Press, 2013), pp. 88-9.

[32] Ibid, p. 89. For more information on the development of light infantry in the British Army, see James R. Mc Intyre, *The Development of the British Light Infantry, Continental and North American Influences, 1740-1765*. (Point Pleasant, NJ: Winged Hussar Publishing, 2015).

[33] Boatner, *Encyclopedia*, p. 523.

[34] O'Schaughnessy, *Men Who Lost America*, p. 90

[35] David Smith, *Howe*, p. 26.

[36] O'Schaughnessy, *Men Who Lost America*, p. 90.

[37] Ibid.

[38] Biographical information of Richard Howe is derived from Boatner, *Encyclopedia*, pp. 520-1.

[39] Frances Vivian, "A Defense of Sir William Howe with a New Interpretation of His Actions in New Jersey, June 1777." in *JSAHR*. 44, 178 (June 1966): 72.

[40] On William Howe's plans for the 1777 campaign, see Ira D. Gruber, *The Howe Brothers and the American Revolution* (New York, Athenaeum: 1972), p. 174.

[41] Ibid, pp. 179-80.

[42] Ibid, p.175, pp. 180-1.

[43] George Germain, or George Sackville (1716-1785), He was known as Lord Sackville until 1770, when he took his wife's surname and became Lord Germain (sometimes rendered as Germaine). The name-changed is usually considered as a part

of his political rehabilitation. Germain served as part of the British expeditionary force that went to the Continent during the Seven Years' War. He commanded the Allied cavalry at the Battle of Minden, August 1, 1759, where he failed to order forward the cavalry which allowed the bulk of the French forces to escape. He was court-martialed and forbidden to serve in the King's armed forces ever again. He became a part of the faction around George III and served as the Secretary of State for the American colonies. In this role Germain exerted the most direct oversight of the running of the war in America of any of the King's ministers. For biographical information on Germain, see Boatner, *Encyclopedia*, pp. 421-4. See also, O'Schaughnessy, *Men Who Lost America*, pp. 165-203. For a complete discussion of Germain's role at Minden, see Piers Mackesy, *The Coward of Minden: The Affair of Lord George Sackville*. New York: St. Martins Press, 1979.

[44] Gruber, *Howe Brothers*, p. 180.

[45] Troyer Steele Anderson, *The Command of the Howe Brothers during the American Revolution* (New York: Oxford University Press, 1936), p. 218.

[46] Ibid.

[47] See Anderson, *Command of the Howe Brothers*, pp. 219-20, and Jackson, *Delaware Defenses*, p. 1.

[48] Anderson, *Command of the Howe Brothers*, p. 220.

[49] Ibid, pp. 221-23.

[50] Ibid, p. 224.

[51] Ibid.

[52] Ibid, pp. 225-27

[53] Ibid, pp. 227-28.

[54] Jackson, *Delaware Defenses*,

[55] Gruber, *Howe Brothers*, pp. 203-4.

[56] The concept of "Center of Gravity" was first developed by the Prussian military theorist Carl von Clausewitz. "What the theorist has to say here is this: one must keep the dominant characteristics of both belligerents in mind. Out of these characteristics a certain center of gravity develops, the hub of all power and movement, on which everything depends. That is the point at which all our energies should be directed." He then went on to note that "For Alexander, Gustavus Adolphus, Charles XII, and Frederick the Great, the center of gravity was their army. If the army had been destroyed, they all would have gone in history as failures." Carl von Clausewitz, *On War*. Michael Howard and Peter Paret, eds. and trans. (Princeton: Princeton University Press, 1976), pp. 595-6. The same observation fits Washington and the Continental Army. If it had disintegrated, the rebellion would collapse, and Washington would be seen as a failure.

[57] Abbot, W.W. and Dorothy Twohig, eds. *The Papers of George Washington, Revolutionary War Series*. vol. 6. (Charlottesville, VA; University of Virginia Press, 1994), p. 249. Hereinafter *Washington, Rev. War*. It is worth noting that the so-called Fabian Strategy adopted by Washington forms the subject of Thomas Fleming's work *The Strategy of Victory: How General George Washington Won the American Revolution* (New York: De Capo Press, 2017).

[58] Concerning Philadelphia as a major production center for the Americans war

effort, see Smith, *Manufacturing Independence.*

[59] Anthony D. Darling, *Red Coat and Brown Bess* (Alexandria Bay, NY: Museum Restoration Service, 1971), pp. 36-7.

[60] Ibid, pp. 10-11. See also

[61] Matthew Spring, *With Zeal and With Bayonets Only: The British Army in North America,1775-1783.* Norman, OK: University of Oklahoma Press, 2008), pp. 245-62.

[62] In the eighteenth century, the terms battalion and regiment were used interchangeably.

[63] On the development of light infantry in North America, see Mc Intyre, *British Light Infantry Tactics* for a solid introduction to the topic.

[64] There is an entire sub-genre of literature concerning the riflemen. For the current purposes, only a small sampling is necessary: Brown, M. L. *Firearms in Colonial America, 1492-1792* (Washington, D.C.: Smithsonian Institution Press, 1980); Samuel E. Dyke, *The Pennsylvania Rifle* (Lancaster, PA: Bicentennial Book, 1974); Arcadi Gluckman, *Unites States Muskets, Rifles, and Carbines.* Buffalo, NY: Otto Ulbrich Co., 1948. Huddleston, Joe D. *Colonial Riflemen in the American Revolution* (York, PA: George Shumway Publisher, 1978); Philip B. Sharpe, *The Rifle in America* (New York: William Morrow and Company, 1938). See also James R. Mc Intyre, "On the Origins and Development of the Pennsylvania-American Longrifle, 1500-1700." *Seven Years War Association Journal.* 14, 1 (Fall 2005): 40-55; George Raudzens, "War-Winning Weapons: The Measurement of Technological Determinism in Military History." *The Journal of Military History.* 54, 4 (October 1990): 403-33; Felix Reichmann, "The Pennsylvania Rifle: A Social Interpretation of Changing Military Techniques." *The Pennsylvania Magazine of History and Biography.* 69, 1 (January 1945): 3-14.

[65] Pruett, "Continental Artillery," p. 35.

[66] While dated, Harold L. Peterson *Round Shot and Rammers.* (Harrisburg, PA: Stackpole Books, 1969) remains a comprehensive discussion of artillery in the period. Unless otherwise noted, the preceding discussion of the field guns is derived predominantly from his work. See also, B.P. Hughes *Open Fire: The Artillery Tactics from Marlborough to Wellington.* (Sussex: Antony Bird Publications, 1983).

[67] John Ellis, *Cavalry: The History of Mounted Warfare.* Yorkshire: Pen and Sword Books, 2004 reprint of 1978 original), pp. 77-108.

[68] Concerning the use of cavalry in the American War of independence, see Jim Piecuch, ed. *Cavalry of the American Revolution* (Yardley, PA: Westholme Publishing, 2014).

[69] Ibid, pp. 7-8.

[70] On the traditional view of the British army, see Sir John Fortescue, *The War of Independence: The British Army in North America, 1775-1783* (Mechanicsburg, PA: Stackpole Books, 2001 reprint of 1911 original); Lynn Montross, *Rag, Tag and Bobtail The Story of the Continental Army, 1775-1783* (New York: Harper & Brothers Publishers, 1952). The first person to really challenge the preceding ideas was Sylvia R. Frey in her *The British Soldier in the American revolution: A Social History of Military Life in the Revolutionary Period* (Austin: University of Texas Press, 1981); Further challenging this idea was J.A. Houlding, *Fit for Service The Training of the British Army, 1715-1795* (Oxford: Clarendon Press, 1981). See also

Spring, *With Zeal and Bayonets Only*; On the professional reading of the officer corps, see Ira D. Gruber, *Books and the British Army in the Age of the American Revolution* (Chapel Hill: University of North Carolina Press, 2014). For an excellent account of the perceptions of common soldier during the war, see Don N. Hagist, *British Soldiers American War: Voices of the American Revolution* (Yardley, PA: Westholme Press, 2012).

[71] Spring, *Zeal and Bayonets Only*, 127.

[72] Ibid.

[73] Ibid, p. 122.

[74] Michael C. Harris, *Brandywine: A Military History of the Battle that Lost Philadelphia but Saved America, September 11, 1777* (El Dorado Hills, CA; Savas Beatie, 2016), p. 314.

[75] Ibid.

[76] Mc Intyre, *British Light Infantry*, p. 18, pp. 34-7.

[77] There is a long historiography of the soldatenhandel, and it is intricately enmeshed in German political trends. For instance, in the nineteenth century, as German nationalism took hold in central Europe, many historians denounced the subsidy treaties as the result of greed on the part of the petty German princes of the previous century. Some good examples of this early trend is Freidrich Kapp *Der soldatenhandel deutscher fürsten nach Amerika. Ein beitrag zur kulturgeschichte des achtzehnten jahrhunderts* (Berling: J. Springer, 1874). See also Carl Presser, *Die Soldatenhandel in Hessen*. Marburg: R.G. Einwert, 1900. In the view of these early historians, the troops from Hesse-Cassel and various other German states that were contracted out to other powers were depicted as little more than military chattels. The trend continued through much of the twentieth century in works such as Philipp Losch, *Soldatenhandel mit einem Berzeidnis der Hessen-Kasselischen Gubdfidienvertrage und einer Bibliographie* (Verlag zu Kassel: Barenreiter, 1933). During the 1980s, a more balanced view of the role of subsidies and subsidy troops began to emerge. One of the key works in this regard was Atwood, *The Hessians.* Following Atwood's work, but expanding on many of the same themes was Charles W. Ingrao, *The Hessian Mercenary State: Ideas, Institutions, and Reform under Frederick II, 1760-1785.* (Cambridge: Cambridge University Press, 1987). Published in the interim between these two works, John Childs, *Armies and Warfare in Europe, 1648-1789.* (Manchester: Manchester University Press, 1982), 46-48 provides a decidedly traditional and negative interpretation of this practice. In this regard, he merely echoes the description given by those such as Kapp and Presser. The most recent of the works survey here, William Urban *Bayonets for Hire: Mercenaries for Hire 1550-1789* (London: Greenhill Books, 2006), which purports to treat of the history of mercenaries, only touches on subsidies and does not contain any discussion of the soldatenhandel.

[78] Peter H. Wilson *War, State and Society in Württemberg, 1677-1793* (Cambridge: Cambridge University Press, 1995), p. 74.

[79] It is worth noting that more works needs to be done concerning the degree to which the men in the ranks understood the service in the context of the policy goals of their sovereigns.

[80] On the origins of the Jägers, see Thomas M. Barker and Thomas M. Huey, "Military Jägers, Their Civilian background and Weaponry." in *The Hessians: The Jour-*

nal of the Johannes Schwalm Historical Association. 15 (2012) pp. 1-15. For a more in-depth study of a particular unit, see Arno Storkel, "The Anspach Jägers." *The Hessians: Journal of the Johannes Schwalm Historical Association.* 14 (2011): 1-31.

[81] Robert K. Wright, *The Continental Army* (Washington, D.C.: Center of Military History, United States Army, 1989), p. 91.

[82] Ibid.

[83] Ibid, p. 92.

[84] Ibid, pp. 98-9.

[85] Ibid, p. 119. See also, Piecuch, ed. *Cavalry of the Revolution*, pp. 7-8.

[86] For an excellent description of this war of posts, see Taaffe, *The Philadelphia Campaign*, pp. 23-28.

[87] Ibid, p. 36.

[88] Ibid.

[89] Ibid, pp. 37-8.

[90] Ibid, p. 39.

[91] Ibid, p. 40.

[92] On the notion of Howe's awaiting the growth of green fodder for the horses, see Marion Balderston, "Lord Howe Clears the Delaware." in *PMHB* 96 (1972): 328.

[93] Lieutenant Colonel Johann Ludwig von Cochenhausen to Major General Friedrich Christian Arnold Baron von Jungkenn-Müntzer vom Mohrenstamm, Germantown, October 9, 1777 quoted in "The Philadelphia Campaign, 1777-1778 Letters and Reports from the von Jungkenn Papers." in *Hessians: Journal of the Johannes Schwalm Historical Association,* 6,2 (1998): 1-2

[94] Richard Howe's nickname derived from his dark complexion.

[95] See chapter two.

[96] Andrew Snape Hamond, *The Autobiography of Andrew Snape Hamond., Bart., R.N., 1738-1828, covering the years 1738-1793.* W. Hugh Moomaw, ed. (MA thesis, University of Virginia, 1953), 73-74. *Roebuck* was on station in the Delaware Capes maintaining the British blockade. As a result, her captain possessed a very thorough knowledge of the defenses the Patriots had developed in the river.

[97] Ibid.

[98] William Howe, *The Narrative of Lt. Gen. Sir William Howe to a Committee in the House of Commons on the 29ᵗʰ of April, 1779* (London: H. Baldwin, 1779), pp. 72-3.

[99] Ibid.

[100] On Howe's call for the inquiry and subsequent defense, see Gruber, *Howe Brothers*, pp. 336-50.

[101] Howe, *Narrative*, p. 23.

[102] Ibid.

[103] Ibid, pp. 23-4.

[104] Ibid, p. 24.

[105] Browne, "Fort Mercer and Fort Mifflin," p. 10.

[106] Lieutenant Heinrich Carl Philipp von Feilitzsch and Lieutenant Christian Friedrich Bartholomai, *Diaries of two Ansbach Jaegers*. Bruce E. Burgoyne, trans and ed. (Bowie, MD: Heritage Books, 1997), p. 11.

[107] Montresor, *Journals*, p. 436.

[108] Ibid.

[109] Ibid.

[110] Browne, "Mercer and Mifflin," p. 11.

[111] It is worth noting that given the late start to Howe's campaign in Pennsylvania, any real chance of aiding Burgoyne in New York was now untenable.

[112] Ewald, *Diary*, p. 76.

[113] The above general description of the Philadelphia Campaign is drawn from Thomas McGuire, *The Philadelphia Campaign, vol.1 The Defeat at Brandywine and the Loss of Philadelphia* (Mechanicsburg, PA: Stackpole Books, 2006). Harris, *Brandywine*.

[114] An excellent discussion of the effects of the British army occupation of the region around Brandywine battlefield can be found in Andrew Outten, "Destruction & Wanton Waste": The Impact of War in a Peaceful Valley. Unpublished paper presented at the Seventeenth Annual Fort Ticonderoga Seminar on the American Revolution. Fort Ticonderoga, New York: September 26, 2021.

[115] On this engagement, see Michael C. Harris, *Germantown: A Military History of the Battle for Philadelphia, October 4, 1777.* (El Dorado Hills, CA: Savas Beatie, 2020), pp. 37-62.

[116] Clausewitz, *On War*, p. 120.

Chapter Four
The Contest for the Delaware Round One: Jockeying for Position

The same day Cornwallis led the advanced elements of the British army into Philadelphia, Lt. Col. Samuel Smith's detachment of some 200 Continentals arrived at Fort Mifflin, relieving the Corps of Invalids already stationed there under Colonel Lewis Nicola. Here was the first positive step in reinforcing the river defenses.

Samuel Smith was born in Carlisle, Pennsylvania on July 27, 1752. He moved with his family to Baltimore, Maryland in 1759. He received a solid education by the standards of the eighteenth century, becoming well versed in Latin and Greek classics. At the age of fourteen, he began working in his father John Smith's counting house. The younger Smith learned the merchants trade there until in May of 1770, when at the age of nineteen, his father sent the young man to London to continue learning the merchant's trade. During his time in Europe, Smith survived a shipwreck and traveled extensively throughout the Continent prior to returning the colonies as the resistance to changes in ministerial policy was reaching its peak.

Smith joined a company of militia raised by a Capt. Mordecai Gist. Later, on January 3, 1776, Samuel Smith received a captain's commission in the Maryland regiment then being raised by Col. William Smallwood. Smith marched with the regiment and took part in the battles of Long Island, Harlem Heights and White Plains. On August 27, he took part in the battle of Long Island. His unit was part of the famed Maryland five hundred, who held off the British attack long enough for much of the American army to extricate itself from disaster. He served during the retreat across New Jersey as well. Shortly after crossing the Delaware into Pennsylvania in December 1776, Smith received promotion to lieutenant colonel in the new Fourth Maryland Regiment under Col. Josias Carvil Hall. He missed participating in the battles of Trenton and Princeton as Smallwood had dispatched him back to Baltimore in order to recruit for the regiment.[1]

He served with the new regiment throughout the Philadelphia Campaign until after the battle of Brandywine. On September 23, 1777, Washington summoned him personally for his assignment to Fort Mifflin.[2] Smith's subordinates at the post included a Maj. Ballard of Virginia, Maj. Simeon Thayer of Rhode Island and Capt. Samuel Treat of the artillery along with a detachment of two hundred infantry.[3] At the age of twenty-five, Smith was being trusted with an independent command of great significance. This was the sort of assignment that could make or break a military career.

Figure 9 Samuel Smith (1752-1839), later in his career, when smith served as a Major General of the Maryland militia during the War of 1812.

Since the battle of Brandywine, Gen. Howe had enjoyed the support of Capt. Andrew Snape Hamond's small force of ships in the Delaware, but it was not until shortly after Cornwallis entered Philadelphia that the main British fleet, with its attendant transports, made its way into the Delaware from the Chesapeake Bay. During the intervening three-week period, Adm. Howe confronted headwinds and gales that substantially slowed his progress out of the Chesapeake and into the Delaware Bay.[4] Once the British fleet entered the Delaware Bay, they quickly established a base at Wilmington, Delaware. Wilmington would remain the main base for the British fleet while they cleared the Delaware River of obstructions.[5] Thus, after throwing away a month of the campaign season, the Royal Navy, at least, returned to where it first touch the theater of operations.

Once the British column entered Philadelphia, the occupiers quickly set about working to secure their prize. One sought after commodity was any type of watercraft, as they would allow the British some operational latitude above the river forts and chevaux de fries. These were in short supply, however, as Washington had already ordered that all boats be taken from the city. Still, in a town as dependent on maritime trade as Philadelphia, this constitute a very tall order, and not all vessels could be secured in time. The Crown forces quickly located about fifty boats. These ranged from a Durham boat capable of transporting roughly fifty men to scows, flatboats and various other vessels.[6]

The British sought to secure their prize from attack in the direction of the Delaware river as well. The began to establish a series of batteries along the waterfront. Capt.-Lieut. Francis Downman of the royal artillery commanded a battery at the southern edge of Philadelphia. His incomplete battery consisted of four 12-pounders and two Royal howitzers. These would be protected by an earthwork thrown up in front of them.[7]

The day following the British occupation of Philadelphia, Downman's batteries, which had only two guns then mounted, underwent a baptism of fire. Coming up the Delaware that morning were a combination of vessels. These included the Pennsylvania State frigate *Delaware* of 24 guns, the 24-gun state ship *Montgomery*, the 8-gun Continental sloop *Fly*, and five row galleys mounting one gun each. The ships were dispatched upriver by Cmdre. John Hazelwood of the Pennsylvania Navy.[8] The commodore seemed unclear on whether the British had taken the city and dispatched this maritime reconnaissance in force to gather intelligence. As John Jackson notes, this lack on information concerning the British occupation of the city stands out as an oddity as "Pennsylvania galleys had been patrolling the river as far as Windmill Island, and as late as the 26th a galley was stationed at Gloucester Point (Pennsylvania)."[9]

Regardless of the reasons, the American ships made their way in close to the city. Hearing the alarm, the commander of British artillery, Gen. Samuel Cleaveland made his way to Downman's battery. The general ordered his subordinate not to open up on the American ships until they fired on him.[10]

The *Delaware* got within 400 yards of the British battery when a Lt. George Wilson, a subordinate of Downman's, who had not received the injunction to hold his fire, ordered his gun to open up on the vessel. His crew got off two shots before Downman ordered him to cease firing.[11]

Taking fire, Capt. Charles Alexander of the *Delaware* opened up on the British positions with his ship's 12-pouders, hurling grape shot at the defenders. Now the remaining British batteries joined in, replying to the fire from the American ship.

Wilson's battery quickly burned through their allotted ammunition, and the lieutenant went off in search of more. At that point, with their position exposed and under fire, some of his gunners abandoned their posts until ordered to return by Downman.[12]

As the British resumed fire on the *Delaware*, more and more of their shots found their mark. Wooden fragments, large enough to maim or kill, burst across and below decks. One shot in particular hit the ship's caboose or cook house, resulting in several fires. Amid the sound and chaos of the fight, orders were likely misunderstood, or not heard at all. As Capt. Alexander sought to bring the ship about, his men mismanaged the sails of the ship, and the Delaware ran aground at the near the lower end of Windmill Island. The crew returned fire as best they could, but they now became an easy mark for the British gunners, who poured iron into her. Stuck fast, and in flames, Capt. Alexander had no choice save to strike his colors and surrender the *Delaware*.[13]

The *Fly* took several hits as well and lost her mast. This led her to run aground on the Jersey side of the river. Her crew managed to refloat the vessel that night and she joined the other ships in returning to Fort Mifflin. Admiral Howe entered the Delaware Bay with elements of the fleet the same day the *Delaware* made its fated run by Philadelphia.

The captain and crew of the *Delaware* became prisoners of the British, save for the ship's cook who was killed in the fighting. The fires on the ship were extinguished, and it was later repaired and taken into the British service.[14]

In itself, the action along the Philadelphia waterfront was a small engagement, it lasted only about an hour, however, it exerted significant operational results. William Howe now had access to the east Jersey and could transport troops there to assault Fort Mercer, or to forage with impunity. It would not be long before Howe took advantage of the possibilities his new control of the ferry opened up.[15]

Washington did not inform John Hancock, the president of the Continental Congress of the loss of the *Delaware* until October 3, which gives some indication of the tempo of the campaign in the Philadelphia area. In the letter, Washington observed

> ...*Since my Letter of the 29th, no favourable change has taken place in our affairs—On the contrary, we have sustained an additional loss in the capture of the Delaware. She fell into the Enemy's hands*

in a day or two after they were in possession of the City, and in a manner not yet well understood. Some have supposed the Crew mutinied, while another report is, that she was disabled in her Rudder by a shot and drove on shore...I will not dwell longer on the subject Congress may rest assured all the means in my power shall be employed to put our affairs in a more agreeable train and to accomplish the end they so earnestly wish.[16]

Before examining the initial efforts of the Howe brothers to open the river to British shipping, it is appropriate to review the overall operational situation of both sides at this point in the campaign. Control of the Delaware River now became of paramount importance for both sides.

For the British, the opening of the river meant being able to retain control of the city of brotherly love. As an interim measure, they resorted to bringing ships up the river to Chester, Pennsylvania, where they were unloaded, and their contents transported overland to Philadelphia. Such a method of supplying the city was both difficult and precarious. The long land line of communications from Chester to Philadelphia, which included movement over a number of poorly maintained country roads, made an easy and appealing target for American raids. As a result, the British were forced to provide substantial escorts to the supplies transported overland, in turn reducing their ability to mount subsequent offensive actions against Washington's beleaguered Continentals or maintain a solid defense of Philadelphia. While a small quantity of supplies was able to get through, and these provided some addition to the commissary stores in Philadelphia, the flow came nowhere near meeting the needs of the British Army and the civilians in the city. The trickle needed to grow to a flood, or the American capital would become untenable. Therefore, it was necessary to break the American hold on the river or the ability of the city to serve as winter quarters for the British Army would be seriously compromised. It is clear William Howe was quite aware of the necessity of opening the Delaware to British shipping. Among his aides, John André, later famed for his role in Benedict Arnold's treason, left this diary entry for October 3, 1777, "Our communication with the ships was only by land."[17] Opening the Delaware River to British shipping would require close coordination between the British land and naval forces, something the British had developed quite thoroughly by time of the American

War.[18]

The Americans, for their part, realized that if they could successfully interdict the flow of necessary supplies to Philadelphia, they could potentially force the British to abandon the city. In essence, maintaining the Delaware River obstructions could potentially force the British to abandon Philadelphia, much as they had evacuated their line of posts in New Jersey in the aftermath of the Trenton and Princeton campaign. As one historian of the Philadelphia Campaign noted, Howe was aware that if he were forced to abandon the city, "Such humiliation, coupled with Burgoyne's failure on the Hudson, might be enough to dissuade Parliament from further support of this costly war."[19] It could be added that the general's reputation would be permanently tarnished. Short of that possibility, the Continentals could certainly curtail the ability of the British to engage in further offensive operations in the Philadelphia area or send troops back to New York to support Burgoyne. In addition, the Americans could make the British stay in Philadelphia far from comfortable by forcing them to live on reduced rations. Such a situation would place Howe in a position Benjamin Franklin would later summarize so aptly, "Instead of Howe taking Philadelphia, Philadelphia has taken Howe."[20] At the very least, a successful delaying action could make Howe's capture of the city an empty victory.

Washington eventually grasped that if he could continue to interdict the flow of supplies into Philadelphia, he might force William Howe to abandon the city, and thus still manage to win the campaign. There were problems with this line of thought. First, the works along the river were far from complete. Likewise, they stood in desperate need of more troops to adequately man them. Thomas Warton, Jr., then president of Pennsylvania, expressed this state of affairs to Washington in a letter dated September 12, 1777.[21]

Moving up the river from the Delaware Bay, the first target of any British attempt to open the waterway to their shipping would be Billingsport. This post covered the southernmost line of chevaux de frise. Once it was dispensed with, the Royal Navy could begin the process of clearing the sunken obstructions and make their way to the port of Philadelphia.

As completed, the fort required a substantial garrison to man it. Due to this, the fort had been reduced several times over the course of 1777. One modification shrank the fort to one-third its original side by enclosing the two bastions facing the riverfront with a connecting wall. The fort was reduced one additional times until only the northeast bastion remained.[22] The northeast bastion was converted into a redoubt and a row of abates was placed in front of the parapet on the landward side.[23] Still, all of these reductions in the size of Billingsport could not make up for the lack of adequate manpower to occupy the post. As of September 5, the garrison of the post consisted of only thirty Continental artillerymen, and fifty Philadelphia militia with a mere eight days left to serve. Fort Mifflin was garrisoned by a similar sized contingent, thirty artillerymen and fifteen militia. Finally, Fort Mercer and the Bush Island battery were completely unmanned.[24]

Nor did the modifications address the primary flaw of the post - it possessed no defense against an assault from the landward side. Bull's focus, and that of all later reformers, including du Coudray remained fixated on an assault form the river. Supplementing the post at Billingsport were two floating batteries moored by Billings Island, one mounting nine 18-pounders and the other ten. Du Coudray hoped the floating batteries would help to ward off and British frigates coming up the river to attack Billingsport.[25] One of Washington's most trusted subordinates, Maj. Gen. Nathanael Greene inspected the works at Billingsport, and wished "them totally demolished." His reasons for this condemnation being "The situation of renders the approaches easy the enemy can make good their landing a little below the work, the ground is very favorable but a small distance from the work to open Batteries Billingsport fortress, the work is not difficult to invest, and once invested it will be difficult if not impossible to keep open a communication as to take of[f] the Garrison..."[26] Greene's damning opinion of the fort laid bare the misconception of du Coudray's efforts. The French engineer focused on the defense of the post from an attack by British shipping in the Delaware to the expense of landward side. By the same token, the Rhode Islander may simply have been expressing an overabundance of caution. After all, he commanded at Fort Washington the previous year and had assured his commander that the fort could hold out. William Howe, on the other hand, determined to take the post by landing troops in New Jersey just below the post.

To take Billingsport, on October 1, Howe detached a force composed of elements of the 10th and 42nd Regiments, as well as some men from the 71st under the overall command of Col. Thomas Stirling. The units moved quickly to their rendezvous near modern Chester, Pennsylvania. Their rapid assembly is underscored by the Master's Journal of the HMS *Roebuck* which recorded that same day, "AM at 9 made Signal for the Troops to embark on boats and afterward the boats were employed landing Troops in the Jerseys."[27]

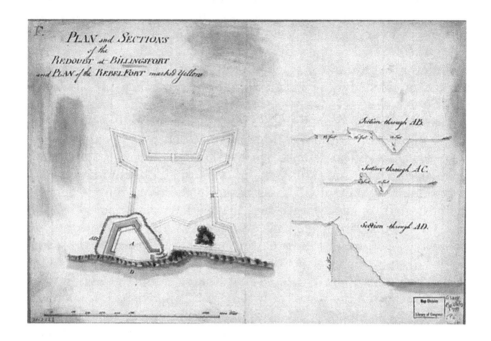

Fig.10. *Plan and sections of the redoubt at Billingsfort and plan of the rebel fort marked yellow.* (1777?). Author unknown. *Source: Library of Congress.*

Concerned that the British might attempt an attack on Billingsport, Washington dispatched Col. William Bradford of the Pennsylvania militia to reinforce the post. The colonel arrived at the fort on September 29. On his arrival, Bradford learned that Brig. Gen. Silas Newcomb of the New Jersey militia, whom he expected to meet at Billingsport, had instead departed with 300 men and one of the fort's guns to engage the British on their march to the post.[28] While Newcomb was within his authority to make such a move, it left the post with a garrison of roughly 100 men of the Fourth Battalion of Pennsylvania militia and 12 artillerists from Capt. Samuel Massey's Company. Desertion had greatly reduced the strength of Massey's contingent unit. He did receive a reinforcement of 100 men later in the day, with an additional 50 coming in on September 30th. Newcomb, seemingly realizing his error, ordered both detachments.

On the morning of October 1, the American troops in the area of Billingsport numbered about 400. There were 300 under Newcomb who established his headquarters at Woodbury. Writing to New Jersey Governor William Livingston, Newcomb explained his dispositions. He detached what were essentially pickets to cover Big Timber Creek Bridge and the Coopers and Gloucester ferries. He noted the reinforcement he sent back to Billingsport to join Bradford as well. He then noted how on October 1 "I was informed that a party of the enemy was landing on this shore, opposite Marcus Hook. Their number said to be about 400." Acting on this information, Newcomb "Immediately called in my out guards & marched to a Height, on the Salem Road, about 15 miles below Philada and about 3 ½ miles from Billingsport [near modern Mount Royal]..."[29]

As the Crown troops approached the defenders of Billingsport, on October 2 Newcomb met with Bradford at the fort before daybreak, still under the assumption that the two men faced a roughly equal number of British forces. Newcomb withdrew the New Jersey militia he had sent to Bradford to join his forces in the field.

Newcomb and his troops collided with the British under Stirling about 9 a.m., and a brisk exchange of fire ensued. Stirling demonstrated his numbers by attempting a flanking maneuver against Newcomb. At that moment, the New Jersey brigadier learned that he was not facing a roughly equal force, but a column of 1500.[30] Newcomb, fearing "[w]e might soon have been surrounded, I thought it prudent to retreat, which we did in tolerable good order, keeping up a constant fire in our rear."[31] Major Joseph Bloomfield of the New Jersey Continentals, recovering from wounds sustained at Brandywine at the nearby home of Dr. Bodo Otto described the engagement in none too flattering terms,

> *Thursday Morning they [the British] appeared near the Docters [sic] and fought the Militia under Genl. Newcomb. This old granny of a Genl. Pretending with 300 undisciplined Men to make a stand, but soon retreated helter skelter with his Men, who eminently distinguished themselves by the swiftness of their heels.*[32]

Stirling's column drove Newcomb and his men back past the Salem Road where it crossed the road leading to Billingsport, a distance of approximately 3 1/2 miles. The New Jersey militia made a brief stand there. Stirling, focusing on his directive to take the fort, disengaged and turned west to deal with his main objective. Newcomb took his command and fell back on Woodbury. In his letter to

Governor Livingston on the action, Newcomb was ambiguous about his losses, "I believe we had none killed, nor many badly wounded..." He did note several missing but assumed they had simply returned home after the engagement.[33]

William Bradford takes up the story of what occurred when the British column approached Billingsport. As he noted in a report to Thomas Wharton, Jr. of Pennsylvania, "...the Enemy were advancing to the Fort, on which I ordered the People into Boats and sent most of them to Fort Island..."[34] In addition, Bradford "spiked up all the Cannon we could not carry off and set the Barracks and Bake House on Fire, but the Dwelling House somehow escaped -."[35] He further noted that the garrison managed to get all their ammunition out of the fort. The travails of the garrison were not over, however, as

> *about 12 o'clock the Enemy come on so close thro' a corn field that they were not more than 30 yards from us, and began to fire on us before our Boat put off the shore, we returned fire with 6 muskets we had on board, and a Guard Boat we had with us also fired on them, and all got off, one man only being wounded.*[36]

The British troops easily gained the fort at Billingsport.[37] Clearly, the small ships of the Pennsylvania Navy played some role in evacuating the garrison of Billingsport to Fort Mifflin. Even the Journal of the HMS *Pearl* noted as she held a position near the chevaux de frise, "A great number Rebels Vessels in sight."[38] While these ships may have rendered invaluable assistance to Bradford and his men, the Pennsylvanian noted in his letter to president Wharton that "Last night Capt. Montgomery's 1st and 2nd Lieut. and 6 Privates deserted and I believe if they could get off, the People on Board the whole fleet would desert, for their spirits are quite sunk ."[39] In an example of the rapidity with which information passed during this period, Elizabeth Drinker, a Quaker woman living in Philadelphia recorded in her diary on October 2, "it is said that the English have taken Billingsport."[40]

From Fort Mifflin, Lt. Col. Samuel Smith reported to Washington the following day, "The Enemy yesterday landed a number of men (below Billingsport and encamp last night within nine miles) ..." His report offers a good example of the uncertain character of American intelligence concerning Stirling's force, "some say 400 others 600, my Opinion is the first as we had intelligence of the

Number having march'd from Wilmington for that purpose."[41] Lt. Col. Smith included his assessment of the situation, which is worth quoting at some length as it provides insight both into the situation along the river and Smith's own perspective,

> *There is now about 250 Militia in that Garrison. It was the Opinion of the Officers Yesterday not to give up that post 'till the last extremity, to remove the heavy Ammunition and if oblig'd to leave the fort (which from the disposition I believe will be the case) to spike up the Cannon and retreat by Water which is safe and easy. Our reason for not dismantling Billingsport was the great discontent in the State fleet who already are much scar'd and from whom the greatest desertions of Captains, Lieutenants and men has been.*[42]

Following the capture of Billingsport, Col. Stirling began dismantling the works there. Likewise, Capt. Hammond and the Royal Navy vessels in the Delaware River could begin the arduous process of removing enough of the sunken obstacles to gain access to the port of Philadelphia without fear of coming under fire from the land batteries. Their efforts are recorded in the Journals of the HMS *Pearl* and *Roebuck*. The *Pearl* under the command of Capt. John Linzee, notes "At 10 AM all the Masters & Pilots in the squadron were sent with two Boats from each Ship to remove the Chivaux de frize..."[43] The Journal of the *Pearl* further notes the actions of the Pennsylvania Navy in harassing their work, "At 3PM two of the Enemies Galleys came down and lay in shore & fired several Guns at the *Dunmore* Brigg."[44] This report is further supported by the Journal of the HMS *Roebuck* under Capt. Hamond for the same day, which recorded "PM two Galleys and some Gun Boats came through the Creek within Hog Island, and fired upon the Tenders and Boats at a great distance."[45] The Journal of the *Pearl* notes the withdrawal of the British troops from New Jersey as well.[46]

Writing on October 6, Lt. Col. Samuel Smith, then in charge of Fort Mifflin, confirmed the British withdrawal from Billingsport, "except for several hundred who seem much discourag'd"[47] The reason for the discouragement among the Crown forces was the belief among them, noted by Smith and his garrison, that they had suffered a reverse at Germantown. The young commander continued,

> *The Commodore and other Officers of the Navy*
> *think Red Bank of the utmost Consequence. I think*
> *from the Situation 400 Men might defend it with the*
> *Assistance of the fleet, without the Enemy possess it,*
> *they never can get the River.*[48]

Some historians assert that if Stirling had pressed onward, he could have taken the fort at Red Bank as well, as it was only weakly held at the time. The loss of Red Bank would have spelled disaster for the Americans, as it would have necessitated abandoning of Mud Island as well since Red Bank stood as its principal conduit supplies and reinforcements.[49] As it was, Stirling adhered strictly to his orders and fell back on Chester, Pennsylvania after dismantling the works at Billingsport.

The loss of Billingsport confirmed the fears of Washington and some of his key officers, principally Nathanael Greene that the forts were more a liability than an asset. In any event, Billingsport was now in British hands, and the work of clearing the first row of sunken obstructions could begin. Simultaneously, the remaining forts guarding the second row of chevaux de frise could now be reduced by the British.

Some portion of the blame for the loss of the post must be doled out to Silas Newcomb. As John Jackson noted, "Newcomb flits across the scene through the defense of the Delaware, never where he should be, and indecisive in the extreme."[50] His troop movements were problematic and indecisive, as was his failure to perform any reconnaissance of the British force under Stirling to verify its strength. At the same time, it is worth pointing out that even had the full strength of Stirling's column been known to the Americans, there was nothing they could have done save abandon Billingsport sooner, possibly salvaging the guns. No additional Continental or militia forces were close enough to support Bradford and Newcomb. All the river defenses were then in the process of receiving additional troops.

Reinforcements stood as the key factor for the success of the American defenders, and Washington remained unable to spare any forces himself until after the failed attack on Germantown on October 4. After the battle, however, Washington began to reinforce the forts that guarded the upper row of chevaux de frise. He sent Brig. Gen. James Varnum and his brigade of New England troops into New Jersey.

James Mitchell Varnum (1748-1789) was a lawyer who graduated in the first class from Rhode Island College (now Brown University) in 1769, after being expelled from Harvard the preceding year. He gained admission to the bar in 1771 and became quite successful and earned reputation for his literary style of oratory. In 1774, he received the colonelcy of the Kentish Guards. He marched in the Lexington alarm in 1775. On May 3, 1775, he was commissioned colonel of the First Rhode Island Regiment. While Varnum participated in the siege of Boston, however, he played no significant role in either the New York or New Jersey campaigns in 1776. On February 21, 1777, Varnum was promoted to brigadier general in the Continental Army. Varnum would play a key role in directing action of Continental troops through the remainder of 1777.[51]

Washington's goal, as expressed to John Hancock in a letter dated September 23, was that "General Howe's Situation in Philada will not be most agreeable for if his supplies cannot be stopped by Water it may be easily done by land." He concluded by stating, "To do both shall be my greatest endeavor, and I am not yet without hope that the acquisition of Philada may, instead of his good fortune, prove his Ruin."[52] Clearly, Washington was beginning to recognize the role the forts on the Delaware could play in an active defense of the region. The British realized these looming possibilities as well.[53]

Clearly, the men on the scene were beginning to appreciate the possible significance of the river forts, and what might be required in manpower for them to hold off the British designs to open the Delaware River and get much needed supplies into Philadelphia. The British were aware of this fact as well, and the diary of Capt. John Montresor reports the dispatch of 100 grenadiers and an engineer to Province Island on October 7 to begin erecting a battery composed of mortars and 8-inch howitzers to bombard Fort Mifflin. In the evening two galleys from the Pennsylvania came down to the mouth of the Schuylkill and took the detachment under fire, forcing its retirement. He noted that between the "Gallies and the Fort together fired one hundred shot at us!"[54]

William Bradford passed information on the British efforts on to Thomas Wharton from Fort Mifflin on October 7. In his letter, he detailed the British efforts to move the chevaux de frise, as well as the American plan to counter their efforts by plugging any channels created with sunken fire ships. [55] He further reported how these vessels were "very badly off for Men."[56]

Bradford followed up this letter with another the following day in which he informed Wharton that the British has already succeeded in moving two of the chevaux de frise. To counter this effort, "A Ship and Brig are now preparing to be sunk in the Gap, which, if we can Effect, will stop the Channel."[57] In addition, he substantiated Montressor's account of the British efforts to erect a battery on Province Island, "Last Night a large body of the Enemy came from Philada [sic], and have erected a Battery near the mouth of the Schuylkill. Our Galleys fired on them in the Night and this Morning, but I believe with very little damage."[58] The preceding demonstrate both the interaction between British and American efforts along the river defenses, and the active role played by the vessels of the Pennsylvania Navy. Both sides agreed that the galleys worked to interdict the British attempts on Province Island. Still, the actions of this force were stymied by desertions, usually and indicator of low morale. In this case, the low morale seemed to stem from lack of pay. Bradford reported the exertions to provide the men of the fleet with a month's wages in his letter to Wharton of the 7th.[59]

That same day, Adm. Howe reconnoitered the position of Billingsport and Fort Mifflin, as well as the river obstructions, in order to gain a better understanding of the overall situation in and along the river. Capt. Henry Duncan accompanied Howe. The captain observed "This evening a smart cannonade from the galleys, and, as we supposed, a battery of ours newly erected at hospital opposite to Mud Island on the Pennsylvania Shore."[60] The battery at the hospital, also known as the Pest House, Duncan refers to consisting of two iron 18-pounders, however, it was not completed until the 14th.

On the 9th, the British Capt. John Montresor commented on the action of the previous night. Writing from his post at Webb's Ferry, the engineer noted, "Nine Rebel Galleys attacked our Battery of 2 medium 12 pounders but were beaten back."[61] He further indicated that the post sustained some casualties to the number of one grenadier killed and three wounded along with a wagoner and two horses killed.[62] That same day, as noted by Capt. James Parker, a trickle of supplies arrived in Philadelphia via wagons from Chester.[63]

Reporting to Washington from Fort Mifflin on the 9th, Lt. Col. Samuel Smith informed his superior that they captured a large scow the previous day after wounding one of the crew. He further passed along "Our Intelligence informs that Six Boats were ready to come down the lower ferry and in the evening we heard that a large Body with 20 pieces of Artillery and Boats on Carriages from the City were marching down to Webbs Ferry, in consequence of these

Accounts the Commodore sent some arm'd Boats and Gondolas in the mouth [sic] Schulkill, who discovered the enemy at work along the bank."[64]

The Pennsylvania Navy ships opened fire on the British force and maintained their fire through the night. Even with this near constant harassment, the British managed to erect a small battery by morning and began to return fire on the Americans. Smith further observed that Hazelwood intended to attack the batteries again at high water.[65]

As noted above, Washington dispatched the New England Brigade to New Jersey to reinforce the river defenses. Once in New Jersey, James Varnum dispatched troops of the First and Second Rhode Island regiments from his brigade to garrison forts Mercer and Mifflin respectively. The Rhode Islanders who garrisoned Fort Mercer were commanded by Col. Christopher Greene.

The third cousin of Nathanael Greene, Christopher was born in Occupessatuxet near Warwick, Rhode Island on May 12, 1737. Christopher Greene became a prominent Rhode Island businessman, owning a number of different concerns. When his father died in 1761, Greene inherited the family's mill and estate. His inheritance included a number of businesses, including forges, anchor works, and sawmills on the south branch of the Pawtuxet River. At this time, Greene also became involved in colonial politics, representing Warwick in the legislature in 1771 and 1772. In 1775 he joined the Kentish Guards. Soon thereafter the unit elected Greene to the post of lieutenant. Promoted to major, Christopher marched with the unit, which included his cousin Nathanael and James Mitchell Varnum, in the Lexington alarm.

Greene served in the siege lines outside of Boston in 1775. He then volunteered to take part in the Quebec expedition led by Benedict Arnold. On volunteering for the expedition Greene was promoted lieutenant colonel and served as second in command of the Rhode Island contingent. Captured in the failed assault on Quebec on December 31, 1775, Greene was held until August of 1777 when he was exchanged and returned to the Continental Army. On his return, Greene received a promotion to full colonel and was placed in command of the First Rhode Island regiment. As noted, in October of 1777, Christopher Greene was ordered with his regiment, as well as the Second Rhode Island Regiment under Col. Israel Angell, to garrison Fort Mercer in Red Bank, New Jersey.[66]

Soon after Varnum dispatched Angell's men to Fort Mercer however, they were recalled. This change in deployments resulted

Figure 11 Colonel Christopher Greene of the Second Rhode Island.

from a profound need for as many troops as possible to remain in the field with the Continental Army combined with Washington's belief that Greene would be able to rely on support for the New Jersey militia to augment his own troops. Washington was terribly mistaken in making this assumption. While New Jersey militia Gen. Newcomb did dispatch approximately 100 militia under Capt. Felix Fisher, to join Greene at the fort, he soon countermanded those orders. It will be recalled that Newcomb had previously exhibited much the same erratic behavior during the defense of Billingsport.[67]

Colonel Greene's men reached the fort at Red Bank on October 11, 1777. One Lt. Robert Rogers of Capt. Thomas Cole's Company in Greene's regiment left the following description of the works as they first appeared to the Rhode Islanders,

> *...The works as laid out and only partly com-*
> *pleted, were sufficiently extensive to require two or*
> *three thousand troops to properly man and defend*
> *them. The number of our men all told were short of*
> *five hundred.*[68]

In addition to the Rhode Islanders, Washington dispatched Capt. Cook's Continental Artillery unit which included some 65 men. These men would provide the core around which the artillery defense of Fort Mercer was developed. The troops arrived at the fort on October 11.[69]

As an additional aid to Greene, Washington dispatched the French engineer Mauduit du Plessis to Fort Mercer as well. The scion of a French noble family situated in Bretagne by the eighteenth century, his roots in the French noble class were shallow, dating back only to the previous century. In his youth, du Plessis and two classmates traveled to visit the battlefields of Ancient Greece. All of them grew ill with an unidentified ailment while in Alexandria. Du Plessis succeeded in traveling on to Constantinople where the French Ambassador aided him in returning to France. His classmates were not as lucky and succumbed to their illness. Du Plessis joined the French artillery on April 11, 1771, being promoted to lieutenant on November 1, 1774. He left France for America at the beginning of 1777, carrying a commission as captain of the artillery. Upon joining the Continental army, du Plessis served as an aid to Gen. Henry Knox, being recognized as one of the foreign officers who brought much-needed technical knowledge to the Continental Artillery. [70]

Once assigned to Fort Mercer, du Plessis contributed significantly to the improvement of the fort's defenses and prepared it to withstand an enemy assault. It seems that from the first, Greene and du Plessis enjoyed a very positive and mutually supportive working relationship. Among the first weak points the two detected in the fort's defenses lay with the artillery at the post.

Trained artillerists were in short supply, therefore, on October 13, Greene ordered "16 Continental Soldiers and 16 Militia will be drafted for the Artillery tomorrow Morning."[71] In addition, he made it clear that both officers and men were to attend when reveille was beaten each morning.[72] Greene and Du Plessis soon turned their attention to the overall structure of the post.

Du Plessis was originally designated simply to command the artillery of the post. He quickly grasped, as did Greene, that the size of Fort Mercer was much larger than the number of troops in their force could hope to defend successfully.

The fort had been designed to hold a garrison of some 1,200 to 1,500 men. The total of Greene's forces with the Continental artillery company lay around 300, with the addition of the militia, perhaps as many as four hundred. Thus, Greene possessed only about a quarter to a third of the men necessary to fully man the defenses of the fort as they currently stood. Greene immediately requisitioned additional tools from the surrounding farms.

By October 15, sufficient tools had been gathered to begin significant alterations to the fort. Du Plessis drew a line across the fort from the river to the eastern rampart, with a double fence being constructed on the line he laid out. He had the space between the two fences filled with any material at hand including construction debris, trees and rocks. Most of the material used came from the nearby farm of Quaker James Whitall. The alterations to the fort had the effect of reducing it to about one third its original size. As Lieutenant Rogers of Cole's company noted, "Daily expecting an attack from the enemy, in our unprepared and almost defenseless situation, officers and men without discrimination set to work with undiminished vigilance night and day to prepare a wing of the fort for defence..."[73]

In addition, the Frenchman sighted fourteen cannons at different angles along the parapet to enable the Capt. Cook's artillerymen to have clear fields of fire on all the land approaches to the reconstituted redoubt. Cook and his men were among the members of the garrison given rapid training as artillerists.[74] Returning to the modifications made in the works, part of the eastern wall was reconfigured as well in order to mount two cannons in a hidden battery and thus provide enfilade fire on any force that entered through the abandoned portion of the fort. Finally, with the height of the parapets being roughly nine feet, Mauduit du Plessis constructed a banquette built into the entire wall to provide a firing step for the infantry and artillerymen manning the fort.[75]

Improvements were made to the outer defenses of the fort as well. Abatis, in some places two rows deep, were added.[76] Additionally, the defenders dug a moat that completely encircled the land side of the fort.[77]

The reconfigured fortification now allowed for an effective defense by the existing garrison, however, it was not without some significant shortcomings. The reconstructed fort was now so small that the majority of the garrison had to be housed outside the works.[78] The troops forced to camp outside the protective walls of Fort Mercer included the Second Battalion of the Gloucester County, New Jersey militia under the command of Capt. Felix Fisher. Fisher raised other local militia contingents as well. Both militia contingents placed themselves under Greene's orders for the duration of their service at Fort Mercer.[79]

As the likelihood of an enemy assault on the fort grew, Col. Greene intensified his efforts at strengthening the post. His preparations demonstrate that Greene seemed to expect a siege of his command rather than an outright assault. For instance, a portion of his order for October 15 commands that "all the troops except Picquet and Main Guard will be on fatigue this day the Carpenters will get a Store Built for Provisions with all possible Expedition."[80]

As time progressed, it became clear to the American command that an attack on Fort Mercer was imminent. Washington received several reports indicating that these were the British intentions from his agents in and around Philadelphia. It is clear that Col. Greene received some intelligence concerning a possible attack on Fort Mercer as well, as demonstrated by the following order of October 16,

> *The Colonel Orders, that as there is the greatest reason to believe that this Garrison will be attacked soon, the whole Garrison, except Cooks and Waiters and the Garrison Guard go on Fatigue this Day in Order to Render the Garrison as defensible as possible.* [81]

That same day, the garrison received heartening news of the surrender of Gen. John Burgoyne's British army to the Americans under Maj. Gen. Horatio Gates on October 7.[82]

Even while he prepared for the possibility of an extended defense of his post, Greene remained a dutiful subordinate and forwarded a detachment under a Lt. Col. Sims to augment the garrison at Fort Mifflin as instructed by Washington. Likewise, Greene dispatched troops, specifically Captain Fisher's company of the Gloucester County militia, to Cooper's Ferry to watch for the expected landing of British troops and send back a dispatch rider to the fort when they arrived.[83]

While for the Americans, the control of the Delaware River revolved around the maintenance of the fortifications at Forts Mercer and Mifflin in order to defend the sunken obstructions, the British efforts at gaining control of the waterway passed through several iterations.

Initially, William Howe attempted to break through the American defenses on the Delaware by simple bombardment. In support of this agenda, the British began erecting batteries on Province and Carpenter's Islands on October 7 with the intended goal of reducing Fort Mifflin solely through artillery fire. Lt. Col. Samuel Smith had already toured both islands with Cmdre. John Hazelwood, and both men determined it would be impossible for the Americans to garrison any posts erected on either of them. In this sense, they yielded valuable positions to the British without a contest. Still, given the numbers they possessed in their respective commands, it stood as a sound tactical decision.

The British forces setting up the batteries were commanded by Capt. John Montresor, the same British engineer who had been asked to design works on Mud Island by the Pennsylvania government after the French and Indian War. At the outset of his operations against the fort, he had approximately 100 troops under his command. They began constructing two batteries, each containing two eight-inch mortars and two eight-inch howitzers. Hazelwood and the Pennsylvania Navy attempted to interdict the movements of the British guns south from Philadelphia but were unsuccessful.[84]

At roughly the same time, on October 8, Montresor began construction of a battery north on the Schuylkill in order to deny the Americans access to the city from the direction of that river. Hazelwood tried to interdict this work as well.[85] Montresor's efforts during this period were impeded by weather conditions which quickly made the labor of constructing the batteries arduous in the extreme. There were heavy rains and winds. It is important to note that both Carpenter's and Province Islands were composed of essentially marshlands and were therefore very open to flooding. Consequently, in order to interdict the British operations, Washington had ordered the dikes on the various streams in the vicinity destroyed to raise the water level in the river. When this was done, men were forced to labor at night waist-deep in water. The difficult conditions were exacerbated by occasional bombardments from Hazelwood's ships of the Pennsylvania Navy. For instance, on October 9th from his vantage point at Webb's Ferry in Pennsylvania the Capt. Montresor recorded in his journal, "Nine Rebel Galleys attacked out Battery of 2 medium 12 pounders but were beaten back." He further recorded that in the exchange, "We lost one Grenadier killed, three wounded and a waggoner and two horses killed."[86]

At this point, much of the contest for control of the Delaware was attritional. Time favored the Americans. If they could prevent or at least slow the construction of the British batteries on Carpenters and Province Islands, the Continentals could hope to prevent the resupply of Philadelphia from the water indefinitely, and thus severely impinge on Howe's ability to hold the American capital. The attritional nature of the struggle is demonstrated in the following actions, which likewise involved both land and maritime assets on both sides.

On October 9, Cmdre. Hazelwood moved a floating battery into position between Little Mud Island and Fort Island to fire on the British batteries under construction. According to Cdr. John Henry on the HMS *Vigilant*, "The Rebel Fleet lying at Anchor near Mud Island consisting of 12 Galeys, One Frigate, 2 Zebecs and several Armed Brigs, Sloops and Schooners, with many half Galleys protected by their Two Forts of Red Bank and Mud Island and by the Chevaux de frize..."[87] Montresor responded by erecting a new battery some 250 yards from the American floating battery in order to challenge it.[88] As Capt. Downman of the Royal Artillery noted in his diary for October 10, "the galleys now and then giving us a shot without effect."[89] Still, due to the increasingly heavy artillery fire civilian laborers from Philadelphia grew more difficult to procure, and British troops had to be used instead in order to construct the batteries. The soldiers as well had to be rotated out routinely as sickness caused by the working conditions began to exact its' own toll.[90]

On October 10, Capt. John Montresor declared that the construction of the British battery on Carpenter's Island was complete. Capt. Francis Downman of the Royal Artillery recorded "A party of our men with engineers passed the ferry this afternoon, and during the night threw up a battery."[91] He went on to describe the difficulties the British encountered in emplacing the guns to fire on Fort Mifflin, noting in his entry for October 11, "In the fore part of the evening [October 10] two twelve pounders had been taken over, and one of them dragged up to the battery through a mile of mud and water, for the whole island is a flat, and from the rain and the rebels cutting the embankment, the whole was nearly under water." Still, they managed to set up the gun emplacement, "The battery is raised within 400 or 500 yards of the fort on Mud Island and open to all the rebel shipping, and their galleys can go within 150 yards of it."[92]

In response to the threat of the new British battery, Cmdre. Hazelwood and Lt. Col. Smith at Fort Mifflin determined to attack Carpenters Island in order to silence the British batteries located there. Their plan called for a joint assault, utilizing both land forces and those of the Pennsylvania Navy in order to achieve a common goal.

At 9:30 AM on October 11, three galleys from Hazelwood's Pennsylvania Navy opened fire on the British position on Carpenter's Island. Lt. Col. Samuel Smith described the assault in his report to George Washington,

> *Last Night the Enemy threw up a Battery in the Rear of the Fort, Close to the Banks of the Meadow within Musket Shot of us & had already got One pc [piece] in it, we attack'd it with the floating Batteries, Block Houses, and Gallies & our 32 pounder from the Battery...*[93]

Capt. Downman of the Royal Artillery described the action, "About 6 o'clock the rebels discovered our work, and began and continued a constant fire from all their vessels and batteries upon it until about 4 in the afternoon."[94] Downman appears to be referring the naval bombardment, which began earlier in the day. The cannonade was followed by the landing of roughly one hundred men from Fort Mifflin's garrison under the command of a Maj. Ballard, some sources give the commander as Lt. Col. Samuel Smith.[95] His men quickly began to exchange small arms fire with the British troops on the island. After roughly an hour of firing, and expending a considerable amount of ammunition, Ballard led his men forward toward the British battery. As Smith reported to Washington, "...in Short time oblig'd them to hoist the white flag, as we were bringing off the prisoners another party run down which the Officer encouraging the Men to Come on & their did not Seem to me to be any Appearance of that Intent..."[96] Smith's account of the British raising a white flag in surrender is supported by the account of William Bradford of the Pennsylvania militia in his report to Thomas Wharton, "After about two hours the Enimy held out a flag and the Soldiers appear'd on the bank with their muskets clubbed..."[97] Interestingly, according to Bradford, Smith had actually undermined the surrender of British troops. Bradford informed Wharton that "Colonel Smith who was in the block house seeing some other coming from the house of Adam Guyer imprudently fird[sic] two shot at them which caus'd the rest of those who had surrendered to run off, and took possession of the battery again and fir'd on us, so that by one imprudent step we lost one half our prisoners and the Cannon which they had in the redoubt..."[98] Bradford then recanted this position in a letter he wrote Wharton the following day in which he explained,

> *My last informed you of our Success in taking 56 of the Enemy Prisoners, and that by Col. Smith's Firing on a Body which we are apprehended are coming down to surrender we lost many Prisoners, but we are since informed it was a large Party [of the enemy] coming down to rescue those that had surrendered...*[99]

As the Americans approached, the British began to come out of their works in order to surrender. According to Capt. Downman, the Americans actually had possession of the battery for a time. He is quick to point out, as well, that "Our force on the island at this time was very small, not above 200 men;"[100] The captain observed a further contributing factor to the initial success of the America attack, panic in the commanding officer, "A Major V[atass] commanded; he was hurrying off the island in the boats as fast as he could, and had he not been prevented, the island would undoubtedly have been in possession of the enemy."[101] Additional British forces from Province Island then launched diversionary attack, allowing many of the men from the battery to escape. Downman credits the activity of Capt. James Moncrieffe with retaking the battery.[102] Still, two lieutenants, one ensign and fifty-six privates were taken in the sortie.[103]

The fighting did not end with the American withdrawal, however, as Smith noted "We open'd fire from all Quarters on them they have yet obstinately refus'd to Surrender. We Shall give them another Attack and try if possible to drive them out."[104]

The above attack demonstrates that during the early phases of the campaign for control of the river, the Americans were mounting an active defense. They sought for opportunities to undermine the British efforts and seized them when they appeared. While the raid did not drive the British from Carpenter's Island, it did serve to make their efforts more costly, Downman noted an ammunition wagon blown up during the fighting.[105] Likewise, the silencing of the batteries, even for a time, gave the garrison in Fort Mifflin some respite. It could serve to boost the morale of the defenders as well, as they saw themselves as striking back at the enemy as opposed to merely enduring the bombardment.

The Americans launched a second attempt on the Carpenters Island battery on October 12, however, this time they found the post much better defended. In this second attack, the Americans lost two killed and five wounded, while the British sustained four killed, two British and two Hessians, and three wounded.[106] William Bradford described this attempt in a report to Thomas Wharton written the following day

> *Yesterday Morning a Party of about 150 Men were landed from this Fort on Province [Carpenters] Island with an Intent to take the Redoubt under the Fire of three gallies and the Floating Battery, but the Number of the Enemy were much more than was expected all under Cover, and a Party full as many as we had on Shore coming down from Adam Guyers, we were obliged to retire with the Loss of two Men killed and five wounded*—[107]

The British vessels in the Delaware recorded the second attempt as well. The Master's Log of the HMS *Roebuck* noted simply "[At] 10 The Enemy [fire] continues and cannonade from fort Island, floating Batterys and Galleys."[108]

Closer to the scene of the action, Capt. Montresor noted that for Sunday October 12, "Weather delightful." He went on the describe the second American attack in the following terms,

> *At 11 o'clock this morning about 500 Rebels landed in front and 2 flanks of the Battery with Bayonets fixed (previous to which they had shelled it with a very heavy cannonade from the Fort, Floating Batteries and Gallies) our detachment of 50 men ½ Hessians and ½ British under a Hessian captain, received them with a well directed fire of [sic] musketery, the attack for ¾ of an hour, the rebels concealing themselves under the Dyke and behind trees and bushes, in the meantime Major Gardiner with 50 Grenadiers moved from his post to outflank the rebels and the battery, which he succeeded in by the rebels taking to their boats, during which the detachment of the battery kept up a smart fire.*[109]

The number Montresor gives in his account of five hundred Americans taking part in the assault seems quite high. Exact numbers for the American attackers are difficult to determine, while casualty figures are well documented. The Americans lost two dead and five wounded, while Montresor acknowledged two British and two Hessians grenadiers killed and three British wounded among the Crown forces.[110]

Concurrent with the American's attempts to silence the first British battery, Montressor and Gen. Samuel Cleaveland, the commander of the British artillery, ordered their men to complete a second work. The men addressed their task diligently and between October 13 and 14, a new battery was completed on the left or northern side of the Carpenters Island batteries, on the point of Province Island, near the hospital. The second battery consisted of two iron 18 pounders. The purpose of this work was to harass the garrison at Fort Mifflin.[111]

On the 12th, the British managed to shift one of the chevaux de frise. Learning of this, Hazelwood dispatched two chains of fire rafts to "drive them from that Place, and a very heavy Cannonade ensued..." between the fire rafts and row galleys on the one side, and the *Roebuck* the armed ship *Vigilant* and two additional vessels on the other. Even with this uneven match up, Cmdre. Hazelwood "obliged them [the British vessels] to fall down the River..."[112] One unfortunate consequence of the night action was that it depleted the ammunition for the galleys. Several men were sent off in search of additional supplies of ammunition.[113]

The Master's Journal of the *Roebuck* recorded first one fire rafts coming down the river, at about 1:30 AM on October 13. In response, the ship dropped down the river about ½ a mile.[114] The Journal of the *Vigilant* is more through, noting as well that the fire rafts were "covered by their Galleys and Gun Boats, who kept a constant fire of Grape Shott on the Rafts to prevent our boats Towing them clear of the Ships..." It further reported "Our Ships also kept a fire on their Galleys, and Gun Boats, which prevented their advancing nearer, and then out Boats Towed the fire Rafts clear of the Ships and grounded them on little Tinicum Island..."[115]

Again, according to the Journal of the *Roebuck*, "about 3 [AM] another fire Raft appear'd sent the Guard boats to tow it on shore..." Then, at about 6 in the morning the *Roebuck* and the other vessels sailed back up-river on the flood-tide to Billingsport and anchored. In the evening, she dispatched some of her crew to assist the Liverpool in shifting one of the chevaux de frise. Likewise, she dispatched other crewmen and a boat to help free the *Vigilant*, which had become stuck in one of the chevaux.[116]

If Hamond's testimony is taken at face value, then the fire rafts sent down river constituted little more than annoyance. However, if the Journal of the *Vigilant* under Cdr. Henry is accepted, it seems the threat posed by these incendiaries was more serious. In either case, this night attack demonstrates that Hazelwood taking aggressive action to interdict the British efforts at removing the sunken obstacles in the river. Still, his efforts were plagued by manpower shortages in his mosquito fleet. So much is evidenced in a letter from George Washington to Christopher Greene the following day. First, the Continental Army commander informed the Rhode Islander "that the desertions from the fleet have left him [Hazelwood] exceedingly deficient in men, which must greatly enfeeble his operations." Washington then got to the heart of the matter, "As I imagine there is likely to be a number of men accustomed to the water in your garrison, I must desire you will immediately draft all such and deliver them for the commodore, for the use of the fleet." Driving home his point, Washington affirmed, "It is essential he should have a sufficiency of hands and the men cannot possibly be more usefully employed than with him." [117] Greene was not the only subordinate Washington tapped for additional men for the fleet. His aid Tench Tilghman wrote the same day to a Maj. Benjamin Eyre to gain any seamen he might have in his command to be sent to Hazelwood as well.[118] Eyre was a member of a family of Philadelphia shipwrights whom the Continental Congress commissioned to help build galleys both in Philadelphia and New York City.[119]

Manpower was not the only difficulty confronting the leadership of the river defenses. For instance, on October 14, Smith's garrison at Fort Mifflin consisted of a mere 173 officers and men, including militia. Over one-third of his garrison was without breeches. Smith acknowledged that without the breeches furnished him by Capt. Blewer of the Pennsylvania State Navy Board, most of his men would have been unfit for duty.[120] Even with the clothing furnished by the local authorities, Smith had thirty-four sick. To address his own manpower problems, Smith first sought to have Col Israel Angell's Rhode Island regiment sent to reinforce his garrison. Then, he suggested that the Pennsylvania Navy should take all the men with seafaring experience from Angell and Greene's regiments and forward the remainder to his command.[121]

In the event, Washington heeded neither of the young colonel's ideas. He did, however, send Smith what proved to be an invaluable asset in the form of Maj. François Louis Teissedre de Fleury. Fleury was the scion of a French noble family and was born in Provencal on August 28, 1749, at Saint-Hippolyte. On May 15, 1768, he volunteered in the Regiment de Rouergue. It was a common practice for young men who sought officers' billets in a regiment where none were currently available to attach themselves to the unit in the hopes of filling a vacancy when one opened up or distinguishing themselves in the eyes of their superiors. Such men were referred to as gentlemen volunteers. In his case, the action proved successful, and Fleury found employment in the regiment.

Fleury attained the rank of sous-lieutenant on August 28, 1768, and sous-aide-major on February 5, 1772. He left France for America with Philippe Tronson du Coudray in 1776. Congress refused employment for Coudray and his entourage, the body having grown jaded towards the numerous foreign officers seeking rank and pay while producing only dubious qualifications. As a result, Fleury joined the Continental Army as a volunteer. He distinguished himself in the fighting at Piscataway, New Jersey on May 10, 1777, and was commissioned a captain of engineers on May 22. His horse was shot from under him at the battle of Brandywine. He was issued a replacement at the behest of Congress. This horse was shot from under him in the fighting at Germantown.[122]

After the battle of October 4, Fleury was ordered to Fort Mifflin by Washington, there to supervise the construction of the works, and make any improvements to its defenses that were feasible. On his arrival at the post, Fleury came across a work that was roughly rectangular in shape, composed of dressed stone on its eastern and southern sides, with simple wooden palisades to the north and west. In addition, the fort possessed wooden blockhouses at all corners save for the southern salient.[123]

Inside, the fort possessed barracks, a magazine, and redoubt designed as the 'last retreat' should an assailant breach the walls of the post.[124] The existence of the last bastion to stand against a land assault underscores the fact that the previous efforts at defending the post were conducted by men whose experience, and therefore thinking, was informed solely by the precepts of land warfare.

On October 15, his first night at the post, major Fleury noted in his diary "...Night pretty quiet except a slight Alarm caused by some Boats of the Enemys Fleet, which had reached the point of Log [Hog] Island and retired after firing upon the boats of our Galleys - a great Noise of Oars heard behind the Island, the cause of it unknown."[125] The sounds of oars were British boats surreptitiously bringing supplies into Philadelphia from Lord Howe's fleet. The relative quite Fleury confided to his diary would not last for long.

CHAPTER NOTES

[1] For biographical information on Smith, see Frank A. Cassell, *Merchant Congressman of the Young Republic: Samuel Smith of Maryland, 1752-1839* (Madison: University of Wisconsin Press, 1971) and John S. Pancake, *Samuel Smith and the Politics of Business: 1752-1839* (University, AL: University of Alabama Press, 1972). See also Samuel Smith, "The Papers of General Samuel Smith." in The Historical Magazine, 2nd Series, 7, 2 (February 1870): 81-92 and Nicholas Sellers, "Lieutenant Colonel Samuel Smith: Defender of Fort Mifflin, 1777." *Cincinnati 14 Newsletter of the Society of the Cincinnati.* 31,1 (October 1994): 17-23.

[2] Nicholas Sellers, "Lieutenant Colonel Samuel Smith: Defender of Fort Mifflin, 1777." *Cincinnati 14, Newsletter of the Society of the Cincinnati.* 31,1 (October 1994): 17-18.

[3] On Simeon Thayer, see Edwin M. Stone, "The Invasion of Canada in 1775: Including the Journal of Captain Simeon Thayer." in *Collections of the Rhode Island Historical Society*, Volume IV, Providence, RI: Hammond, Angell and Company, Printers, 1867, pp. 70-79. On Treat, see Jackson, *Pennsylvania Navy*, p. 129.

[4] Gruber, *Howe Brothers*, p. 248.

[5] Gregory T. Edgar, *The Philadelphia Campaign 1777-1778* (Westminster, MD: Heritage Books, 2004), p. 42.

[6] Harris, *Germantown*, p. 142.

[7] Ibid, p. 155.

[8] Ibid, pp. 154-5.

[9] Jackson, *Pennsylvania Navy*, p. 124.

[10] Harris, *Germantown*, p. 155. See also McGuire, *Philadelphia Campaign*, vol. 2, p. 31.

[11] Harris, *Germantown*, pp. 155-6.

[12] Ibid, p. 156.

[13] Ibid, pp. 156-7. See also Jackson, *Pennsylvania Navy*, pp. 124-5.

[14] Jackson, *Pennsylvania Navy*, p. 124.

[15] Ibid, p. 125.

[16] George Washington to John Hancock, Camp 20 Miles from Philadelphia, October 3, 1777, quoted in *NDAR*, vol. 10, p. 28.

[17] John Andre, *Major Andre's Journal: Operations of the British Army under General Sir William Howe and Sir Henry Clinton, June 1777, to November, 1778* (William Abbatt, ed. New York, 1930), p. 54.

[18] See Molyneux, *Conjunct Expeditions*. See also, Syrett, "Methodology"

[19] Edgar, *Philadelphia Campaign*, p. 71.

[20] Walter Isaacson, *Benjamin Franklin, An American Life* (New York: Simon and Schuster, 2003), p. 342.

[21] Thomas Warton to George Washington, September 12, 1777 in W.W. Abbot, and Dorothy Twohig, eds. *The Papers of George Washington, Revolutionary War Series.* Volume 11. Charlottesville, VA; University of Virginia Press, 2001,

[22] Browne, "Fort Mercer and Fort Mifflin," p. 65.

[23] Jackson, *Fort Mercer*, p. 12.

[24] Ibid, p. 11.

[25] Philippe du Coudray, A definitive Project upon the Defense of Philadelphia in the Present State of Affairs," quoted in Worthington C. Ford, ed. *Defenses of Philadelphia in 1777* (Brooklyn, Historical Printing Club, 1897. Reprint, New York: DeCapo Press, 1971), p. 12.

[26] Nathanael Greene to George Washington, n.d. quoted in Ibid, pp. 8-9.

[27] Master's Journal of the HMS *Roebuck* under Captain Andrew Snape Hammond, October 1, 1777, quoted in *NDAR*, vol. 10, p. 13.

[28] Harris, *Germantown*, 176. See also, Jackson, *Pennsylvania Navy*, p. 131.

[29] Silas Newcomb to William Livingston, October 4, 1777 quoted in Harris, *Germantown*, 1777.

[30] Smith, *Fight for the Delaware*, p. 10.

[31] Newcomb, Letter, quoted in Harris, *Germantown*, pp. 177-8.

[32] Joseph Bloomfield, *Citizen Soldier: The Revolutionary War Journal of Joseph Bloomfield*. Mark Edward Lender and James Kirby Martin, eds. (Yardley, PA: Westholme Press, 2018), p. 129.

[33] Ibid, p. 178.

[34] William Bradford to Thomas Wharton, Jr. Fort Mifflin, October 3, 1777, quoted in *NDAR*, vol. 10, p. 29.

[35] Ibid.

[36] Ibid.

[37] Stirling's command of the detachment is covered in Lender, *River War*, p. 17. On the units that composed his striking force, see John Peebles, *John Peebles American War: The Diary of a Scottish Grenadier, 1776-1782*. Ira D. Gruber, ed. (Strand, Gloucestershire: Published by the Sutton for the Army Records Society, 1997),p. 140. Peebles's account should be taken with some circumspection, as he was not a participant in the attack.

[38] Journal of the HMS *Pearl*, October 3, 1777, quoted in *NDAR*, vol. 10, p. 29.

[39] Bradford to Wharton, October 3, 1777, quoted in Ibid.

[40] Elizabeth Drinker, *The Diary of Elizabeth Drinker: The Life Cycle of an Eighteenth-Century Woman*. Crane, Elaine F. ed. (Boston: Northeaster University Press, 1994), p. 238.

[41] Lieutenant Colonel Samuel Smith to George Washington from Fort Mifflin, October 2, 1777, quoted in *NDAR*, vol. 10, p. 16

[42] Ibid.

[43] Master's Journal of the HMS *Pearl* under Captain John Linzee, October 4, 1777, quoted in Ibid, p. 39.

[44] Ibid.

[45] Master's Journal of the HMS *Roebuck* under Captain Andrew Snape Hammond, October 4, 1777 quoted in Ibid, p. 40.

⁴⁶ Master's Journal of the HMS *Pearl* under Captain John Linzee, October 4, 1777, quoted in Ibid, p. 39.

⁴⁷ Lieutenant Colonel Samuel Smith to George Washington, Fort Mifflin, PA, October 6, 1777, quoted in Ibid, p. 50.

⁴⁸ Ibid.

⁴⁹ Mark E. Lender, *The River War*. Trenton, NJ: New Jersey Historical Commission, 1979, p. 14.

⁵⁰ Jackson, *Pennsylvania Navy*, p. 133.

⁵¹ Biographical information on James Mitchell Varnum is derived from Boatner, *Encyclopedia*, pp. 1143-4.

⁵² George Washington to John Hancock, September 23, 1777, in *Washington, Rev. War*. p. 11, p. 302.

⁵³ Stryker, *Forts*, p. 14.

⁵⁴ Montressor, Journal, October 7, 1777, Webb's Ferry, PA, quoted in *NDAR*, vol. 10, p. 62.

⁵⁵ William Bradford to Thomas Wharton, October 7, 1777, Fort Mifflin, quoted in Ibid, pp. 62-3.

⁵⁶ Ibid, p. 63.

⁵⁷ William Bradford to Thomas Wharton, October 8, 1777 Fort Mifflin, quoted in Ibid, p. 74.

⁵⁸ Ibid.

⁵⁹ Specifically, Bradford relates:"Mr. Samuel Massey having a sum of Money by him near this Place, we have browd [borrowed] it, and have ordered the Fleet to be paid their Months Wages..." Bradford to Wharton, Fort Mifflin, October 7, 1777, quoted in Ibid, pp. 62-3.

⁶⁰ Journal of Captain Henry Duncan, RN, October 8, 1777 quoted in *NDAR*, vol. 10, p. 75.

⁶¹ Montresor, *Journal*, quoted in Ibid, p. 102.

⁶² Ibid.

⁶³ Journal of Captain James Parker, October 9, 1777, quoted in Ibid, vol. 10, p. 102

⁶⁴ Lieutenant Colonel Samuel Smith to George Washington, Fort Mifflin, October 9, 1777, quoted in Ibid.

⁶⁵ Ibid, pp. 102-3.

⁶⁶ The biographical information on Christopher Greene is drawn from George S. Greene, *The Greene's of Rhode Island, with Historical records of English Ancestry, 1534-1902.* (New York: The Knickerbocker Press, 1907) as well as Marcius S. Raymond, "Colonel Christopher Greene." *Magazine of History, with Notes and Queries.* (September/October, 1916): pp. 138-49.

⁶⁷ It should be stated that Newcomb remained a problem for both the Continental and State military leaders until his relief from command. In this regard, see Jackson, *Fort Mercer*, p. 14.

⁶⁸ Lieutenant Robert Rogers, pension file application, quoted in Daniel M. Popek,

They *"...fought bravely, but were unfortunate:" The True Story of Rhode Island's "Black Regiment" and the Failure of Segregation in Rhode Island's Continental Line, 1777-1783* (Bloomington, IN: Authorhouse, 2015), p. 74.

[69] Jackson, *Fort Mercer*, p. 14.

[70] Captain Gilbert Bodinier, *Dictionnaire des officiers de l'armee royale qui ont combattu aux Etats-Unis pendant la guerre d'independence, 1776-1783 suivi d'un supplement a Les Francais sous le trieme etoiles du commandant Andre Lasseray* (Chateau de Vincennes, 1982), p. 339.

[71] Greene, Garrison Orders, Red Bank, October 13, 1777 in Christopher Greene, *Papers of Christopher Greene, Lieutenant Colonel of the First Regiment, Rhode Island Infantry, 1776-1781* (Microfilm. Rhode Island Historical Society, Manuscript Division, MSS 455), pp. 93-94.

[72] Ibid.

[73] Rogers, quoted in Popek, *Brave but Unfortunate*, p. 74.

[74] Jackson, *Pennsylvania Navy*, p. 153.

[75] Jackson, *Fort Mercer*, p. 16.

[76] An abatis was a defense composed of felled trees, usually with their branches pointed outward, and the tips sharpened to a point. See Christopher Duffy, *Fire and Stone: The Science of Fortress Warfare, 1660*-1860 (Edison, NJ: Castle Books reprint of 1975 original), p. 183.

[77] Jackson, *Fort Mercer*, p. 6.

[78] Ibid.

[79] Stryker, *Forts*, p. 12.

[80] Greene, Garrison Orders, October 15, in *Christopher Greene Papers*, p. 96

[81] Greene, Garrison Orders, October 16, 1777, in Ibid, p. 97.

[82] Ibid.

[83] Stryker, *Forts*, p. 13.

[84] Smith, *Fight for the Delaware*, p. 13.

[85] Ibid.

[86] Montresor, *Journal*, pp. 463-4.

[87] Journal of the Armed Ship *Vigilant*, Commander John Henry, October 10, 1777 quoted in *NDAR*, vol. 10, p. 112.

[88] Smith, *Fight for the Delaware*, p. 13.

[89] Francis Downman, *The Services of Lieut.-Colonel Francis Downman, R.A., in France, North America, and the West Indies, between 1758 and 1784* (F. A. Whinyates, ed. Woolwich: England: Royal Artillery Institution, 1898), p. 40.

[90] Jackson, *With the British Army*,

[91] Downman, *Services of Lieut.-Colonel Downman*, p. 40.

[92] Ibid.

[93] Lieutenant Colonel Samuel Smith to George Washington, Fort Mifflin, October 11, 1777, quoted in *NDAR*, vol. 10, p. 119.

[94] Downman, *Services of Lieut.-Colonel Downman*, p. 40.

[95] Sellers, "Lieutenant Colonel Samuel Smith," 20 gives Smith as the leader of the raid.

[96] Smith to Washington, quoted in *NDAR*, vol. 10, pp. 119-20.

[97] William Bradford and Commodore John Hazelwood to Thomas Wharton, Jr. Fort Mifflin, October 11, 1777, quoted in *NDAR*, vol. 10, p. 120.

[98] Ibid.

[99] Bradford to Wharton, October 13, 1777 quoted in *NDAR*, vol. 10, p. 146.

[100] Downman, *Services of Lieut.-Colonel Downman*, p. 40.

[101] Ibid.

[102] Ibid.

[103] Smith, *Fight for the Delaware*, p. 14.

[104] Smith to Washington, quoted in *NDAR*, vol. 10, p. 120.

[105] Downman, *Services of Lieut.-Colonel Downman*, p. 40.

[106] Ibid.

[107] Bradford to Wharton, October 13, 1777 quoted in *NDAR*, vol. 10, p. 146.

[108] Master's Log of the HMS *Roebuck*, Captain Andrew Snape Hammond, Sunday, October 12, 1777, quoted in Ibid, p. 130.

[109] Montresor, *Journal*, p. 465.

[110] The American casualty figures derive from Jackson, *Pennsylvania Navy*, p. 144, while those for the British are taken from Montresor, *Journal*, p. 465.

[111]Downman, *Services of Lieut.-Colonel Downman*, 40. Stryker has the order for these additional batteries coming from Howe. See Stryker, *Forts*, p. 12.

[112] Bradford to Wharton, October 13, 1777, quoted in *NDAR*, vol. 10, p. 146.

[113] Ibid.

[114] Master's Journal of the HMS *Roebuck*, October 13, 1777, quoted in ibid, p. 147.

[115] Journal of H.M. Armed Ship *Vigilant*, Commander John Henry, October13, 1777, quoted in Ibid, pp. 147-8.

[116] Master's Journal of the HMS *Roebuck*, October 13, 1777, quoted in Ibid, p. 147.

[117] George Washington to Christopher Greene, Headquarters Towamencin, PA, October 14, 1777, quoted in Ibid, vol. 10, p. 162.

[118] Tench Tilghman to Benjamin Eyre, from headquarters at Towamencin, PA, October 14, 1777, quoted in Ibid, p. 163.

[119] Jackson, *River Defenses*, p. 18.

[120] Ibid, p.145.

[121] Ibid, p. 147.

[122] Bodinier, *Dictionnaire*, p. 452.

[123] Jackson, *River Defenses*, p. 18.

[124] Ibid.

[125] Journal of Major Francois Fleury, October 15, 1777, Fort Mifflin, quoted in *NDAR*, vol. 10, p. 1777.

Chapter Five
The Contest for the Delaware
Round Two: The Battle of Red Bank

Capt. John Montresor's initial efforts at reducing the American forts proved bitterly disappointing. The American works had not crumbled under the cannonade. Instead, more troops were being drawn into the efforts to reduce them, and the Americans had even launched several soties against the British works with varying degrees of success. William Howe's impatience with the lack of any headway in the assault was so profound that on October 16, he visited Province Island to reprimand Montressor and Cleaveland for their lack of progress on the siege.[1]

While the initial British assault revealed some of the weaknesses in the American defenses, they likewise disclosed the general weakness of Howe's position in Philadelphia without the means to resupply his forces. The failure of the bombardment demonstrated to Howe that the only way to break through the American defenses would be through a direct assault, something he was loath to do in consideration of the large number of casualties such an action would surely generate.[2]

The same day Howe harangued his engineer officers, residents in Philadelphia, as well as members of the occupation force, heard a cannonade from the river. Capt. James Parker recorded that "the Rebel fleet move from mud island to the Jersey shore near to red bank, many salute guns are fired by them this day."[3] The guns were fired in celebration of Maj. Gen. Horatio Gates victory over British Lt. Gen. John Burgoyne at Saratoga on the seventh, news of which had just reached the American forces.

Even as the Americans celebrated their victory, the British continued their efforts to open the river. For instance, the Journal of the HMS *Vigilant*, which lay anchored off Billingsport, recorded that the ship "got 2 Nine Pounders off the Forecastle on the Quarter Deck and 2 Twenty four Ponders off the Main Deck on the Forecastle to keep off the Galleys, Boats rowing guard."[4] The reason for shifting the canon around on board the ship was to allow the vessel to throw heavier shot at the Americans while remaining in position to try and shift the chevaux de fries.

Locals continued to implement Washington's directive of removing all the boats from the vicinity of Philadelphia as well. Benjamin Eyre reported to the Commander-in-Chief from Bordentown that "Agreeable to your orders I have Collected all Shallops and flats in Bordentown Creek..."[5]

The defenders of the river forts remained on their guard. As Maj. Fleury reflected in a letter to Lt. Col. Alexander Hamilton, written on the 17th,

> *...Our greatest Uneasiness is occasioned by the dread of Surprise - the Channel between Pennsylvania and the Fort is altogether clear, the Galleys have removed to the Jersey Side out of all distance for annoying the Enemy and Seconding us, the nights are darken'd by Fogs and all our Garrison must be on the watch to avoid being carried by storm -* [6]

The following day, Howe issued orders to move his headquarters into Philadelphia. The move could have been due to dissatisfaction over the efforts to open the Delaware, or simply moving the troops into planned winter quarters, or a combination of both.[7] Once in Philadelphia, William Howe decided that the next logical step in opening the Delaware River to British shipping would be to seize Fort Mercer in Red Bank, New Jersey. This stood as a logical conclusion, considering that Fort Mercer served as the staging area for supplies and reinforcements for Fort Mifflin on the Pennsylvania side of the river. Without Fort Mercer, Fort Mifflin would then become untenable, and the British could focus their efforts on removing the chevaux de frise in order to open navigation of the river to their shipping. In order to seize Fort Mercer, Howe determined on a joint land and water assault.

The land assault would be conducted much like the attack on Billingsport further south in New Jersey had been. The principal difference in this enterprise would be that this time the troops would cross the Delaware from Philadelphia to Cooper's Ferry (modern Camden), and then march southward to attack the post.

Occurring simultaneously with the land attack on Fort Mercer, ships from the Royal Navy as well as land batteries then under construction in the area would bombard Fort Mifflin in turn softening up that post so that it could be taken by storm once the British cut it off from its support.[8] At first, Howe planned to send a British force to seize the Fort Mercer, however, Col. Count Carl Emil von

Donop intervened and asked to make the attack with his Hessians.

The son of a noble family from Hessen-Cassel, von Donop entered the service of the Landgraf and won distinction in the Seven Years War. He rose to become the personal adjutant to the Landgraf of Hessen-Cassel by the outbreak of the American War of Independence. He maintained a correspondence with both Prince Henry and Frederick William of Prussia, the heir apparent. It seems the count would have preferred to take service in the Prussian army, however, since this was not possible at the time, he took service in North America. Due to his distinguished service record, he was placed in command of the elite troops that would make up the Hessian contingent. These included the three grenadier battalions and the *Jäger* Corps.[9] His impetuous nature stands out as one of von Donop's more pronounced character traits. Some accounts describe him as less than kind to enlisted men, however, Johann Conrad Dohla, himself a private throughout his service in America referred to von Donop as "an excellent man, experienced in war; above all polite and compassionate towards officers and men."[10]

Von Donop's Hessians served at the battle of Long Island and Kip's Bay, and von Donop himself was recognized for his personal bravery in leading troops at the battle of Harlem Heights. His troops played a part in the pursuit of Washington's Continentals across New Jersey in the fall of 1776 as well. As a result, they garrisoned the southern New Jersey towns of Trenton, Burlington and Bordentown. Col. von Donop was the ranking Hessian in the area when Washington surprised Rall's troops at Trenton, and therefore fell in for a measure of the disgrace attending the defeat.[11]

Through much of 1777, he sought for an opportunity to restore the honor both of himself and of the troops under his command. Thus, when the opportunity to lead the assault on Fort Mercer presented itself, von Donop was quick to secure the mission for himself.

To some extent, the Crown forces signaled their preparations for a major assault on the river defenses. Writing in his journal from Fort Mifflin of October 20, Maj. Fleury observed "...The enemy appear to be raising a work at near a mile and a half from us at the point of Tinicum, in the direction of Hog Island—there are a great many people there..." He likewise observed that Cmdre. Hazelwood, while informed of the British efforts in Tinicum instead used his ships to attack the British fleet as well, an assault the Frenchman called a "fruitless Cannonade."[12] Hazelwood maintained throughout that he believed his galleys were useless against fixed shore emplacements, but he eventually agreed to night patrols.[13]

The troops in Fort Mifflin, for their part, were far from idle. Fleury continued,

> *For want of Pickets, we have begun a Ditch to surround the Battery—to-morrow night we shall endeavour to make a double Chain of floating Timber, or of Iron Chains taken from the Fire-Ships, to hinder the Enemys Landing.*[14]

The same day as Fleury recorded his observations, the *Vigilant*, *Zebra* and the galley *Columbus* sailed up the western channel and took up positions off Hog Island. Some of Hazelwood's galleys moved in to challenge the advance of the British vessels but were forced to retire as they came under fire from the newly-constructed shore batteries as well.[15] From the British perspective, the Journal of the Armed Ship *Vigilant* recorded that

> *The Fort at Mud Island fired at us, and the Galley's rowed over from Red Bank to Assist the Fort, we returned their fire, as we dropped down all the Damage they did us was Sinking a Flat Boat and breaking some Oars. we [sic] Towed the flat Boat on shore and repaired her ...when the Tyde rose, the Camilla being with us got aground also.*[16]

The Journal of the HMS *Camilla*, under Capt. John Phipps substantiated the clash between the Royal Navy and the Pennsylvania galleys. The journal further reported that the *Roebuck*, *Pearl* and *Liverpool* got above the lower chevaux de frise that day.[17] Finally, the Journal of the sloop *Zebra* under Cdr. John Orde recorded that "At 4 Came down 13 Rebel Gallies & Fired on the Ships in the other Channel as also at the *Vigilant* in this Channel which fire was returned..."[18] The British vessels were moving into position for the planned grand assault on the American river forts.[19]

The following day, October 21, Washington wrote to Hazelwood to inform the latter that he had appointed a new commander for Fort Mifflin, Col. Baron Heinrich Leonard Philipe d'Arendt. Little is known about d'Arendt's background, aside from that he was a veteran of the Prussian Army and served as colonel of the German Regiment of the Continental Army. Samuel Smith left the following, opinionated, description of him, "He was a Prussian, a very military-looking man, six feet high and elegantly formed." Smith continued, "Indeed, his whole appearance was that which would comment him to command where personal bravery was not required."[20] Part of his lack of bravery as Smith describes it might have stemmed from the fact that d'Arendt had been ill for the preceding month. His sickness precluded him from assuming command when initially ordered to do so by Washington on September 23. Even during his tenure in command, the Prussian officer remained so ill that Smith carried out most of the day-to-day duties of command at Fort Mifflin.[21] Certainly Washington painted a very different picture of the Prussian officer in a note to Cmdre. John Hazelwood, "This gentleman's knowledge of and experience in war, which has been the study and business of his life, induce me to expect, with [sic] intire confidence, that he will acquit himself in his command in a manner that will do him honor." Likewise, the Continental Army commander seemed to presage the difficulties between Smith and d'Arendt noting "the best designs and most important pursuits have been and ever will be defeated by foolish differences when the exist between those engaged in them."[22]

In all likelihood, however, Washington was referring the contemporaneous dispute between Smith and Hazelwood. He mentioned the issue in a letter to Smith of the same date, observing, "This circumstance, I confess, gives me great uneasiness, as I well know that a good agreement between the Navy and Garrison is of the last importance, and that a want of cooperation and every possible - mutual aid may involve the most unhappy consequences."[23] The commander went on to play the conciliator between two warring officers as he had in the past and would again in the future. He notified Smith that he had appoint d'Arendt to act as something of an arbiter in any disputes between him and Hazelwood and enjoined his subordinate to defer and further concerns with the naval forces to the Prussian. He closed by reaffirming the importance of a cooperative relationship between the two forces in the most glowing terms, "Hitherto a happy agreement has done much - It has disappointed the Enemy from effecting, notwithstanding their repeat efforts, what they seemed to consider without difficulty; And should the same spirit and disposition continue, I flatter myself, they will produce the same ends."[24]

That same day, Gen. William Howe ordered von Donop to march into New Jersey and take the fort at Red Bank.[25] The Hessian column that was to assault was one part of a multipronged effort by the Crown forces. As the Hessians attacked Fort Mercer, ships of Lord Howe's squadron were to sail up the Delaware and engage

Fort Mifflin and the Pennsylvania Navy. Finally, the British batteries on the Pennsylvania shore were to contribute their weight of
shot to the undertaking as well. Thus, the effort constituted a joint
venture between land and maritime forces. If all went as planned,
Fort Mercer would be seized by ground assault as the bombardment
reduced Fort Mifflin. With both posts either captured or destroyed,
the obstacles blocking the fleet could be removed in relative safety.
The simultaneous assaults were planned for Thursday, October 23.

Donop's impetuous streak revealed itself in the preparations
the colonel made for the assault on the fort at Red Bank as will be
seen below. At the same time, one of the junior officers who took
part in the expedition, Maj. Carl Leopold Baurmeister, noted in his
journal that Howe had ordered von Donop to "capture Fort Redbank
on the Jersey shore by *coup de main*," or frontal assault.[26] The British did not possess any clear intelligence concerning the strength
of the works at Red Bank, nor did they seem to be aware of any of
du Plessis's modifications. The order to attack the post in such a
manner coming from Howe disclosed the British commander's ex-
asperation and reduced the options available to his subordinate in
carrying out his mission. Thus, some of the censure for subsequent
events must fall on William Howe as well.

The expedition to take the Fort at Red Bank left Philadelphia from the Arch Street Ferry in Philadelphia on October 21. The
force consisted of the Hessian and Ansbach *Jäger* Corps under Col.
von Würmb, and Donop's three Hessian grenadier battalions, von
Linsing, von Minnigerode, and von Lengerke respectively, as well
as the infantry regiment von Mirbach. In addition, he brought the
battalion artillery of ten 3-pounders. A request for additions artillery from the British, including howitzers to lob shells over the walls
of the fort had been turned down. One key element the force lacked
were scaling ladders to ascend the walls of the Fort. Other logistical shortcomings existed in the composition of the expedition as
well. Chief among these stood the lack of wagons to carry additional
supplies with the force, and to help return the seriously wounded to
Cooper's Ferry.[27]

The men were to be ferried across the river in twelve flat
boats that had been brought up the Delaware River on the night of
October 20 under the command of a Capt. Clayton.[28] The boats were
transported along the Pennsylvania side of the river, between Fort
Mifflin and the riverbank. Since they were flat-bottomed, they drew
a shallow enough draft not to be damaged by the chevaux de frise.
It also seems that the narrow strip of water between Fort Island

and the shoreline was considered too small for enemy ships to get into and had therefore been left open. The sinking of the chevaux de frise in the river altered the depth of the water in the channel as well, thus making the transit of the flat boats easier. The change in depth would play a significant role in the fighting at Fort Mifflin in the following month.

The boats did not make the journey without incident. According to Staff Capt. Levin Friedrich Ernst von Munchhausen of the Leib Regiment, some British pickets, not knowing of the plan, fired on the boats passing their post in the dark. Their fire, in turn, alerted the ships of the Pennsylvania Navy, who also fired on the boats, likely assuming that they were transporting supplies into the city under cover of the night. Still, it appears that the boats succeeded in getting to Philadelphia undamaged.[29]

It appears that the movement of the troops across the river occupied much of the day on October 21. Following British protocol, von Donop's men would fall under Clayton's command during their movement across the river.[30]

Once across the Delaware River, the Hessians made their way towards Haddonfield, New Jersey. As they proceeded along the road, they encountered some sniping fire from local militia, however, the Jägers quickly drove these forces off. As noted in the journal of Maj. Baurmeister, who was then serving with the regiment von Mirbach, "They were met by about 20 light horse who fired at the boats without results, and then retired."[31] This view is reinforced by Feilitzsch, who recalled "Underway we received a few shots."[32] The resistance the Hessians encountered was composed of men of the Salem and Cape May County militias. Still, the Jägers, led by Capt. Ewald, brushed them aside. They may have belonged to the Gloucester County militia as well, as Col. Greene dispatched a contingent under a Capt. Fisher to observe the river crossing and report back on the size and composition of the force headed his way.[33] By the evening, about 7 o'clock according the Feilitzsch, the Hessians reached their objective of Haddonfield where they camped for the night.[34]

It is often argued that von Donop was very lackadaisical in his conduct during the march and took few precautions to guard information concerning his numbers and equipment.[35] Still, it appears that during their bivouac in Haddonfield, the Hessian commander did take some precautions to preserve the security of his camp. He ordered that all of the young men of the town who possessed Patriot leanings be gathered in the center of Haddonfield and remain there until after the Hessians departed the following morning. The Loyalists of the town aided in the endeavor of rounding up the suspected rebel sympathizers. Still, quartering an army in a town in the eighteenth century meant that the perimeter would remain somewhat porous. Due to the gaps in security New Jersey militia forces operating in the area were able to warn Col. Greene of an imminent attack. For his part, Donop spent the night of Monday, October 21 at the house of local Loyalist John Gill.[36]

Meanwhile, activity continued in and around the Delaware River. During the night, Fleury observed "no fire from the Enemy." Still, the work continued at Fort Mifflin. The engineer continued his journal entry, "we have driven down large Pickets in the bed of the River, at the distance of 20 feet from the Battery and at the distance of 15 feet from each other - they are intended to support the double Chain..." Concerning the chain, Fleury noted that weather was making it difficult to stretch the chain across the river, and so the defenders resorted to the expedient of fastening together wooden beams to extend the length of the chain.[37]

On the British side, the Journal of the Armed Schooner *Viper*, under Lt. Edward Pakenham noted the movements of various Royal Navy Vessels to better position themselves for the coming bombardment of Fort Mifflin. In addition, the Journal recorded that at 6PM "The Rebel Galleys began to Engage us as did Mud Island Fort against our Shipping."[38]

Still, the main scene of the coming action lay not in the river or by Fort Mifflin, but at Red Bank. Upon receiving intelligence that a Hessian column was operating in the vicinity of Fort Mercer, Greene ordered his men to strike their tents and take up positions within the cramped confines of the post. The fort could only accommodate the Rhode Islanders of Greene's command, so he dispatched the men of Fischer's Gloucester County militia to destroy the bridges over the intervening creeks and take whatever opportunities they could to harass the advancing column. It does not appear that any of these directives were followed by the militia under Fisher.[39]

Learning of the British plan through his network of informants, on October 18 Washington had dispatched Lt. Col. Charles Simms and the Sixth Virginia Regiment to reinforce the river forts.[40] The unit, which included 120 rank and file, marched to Bristol, Pennsylvania where they crossed the Delaware River and continued through Moorestown, New Jersey to Cooper's Ferry. They reached this point at 10 PM on the night of October 20. The unit then pressed their march and arrived at Fort Mercer before daylight on October 21. Once there, Col. Greene forwarded this unit to Fort Mifflin, as these were Washington's orders, and even with the imminent danger to his command, Greene was uncertain as to whether he could alter the orders of the army commander. Simms men, therefore, played no role on the defense of Fort Mercer. His concern for following Washington's orders may have combined with the cramped surroundings of the fort to convince Greene to forward Simms's Regiment over to Fort Mifflin.

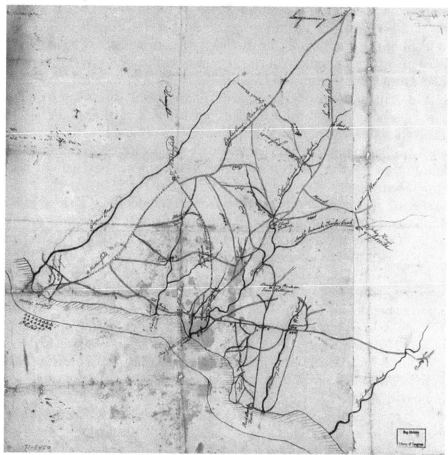

Fig.12. Scale not given. Title from verso. Manuscript, pen-and-ink. Has water-marks. Shows roads of Camden and Gloucester counties, New Jersey. Described in Samuel S. Smith's The fight for the Delaware, under the title Route the Hessians took from Coopers Ferry to Red Bank. *LC Maps of North America, 1750-1789, 1263* *Available also through the Library of Congress Web site as a raster image.*

As morning dawned on October 22, the German column was already in motion on their way to Fort Mercer. Von Donop had roused his troops at 4 AM in order to begin preparations for the march. In addition, he did recruit some local Loyalists to serve as guides for his force on their way to Red Bank. The route they followed closely parallels modern King's Highway, and leads to a bridge over Timber Creek, near modern Westville, New Jersey.[41] As the Hessians made their way to the fort, they again encountered some resistance from the militia of Salem and Cape May Counties, but this was driven off fairly quickly. It seems that the poor condition of the roads may have slowed the pace of the march, as von Donop's column did not reach Fort Mercer until mid-day.[42]

As they came within range of the fort, the *Jägers* fanned out in front of the main column to act as a screening force. These troops were under the command of the esteemed military analyst and commentator Capt. Johann von Ewald. The captain provided a very clear and insightful description of the Hessian attack. First, he recalled how he reconnoitered the American position, "I approached the fort up to rifle-shot range and found that it was provided with a breastwork twelve-feet high, palisaded and dressed with assault stakes."[43] In addition, Donop, as well as his artillery officers performed their own reconnaissance of the fort.[44] To some extent, during their advance the Hessians were screened from the defenders of the fort by some woods as they made the initial deployments.

Col. von Donop then dispatched a deputation to the fort in order to call on it to surrender. Instead, the defenders announced that they would hold the fort to the last man. With the receipt of this response, von Donop ordered each of his battalions under his command to begin making one hundred fascines. These would be thrown into the ditches surrounding the fort when the men launched their assault. These preparations, within sight of the objective, took an additional four hours, and it was not until 4PM that the Hessians were in readiness to initiate their attack. Clearly, even the remotest chance at surprise of the garrison was now completely lost.

Even at this juncture, with the element of surprise lost, and the daylight growing short, von Donop decided to attempt one last time to receive the fort's surrender without engaging in what would surely be a bloody attack, dispatching British Maj. Stuart and a drummer to call on the fort once again to surrender. Once more, the defenders refused. Ewald, again, offers a candid description of the demeanor of the officers as they prepared to lead their men forward. His entry is worth quoting at some length as it provides an astute account of the preparations for the assault from the perspective of some of von Donop's more experienced subordinates:

> *On my way back, I met Colonel Stuart with a drummer who was to summon the fort, and right behind them I met Major Pauli, Captain Krug, and both adjutants of the colonel. All these gentlemen regarded the affair with levity. The only man who had any real knowledge, and looked upon the business as serious, was worthy old Captain Krug. I took this man aside and asked him what he thought of the undertaking, whereupon he answered: 'He who has seen forts or fortified places taken with the sword in hand will not regard this affair as a small matter, if the garrison puts up a fight and has a resolute commandant. We have let luck slip through our fingers. We should not have summoned the fort, but immediately taken it by surprise on our arrival.*[45]

Almost prophetically, the captain continued, "But now they will make themselves ready, and if our preparations are not being made better than I hear, we will get a good beating."[46]

Colonel Jeremiah Olney was sent to receive the flag of truce and listen to the enemy's latest demands a short distance outside of the fort. He met the deputation outside the fort in order to prevent the enemy troops from gaining any intelligence of the works. Olney recorded his response to the demand for surrender, "We shall not ask for nor expect any quarter and mean to defend the fort to the last extremity."[47]

The deputations returning to their respective lines, the Hessians proceeded to attack the garrison. They began with an opening artillery bombardment, which lasted about ten minutes. Considering the garrison were already aware of the presence of the attack column, this cannonade fell far short of any real purpose. It was not enough to batter down any section of the fort, nor did it throw an unsuspecting garrison into confusion. The sound did alert the British ships in the river that the action was taking place, but otherwise proved ineffectual. At the same time, the noise attracted the attention of some of Hazelwood's galleys as well.

As the cannonade ended and the Hessian troops began their advance on Fort Mercer, many of the critical omissions concerning the organization and equipping of the expedition manifested themselves. The guns the Hessians had brought with them were of insufficient size to do any real damage to walls of the fort, and the time spent in bombarding the works only served to alert the small vessels of the Pennsylvania Navy that the post was under attack. If that were not enough, defenders raised a flag in the fort to signal Hazelwood of the need for galleys to come to the aid of the garrison. Several vessels moved toward the Jersey side of the river in order to lend their support to the defenders of Fort Mercer.[48]

As the Hessian columns moved out, they were attacking an intact post with a determined garrison and naval support. Donop divided his force into three columns that were to make their attacks simultaneously, one from the north (von Minnegerode), one from the center (von Mirbach), and the other from the south (von Linsing). The Grenadier Battalion von Lengerke, and the Jägers were held back in reserve. The three infantry regiments were to jump off at 5 PM.

For reasons that remain unknown, the von Linsing Battalion jumped off prematurely and began to storm the outer works of the fort ahead of the other units. These men slowly pushed their way through the abatis. The lack of saws and axes for such work slowed their progress. As the assailants attempted to drag themselves up the wall by hand, musketry erupted across wall and threw back the assault.

Chaplain Feilitzsch of the Anspach Jägers left his perspective of the action,

> *at about four o'clock, it began. However the commandant would not surrender so the attack was launched. The cannonade was severe and the small arms fire very heavy. In addition, several rebel ships joined in which fired against us on both sides and did great damage.*[49]

While Feilitzsch's account is fairly general concerning the ground assault, it does include the role played by the galleys of the Pennsylvania Navy. A number of contemporary accounts single out the support given by the small ships of Hazelwood's fleet and the havoc their artillery wrought among the advancing Hessians as an additional contributing factor the defeat of this assault. The Journal of 2nd Lt. Carl Wilhelm von Bultsingsloewen of Regiment von Mirbach reported "To our great misfortune the (enemy) row galleys and ships off shore could fire on both our flanks with grapeshot."[50] Likewise, the official Journal of the Regiment von Würmb had the troops being fired upon by the galleys "in the flank and in the rear."[51] Finally, Jacob Martin, recorded in his diary that "the row galleys

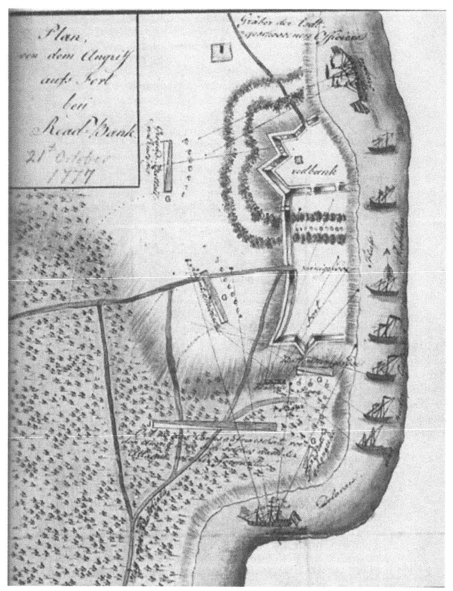

Fig. 13. Sketch of the attack on Red Bank by Johann Ewald, from his *Diary of the American Revolution*, p. 101. The Gs are for German troops, while the Js designate Jäger.

had advanced still nearer, and were pouring a most terrific fire of grapeshot into our troops on the left and flank;"[52] Martin continued, providing a valuable first hand narrative of the action from the perspective of the assailants,

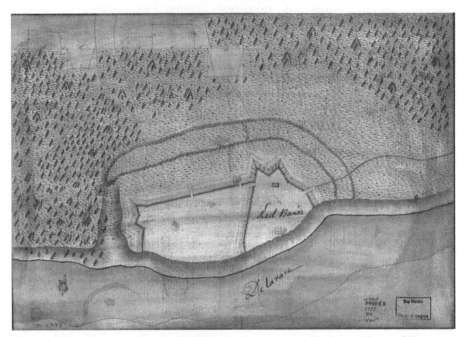

Fig. 14 Map of Fort Mercer in Red Bank, New Jersey. It shows the modifications made by du Plessis and how they contracted the size of the works. Scale not given. Manuscript, pen-and-ink and watercolor. Has watermarks. Oriented with north toward the lower right. Relief shown by hachures. Shows fortifications of Fort Mercer, N.J. currently located in Red Bank Battlefield in the borough of National Park, Gloucester County. Includes profile. *LC Maps of North America, 1750-1789, 1275 Available also through the Library of Congress Web site as a raster image.*

> *Notwithstanding this they took possession of the greater part of the main ditch, and a number of our men had already climbed up as far as the parapet; however, as the uninterrupted fire of grapeshot from the row galleys tore down whole rows of our men and ...the above named battalions could not maintain the advantages they had gained, but had to retire to the wood behind them in order to gather their forces.*[53]

Martin's account is bolstered by that of 2nd Lt. Carl Friedrich Rueffer of the Regiment von Mirbach, who was wounded in the assault on Fort Mercer. He stated,

> *We took both the outer defenses with little effort. This had hardly occurred when, because of the extensive losses and the indescribable cannonade and*

small arms fire from the fort and from the enemy ships lying on the water side, which fired on our right wing... necessitated a withdrawal without accomplishing our purpose.[54]

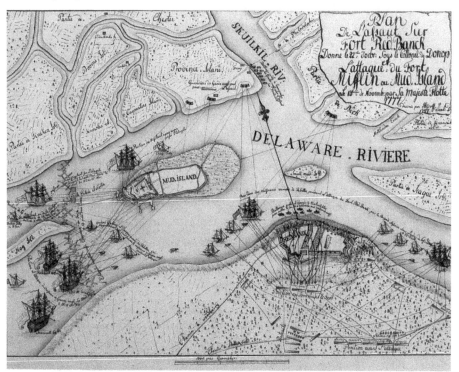

Fig. 15. Plan zum Aufstieg zum Fort Redbank am 22. Oktober 1777 unter Colonel de Donop und der Angriff der Briten von Fort Mifflin oder Mud-Island am 15. November 1777; or the plan for the ascent to Fort Redbank on October 22, 1777 under Colonel de Donop and the attack of the British on Fort Mifflin are or Mud-Island on November 15, 1777. *(Courtesy the Hessische Staatsarchive, Marburg, HStAM Order. WHK No. WHK 29 / 64a)*

The momentum of the attack collapsed, and the survivors sought to escape the withering fire reigning down on them. With the prematurely launched assault thus driven off, Greene and Du Plessis quickly repositioned the defenders in order to meet the other columns moving on the fort.

The defenders finished repositioning themselves just as the second attack began to clear the obstructions on the inner wall of the fort. This inner wall stood where du Plessis had reduced the overall size of the works to more effectively defend it with the garrison available. Once they pushed through the obstacles, the Hessians entered the outer works and found them empty. As the men

cleared the abatis and made their way up the inner wall, they were
greeted with a massive volley from the defenders. Von Donop went
down in this assault. Lacking command and control, this attack
soon collapsed as well, and the troops began to retreat, taking off
their wounded as best they could.[55]

Israel Angell of the Second Rhode Island Regiment left a
gripping account of the fighting from the perspective of the defenders of Red Bank fort,

> *About one o'clock, when the Enemy Arrived
> within musket Shot of our fort, we fired a Cannon or
> two at them on which they Retired, and kept Skulking
> in the woods until half After four o'clock, when they
> sent in a flagg demanding the fort but answered the
> fort was not to be given on any terms, they answered
> that if we still remained obstinate, our blood might
> be upon our own heads, for we Should have no Mer-
> cy Shone us, our Answer was we asked for none; and
> Expect none, so parted, and in about ten minutes after
> there began a smart fire as ever I heard from eight
> field pieces and two [sic]hoets they had placed against
> us, at the Same time Advanced in two [sic] Colems to
> attack our fort by Storm, when there begun an inces-
> sant fire of Musketery which Continued forty minutes
> when the hessians Retreated in the most Prescipited
> manner leaving 200 killed and wounded in the field.
> We spent the greatest part of the Night in bringing in
> the wounded.[56]*

It is likely that due to his location in the fort, Angell could
only see two of the attacking columns. While the repulse of the Hessian attack stood as an amazing accomplishment for the defenders,
the officers and men of Donop's command quickly sought to explain
their defeat. From their accounts, several factors for the failure of
the assault emerge. For his part, Bultsingsloewen commented on
the futility of the assault with the materials the Germans brought
with them, "Although our eight cannons did what they could, the
two howitzers were placed too close to the fort-both were like nothing."[57] He added a sentiment that likely entered the hearts of many
of the officers as they saw what they had believed would be an easy
victory morph into an ignominious defeat, "There was nothing to do
but die or retire."[58] On a more practical note, he added "We could not

become master of the fort since we did not have any heavy artillery to breach the walls."[59] Second Lieutenant Carl Friedrich Rueffer added several other factors that, in his estimation, contributed to the Hessian defeat. These included, "the almost impassable abates before the main fort," as well as that fact that the fascines that had been hurriedly made prior to launching the assault proved "of little value at the eighteen-foot high parapet."[60]

Bultsingsloewen concluded his account of the attack with the sentiment, "Our bravery was for nothing." He continued, "In the American war no attack was more furious than this one. The assault lasted 75 minutes and that was all that was possible."[61] The sentiment of failure was mollified here, at least to an extent, by the thought that the men had done all they could against extremely difficult odds.

The fighting outside Red Bank was so intense that the sounds carried down the Delaware River as well. For instance, the Journal of the HMS *Camilla*, holding station off Billingsport, included in the entry for the day "from 5 to 8 a Heavy Canonading [sic] from Our Ships and the Rebel Floating Batterys and Gallies same Time heard a Number of Small Arms fired at Red Bank. Supposed to be our Troops Storming the Fort at Red Bank."[62]

In the end, both attacks were driven off with heavy losses to the Hessians. During the retreat, the lack of wagons for the transportation of the wounded became a serious issue, and many of the men had to be abandoned to the Americans. Among those taken prisoner was von Donop, who was transported to the nearby farm of James Whitall.[63]

With von Donop a prisoner, the command of the remnants of the column passed to Lt. Col. von Linsing.[64] He gathered up the wounded as best he could and began the long march back to Philadelphia. A brief description of the retreat is presented by 1st Lt. Friedrich Wilhelm Werner of the Feld-Artillerie Corps in his report of the action of the 22nd,

> *At nightfall all the troops reassembled in the woods, on the rising ground, and at once set out on the return march by the same route. At eleven o'clock we reached the new bridge over Timber Creek, crossed it, pulled down part of it, and at three in the morning we made a halt. After a rest, we continued on to Haddon-field and to Cooper's Ferry.*[65]

The fact that Werner refers to the bridge over the Timber Creek as being only partially torn down speaks to the precipitous nature of the retreat. At the same time, the retreating troops may have spared the bridge complete destruction for another purpose. Rueffer notes in his diary that many of the wounded had been left lying in a house near the battlefield, and that "Lieutenant Pertot, with some jaegers, risked returning to them, pressed some wagons, and fortunately brought them back to us."[66] If it were planned to return and recover the wounded left behind during the initial retreat, it would make sense not to destroy the bridge completely. The men may have left the bridge intact out of sheer exhaustion as well, considering they had marched early in the morning, attacked the post and suffered a rout all in the space of approximately thirteen hours, fatigue likely ran rampant through the ranks.

Also of interest in Rueffer's account is the mention that these men were left in a nearby house. The closest house to the scene of the battle was that of James Whitall, on whose property Fort Mercer was constructed. The Americans pressed the Whitall residence into service as a hospital in the aftermath of the engagement. Given its close proximity to the fort, and the heightened alert on which Greene kept the garrison that night, it is unlikely that this was the location. It is a more likely that the force under Pertot made their way to a residence along the line of retreat where troops unable to keep up with the column were left with the intent of returning for them.

For his part, Werner noted that the force arrived back at Cooper's Ferry at noon on October 23, where they "ended this fruitless expedition."[67] The preceding, as well as the other German accounts of the battle and subsequent retreat demonstrated the impact of the loss on their morale.

In the aftermath of the fighting, the American victors now undertook the gruesome duty of separating the living from the dead and offering whatever comfort they could to the former. A private Smith of the Second Rhode Island records, "The night following the battle we were all on duty, either in scouting parties or on trails."[68] He goes on to describe how his patrol found Count von Donop, with two waiters, hiding behind a pine tree. He further noted how, "The next day the whole regiment was employed, except those on guard and scouting parties in digging a trench and burying the dead."[69] He placed the number interred at somewhere between four and five hundred. A recent study places the overall losses to von Donop's expedition as 370 killed, wounded or missing. The same author places the American casualties at fourteen killed, twenty-three wounded and one missing.[70] In addition to the wounded and prisoners secured by the garrison, the men were able to exchange their muskets for those of the fallen Hessians, which appeared to be of superior manufacture. So great was the bounty of weapons that there was a surplus, which the colonel forwarded to the Continental Army in accordance with Washington's orders.[71]

Persons captured near the fort who were believed to have aided to the Hessians on their march were dealt with as well. Smith recalled the fate of three such men: "Having buried the dead, we hung three spies - one white man and two negroes. The white man confessed that he had taken pay of the British, (a tankard full of guineas,) for conducting Hessians to Red Bank."[72]

Even with the repulse of the Hessian attack on the 22nd, there remained the fear that a subsequent assault would be undertaken by the Crown forces. Such was evidenced in the letter of Washington to Christopher Greene dated October 26, "I have sent down Lt. Colo. Rollston with three hundred Pennsylvania Militia to reinforce Forts Mercer and Mifflin. I therefore desire that you and Baron Arent [sic] will settle the proportion that each is to have upon the most equitable terms. If you should have been joined by such a Number of New Jersey Militia as will render your post quite secure, you are to permit the Pennsylvania Militia to pass over to Fort Mifflin."[73]

During this same period, Washington received intelligence as to the fate of the Hessians who had taken part in the failed attack. From Maj. John Clark, Jr, stationed at Goshen, Pennsylvania, Washington learned that thirty boatloads of wounded had been brought into Philadelphia, and that the Royal Marines were being forced to fight as infantry. The major passed on the additional report that the Marines "curse Fort Mifflin heartily, & say it has given them more trouble than anything they ever met with."[74]

Some argue that a determined follow-up assault by Col. Greene or the New Jersey militia, at this juncture, could have transformed the defeat of the Hessian attack into a complete rout.[75] While the possibility exists, it is far from likely. The men in the fort had just repulsed two major assaults. Ammunition had to be tallied, and damage to the garrison assessed. At the same time, the New Jersey militia forces were conspicuous by the absences up to this point in the campaign. Given their uneven record of activity against the Hessians thus far, the chance of them coming out to fight remained far from certain. Finally, it was unclear if there were any Hessian reserves waiting that could attack a force sent from the fort. In the end, Greene determined to hold his position. A conservative decision to be sure, but one that prevented his success from possibly turning to a defeat, a fate which had all too often befallen Continental designs up to this point in the war.

The Hessians, as noted above, marched through much of the night, and returned to Cooper's Ferry by the morning of October 23. From there, the British sent across reinforcements, specifically, elements of the First Battalion of Light Infantry, and the 27th Regiment, to cover the embarkation of the Hessians and their wounded.[76]

As word spread of the defeat of von Donop's Hessians, a variety of reactions emerged among the various combatants. The repulse served as a tonic to Washington and the forces under his command. Writing from his headquarters at Whitemarsh to George Clinton, governor of New York, on October 26, 1777 Washington passed along news of the success, "I have the pleasure to inform you that on the 22d Inst., about 1200 Hessians under the command of Count Donnop, attempted to storm our Fort at Red Bank and were repulsed with the loss of about 400 killed."[77] Washington sent additional notes to Israel Putnam and Jonathan Trumball, Sr. informing them of the victory as well.[78] Likewise, Benjamin Tallmadge, one of Washington's spymaster's observed to Gen. Samuel Webb,

> *The noble defense lately made at the important post on Red-bank you have doubtless been apprized of. By a gentleman from Philadelphia I am told that nothing could equal the mortification and disappointment of the enemy on that repulse, as they expected but little resistance would have been made, and on setting down and counting the cost it has been the amount of five hundred men to them.*[79]

The success of Greene and his Rhode Islanders at defending against the Hessian assault continued to resonate within the Patriot ranks even weeks after the event.

Residents in Philadelphia quickly learned of the Hessian repulse and reacted to the news in various ways depending on their political leanings. For instance, Elizabeth Drinker, a Quaker, noted matter-of-factly in her diary the following day, "this day will be remembered by many; the 2,500 Hessians who cross'd the River the day before yesterday, were last Night driven back 2 or 3 times, in endeavouring to Storm the fort on Red Bank, 200 slain and great

Numbers wounded..."[80] For the Crown forces, the reaction was quite different.

From the British perspective, the attack was understood differently by many of the soldiers, as evidenced in the entry in John Peebles diary, he states that "In going up to the works, they were gall'd on their flanks by a fire from the Enemys Vessels in the river and notwithstanding that & a heavy fire in front they persevered in the attack & carried some of the out works but others were so high & were obliged to withdraw..."[81] Perhaps more telling on this occasion are the remarks left by Thomas Sullivan in his journal, that "There were several brave Officer lost upon this occasion in which the utmost ardor and courage were displayed by both Officers and Soldiers."[82] Thus in the perceptions of Peebles and Sullivan, the attack was carried out with bravery and met with overwhelming resistance. Its failure was therefore not due to any lapses in judgment on the part of von Donop.

William Howe's report is perhaps the most intriguing. In a letter dated October 25th to Lord George Germain, Secretary of State for the Colonies, later printed in *The Westminster Magazine; or The Pantheon of Taste*, the general recounted how Donop

> *...on the 22d in the afternoon was before Red Bank; Colonel Donop immediately made the best disposition and led on the troops in the most gallant manner to the assault. They carried an extensive out work, from whence the enemy were driven into an interior intrenchment, which could not be forced without ladders, being eight or nine feet high with a parapet boarded and fraised. The detachment in moving up, and returning, was much galled by the enemy's gallies and floating batteries.*[83]

Howe's letter is interesting in several respects. He praised Donop's dispositions and attributed a partial victory to the Hessian colonel. Clearly, there were enough reports of the action at Red Bank to provide the British commander with a more accurate picture of what actually transpired. Likewise, he attributes the repulse of the Hessian strike to the gallies and floating batteries, factors that the land forces had no control over. While it is clear that some of Hazelwood's ships contributed their weight of shot to the fighting, it is clear from the accounts of the survivors that the devastating fire of the fort's garrison had the greatest effect. Finally, Howe did not mention the fact that Donop launched his attack earlier than the agreed upon time. This all begs the question of why Howe would distort the assault in what was essentially his report to his political superior in London?

There are several plausible reasons. First, to cover Howe's own role in the Hessian defeat. He was, after all, the overall commander in the theater, and as such bore final responsibility for the defeat. Second, Howe may have felt the loss of the subordinate he dispatched without adequate artillery and sought to make good by preserving the man's honor in death. In the end, however, all of this is mere supposition.

Interestingly, Hessian contemporaries were not so kind to Donop as the British officers. For instance, the *Journal* of the Grenadier Battalion von Minnigerode stated,

> *Despite the fact that Colonel v. Donop ought to have passed the night of 22nd October a certain distance off in order not to be discovered by the rebels, and although he ought to have waited for the arrival of the ships next day in order that he might not be exposed to a cannonade from the latter's ships, he did not consider the matter to be of supreme importance...*[84]

The assessment is accurate, in that von Donop did not adhere to the plan as developed by the Howe brothers for the storming of the fort. In going it alone, he deprived himself of the support of the Royal Navy ships in the river. On the one hand, it is doubtful that these vessels could have provided truly effectual support to the Hessian attack given the distances from which they would be firing. At the same time, their presence could have prevented the galleys of the Pennsylvania State Navy from supporting the defenders of Fort Mercer, by many accounts a crucial contribution to the American success. The more damning criticisms contained in the account concern Donop's actions when he approached Fort Mercer on October 22nd, "If he had attacked and stormed it at once, he could have effected an entry forthwith and put the garrison to death at the point of a bayonet." This was so according to the author of the journal because "the door of the fort stood open and the sentinels at the gate and in the fort were pacing quietly up and down with the guns on their shoulders, probably unloaded."[85] Again, the conditions set down in the official record of the von Minnigerode Battalion are patently false based on reports from both sides. This conflicting account begs the question as to why the Hessians would saddle the blame on one of their own officers for the debacle and essentially label him an incompetent. The answer might be that they could not accept the fact that they had actually been beaten by the Americans in an open fight. The only major defeat suffered by the German forces in America prior to this was the attack on Trenton. To a certain extent, the Hessian defeat at Trenton could be mitigated in their sense of pride by the fact that it was surprise assault. At Fort Mercer, however, the Hessians were prepared for battle, and in fact initiated the clash. They had attacked and been beaten in an open fight of their own choosing.

The preceding begs the question of why von Donop attacked when and how he did. A letter written by Lt. Col. Ludwig Johann Adolph von Würmb to Maj. Gen. Freidrich Christian Arnold Jungkenn on October 25 may shed some additional light on how von Donop perceived his situation. Würmb began by noting that on meeting von Donop, the latter informed him that he had orders to take Red Bank in New Jersey. He went on to note, "I asked him what instructions he had, he said none, he was told to improvise."[86] It appears then, that von Donop either did not receive or did not understand the overall plan for the assault on the river defenses scheduled for October 23. Würmb added that Donop further informed him, "If he were to fail, he also had no instructions."[87]

Subsequent historians have not been so kind in their assessment of von Donop's performance either. Among the more prolific authors on the river campaign, John W. Jackson rendered this verdict in von Donop, "By not attacking all faces of the fort simultaneously, Donop exposed each separate attack to the devastating fire of almost the entire garrison and was defeated in detail." Likewise, Thomas Mc Guire makes the following judgment of attack on Fort Mercer, "the behind-the-scenes tensions of an honor bound, obsessed commander, combined with a lack of basic professionalism by some of his subordinates at that moment, was a formula for disaster." In assessing the failure of the Hessian assault on Fort Mercer, Ira Gruber goes beyond the failures of von Donop and notes, as well, the failure of Gen. William Howe to ensure that the force possessed the correct equipment for its proposed mission. He likewise faults Howe for not determining whether his brother's ships in the Delaware were in a suitable position to support the attack. [88]

Each of the above criticisms holds merit. Von Donop's force was, in fact, defeated in detail, due to the fact that the commander was unprepared, and did not keep his men under close coordination. To this could added von Donop's own delay in launching the assault, as it allowed the garrison to prepare to repulse the Hessian onslaught when it came, and to raise the signal flags which alerted the small ships of the Pennsylvania Navy, allowing them to lend the weight of their artillery to the defense. Still, the final burden of responsibility resides with William Howe as he held the overall command of land forces. His culpability in the failed assault will be discussed in the concluding chapter.

In his General Orders for October 24, Howe tried, to the best extent he could, to be magnanimous in defeat, stating

> *The Commander in Chief returns his thanks to Col. Donop and to all the Officers and Men of the Hessian Detachment under his Command, for their Gallant and Spirited attempt in the attack of the Evening of the 22nd Instant, which, though not attended with the success it merited, reflect great honour and credit upon them.*[89]

While William Howe attempted to portray the defeat in the most positive light possible, it remained a defeat. The repulse of the Hessian attack on Fort Mercer was not the end of the British woes, however. It should be recalled that von Donop's expedition was only one portion of a larger overall joint assault on the American defensive network. The Royal Navy was slated to move ships into position and bombard Fort Mifflin at the same time that Fort Mercer was under attack from the land side. This was if the attack had gone according to plan on October 23. This would have two potential consequences. First, it would prevent the Americans from being able to shift troops and ships to meet the twin assault. Second, it would reduce the works at Fort Mifflin and prepare them for an assault by British ground forces.

Among the naval vessels slated to bring their guns to bear on Fort Mifflin were the HMS *Augusta, Pearl, Liverpool, Roebuck, Merlin* and the galley *Cornwallis*. These vessels were in motion of the 22nd, as attested to by the Journal of the HMS *Vigilant*,

> *At Anchor in Tinicum Channel at 4AM weighed and Towed up to Hog Island intending to get into the Pool between Hog and Province Islands, to be ready next morning to go against Mud Fort, while the Augusta, Roebuck, Liverpool and Pearl were to Act*

> *against it and the Galleys in the Eastern Channell,*
> *but there not being Water enough for us at High water*
> *got aground on the Bar...*[90]

When it became apparent that Donop was in fact attacking on October 22 instead, Capt. Francis Reynolds of the *Augusta*, a sixty-four-gun ship of the line, who had replaced Hamond in charge of the squadron, ordered the fleet to move into position to bombard Fort Mifflin.[91] The Americans in the fort returned fire, and an intense artillery duel ensued that continued over the next two hours. The smaller vessels of the Pennsylvania Navy joined in the fighting as well, after they had helped to drive off the Hessian attempt on Fort Mercer. The *Vigilant's* Journal noted briefly, "6 the firing began between the Galleys and Ships..."[92] At roughly 8PM the firing ceased on both sides, and the British ships began to retire southward in the river. As they did so, the *Augusta* ran aground. The *Vigilant*

> *sent out Boats to Assist them, but could not get*
> *them Off, the enemy firing on them very Hot, we fired*
> *some Shott at the Galleys over Hog Island, our Boats*
> *rowing guard, sounding our Channel up to Mud Fort.*[93]

The *Augusta* remained stuck fast through the night, during which Hazelwood dispatched three fire ships downriver in an attempt to set the man of war on fire. They were the *Comet, Hellcat* and *Volcano*.[94] The following day, October 23, the British ships returned upriver to provide cover for their stranded comrades and assist in efforts to try and free the *Augusta*. An intense artillery exchange again developed, between the garrison of Fort Mifflin and the vessels of Hazelwood's Pennsylvania Navy on the one side, and the Royal Navy ships on the other. The intensity of the fire eventually forced the British warships to withdrawal downstream.

Somewhere between 10:30 and 11 AM on October 23, the *Augusta* caught fire.

As the fire spread out of control, British efforts turned to evacuating the crew of the vessel. Various boats from the *Augusta* herself as well as the *Roebuck* and the attending transports were pressed into service to remove the crew from the burning ship. Some accounts attest that fire from the American batteries hampered the British relief efforts of the crew of the *Augusta*. At about noon she exploded. The sound of the explosion was heard as far north as the road between Germantown and Whitemarsh. That was the location of Thomas Paine, who recorded his impression of the incident in a letter to Benjamin Franklin, "we were stunned with a report as loud as a peal from a hundred cannon at once…" He continued, "turning round I saw a thick smoke rising like a pillar and spreading from the top like a tree."[95] Paine confirmed that this was the explosion of the *Augusta*, and that he did not hear any explosion of the *Merlin*.[96]

Likewise, Capt. Fleury, writing to Alexander Hamilton on October 23, offered a thorough summary of the day's events,

> *…The morning of the 23rd, the Enemy began a heavy fire from their batteries—their Vessels which had pass'd the Billingsport Chevaux de fries kept up a Cannonade part of the morning and our situation began to be very critical when luckily one of our Bullets or one from the Fleet set fire to the Augusta, a 64 Gun Ship which was nearest our battery and did most mischief—another Vessel of 20 Guns was likewise burnt, the firing from the Land ceased, the Enemys Fleet retired and we had the Victory…*[97]

Additional testimony from the perspective of Fort Mifflin derives from a letter by Lt. Col. Robert Ballard to George Washington. Ballard had just left the garrison at Fort Mifflin and found that Greene and Hazelwood were in the process of composing an express to the commander in chief to inform him of the "Glorious Event of last Evening," and decided he would contribute the "particulars from our Garrison." He described how the previous morning the batteries on Province Island and later the British vessels in the river began a bombardment of Fort Mifflin. Ballard continued,

> *Our Battery in Consort with the Commodores Fleet playing on them with 18 and 32 lb Shott so closely that they I believe began to give ground, however they ran a Sixty four Gun Ship and a Twenty Gun Frigate a ground and after fruitless attempts in vain to get them off, they set fire to them both, to our small satisfaction as it was out of the Power of our Fleet to take them. We sustain'd no Damage except a Capt. and 1 private slightly wounded.*[98]

Significant in Ballard's account is the inclusion of the ships from Hazelwood's fleet in the fighting. Once again, they joined in the defense of the forts, contributing their firepower, little as it often was, to aiding the garrisons. Ballard further noted that fallowing the destruction of the *Augusta* and *Merlin*, the remaining British ships fell back down the river. He did stress that to continue the defense, the fort required ammunition for its guns.

Among the more dramatic accounts of the death of the *Augusta* is that of Col. Thomas Hartley of Hartley's Additional Continental Regiment.[99] Writing to Thomas Wharton, President of the Supreme Executive Council from camp, probably at Whitpain, the colonel described how "About eleven o'clock we heard a monstrous explosion which shook the [sic] neighbouring country and a prodigious column of smoak rose towards the heavens." Initially, "we feared that it might be the magazine at the fort." However, "better fortune awaited America."[100]

Likewise, there is the account of an unidentified defender of Fort Mifflin who noted that "Yesterday Morning they began a Cannonade from a 64, a 20 and a 50 Gun Ship..." and that the fire from these vessels was supplemented by the various shore batteries. They observed, "We suffered from the Shore, and directed out whole Attention to the Ships, assisted by our Gallies, who sent 4 Fire Rafts, without any success." Most importantly for the present inquiry, this account states, "A lucky Shot set Fire to the 64's Stern, and she burned down;"[101] Three of these fire rafts were the ones noted above, the fourth, dispatched later on Hazelwood's orders, was actually the sloop *Aetna*.[102] More importantly, it credits the destruction of the *Augusta* to a shot from Fort Mifflin, a possibility which will be examined in greater depth below.

On the British side, Archibald Robertson reported that on the 23rd,

> *Some men of War Came up the River this morning on Intention to Cannonade Mud Island while some of our Grenadiers Storm'd it but after a great Deal of firing from the Rebel fleet and ours, the Augusta, a 64 Gun Ship, Captain Reynolds, got aground and afire by Accident. She was burnt; the Crew saved except some sick and Wounded. The Merlin Sloop likewise got Aground and was burnt.*[103]

Robertson's account is useful as it notes the role played by the Pennsylvania Navy, a factor often overlooked in other descriptions of the fighting. British Capt. John Montresor described the circumstances as follows, "Before the Explosion of the *Augusta's* Powder Magazine which was at ½ past 10 A.M. many of the seamen jumped overboard apprehending it, some were taken up by our ships boats, but the Chaplain, one Lieutenant and 60 men perished in the water." Jackson combines these numbers to give a total loss of 62. He further attributed these casualties more to the damage sustained by the ship as a result of rebel canon fire as it was abandoned prior to exploding.[104] Montresor further noted how the HMS *Merlin*, coming to the aid of the *Augusta* became stuck as well, "The *Augusta* was got aground, but not on the Chevaux de frises as did the *Merlin* sloop of war but nearer the Jersey shore."[105]

Finally, from Philadelphia, Elizabeth Drinker recorded "the fireing [sic] this morning seem'd to be incessant, from the Battry, the Gondelows, and the Augusta, Man of War, of 64 Guns, she took fire, and after burning near 2 hours, blew up, the loss of this fine Vessel is accounted for in different ways -"[106] The last phrase of Drinker's entry belies a significant point.

There exists some degree of controversy as to what exactly caused the explosion that destroyed the *Augusta*. Some sources assert that it was a heated canon ball from Fort Mifflin, referred to as a hot shot. This version is supported by the testimony of the anonymous witness from the fort given above. Others state that it was the wadding from the one of the *Augusta's* own canon that fell on the gun deck and began a fire.[107]

Considering the proposition that the shot came from the American batteries, some authorities contend that a special type of furnace, referred to as a hot shot furnace, was necessary in order to heat the projectile. Harold Peterson, however, maintains that all that was needed was a hole in ground six feet in diameter and roughly four feet deep. The hole would contain a fire built by the gun crew, and the balls would be heated atop the fire. A wooden disc or piece of sod would be placed in the artillery piece, between the charge and the hot shot to prevent the weapon from discharging prematurely. It would be fired shortly thereafter so that the heated round would have as little time as possible to begin to cool.[108]

To date, no archeological evidence of a hot shot furnace has come to light at the site of Fort Mifflin. It is important to bear in mind, however, that following the war, a new fort was constructed over the remains of the older one. The construction of the new fort, which remains standing to the present, may have effaced any traces of an ad hoc furnace such as the one Peterson describes. Given the simplicity of the method of manufacturing the hot shot described above, it may have been possible for the artillerists at Fort Mifflin to improvise such a round, even without a specially designed furnace.

The notion that the fire developed from wadding on the Augusta herself is equally plausible. At the same time, the only one to advance this theory was Gen. Howe, and so it may be considered as an attempt to deny that the American gunners were capable of such a feat.[109]

In any case, with the destruction of the *Augusta*, Adm. Lord Howe ordered the *Merlin* burned to prevent her or her weapons and stores from falling into the hands of the Americans. In the wake of these losses, the concern of paramount importance to Adm. Howe encompassed the preservation of the remaining ships in his flotilla. Such is evidenced in his instructions to Capt.-William Cornwallis. He began by giving the captain a brevet promotion of sorts, 'The Command of the Ships off Billins Port [sic] by the unfortunate accident to the Augusts devolving on you..." The admiral then cautioned his subordinate, "Your attention will be requisite for preventing as much as may be the Effect of any attack attempted to be made on the *Vigilant* in the situation where she is now placed." At this time, the *Vigilant* had had most of her sails removed as well as her guns on the landward side. These modifications were made in to reduce her draft and allow her to get into the shallow channel between Fort Mifflin and the Pennsylvania shore. The *Vigilant* slowly made her way to this position during the intense cannonade which resulted in the loss of the *Augusta*. Adm. Howe further enjoined Capt. Cornwallis, "She will be towed forward through the Channel to the W[t]ward [westward] of Hog Island, or back to her former Station off of Tinicum Island, where she may lye afloat at all times of the tide, in readiness however to proceed up against the Fort, as circumstances may induce, and of which Captain Henry will be duly informed."[110] However, strong winds led to the vessel becoming stuck on a reef and therefore failing to get between the fort and the Pennsylvania shore. For the Crown forces, October 22nd and 23rd were dark days indeed. Likewise, they stand as prime examples of the Prussian military theorist Carl von Clausewitz concept of friction in war.[111]

The admiral, in relating the loss of two of his ships to one Philip Stephens in a letter dated October 25. After describing, in general terms, the Hessian assault on Fort Mercer, Howe continued,

The Attack of the Redoubt being observed to take place the Evening of the 22d, just upon the Close of Day, Captain Reynolds immediately slipped and

*advanced with the Squadron (to which the Merlin had
been joined) as fast as he was able with the Flood; to
second the Attempt of the Troops which were seen to be
very warmly engaged. But the Change in the natural
Course of the River caused by the Obstructions, ap-
pearing to have altered the Channel, the Augusta and
Merlin unfortunately grounded some distance below
the second Line of Chevaux de Frize.*[112]

The Admiral's account sheds some light on why the two
vessels became trapped in the first place. First, the course of the
sinking of the chevaux de frise had altered the course of the river
in the area. Likewise, any pilots on board may not have been aware
of these changes. The time of day is important as well. Col. von
Donop launched his attempt to storm Fort Mercer at approximately 4 PM. In late October, the sun would already be setting, which
would make finding the safe course through the eastern channel
even more difficult. Combining these factors helps to explain in
some degree why the *Augusta* and later the *Merlin* grounded. As
for what began the fire that consumed the former ship, the precise
cause remains unsettled.

The loss of the *Augusta* and the *Merlin*, as well as over 300
Hessian casualties, brought the British no closer to opening the Delaware River. A new plan of attack was needed. The new approach to
the opening of the river, as will be seen, would focus on Fort Mifflin.

On the American side, the destruction of the British warships
stood as further cause for celebration. News of the victories dissem-
inated rapidly within the Continental Army. Joseph Clark wrote
in his diary on October 24 from Whitpain, Pennsylvania, the information being given out in the General Orders: "The battle was on
the 22d of October. Count Donop was wounded and taken; likewise,
his Brigade Major taken. The two ships were destroyed on the 23d,
being set on fire by their own men after they had run aground."[113]

Thomas Wharton, writing to John Hazelwood on October 24
concerning pay for the sailors in the Pennsylvania Navy could not
resist adding the post-script, "Since writing...we have the glorious
news that you repulsed and destroyed two of the King of Great Brit-
ains ships in their attempt to weight the Chevaux de Frize..."[114]
Likewise, John Laurens of South Carolina wrote to Robert Howe
from York on October 25 "The Delaware affair which you will find
upon another piece is Glorious." He could not resist a bit of play on
words, "Don't you think those Canoniering Heroes Commodore Ha-

zelwood of the little Fleet, Colonel Smith at Fort Mifflin and Colonel Green of Rhode Island, at Red Bank, deserve to be Canonized?"[115] John Harvie wrote Thomas Jefferson the same day. After providing a somewhat muddled account of the defense of Fort Mercer and the sinking of the British vessels, he positively gushed to the Virginian, "Could you have thought these Forts and Batteries were so formidable?"[116] The following day, John Adams wrote his wife Abigail, "The Forts at Province Island and Red Bank have been defended, with a Magnanimity, which will give our Country a Reputation in Europe."[117] Such soaring praise from someone so irascible as John Adams was not easy to come by. Finally, Elbridge Gerry described the repulse of the Hessians to James Warren on the 28th, noting "The Enemy We are informed did not recover their Fright until they had recrossed the Ferry & joined their main army." [118] Clearly the successes along the Delaware excited the members of Congress.

The defense of Fort Mercer exerted international as well as domestic effects. Writing to their agents in Paris on October 31, 1777, the Continental Congress' Committee for Foreign Affairs informed, in part 'a general and very powerful attack was made upon the 22d & 23d of this month on Red Bank by twelve hundred Hessians and on Fort Island by several Ships of war which approached as near as the Frize would admit..."[119] The letter continued, informing of the repulse of von Donop and his Hessians as well as the sinking of the *Augusta* and the *Merlin* (misidentified in the letter as the *Liverpool*). The Committeemen continued with the injunction "We rely on your wisdom and care to make the best and most immediate use of this intelligence to depress our enemies and produce essential aid to our cause in Europe."[120] Clearly, the members of the committee understood the propaganda value of these successes in convincing the European powers, especially France to provide aid.

The repulse at Fort Mercer served as an important tonic for the men under Washington's command. They had lost two battles to the British in the campaign season just ending. While they had acquitted themselves well in both instances, they remained on the losing side. Meanwhile, the troops of the northern army under Gates had the stunning success of Saratoga to their credit. As previously noted, Washington, Greene, and other commanders hailed the success in their correspondence, and quickly broadcast it out to other leaders, both political and military.

For the Hessians, however, Fort Mercer had a very different meaning. As historian Rodney Atwood is quick to point out, "Redbank marks a turning point for the Hessian corps in America. If

Trenton destroyed the myth of Hessian invincibility, Redbank shattered the physical reality."[121] Summing up, he declares, "Their best troops had suffered devastating losses."[122] One look at the casualty figures for the specific units engaged in the Fort Mercer attack is enough to confirm Atwood's analysis. Such an appraisal begs the question of why such professionals were defeated by a fairly new force. The Rhode Island regiments had been rebuilt earlier in the year.[123]

After intensive analysis, historian Robert K. Wright lays the blame for the Hessian defeat at Fort Mercer squarely on the shoulders of the Hessian's allies, "The only explanation left is the British."[124] Wright further observes that the British role was one of poor leadership, referring to William Howe as only an "average general."[125] Based on his examination of the assault, Wright observes that Howe believed von Donop "could abort the mission if necessary; whereas von Donop thought that he had to persevere at all costs."[126]

Wright is quick to note, however, concerning the loss at Fort Mercer, that it was von Donop who asked for the command of the assault. He further notes that "...Howe gave von Donop a free hand in making his tactical decisions." Therefore, to some extent von Donop contributed to his own defeat at Red Bank. Still, Wright is quick to point out that what Howe did not provide for Donop was the naval support, "that was a key part of his own plan—attacking both forts and the obstacles simultaneously and getting a warship into position to neutralize the galleys." [127] This part Wright's assessment is problematic in that naval support would be available, at the appointed time for the assault. Von Donop's impatience comprised a major contributing factor in his defeat. Lastly, Wright observes that "That offensive stroke collapsed in a large part when Lord Richard's ships couldn't break through. That missing part turned Fort Mercer into a virtual shooting gallery."[128] While critical of their leadership, Wright praises the courage of the Hessian soldiers who took part in the assault, noting that all three of von Donop's attack units made it to the ditch around Fort Mercer.[129]

As noted previously, the success at Fort Mercer, along with the destruction of the *Augusta* and the *Merlin* raised the spirits of both the army and the men in the Continental Congress, especially after the defeat suffered at Brandywine and Germantown. Many in both bodies believed that the forts could hold until the river froze, and in so doing, force Howe to abandon Philadelphia for lack of supply. By the same token, following these disasters, William and Richard Howe focused their attention on Fort Mifflin, rightly surmising that this post was the true key to the Delaware River defenses. Without Fort Mifflin, the obstacles in the river could be removed, and British shipping could bring the much-needed supplies to the beleaguered city. They then determined to focus their attention Fort Mifflin, and thus began the siege of that post.

Finally, a number of histories that discuss the Hessian assault on Fort Mercer tend to focus on the brilliant defense of the post conducted by Greene and Du Plessis. In doing so, they conversely highlight the critical flaws in von Donop's conception of the attack on the post. Both of these approaches fail to take into account the role played by the ships of the Pennsylvania Navy who contributed their support from the direction of the Delaware River.[130] The above should make it clear that according to a number of contemporaries, the galleys of the Pennsylvania Navy contributed significantly to the defeat of the Hessian assault.[131]

CHAPTER NOTES

[1] Smith, *Fight for the Delaware*, p. 15.

[2] This appraisal of Howe's initial efforts is contained in Gruber, *Howe Brothers*, p. 247. On the option of direct assault, Lender, *River War*, p. 23.

[3] James Parker, Journal of Captain James Parker, Philadelphia, October 16, 1777, quoted in *NDAR*, vol. 10, p. 186.

[4] Journal of the HMS *Vigilant*, Captain John Henry, October 16, 1777, quoted in Ibid, p. 187.

[5] Benjamin Eyre to George Washington, October 16, 1777 quoted in Ibid, p. 186.

[6] Major François Fleury to lieutenant colonel Alexander Hamilton, Fort Mifflin, October 17, 1777, quoted in Ibid, p.195.

[7] Jackson, *British in Philadelphia*, p. 61.

[8] Jackson, *Pennsylvania Navy*, pp. 230-31.

[9] On Colonel von Donop's background, see Wilhelm Gottlieb Levin von Donop, *Des Obermarschalls und Drosten Wilhelm Gottlieb Levin von Donop zu Lüdershofen, Maspe Nachricht von dem Geschlecht der von Donop.* (Paderborn 1796), pp. 21-22. See also Atwood, *The Hessians*, pp. 102-3. On his correspondence with Prince Henry and Prince Frederick William of Prussia, see Carl Emil von Donop, Letters from a Hessian Mercenary." C.V. Easum and Hans Huth, trans., and eds. in *PMBH* 62, 4 (October 1938): 490.The Jäger were considered elite riflemen of the Hessian forces.

[10] Johann Conrad Dohla, *A Hessian Diary of the Revolution*. Bruce E. Burgoyne, ed. trans. Norman, OK: University of Oklahoma Press, 1990, p. 44.

[11] A number of works have been written concerning the battle of Trenton. Among the most useful are: William S. Stryker, *The Battle of Trenton and Princeton* (Trenton, NJ: The Old Barracks Association, 2001 reprint of 1898 orig.) and David Hackett Fischer, *Washington's Crossing* (New York: Oxford University Press, 2004).

[12] Fleury, Journal, Fort Mifflin, October 20, 1777, quoted in *NDAR* vol. 10, p. 226.

[13] Jackson, *Pennsylvania Navy*, p. 219.

[14] Ibid.

[15] Jackson, *Pennsylvania Navy*, p. 171.

[16] Journal of HM Armed Ship *Vigilant*, Commander John Henry, Monday October 20, 1777, quoted in *NDAR*, vol. 10, p. 228.

[17] Journal of the HMS *Camilla*, Captain Charles Phipps, Monday, October 20, 1777, quoted in Ibid, p. 229.

[18] Journal of HM Sloop Zebra, Commander John Orde, Monday October 20, 1777 quoted in Ibid, pp. 228-9.

[19] Journal of the HMS *Camilla*, Captain Charles Phipps, Monday, October 20, 1777, quoted in Ibid, p. 229.

[20] Ibid.

[21] McGuire, *Philadelphia Campaign*, vol. 2, p. 185.

[22] George Washington to Commodore John Hazelwood, HQ, Whitepain, PA, October 21, 1777, quoted in *NDAR*, vol. 10, pp. 233-4.

[23] George Washington to Lieutenant Colonel Samuel Smith, Headquarters Whitepain, PA, October 21, 1777, quoted in Ibid, p. 234.

[24] Ibid.

[25] While he could work well with superiors, he was often harsh on his subordinates. This could account for some of the censure heaped upon him following the battle.

[26] Journal of Major Carl Leopold Baurmeister, October 21, 1777, quoted in Lieutenant Colonel Donald M. Londahl-Schmidt ed. trans., "German and British Accounts of the Assault on Fort Mercer at Redbank, NJ in October 1777." *The Hessians: Journal of the Johannes Schwalm Historical Association.* 16 (2013),:26. Hereinafter Hessians

[27] McGuire, *Philadelphia Campaign*, vol. 2, p. 154.

[28] Jackson, *Fort Mercer*, 17. On the command of the flatboats, see Thomas Sullivan, *From Redcoat to Rebel: The Thomas Sullivan Journal.* Joseph Lee Boyle, ed. (Bowie, MD: Heritage Books, 1997), p. 148.

[29] Diary of Staff Captain Levin Friedrich Ernst von Münchhausen of the Leib Regiment quoted in Lieutenant Colonel Donald M. Londahl-Schmidt ed. trans., "German and British Accounts of the Assault on Fort Mercer at Redbank, NJ in October 1777." *The Hessians: Journal of the Johannes Schwalm Historical Association.* 16 (2013), p. 23.

[30] David Syrett, "The Methodology of British Amphibious Operations during the Seven Years' War" in *The Mariner's Mirror.* 58, (1972): 272.

[31] Journal of Major Carl Leopold Baurmeister, October 21, 1777, quoted in Londahl-Schmidt, "German and British Accounts," p. 27.

[32] Feilitzsch, *Diary*, p. 23.

[33] Smith, *Fight for the Delaware*, p. 18. Stryker, *Forts*, p. 13.

[34] Feilitzsch, *Diary*, p. 23.

[35] Mc Guire, *Philadelphia Campaign*, vol.2, *p.* 156, and Stewart, *Battle of Red Bank*, 10, make the claim that the Hessian security was quite lax. On the other hand, Jackson, *Mercer*, p. 19; Lender, *River War*, p. 24; Browne, Thesis, p. 106, all note the security precautions taken by Donop. Of these accounts, Jackson's is the most detailed.

[36] On the Hessians security precautions, see, Jackson, *Mercer*, p. 19. Concerning their limitations, see McGuire, *Philadelphia Campaign*, p. 156.

[37] Fleury, *Journal*, October 21, 1777, quoted in *NDAR*, vol. 10, p. 235.

[38] Journal of HM Armed Schooner *Viper*, LT Edward Pakenham, October 21, 1777, quoted in Ibid.

[39] Stryker, *Forts*, p. 13.

[40] Jackson, *Pennsylvania Navy*, 175. Jackson gave the date of the 19th but admitted that no written order had been located at the time of his writing.

[41] The men were actually John Mc Ilvaine, at Tory, and one known only as Dick, a runway slave. Browne, "Fort Mercer and Fort Mifflin," p. 105. On the route taken by Von Donop's troops, see Jackson, *Mercer*, p. 19.

[42] Stewart, p. 11.

[43] Ewald, *Diary*, p. 58.

[44] Diary of Lieutenant Colonel Levin Carl von Heister, quoted in Londahl-Smidt, Lieutenant Colonel Donald M. ed. trans., "German and British Accounts," in *Hessians*. p. 16 (2013), p. 14.

[45] Ibid.

[46] Ibid.

[47] Catherine R. Williams, *Biography of Revolutionary Heroes: Containing the Life of Brigadier General William Barton, and also, of Captain Stephen Olney*. (Providence, RI: Privately Printed, 1839), p. 233.

[48] For the use of the signal flag, see Browne, Fort Mercer and Fort Mifflin," 111. On the notion of the bombardment alerting the ships, see McGuire, *Philadelphia Campaign*, p. 162.

[49] Chaplain Feilitzsch in Bruce E. Burgoyne, ed. Trans. *Diaries of Two Ansbach Jaegers*. Bowie, MD: Heritage Books, 1997, p. 23.

[50] Journal of Second Lieutenant Carl Wilhlem von Bultsingsloewen for October 22, 1777, Londahl-Schmidt, "German and British Accounts," p. 8.

[51] Journal of the Regiment von Würmb, quoted in Ibid, p. 13.

[52] Diary of Jacob Martin quoted in Ibid, p. 11.

[53] Ibid.

[54] Diary of Second Lieutenant Carl Freidrich Reuffer quoted in Ibid, p. 9

[55] Lender, *River War*, pp. 26-27.

[56] Joseph LaBoyle, "The Israel Angell Diary, 1 October 1777- 28 February 1778." in *Rhode Island History* 58 (2000):113.

[57] Bultsingsloewen, quoted in Londahl-Smidt, "German and British Accounts," p. 8

[58] Ibid.

[59] Ibid.

[60] Rueffer, Diary, quoted in Ibid, p. 9

[61] Bultsingsloewen, quoted in Ibid, p. 8.

[62] Journal of the HMS *Camilla*, October 22, 1777 quoted in *NDAR*, vol. 10, p. 239.

[63] Lee Patrick Anderson, *Forty Minutes by the Delaware: The Battle for Fort Mercer* (n.l., Universal Publishers, 1999), p. 131.

[64] William S. Stryker, *The Forts on the Delaware in the Revolutionary War*. (Trenton, NJ: John L. Murphy Publishing Co., 1901), p. 20.

[65] Report of First Lieutenant Friederich Wilhelm Werner of the Feld-Artillerie Corps quoted in Londahl-Smidt, "German and British Accounts," p. 6.

[66] Reuffer diary, quoted in ibid, p. 9.

[67] Werner, report, quoted in ibid, p. 6.

[68] Smith, *Memoirs*, p. 10.

[69] Ibid.

[70] Robert K. Wright: "A Crisis of Faith: Three Defeats that Cost a Reputation." in *The Hessians: Journal of the Johannes Schwalm Historical Association*. 21, (2018): 63.

[71] Stewart, *Battle of Red Bank*, p. 15.

[72] Ibid.

[73] George Washington to Christopher Greene, October 26, 1777, quoted in *Washington, Rev. War*. Vol. 12, p. 17.

[74] Major John Clark, Jr. to George Washington, October 22, in Ibid, p. 27.

[75] Anderson, *Forty Minutes*, p. 130.

[76] On the specific units involved in the evacuation of the Hessians, see Henry Stirke, *Journal of Henry Stirke, Light Infantry Company, 10th Regiment of Fort 1st Battalion of Light Infantry*, quoted in Londahl-Schmidt, "German and British Accounts," p. 20.

[77] George Washington to George Clinton, October 26, 1777, quoted in *Washington, Rev. War*. vol. 12., p. 6.

[78] Ibid, p. 20 and p. 24 respectively.

[79] From Major Benjamin Tallmadge to General Samuel Webb, Upper Dublin new

Germantown, PA, November 13, 1777. Quoted in J. Watson Webb, ed. *Reminiscences of Gen'l Samuel B. Webb of the Revolutionary Army.* (New York, Globe Stationary and Printing, 1882), 292. For more information on Benjamin Tallmadge, see Richard F. Welch, *General Washington's Commando: Benjamin Tallmadge in the Revolutionary War.* (Jefferson, North Carolina: McFarland and Company, Inc., Publishers, 2014).

[80] Elizabeth Drinker, October 23, 1777, *The Diary of Elizabeth Drinker: The Life Cycle of an Eighteenth Century Woman.* Elaine F Crane,. ed. (Boston: Northeaster University Press, 1994), p. 247.

[81] John Peebles, *John Peebles American War*, p. 144.

[82] Sullivan, *Redcoat to Rebel*, p. 150.

[83] William Howe, "Copy of a Letter from General Sir William Howe to Lord George Germain, dated Philadelphia 25 October 1777." in *The Westminster Magazine; or The Pantheon of Taste.* 5, 2 (June 1777): 652.

[84] Journal of the Grenadier Battalion von Minnegerode, quoted in Londahl-Smidt, "German and British Accounts," p. 10.

[85] Ibid.

[86] Lieutenant Colonel Ludwig Johann Adolph von Würmb to Major General Friedrich Christian Arnold Jungkenn, October 25, 1777, quoted in Londahl-Smidt, "German and British Accounts," p. 13.

[87] Ibid.

[88] Jackson, *With the British*, 65. See also Mc Guire, *Philadelphia Campaign*, vol. 2, p. 158 and Gruber, *Howe Brothers*, 252.

[89] William Howe, General Orders, Head Quarters, Philadelphia, October 24, 1777 quoted in Londahl-Smidt, "German and British Accounts," p. 2.

[90] Journal of HM Armed Ship *Vigilant*, October 22, 1777 quoted in *NDAR*, vol. 10, p. 239.

[91] Browne, "Fort Mercer and fort Mifflin," p. 117.

[92] Journal of HM Armed Ship *Vigilant*, October 22, 1777 quoted in *NDAR*, vol. 10, p. 240.

[93] Ibid.

[94] Jackson, *Pennsylvania Navy*, p. 197.

[95] Thomas Paine, "Military Operations near Philadelphia in the Campaign of 1777-8." *PMHB*, 2, 3 (1878): 291-92.

[96] Ibid.

[97] Fleury to Alexander Hamilton from Fort Mifflin, October 28, 1777, quoted in *NDAR*, vol. 10, p. 234.

[98] Lieutenant Colonel Robert Ballard to George Washington, Red Bank, October 23, 1777, quoted in Ibid, pp. 248-9.

[99] Thomas Hartley was born in Pennsylvania on September 7, 1748. At age 18 he moved to York, Pennsylvania, where he joined the local Associators in 1774. With the outbreak of hostilities between Britain and the colonies the following year, he served first with the Sixth Pennsylvania Regiment of the Continental Line, and then, in January 1777 raised Hartley's Additional Regiment, which took part in the battles of Brandywine, Paoli and Germantown. See John Jordan, "Biographical Sketch of Colonel Thomas Hartley of the Pennsylvania Line." In *PMHB* 25 (1901): pp. 303-6.

[100] Colonel Thomas Hartley to Thomas Wharton, Whitpain, October 24, 1777 quoted in Ibid, p. 261.

[101] Extract of a Letter from Fort Mifflin, October 24, 1777, quoted in Ibid, p. 264.

[102] Jackson, *Pennsylvania Navy*, p. 197.

[103] Archibald Robertson, *Archibald Robertson: His Diaries and Sketches in American, 1762-1780*. Edited by Harry Miller Lyndenberg (New York: Arno Press, 1971), p. 153.

[104] Jackson, *Pennsylvania Navy*, p. 199.

[105] Montresor, *Journal*, pp. 469-70

[106] Drinker, *Diary*, p. 248.

[107] Jackson, *Pennsylvania Navy*, p. 199.

[108] Peterson, *Round Shot and Rammers*, p. 64.

[109] Jackson, *Pennsylvania Navy*, p. 199.

[110] Vice Admiral Viscount Howe to Captain William Cornwallis, HMS *Eagle*, October 23, 1777 quoted in *NDAR*, vol. 10, pp. 254-5.

[111] For Clausewitz, friction is that quality which makes even the simplest acts difficult.

[112] "Viscount Admiral Richard Howe to Mr. Stepehns," quoted in *The Westminster Magazine; or the Pantheon of Taste*. 5, 2 (1777): 654.

[113] Joseph Clark, "Diary of Joseph Clark" *Proceedings of the New Jersey Historical Society*. 7 (1853-56): 102.

[114] Thomas Wharton to John Hazelwood, Lancaster, October 24, 1777 quoted in Ibid, p. 260.

[115] Henry Laurens to Robert Howe, York, PA, October 25, 1777, quoted in *Letters of the Delegates of the Continental Congress*, Paul H. Smith, ed. volume 8, September 19, 1777-January 31, 1778, (Washington, DC: Library of Congress, 1981), p. 184. Hereinafter *LoD*

[116] John Harvie to Thomas Jefferson, York, PA, October 25, 1777, quoted in Ibid, p. 182.

[117] John Adams to Abigail Adams, York, PA, October 26, 1777, quoted in Ibid, p. 187.

[118] Elbridge Gerry to James Warren, York Town, October 28, 1777, quoted in Ibid, p. 205.

[119] Committee for Foreign Affairs to the Commissioners at Paris, October 31, 1777, quoted in Ibid, p. 215.

[120] Ibid.

[121] Atwood, *Hessians*, p. 128

[122] Ibid.

[123] See Popek, *They "...fought bravely..."*

[124] Wright, "Crisis of Faith," 65.

[125] Ibid.

[126] Ibid, p. 64.

[127] Wright, "Crisis of Faith," p. 66.

[128] Ibid.

[129] Ibid, p. 62.

[130] The accounts that fall into this category include: Browne, "Fort Mercer and Fort Mifflin"; Anderson, *Forty Minutes*, 119-23; Lender, *River War*, pp. 26-7; and Ward, *War of the Revolution*, pp. 374-6.

[131] Jackson, *Pennsylvania Navy*, pp. 282-3, makes this assertion as well.

Chapter Six

Tightening the Noose - Preparations for the Siege of Fort Mifflin

On the failure of the British attempt to take Red Bank in New Jersey by storm, as well as the loss of the *Merlin* and the *Augusta*, the Howe brothers adopted a different approach. They now focused their principal efforts on the Fort Mifflin. The goal was to reduce the fort with artillery fire, and then possibly seize the remainder of the garrison through an amphibious assault. This approach made sense, as Fort Mifflin sat south of Fort Mercer, and was therefore more easily in range of the British guns. In addition, Fort Mifflin sat at the very end of the chain of American river defenses as they currently stood. Without it, the British could begin to remove the chevaux de frise, which would in turn negate the importance of Fort Mercer and open the all-important water route to Philadelphia. Such an approach would likely have appealed to Gen. William Howe as it implied fewer casualties than a direct assault such as the one previously attempted on Fort Mercer.

The weight of the British effort would be extensive, as they would bombard the weakly constructed post from batteries on the Pennsylvania shore, from the islands in the Delaware, and from Royal Navy ships as well as floating batteries in the river. Again, this would constitute a "joint" activity in the modern parlance, with both land and naval forces cooperating to achieve a shared outcome. What emerges from a close examination of the siege of Fort Mifflin is that victory went to the side with the better organization and combination of naval and land forces, in this case the British. It is also worth noting how this integration occurred as their existed no formal institutional structure to support it.

As previously noted, the British had refined their techniques for cooperation between land and naval forces during the Seven Years' War. The collaboration between the army and navy had reached a very high degree in that conflict, especially within the realm of conducting amphibious operations. The siege of Havana in 1762 stands as a prime example of British proficiency in amphibious operations.[1] Organizational principles were developed for landing of troops and supplies, as well as clear divisions of command between the land and naval forces. They had even, as discussed previously, specialized boats for the transportation of troops and supplies from ship to shore. These principles were employed to good effect in the landings at Havana in 1762 during the Seven Years War, as well as on Long Island and at the Head of Elk during the current conflict.[2] The reduction and occupation of Fort Island could potentially require the use of all of these practices as well.

British batteries had already kept Fort Mifflin under some level of bombardment from October 10. In addition, concentrated efforts at a naval and land assault on the fort began as the wrecks of the *Augusta* and the *Merlin* still lay smoldering in the Delaware.

A key figure in the British planning of the assault was Capt. John Montressor of the Royal Engineers. Still, the overall commander of the British land operations against Fort Mifflin was Gen. Samuel Cleaveland or Cleveland of the Royal Artillery.[3] It will be recalled that Montressor

Fig. 16. British iron canon recovered from the Delaware River and mounted on a naval carriage. This gun may have come from the HMS Augusta or the Merlin. Currently on display at Fort Mifflin on the Delaware. *Author's photograph.*

played a role in the initial plans for fortifying Mud Island in the aftermath of the French and Indian War, however, this did not give him any particular insight into the weaknesses of the post. The works developed by the Americans on Mud Island differed considerably from those he had recommended to the colonial leadership.

In reality, the post possessed a great many weaknesses. Baron d'Arendt made these abundantly clear in a long missive he composed to
Washington on October 24,

> *Now a word respecting this Place and its De-*
> *fense - The Fort is the worst constructed that I have*
> *ever seen; it would require 800 men, to defend it, and*
> *then there would not be sufficiency for a necessary Re-*
> *serve, and the Line of Troops would for the most part*
> *be only a single Rank - besides this there is no Ram-*
> *part, the inclosure for the most part being of Palisades*
> *- no works to flank - in a word there are too many De-*
> *fects to enumerate here.*[4]

The Prussian officer continued,

> *The Battery which seems to be the strongest*
> *part, is in effect the weakest - for there the Enemy*
> *could land most readily-it could be defended but fee-*
> *bly by small Arm and the Enemy once landed would*
> *be out of danger from the Canon.*[5]

D'Arendt went on to inform the Continental commander in
chief that he had initiated some efforts to strengthen the defenses,
however lack of manpower and materials stymied the work. The
baron stressed what he perceived as a key point to his superior, "the
Defense of this Place consists principally in this point, to hinder the
Enemy from closing in upon us, it will be necessary for the Fleet to
give us the assistance to the utmost, in firing upon the Boats des-
tined to make a Descent upon us."[6]

A few points stand out in d'Arendt's letter. The first is that
the Prussian seemed more of an infantry commander than a military engineer, for example, his expression that 800 men would only
make a single rank in defense of the post. More importantly, his
stress on the importance of cooperation between the defenders of
the fort and the ships of the Pennsylvania Navy to stage a successful defense. Still, the baron's views on the construction of the fort
and the necessities for its successful defense should be taken with
some apprehension. Numerous historians have observed various deficiencies of the post as well.

One of the key weaknesses of the fort was that it had been
laid out with an eye to defending the Delaware from ships coming

up the river. No thought had been given to the possibility of an ene-my coming attacking the post from the landward side, therefore its western side was very weakly fortified, consisting only of wooden palisades. If canon could be brought to bear on this side of the fort, they could easily blast through these defenses. That accomplished, an assailant could easily rake the interior of the post with enfilade fire, thus making it untenable to any defenders inside.

In order to exploit the weaknesses of Fort Mifflin, Montress-or ordered constructed a number of batteries just below Fort Mifflin, the largest of these sat just below Mingo Creek. In addition, the engineer constructed epaulements, earthen barriers to protect the British infantry who were guarding the artillery pieces.[7] Work on the British batteries progressed slowly, much to the frustration of Gen. Howe.

John Peebles gives some indication of the difficulties the weather brought upon the British at this time, noting on Saturday, October 25, that there was "very little firing below, 4 large men of war came up this morning near to Mud Island, but the tide turned & the wind died away..." As a result, the British ships dropped down the river again.[8] These maneuvers were in keeping with directives from Adm. Richard Howe, as noted in a report to the admiral from his subordinate, Capt. William Cornwallis. Cornwallis letter to the admiral provided a clear description of the British naval deploy-ments in the upper Delaware in late October, and therefore merits quoting at some length:

> *Upon receiving your Lordships Commands from Cap[t] Hammond, the Roebuck and Isis dropt below the Chevaux de frieze Yesterday Evening the Liverpool and Pearl remain'd as high up as your Lordship saw them yesterday, but it being foggy this Morning and hearing a [sic] fireing from those Ships, I sent the Boats to their Assistance and directed them to fall down so as to remain just above the Chevaux de frieze, which I understood from Cap[t]* [9]

Following his report detailing the locations of the various vessels as they positioned to renew their efforts against Fort Miff-lin, the captain informed his superior of American efforts to salvage whatever they could from the wrecks of the *Augusta* and *Merlin*, "The Rebels here had many men upon the wrecks this Evening, but from the Size of their Boats, I do not apprehend, they got any thing of Consequence out of them..."[10] In fact, once the fires on the wrecks subsided, Hazelwood ordered Col. Bradford with five galleys down to scavenge the whatever was useful. Apparently, they were successful, as the militia colonel wrote on October 26, "I had the pleasure of being on part of a 64 Gun Ship—most of her guns are in the wreck and we brought off two of here 24 pounders..."[11] They planned to return for the remaining guns the following day if the British ships did not interdict their efforts.

John W. Jackson, following work done at the beginning of the twentieth century by Dr. Wallace McGeorge, noted that according to the latter's research the *Augusta* mounted twenty-six twenty-four pounders on her lower deck, twenty-six eighteen-pounders on her upper deck: ten nine pounders on the quarter deck and two nine-pounders in her forecastle. However, when the vessel was raised and the river dragged in 1876, only a few twenty-four pounders were discovered. It remains unclear what became of the other guns from the *Augusta*. An account book, later lost, Mc George examined noted all the other articles taken from the *Augusta* aside from the guns. It seems possible, then, that at least some additional guns were salvaged either by the rebels during the fighting or the British between when they secured control of the river and when the abandoned Philadelphia the following June.[12]

Even with the British warships shifting their location, the vessels of Hazelwood's mosquito fleet continued to harass the British warships in the river. If anything, their perceived success against the *Augusta* and the *Merlin* seemed to embolden these vessels somewhat. For instance, the Lieutenant's Journal of the HMS *Isis* under Capt. William Cornwallis recorded for October 25 that they fired on some rebel boats in the afternoon.[13] That same day, the HMS *Camilla* transferred some of the men rescued from the Augusta to Lord Howe's flagship the HMS *Eagle*.[14]

While the weather impeded British efforts to position their forces for a joint assault on Fort Mifflin, this delay provided valuable time to the Americans to strengthen their own defenses to defy the impending British attack.

While work commenced on additional batteries for the assault on Fort Mifflin, the British took precautions to guard the flanks of their forces against a renewed assault. Once again, on October 26, British forces occupied the works at Billingsport. As Montressor recorded in his journal, "This day, the marines of the Fleet took possession again at Billingsport in New Jersey."[15]

The same day that the British reoccupied the remnants of Billingsport in New Jersey, rains began to fall. The rains, along with strong winds, continued between October 26 and October 30. The weather impeded efforts on both sides to strengthen their respective works and prepare for what would be the central drive to open the river to British shipping.[16]

In the aftermath of the assault on Fort Mercer, anxiety pervaded among the Americans concerning a renewed British offensive on the river forts. The concern is demonstrated in a letter from George Washington to New Jersey Militia Gen. David Forman from Continental Army headquarters at Whitpain Township on October 28. He declared,

> *I wrote you last evening with respect to reinforcing Red Bank, & Fort Mifflin, my anxiety from the importance of those places, is so great that I cannot help urging you again to throw in without loss of time, what assistance the Commanding officers think necessary, and such as you may be able to afford them.*[17]

Interestingly, in his letter to Forman, Washington explicitly reiterated his desire that reinforcing the posts be kept secret so as not to leak out to the enemy.[18] Additional work went on in the American forts as well, to prepare as much as possible for the expected onslaught. John Peebles noted in his diary entry for the October 25, that the "Rebels working at Red bank."[19]

The labor of both sides on their respective positions was time consuming and had different meanings for the respective combatants. In essence, for the Americans each day without an assault was another small victory. For the British, on the other hand, it challenged their ability hold the city of Philadelphia through the winter. Considering that the occupation of the rebel capital stood as the only concrete achievement of Gen. William Howe, it was imperative that it not be allowed to slip away.

During this preparatory period, both sides continued to engage one another in the river. For instance, during the fighting on October 23, the British set fire to a block house at Fort Mifflin which was fully occupied at the time. However, the defenders quickly extinguished the flames sustaining only one man wounded. As the anonymous reporter observed, "All inside of the Fort torn up as if ploughed, or rather as if dug in Holes."[20]

These intermittent clashes generated some friction between the land and naval forces on the American side. Major Fleury, writing to Alexander Hamilton from Fort Mifflin on October 28 asserted that "The Galleys which ought to be a Security to us, are absolutely useless - they have withdrawn to the Jersey Shore, the Channel between us and Province Island is perfectly clear and if the enemy choose to make a descent here as I have no doubt they will do - we cannot hinder them."[21]

What Fleury seemed to miss in his condemnation of the galleys was that the same conditions which prevented the *Vigilant* from taking up a station between the fort and Providence Island kept the galleys out of the area as well as the tides generated by the strong winds were likely to cause them to swamp. By now, Washington seemed to have a better grasp of the situation developing on the river and the growing British commitment of resources there. The American commander worked to counter his adversary's moves.

As the focus of the British efforts to open the Delaware to river traffic began to concentrate on the reduction of Fort Island, Washington ordered the remainder of Varnum's brigade into New Jersey at Burlington, then to march down to Woodbury, a few miles north of Red Bank. Once Varnum established his post there, he was to form a reserve that could be dispatched to trouble spots as needed.[22] In giving these orders, Washington allowed Varnum a great deal of operational latitude, stating, "I cannot delineate particularly the line of conduct you are to observe. I leave it to your discretion to be adapted to circumstances."[23] At the same time, Washington sketched some overall parameters to guide Varnum's actions,

> *These general ideas, I would however, throw out; That you are in conjunction with the Jersey Militia, to give the garrisons all the assistance and relief in your power. That as the men in them must be greatly harassed by labor and watching, and in need of rest and refreshment, you are to send detachments, from time to time to relieve and replace an equal number from the garrisons, who are occasionally to reinforce them with additional numbers, as they may stand in need of it. That in case of an attack upon or investiture of Red-Bank, you are to act upon the rear or flanks of the enemy; not to throw your troops into the Fort, except such reinforcements from them, as may really be wanted, in defense of the works.[24]*

Washington closed the main set of instructions with a caution to Varnum against allowing himself to be surprised in his camp. To some extent this was probably in reaction to the surprise suffered by Wayne at Paoli just over a month previously.[25] The injunction not to throw his men into the fort may also be based on the Continental Army commander's experiences, for it was approaching the anniversary of the British capture of Fort Washington in New York, with the bulk of its garrison and a vast stockpile of supplies. Washington had no desire to repeat that experience.[26]

With Varnum in effective tactical command of the river defenses, there occurred some unconnected changes in the leadership at lower levels. During the assault on Fort Mercer, Fort Mifflin was under the command of Col. Baron d'Arendt. Some friction existed between him and his second in command, Lt. Col. Samuel Smith of Maryland over the command of the fort.[27] On October 29th, however, d'Arendt's illness flared up once again and the Prussian was removed across the Delaware to Fort Mercer and eventually to the Whitall house for medical care.[28] Prior to leaving the fort, d'Arendt asked Washington that the garrison there be completed to 700 infantry, and that at least seventy artillerists be included in the fort's complement as well.[29] At this juncture, command devolved upon Lt. Col. Smith, an officer referred to by one historian of the campaign as a man of "uncommon patience and fortitude."[30] His contemporary, Henry "Light Horse Harry" Lee observed of him, "Smith felt the high responsibility devolved upon him, and was well apprised of the vast odds with which he had to contend."[31] He remained in command of Fort Mifflin until November 11.

Smith informed Washington of his assumption of command of Fort Mifflin in a letter dated October 30. Detailing his situation, Smith seemed confident of his men's ability to hold the post at the time. He laid out plans to defend the fort against possible British efforts to overrun it. The major concern voiced by Smith in his letter was with the Pennsylvania Navy. He stated, "I shall do everything in my power to keep amity with the navy." He went on to assert, "However, when the gallies [sic] are manned by soldiers, then we may expect every assistance, and then the fort will be impregnable."[32] The last denotes that there existed a tension between the commanders of the respective land and naval forces on the American side. This tension appeared already in the letter of Fleury to Hamilton quoted above. The tension between Smith and Cmdre. John Hazelwood of the Pennsylvania Navy would persist throughout the siege of Fort

Mifflin and later proved to be one of the contributing factors in the American loss of the post.

With Smith in command, Washington sought to make good on d'Arendt's parting requests. He sent orders that clothes and ammunition be forwarded into Fort Mifflin. In addition, he dispatched orders to Col. Christopher Greene that he was to send on any reinforcements he could into the fort.[33]

It should be recalled that following the attack on Germantown, Washington dispatched Maj. François Fleury to Fort Mifflin to aid in strengthening the defenses. Fleury worked hastily to improve the defenses of the fort. He completed traverses in the main battery. In addition, he dug ditches in front with a fraised (an earthwork built around fraises) earthen rampart on the southwest salient. He did this in order to protect the gunners from enfilade and ricochet fire. Furthermore, Fluery had installed a double chain by the water's edge to provide some degree of security on the right of the battery.[34]

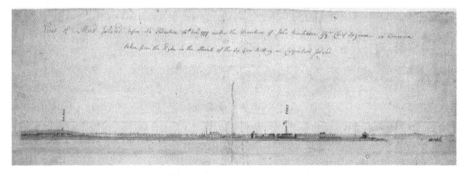

Figure 17 View of Mud Island before its reduction, 16th Novr., 1777, under the direction of John Montresor, Esqr., chief engineer in America, taken from the dyke in front of the six gun battery on Carpenter's Island. DRWG/US - *Unattributed, no. 51 (D size) [P&P] Library of Congress Prints and Photographs Division Washington, D.C. 20540 USA.*

In order to offer some degree of defense against any British storming parties, Fleury ordered further fraised works placed on the north and west sides of the post as well. These works complemented a series of wolf pits that had already been placed in the fort.[35] The demi-lune battery he ordered constructed would allow infantry to rake the flanks of the northern rampart.[36]

These changes complemented work already done by Smith prior to Fleury's joining the garrison. The works Smith ordered built consisted of a battery of two eighteen-pounders near the northwest blockhouse, and another of two four-pounders at the ferry wharf.

Still, the defenses of Fort Mifflin possessed some significant weaknesses. The ramparts on the north and west sides had been poorly conceived and could not provide adequate defensive fire on either of those fronts.[37] Considering that the walls of the fort were of uneven quality, there existed the real possibility that they could be breached in some areas, and the post stormed by British infantry, which was in fact the enemy's plan. Approximately two hundred British grenadiers had been sent to the ferry on Providence Island with the intent of storming the fort once the *Vigilant*'s bombardment of the post softened its defenses sufficiently to make the assault practicable. The contrary winds which prevent the hulked ship from taking up its station likewise prevented the implementation of the amphibious assault.[38]

Still, the modifications made to the post took into account the possibility of an amphibious attack. Should the walls of the fort be breached, and a storming party entered the post, the garrison could fall back to a rally point that included the north and west barracks. A last stand could be then made in a redoubt situated at the center of the parade ground.[39] Even with the efforts of Smith and Fleury, it was no certainty that post would hold out.

In addition to the physical weaknesses of Fort Mifflin, there was the continuing deterioration in the relationship between Smith and Hazewlwood. On October 26, Washington received a letter from Lt. Col. Smith, in which the latter informed him, "...I am clearly of the Opinion if we had a Commodore who would do his Duty, it would be impossible for the Enemy ever to get Possession of this fort, without we are improperly guarded and the Enemy may be with us before we can form."[40] Clearly the relations between Smith and Hazelwood were not improving, in fact quite the opposite was the case.

A major concern for Smith and d'Arendt lurked in the close proximity of the British batteries on the Pennsylvania side of the river. The nearness of the guns fed a fear that the British would launch both an artillery and infantry assault on the fort before the garrison had time to respond. Smith continued, informing Washington of a request from Col. d'Arendt for six galleys to guard the channel behind the fort and enclosing Hazelwood's response.[41]

The Continental commander in chief followed up with a letter to Hazelwood, in which he reminded the commodore of the importance of close cooperation between the two services in denying the British access to Philadelphia. Hazelwood responded to Washington the same day, beginning with, "By you Excellency's pressing in your last letter, so much for me keeping up harmony with the Fleet and Army, I apprehend some letters had been wrote as tho' a difference subsisted here..."[42]

If the acrimony between the American commanders were not enough, there were problems in the naval arm of the river defenses as well. Writing to Washington from the *Chatham* galley on October 26, Cmdre. John Hazelwood expressed his concerns over the conditions in the Pennsylvania Navy, "The Fleet is now so poorly Mann'd, & the constant cry from Fort Mifflin is to guard that Post, that I know not how to act without more assistance." He went on to inform the general that the vessels stationed further up the Delaware at Bordentown had lost twenty men and could therefore not be relied upon for support.[43]

At the same time, Washington grew increasingly concerned, almost obsessed, with the fate of two Continental Navy frigates, the *Washington* and the *Effingham*. Both vessels were above Philadelphia at Bordentown, and Washington worried over the possibility of their falling into British hands, as neither was fully armed or manned. If the British gained possession of these vessels, they could could arm and crew them, and then utilize the ships to trap Hazelwood's forces in between themselves and the remainder of Lord Howe's warships further down the Delaware. The more Washington considered the possibility, the greater his alarm. He wrote the Continental Navy Board on October 25th, and again, without waiting for a reply on the 27th. In his second letter, he asked that the two ships, as well as any other vessels that could be converted to warships be scuttled to prevent their falling into the hands of the British, and asked forgiveness if he had overstepped his bounds. The Navy Board complied with Washington's request only on November 5. Further, Washington sought to get the sailors assigned to the ships sent to Hazelwood to help assuage some of his manpower problems.[44] On this point, the Navy Board demurred informing the commander that the men were needed to sink the vessels in Crosswicks Creek, and then to help with scuttling a larger vessel across it to prevent the British from raising the ships concealed there.[45]

If nothing else, the preceding, albeit minor drama testifies to the strain the commander in chief labored under at this point in the campaign. Still, it is worth noting, as Jackson does, that the dilatory approach taken by the Navy Board in implementing Washington's directive could have turned this minor annoyance into an operational catastrophe for the Americans. If the British had sent a raiding force out of Philadelphia and secured the ships, they could have caught the Pennsylvania mosquito fleet between a hammer and an anvil and reduced the river forts several weeks sooner.[46]

Returning to the state navy, the Pennsylvania Supreme Executive Council worked to alleviate at least some of Hazelwood's concerns. Sensing that lack of provisions for his crews were a contributing factor to the continuing loss of sailors through desertion, on October 27, they ordered that the commodore "be authorized and empowered to seize and take the necessary Provisions for the Fleet under his Command where it may be found in this State giving to the Owners Certificates for the same, which shall be paid for at rates hereafter to be fixed by the council."[47]

The sailors of Pennsylvania were not the only ones suffering for want of provisions. That same day, Capt. Henry Bellew of the HMS *Liverpool* wrote to Capt. Cornwallis on the *Isis* bemoaning the situation of his crew, many of whom lacked articles of clothing or bedding. Bellew then requested "a small supply of each from the Isis."[48] Cornwallis replied the same day stating, "I should have great Pleasure in complying with your request if it were in my Power; we have a Number of men in the same situation and no slops to give them."[49]

These difficulties did not deter the British from continuing their arrangements. On October 26, just before a major storm set in, a force of roughly 100 Royal Marines re-occupied Billingsport. The Marines were reinforced the following day with 200 men from the 71st Regiment amid heavy rains. The troops dispatched to Billingsport were to rebuild the redoubt there in so as to offer protection to the larger British ships of the line as they passed through the lower chevaux-de-frise.[50]

Washington, for his part, enjoyed at least some success in remedying the manpower issues in the river defenses. He managed to locate over one hundred sailors in the ranks of the Continental Army. He informed Hazelwood on October 26 that he was forwarding them to help man the fleet. Still, rain and winds slowed the movements of these troops, much as it hampered operations in the river.[51] Hazelwood offers some idea of the dire manning situation of the ships under his command in a letter to Thomas Wharton, dated October 29. In it he confided that the fleet had already lost over 250 men "thro cowardice or disaffection..." He then reassured Wharton that "the remaining few we have left we are determined to spend the last drop of our blood in defense of this pass..."[52] Posturing aside, the losses to the fleet through desertion were significant.

The true causes were likely low morale due to low or non-existent wages, lack of provisions and the overall conditions the men worked under. The men Washington forwarded provided at least some relief to the commodore. If the Americans were to hold back the British in the Delaware, relief of the garrison at Fort Mifflin every twenty-four to forty-eight hours would be imperative given the nature of the duty and the conditions under which they labored.[53]

Likewise, the previous day, the Continental commander took the opportunity, while telling Hazelwood that reinforcements should assuage the manpower crisis, to reinforce the importance of the various services working in tandem, "it is my most earnest desire that every mode may be adopted by which your force may be brought to Co-operate against the designs and approaches of the Enemy, and that a mutual Confidence and perfect understanding may take place."[54] Washington further relayed the concerns expressed to him by d'Arendt and Smith concerning a rapid descent on Fort Mifflin, "As there is a greater possibility that the reduction of the Forts might be effected by surprise than any other means, you will see the necessity of giving them every Aid by your Gondolas and Guard Boats, as may effectually prevent any mischance of this kind."[55]

The same day, Washington informed Lt. Col. Smith at Fort Mifflin of the coming reinforcement as well. Continental army commander seemed to be realizing the source of the interservice disfunction in the river defenses, as he took the opportunity to inform Smith, "You seem to have mistaken the Commodore's meaning. From his letter I understand he will always assist you whenever it is in his power." Washington continued, "He tells you that in rough Weather his Gallies and armed Boats cannot live and therefore guards you against expecting much assistance from them at such times." He then came to the crux of his appeal, "I beg you of all things, not to suffer any Jealousies between the land and sea service to take place. Consider that your mutual security depends upon acting perfectly in concert."[56] Clearly, Washington was calling on both men to work jointly and focus on the common task.

Crews would be needed for the ships, as the British stepped up their activities in preparation for a major attack on Fort Mifflin. On October 26, Capt. Cornwallis in the HMS *Isis* reported to Adm. Howe from off Billingsport, "The Detachment of Marines and 71st regiment had taken Post at Billingsport."[57] These troops were being positioned for a second attack on Fort Mercer.

Throughout this period, there was a heavy storm in the Delaware, as engineer Capt. Montresor noted in his journal entry for October 29, "The weather too bad for work."[58] The inclement weather hampered the British in moving ships into position to bombard Fort Mifflin, as well as their attempt to remove the chevaux-de-frise. In addition, it hampered the British in their construction of floating batteries to aid in the bombardment of the post.[59]

The weather interfered with Maj. Fleury's efforts at repairing the fort as well. In fact, on October 29, the rains cut the banks around the fort in several places leading to flooding which placed the entire fort under water. The rain, in effect, halted all operations for a time as the British land batteries were flooded as well, and the river was too choppy for Hazelwood's guard boats and gondolas to render any assistance to the fort.[60]

The most significant damage inflicted by the rains befell the British, as the bridge of boats they had previously constructed across the river was washed away. The loss of this passage, which was formed by boats with planking spread across their tops and thus forming something of a rough pontoon, in effect severed an important line of communication between Philadelphia and the hinterland.

Throughout the halt in operations brought on by the elements, conditions in Philadelphia worsened. On October 30, the Hessian Lt. Feilitzsch reported "There is a shortage of provisions and food which can be bought." He went on to note how "The inhabitants bring us nothing and the rations are the worst imaginable." [61]

As it grew more apparent that the British were becoming desperate for supplies, Washington tightened the logistical screws on his foes. He ordered the millstones removed from all the mills between Philadelphia and Elkton, Maryland. In addition, there were heavy patrols in the countryside. These patrols effectively sealed off the city from American farmers, either those loyal to the Crown in their political leanings, or those simply tempted by British specie. The British did have a route for transport of some supply into the beleaguered city, over land and under heavy escort, first from Elkton, and then, as the British fleet under Lord Howe made its way into the Delaware Bay, from Newcastle. This route resulted in only a trickle of material getting through.

The British tried to bring supplies via the river exploiting the passage between Tinicum and Billings Islands as well. However, the Americans cut up the road from this landing. They had an overland route as well that had supplies offloaded in Chester, and then transported overland and into the city via the floating bridge in the Schuylkill, a distance of roughly fifteen miles.[62] Again, while the British were able to bring a fair number of supplies into the city through the various overland routes, it was both labor intensive and provided nowhere near enough consumables to meet the needs of the city.[63]

Many in Washington's army were aware of the British predicament. One of Washington's more gifted partisans, Capt. Henry "Lighthorse Harry" Lee, then patrolling along the banks of the Schuylkill River observed that the British had men posted on Carpenters Island, by his count less than five hundred and that these troops kept open a constant flow of provisions brought by water from the fleet off Chester.[64] This operation was overseen by Capt. Henry Duncan of the HMS *Eagle*. These provisions were then brought to the island from whence they were taken by the lower ferry into the city. He further noted an illicit commerce in beef between the people in the countryside taking place south of Chester at a location known as Grubs Ferry. The captain had already dispatched some dragoons to interdict this commerce.[65] According to at least one historian of the campaign, the amount of supplies reaching Philadelphia, especially from the British fleet, while quite substantial, still fell far below the needs of the garrison as well as the civilian populace.[66]

On November 1, Washington once again intervened in the ongoing dispute between Smith and Hazelwood. After informing Varnum of Smith and d'Arendt's complaints against the Pennsylvania Commodore's inattention to the defense of Fort Mifflin, he confided "I do not know whether with just Grounds." Washington then ordered that Varnum to "do all in your power to reconcile any differences that may have arisen, not by taking notice of them in a direct manner, but by recommending unanimity and demonstrating the manifest advantages of it."[67] He closed with the hope that Hazelwood would be more active in his defense of the fort once he received the reinforcements Washington forwarded to him.[68]

For their part, the British vessels in the Delaware spent much of the day removing an anchor from the *Merlin* in order to be able to salvage some of her guns.[69] They continued work in trying to shift the chevaux de frise as well.

As the reality of a major push by the British for control of the Delaware, Washington seemed to give in somewhat to his propensity to micro-manage.[70] On November 2, he wrote a long missive to Cmdre. Hazelwood detailing his ideas on the role of the Pennsylvania Navy in the coming contest. This communique warrants quoting at length as it reveals both the strengths and weaknesses of Washington's understanding of the contest for control of the river:

Upon maturely considering the nature of the Fortress on Mud Island incomplete in such works as would secure it against Storm, and investigating what mode of defence is best adapted to its deficiency in this respect - it appears absolutely necessary to keep the Enemy at bay as much as possible and confine them to distant combat--this can only be effected by the co-operation of the Fleet under your command or such part of it as may appear proper to you to be detached for the purpose - Nothing but the Fire of your Vessels and Galleys can prevent the Enemys making a descent upon the Island, if they are determined to effect it by such a Sacrifice as the importance of the object to hem certainly deserves - I would advise therefore in case of the Enemys attempting to throw a number of men over in boats, not to suffer the attention of the Fleet to be intirely call'd by any concerted attempt which may be made on the Chevaux de fries at the same time - but to order a sufficient number of Galleys to meet their boats and keep up as directed fire, or board them as Circumstances may require - in a word every measure should be taken which your Skill in naval maneuvers can dictate to prevent them from getting footing on the Island, a fire of Red-hot balls thrown with Judgement from a few Vessels, and the solidity of the work itself will be sufficient Security in the mean-time to the Chevaux de fries—there will be but one way left them which is to attempt a Landing by night how necessary the Guardianship of the Galleys will be in such case, must be obvious - If a sudden Assault from superior numbers, taking the advantage of weak parts, would be dreadful by day, when something of the Enemys designs is to be discover'd - how fatal might it be in the confusion of darkness when the Guns of the fort could not be brought to bear.[71]

The commander in chief continued,

Galleys stationed between the Fort and province Island at night are the only Security which the garrison could have in such case against a sudden de-

scent from the Enemy, cover'd perhaps by false Attacks and Demonstrations from the Shipping. [72]

It would seem that this long missive on the part of Washington might betray a lack of faith in the Pennsylvania Navy commander. However, as will be discussed below, it constituted more of a trait of the Continental commander's personality when he could not be in the thick of the fighting himself. Ironically, Washington closed his letter to Hazelwood with the reassurance "You're the best Judge of the most proper situation for the Galleys." Still, he could not resist offering one further bit of unrequested advice, "however if there is no cogent Reason for keeping the whole of them on the Jersey Side, it appears to me that stationing them or part of them where they will be within distance for giving immediate support to the Garrison on Mud Island would be turning their services to the best account - "[73]

The same day Washington detailed his thoughts to Hazelwood, the Continental Navy Board of the Middle Department acted belatedly on a previous nagging concern of the army commander. They ordered Capt. John Barry to scuttle the frigate *Effingham*, then above Philadelphia, to prevent its being taken by the British.[74]

Finally, on the 2nd, Brig. Gen. James Mitchell Varnum established his headquarters at Woodbury, New Jersey. Varnum had left the main Continental encampment at Whitpain on October 28, bringing with him the Fourth and Eighth Connecticut Regiments. The other two regiments in his brigade, the First and Second Rhode Island were already operating in the state. Washington entrusted Varnum with overall command of the military operations in New Jersey. The brigadier quickly made a survey of his new area of operations and determined on setting up a battery on the east side of Mantua Creek, about a mile north of Billingsport.[75] His survey further convinced Varnum that the British would not take Fort Mifflin by storm, even if they battered down the palisades. He therefore placed the onus for the defense of the post on Hazelwood's galleys. Interestingly, he fell into the same misunderstanding of the river defenses as had du Coudray previously, in that he perceived Billingsport as the key fortification. He seemingly did not appreciate the fatal flaws inherent in the works as noted above.[76]

The following day, the 3rd, Washington received intelligence from Pennsylvania Brig. Gen. James Potter that the British were constructing two floating batteries, and that with these, the British, once in possession of Carpenters Island would make Fort Mifflin untenable, even with the assistance of the galleys.[77] He was further informed by Lt. Col. Samuel Smith at Fort Mifflin that the British had secured the canon for the floating batteries from "the 64 Gun Ship," referring to the *Augusta*. He believed that the British would begin their bombardment with the floating battery the following day, unless they were driven from Billingsport, a move he suggested to Brig. Gen. James Varnum.[78]

Potter's suspicions were confirmed by Maj. Fleury in his Journal for November 3, "they [the British] are raising a battery of heavy Cannon upon the hulk which is aground on the Sand bank, the Galleys do not disturb them in their work..." He further commented that if the British were allowed to complete the emplacement it would "do great injury to our fort." He believed that thirteen of the galleys and two floating batteries could drive the British from the new emplacement if they were so inclined.[79] The French engineer either did not know or did not pay heed to Hazelwood's belief that the guns on his galleys were useless against fixe positions on land. The battery in question was being raised near the dike on Carpenter's Island and was to contain six twenty-four pounders, the guns being taken from Lord Howe's flagship, the Eagle.[80]

Not only were the British constructing new batteries, the flow of supplies past Fort Mifflin generated a growing concern. Fleury noted in his journal that night that "a considerable number of the Enemy boats, pass'd and repass'd in the course of the night, near the shore of Province Island. - it appears that this Communication between their Fleet and Philadelphia is established." [81] Meanwhile Hazelwood's ships continued to harass the British efforts below the fort, the Journal of the HMS *Pearl* for November 3 reported that at 5 PM the galleys came down and fired several shots, which the British vessels then returned.[82] Still, the communication between the fleet and Philadelphia quickly became a major source of anxiety for Washington. The entire reason for dedicating scant Continental resources to the forts and the Pennsylvania Navy was to prevent supplies from getting through to the city and make it untenable for the British occupiers. If the Crown forces had found a hole in the cordon, then the whole campaign was a failure. This reverse, combined with his recent battlefield defeats at Trenton and Germantown could lead to significant political repercussions.

Washington passed along this information concerning the British communications with the city in a letter of November 4 to Cmdre. Hazelwood.[83] Once again, the general could not resist specific direction. After stating, " I will not undertake to point out to you the mode of doing this," he continued, "but in my opinion the most probable is, to keep small Boats rowing guard between the south end of Mud Island and the Pennsylvania [sic] shore, and a Galley or two under the north end of Mud Island, when the weather will permit."[84] If they sighted any enemy row boats, they were to fire a signal and alert the other ships and the fort. Washington believed the British would refrain from firing in the dark for fear of hitting their own vessels.[85] Once again, the ships of Hazelwood's command were being asked to undertake an additional duty. Not only were they being asked to defend the fort and interdict the movements of the warships of Admiral Howe's fleet during the day, but they were also to patrol at night.

Concerning Hazelwood, Capt. John Montresor recorded in his *Journal* that as shot from of the British medium twelve pounders hit the former's flag ship, the Pennsylvania vessel *Montgomery*.[86] Likewise, the British ships below Fort Mifflin continued to work on moving the chevaux de frise, as recorded in the Journal of the HMS *Liverpool*. While they were able to move one of the obstructions, this did not widen the passage any further.[87]

Added to these developments, the likelihood of a renewed assault on Fort Mifflin grew more pronounced. The bold partisan Henry Lee, at this time very active along the banks of the Delaware and Schuylkill rivers, wrote Washington on the 3rd, "It is a certainty from the intelligence received from various characters that the enemy design shortly to make a push on fort Mifflin." Lee continued, adding his own assessment of the situation "Their only possible mode, by which they can promise themselves success is their floating batteries." Beyond merely identifying the problem, Lee further added a potential solution, "In this they may be totally blasted if we take possession of Carpenters Island." He suggested then placing a strong battery on the island. However, the cavalry commander did not provide specifics on how this could be done.[88]

Finally, the ongoing controversy between Smith and Hazelwood continued to draw in the attention of Washington and now Varnum as well. Once established at his headquarters in Woodbury, the latter could gain a more direct perspective on the relationship between the two commanders. He passed his own impressions on to Washington in a letter dated November 3 "...The Want of Confidence between the commodore and Col. Smith is very great." He further reassured his superior "I shall do every Thing in my Power to cause that mutual Support between the Land and Water Forces, which appears very essential for the Security of Fort Mifflin..."[89]

Clearly, the general understood the importance of joint cooperation if the Americans were to keep the river closed to British shipping.

As the aforementioned actions were taking place along the Delaware River, the Continental Congress, meeting in the courthouse in York, Pennsylvania on November 4, awarded Hazelwood a silver sword for his services in the sinking of the *Augusta* and *Merlin*. They voted similar swords for Col. Christopher Greene and Lt. Col. Samuel Smith as well. According to one contemporary, this touched off an additional controversy between Smith and Hazelwood, as Smith supposedly refused to accept the sword if one were given to the Pennsylvania navy commander. There exists, however, no evidence to support such a dispute arising.[90]

In addition, the Marine Committee responded to Washington's call on the Continental Navy to scuttle the frigates hidden north of Philadelphia in the Delaware to prevent them from falling into British hands. Those on the scene proposed instead that the vessels be lightened as much as possible and then dragged on shore and a battery erected to defend them and prevent the British from taking them. As an additional measure, they proposed to load the ships with combustibles in order to destroy them if they should be in danger of capture. Failing the previous measure, a number of smaller vessels should be sunk in whatever creek the ships were hidden to block off the body and prevent the ships' removal. The body referred the matter back to Washington.[91]

On that same day, the Americans began to fire on the British ships from the new battery situated near Manto Creek. Capt. James Lee of the Second Continental Artillery commanded the battery, which was composed of one eighteen and one twelve-pounder gun. The former only joined in the action the next day as it upset on its way to the battery.[92] The Lieutenant's Journal for the HMS *Isis*, stationed off Billingsport, noted, "AM the Rebels open'd up a Two Gun Battery on us...engaged them for some time with the *Pearl* and Galley [*Cornwallis*] and then drop's down."[93] The galleys of the Pennsylvania Navy sortied to attack the British shipping as well. Hazelwood's ships were driven back by the heavier guns of the Royal Navy vessels in the vicinity.[94] As Francis Downman observed, "This afternoon about 5 o'clock all the rebel galleys drew up in formation and went down and began a very heavy fire at out two uppermost men-of-war. They continued near and hour firing, but at such a distance that they did little or no execution."[95] While Downman asserted that this action failed to do any damage, accounts from the ships in the river contradict his report. The Lieutenant's Journal of the

Isis observed that Hazelwood's galleys were "draw'd up in a Line" when they began their advance. It further noted that "our Hull and rigging much damaged."[96] The HMS *Pearl*, operating alongside the *Isis* sustained damage to her rigging as well.[97] An anonymous officer serving at Fort Mercer writing a letter to Col. Hugh Hughes, related how the British had boats out working to get the Isis "plugging her during the whole time..." It seems more likely that they were working to refloat the ship off the sandbar on which it had become stuck. The author went on to describe how while making these efforts, two of the ships' boats, "happened to fall in line of a shot which cut one in two, left the other Floating, which drifted some distance..." before being recovered.[98] Interestingly, the British had not wanted to engage in the long-range cannon duel with the gallies, rather they sought to lure them in to draw the vessels closer where their main guns could do more damage.[99] The efforts of the Americans made it clear that reducing Fort Mifflin would be no easy task.

The fighting ended at sunset. The precise number of galleys that took part in the attack is difficult to determine. The Master's Journal of the HMS *Roebuck* places it at five, while the *Pearl*, which was directly engaged in the fighting places it at twelve.[100] It is most likely that the number of galleys which took part in the attack that day lies somewhere between the two figures. Given the fact that the British vessels were under fire both from the Pennsylvania navy ships and the battery at Manto Creek as well as Fort Mifflin intermittently, something of a fog of war enveloped the river, making the determination of actual number difficult, especially given the ranges and the small size of the galleys. Twelve seems too high a number given the continuing manpower shortages, while five seems fairly small to launch such a sustained attack and employ a linear formation visible at some distance. Francis Downman noted that the American galleys came down river in two divisions, which would support the notion of more than four galleys. Further, he recorded that "though the smoke had a great effect their fire was incessant."[101] Likewise, Brigadier Gen. Varnum in his report to Washington, which will be discussed in greater detail below, noted only that Hazelwood moved downriver with "a great naval Force," without giving specific numbers.[102] The smoke produced not only by the guns of the galleys, but by the American battery, as well as the return fire from the British warships would serve to obscure the battle area to an extent and make the exact count of the small ships difficult, especially at a distance.

In the evening the *Pearl* dispatched one of her boats upriver to attempt to gain some intelligence as to rebel intentions. As Capt. Linzee reported to Capt. Cornwallis, his other motive was to determine whether it was safe to send the nightly squadron of provision boats up past Fort Mifflin to Philadelphia. The officer commanding the scout boat informed that the rebels were "perfectly quiet," thus the supply mission could continue as planned.[103]

Another significant event occurred along the river on November 5. Gen. Howe visited the works on Province and Carpenter's Islands, in order to oversee the efforts at reducing Fort Mifflin. The general had already expressed displeasure with the efforts of the troops along the banks of the Delaware on his previous visit the preceding month. The passage of time and lack of progress did nothing to improve his sentiments. At the same time, Howe witnessed the most violent assault to date on Fort Mifflin.[104] Samuel Stelle Smith notes, without naming a source, that on this day Capt. Montresor of the Royal Engineers submitted a new plan for reducing Fort Mifflin. The plan called for a softening up of the fort for some three or four days beginning on November 9. Once the fort's defenses were deemed sufficiently reduced, it would be taken by storm.[105] Montresor, while he noted Howe's visit in his journal, made no mention of a new plan for the reduction of the fort. He did note, "The rebels opened a Battery of two Guns near Manto Creek, against our shipping which was retuned by them. Rebel Gallies at the same time went down and attacked the Fleet and were beat back."[106] He added that "The Battery on the Front dam being found too miry this night, the working party continued on the work of the night before last."[107] Regardless of where Smith came by his information, or even whether a formal plan was submitted by anyone on the British side, it summarizes what the British did over the following days.

On November 6, Varnum composed a long letter in which he informed Washington of the preceding day's events. He reported the construction temporary battery on the north side of Manto Creek as well as is role in the action against the British shipping in the river. Varnum credited the cannonade with driving the *Roebuck* and another British frigate from their stations. In actuality, the British vessels engaged were the *Isis*, *Pearl* and the galley *Cornwallis*.[108] Likewise, he thought their fire drove the *Somerset* [actually the *Isis*] down river until it beached and was forced to take their fire. The shore battery was then joined by four of Hazelwood's galleys, which opened up at a distance of two miles. As a result, the galleys expended a great deal of ammunition, but to little purpose. The galleys were driven off when the *Somerset* and *Roebuck* [actually *Isis* and *Pearl*] opened fire on them with their bow guns. The incoming tide then refloated the *Isis*, but the absence of any wind prevented the ship from moving out of range and it continued to endure a pounding from the two-gun battery. Hazelwood committed additional ships, which added their firepower to the attack on the British vessel. Having expended their ammunition, the galleys returned back upriver. In reporting the incident to Washington, Varnum insisted that if Hazelwood directed his galleys to fire at closer range, they would have sunk the *Isis*.[109] His last comment provided further evidence of Varnum's concern over the inability of the Pennsylvania Navy vessels to provide adequate support for the land batteries. Downman as well observed that the fire was "at such a distance that they did little or no execution."[110]

By the same token, it should be borne in mind that due to the recent reinforcements, many of the crews of Hazelwood's galleys were new and therefore inexperienced in handling their ships. They were very likely nervous as well, considering they were taking their small craft up against British men-of-war bristling with heavy guns. Given the context, it should come as no surprise that the ships began firing at extreme range. It seems plausible that they did so, at least in part, to steady the crewmen's nerves, much as the crews had done in their first encounters with the British firgates in 1776.

In addition to the previous day's fighting, the issue of cooperation with the garrison at Fort Mifflin arose once again in Varnum's report to Washington,

> *Col. Smith is continually complaining of the Remisness of the Fleet. I have conversed freely with the Commodore upon the Subject of Defence which he ought to afford. He has pointed out to me the Places where he has ordered his Guard Boats and some of his Gallies stationed by Night. His Plan, it spiritedly executed, would sufficiently Aid Fort Mifflin, and Prevent the Enemy from making a Lodgement [sic] in its rear. The Commodore says he cannot prevent the Enemies Boats from passing up and down the River as they are covered by their Batteries upon Province Island [Carpenters Island] and at the Mouth of the Schuylkill. In short, the Commodore appears to be a very good kind of Man, but his extreme good Nature gives too great a license to those under his Command, who would obey only from Severity, if any such he has,*

to their [shame?] their Duty.[111]

From the preceding, Varnum appeared to be gaining a perspective on the dysfunctional relationship existing between the two commanders, and at the same time pointing out to his superior where each was at fault. His portrayal of Hazelwood is particularly interesting, a commander who was essentially too compassionate towards his subordinates to push them to take risks deemed necessary to hold back the adversary. Varnum continued, declaring "I shall religious avoid any personal Disputes myself, where I cannot be of Service by them, to the public; I shall continue however, to create, if possible, greater Harmony between the Fleet and Garrisons."[112]

On the same day Varnum made his report to Washington, Adm. Howe wrote to Capt. Cornwallis of the *Isis*, impressing his subordinate with the importance of keeping open the line of communication between the fleet and Philadelphia.[113]

Both sides spent the following day in preparations. On the British side, Adm. Howe passed along instructions to Capt. Cornwallis. In these, he notified that captain that the *Somerset* was moving into position to begin the planned bombardment of Fort Mifflin the following day, and to furnish Capt. Ourrey with all the information he would need to complete his assigned task.[114]

Meanwhile, at Woodberry, Varnum passed additional information on to Washington concerning reported British strength at Billingsport, and what his informants gleaned for him concerning the British plans for the coming assault on Fort Mifflin. He assured his superior that he would forward reinforcements into the fort, though he believed it sufficiently manned at the moment. Further, he declared that "Fourteen Gun Boats will lay in the Passage,-- They[sic] Floating Batteries, and Xebecks, to guard the Chievaux de Frize, and oppose the Shipping, should they attempt to advance..." Not only would the vessels of the Hazelwood's command take part in the defense, but "the continental Vessells under Capt Robinson's Command will lay at the Mouth of the Schuylkill and at the mouth of Timber Creek." The latter consisted of the brig *Andrew Doria* and the sloop *Fly*.[115]

Capt. Isaiah Robinson would play a significant role in the latter stages of the fighting for control of the Delaware. He was born in Philadelphia and was a member of the city's Ship Master's Association. Robinson was an early supporter of the revolution and joined the Continental Navy almost at its inception. He took part in several successful cruises with smaller vessels including the 10-gun sloop of war *Sachem*, with which he captured a six-gun British privateer off the Virginia Capes. In recognition of his services, he was given command of the brig *Andrew Doria*, then building.[116]

It is fairly evident from the sources that the British intentions were well known within the American camp. Several sources were responsible for providing this information. As noted previously, Washington enjoyed a remarkable network of spies scattered throughout the area, and these provided him with an abundance of information on British movements and, at times, even intentions. Over time, Washington's ability to make sense out of the information he received from various sources and pass along usable intelligence to his field officers improved as well. For instance, writing to Gen. Varnum on November 7 from his headquarters as Whitemarsh, Washington informed his subordinate, "From various accounts I am convinced that the enemy are upon the point of making a grand effort upon Fort Mifflin."[117] Based on this idea, Washington directed Varnum, "No time is therefore to be lost in making that Garrison as respectable as your numbers will admit," explaining, "for should the attack commence before they are reinforced, it may probably be out of you power to throw them in."[118]

Interestingly, Washington drew an important distinction as to which troops should be brought into the forts,

> *I think you had better, for the present, draw all the Continental Troops into or near Forts Mercer and Mifflin, and let what Militia are collected, lay without; for I am of opinion that they will rather dismay than assist the Continental troops if shut up in the forts.*[119]

Washington went on to provide Varnum with intelligence concerning three floating batteries and several fire rafts that the British were planning to send down from Philadelphia to attack the fleet while they made their attempt on Fort Mifflin. He instructed Varnum to pass this information on to Cmdre. Hazelwood. Finally, he cautioned the general, "As Fort Mercer cannot be attacked without considerable previous notice, I would have you spare as many men to Fort Mifflin as you possibly can, for if accounts are to be depended upon, that is undoubtedly the post the Enemy have their designs upon."[120]

By now, Washington understood the roles of the respective

forts in the network of river defenses. It is worth noting that while Washington was giving these orders to Varnum, he was simultaneously considering how to make the best use of a British attempt on Fort Mifflin, to the extent that he called a council of war on November 8 to consider the options. One of the possibilities discussed involved taking advantage of the British focus on the river forts to launch an attack on Philadelphia with the object of driving Howe and his troops from the city. The council universally rejected this option.[121] Washington then asked whether those present felt that they could safely send further reinforcements to the fort without endangering the safety of the army. On this point, the members of the council held mixed opinions, however, Washington did continue to send some reinforcements. While the options were being weighed by Washington and his senior staff, the British continued to prepare their assault on the fort.

While Washington and his staff debated the army's options, Henry Lee transmitted additional intelligence to Washington, that the British launched one of their floating batteries two days' past, and that the other was nearing completion. The partisan outlined the British method of transporting supplies overland, as well as his thoughts on how to interdict this activity.[122]

For their part, the British squadron warped over the lower chevaux de frise off of Billingsport on the same day. The ships were moving into position in order to be prepared for the grand assault on Fort Mifflin scheduled to begin two days later. These ships remained in the lower Delaware, out of range of the two-gun battery north of Manto Creek.[123] Preparations continued on land as well, several captains and a working party of 160 men labored to get a British battery of 24-pounders in readiness "for the day of opening."[124] Francis Downman wrote worriedly that morning, "I went down to the island. The 24-prs. not yet ready. The rebels seem very busy in their fort."[125] During this time, the British working parties suffered as well. Flooding and rain made quagmires of the dikes and high ground. Still, they did at least have some comfort from the elements in their uniforms, something the defenders of Fort Mifflin could only dream of possessing.[126]

By November 9, both sides felt they had made all the preparations possible.[127] On that day, Col. Smith wrote Washington to inform him that he believed the British were preparing a bombardment to be followed up by storming the post.[128] Likewise, the HMS *Somerset* made her way over the upper chevaux de frise and could add the weight of her broadsides to the coming bombardment.[129]

Both sides seemed prepared for what they believed would be the climactic assault on the river defenses. Some notion of this back and forth is given in the following account from the journal of Maj. Fleury,

> *9th [November] at night. The Enemy appearing ready to open their batteries, we raised the bank which covers our Palisades on the west Front, against which the whole Fire of the enemy is directed, and which will be the point of attack in case of their storming the Fort.*[130]

Writing from Fort Mifflin on November 9, Col. Smith updated Washington on British activities in the surrounding area,

> *The enemy since I wrote you last have been fortifying their Island for an advanced post and for a pass to the City, they have strengthened the first work which they made on the height with Pickquets and Abbatees, and yesterday threw up a breast work or Redoubt, a quarter of a mile below that, I imagine to defend some narrow part of the Creek where you might pass to repossess the Island.*[131]

As Washington labored to place the river defenders in the best possible state of readiness for what all concerned believed to be the decisive assault, he was once again torn away by a subsidiary matter. The controversy over the fate of the Continental ships stranded further up the Delaware once again reared its head. The Continental Navy Board of the Middle Department wrote Washington on November 8, asking him for troops to man planned defenses to be erected at the mouth of the creek harboring the vessels. Washington responded that he did not possess enough troops to send the requested detachment. He took the issue a step further, and wrote Henry Laurens, the president of the Continental Congress, laying the situation before him. [132]

Varnum reported to the commander in chief as well on the 9th. In his letter he mentioned that he had been to Fort Mifflin that day. He did not include any details concerning the state of the post. He did inform his commander that the British appeared ready to open a new battery, he believed of eighteen or twenty-four pounder guns either that night or the following morning. He further informed Washington that two more larger vessels, "double deckers" as he referred to them, had crossed over the chevaux de frise. The one was the *Somerset*, though the identity of the other remains a mystery. These ships stayed out of range of the new battery Varnum had recently ordered erected at the Mantua Creek.

The brigadier further reported that there appeared to be significant activity on land as well by the mouth of the Schuylkill, with the movements of wagons and fascines. Likewise, one of the British floating batteries that were under construction in the Schuylkill was launched the preceding Thursday and sunk with its guns.

CHAPTER NOTES

[1] The most recent work n the siege of Havana is Elena A. Schneider, *The Occupation of Havana: War, Trade, and Slavery in the Atlantic World*. (Chapel Hill: UNC Press, 2018). More detailed on the technical aspects is David Syrett "The British Landing at Havana: An Example of an Eighteenth-Century Combined Operation." in *The Mariner's Mirror*. 55(1969):325-32. As noted in the title, the author uses the term combined in the manner in which it was understood at the time. In today's military lexicon, it would be considered a joint operation.

[2] On the methodology of British amphibious operations, see David Syrett, "The Methodology of British Amphibious Operations during the Seven Years' War" in *The Mariner's Mirror*. 58, (1972): 269-280.

[3] Samuel Cleaveland (ca. 1727 – 1794) was a British artillery officer. He took command of the First Royal Artillery Company in India in 1748 and continued serving with that unit until 1762. Promoted to major for his part in capture of Havana in that year, he transferred to the 4th Battalion Royal Artillery. Following the end of the Seven Years' War, he served intermittently in North America until his final return to England at the end of the 1777 campaign. In 1781, Cleaveland commanded the 3rd Artillery Battalion and eventually rose to the rank of lieutenant general.

[4] Colonel Baron d'Arendt to George Washington, Fort Mifflin, October 24, 1777, quoted in *NDAR*, p. 263.

[5] Ibid.

[6] Ibid.

[7] Jackson, *Pennsylvania Navy*, p. 230.

[8] John Peebles, *John Peebles American War*, p. 145.

[9] Captain William Cornwallis to Vice Admiral Viscount Richard Howe, October 25, 1777, on board HMS *Isis*, quoted in quoted in *NDAR*, vol. 10, p. 286.

[10] Ibid.

[11] Bradford to Wharton, October 26, 1777, quoted in Ibid.

[12] Jackson, *Pennsylvania Navy*, pp. 202-4.

[13] Lieutenant's Journal of the HMS *Isis*, Captain William Cornwallis, October 25, 1777, quoted in Ibid.

[14] Journal of the HMS *Camilla*, Captain Charles Phipps, October 25, 1777, quoted in Ibid.

[15] Montressor, *Journal*, p. 53

[16] Samuel S. Smith, *Fight for the Delaware*, p. 28

[17] George Washington to Brigadier General David Forman, October 28, 1777, quoted in *Washington, Rev. War*, vol. 12, p. 37.

[18] Ibid, p. 38.

[19] Peebles *American War*, p. 145.

[20] Extract of a Letter from Fort Mifflin, October 24, 1777 quoted in *NDAR*, vol. 10, p. 264.

[21] From Fort Mifflin, Fleury to Hamilton, October 28, 1777 quoted in *NDAR*, vol.7, p. 334

[22] Stryker, *Forts*, p. 28.

[23] Writing from his headquarters in Whitpain Township, George Washington to Brigadier General James Varnum, October 28, 1777 in *Washington, Rev War, vol. 12*, p. 44.

[24] Ibid.

[25] Ibid.

[26] Fort Washington fell on November 16, 1776.

[27] John F. Reed, *Campaign to Valley Forge, July 1, 1777-December 19, 1777* (Philadelphia: University of Pennsylvania Press, 1965), p. 283.

[28] Stryker, *Forts, p.* 28.

[29] Stryker, *Forts*, pp. 28-29.

[30]   Isidor Paul Strittmatter, *The Importance of the Campaign in the Delaware...(*Philadelphia: The Medical Club of Philadelphia, 1932), p. 11.

[31] Henry Lee, *The Revolutionary Memoirs of General Henry Lee.* Robert E. Lee ed. (New York: De Capo Press, 1998 reprint of 1812 original), p. 102.

[32] Smith to Washington from Fort Mifflin, October 30, 1777 quoted in *Washington, Rev. War*, vol. 12, p. 64.

[33] Browne, "Fort Mercer and Fort Mifflin," p. 97.

[34] Jackson, *The Pennsylvania Navy, p.* 227.

[35] Wolf pits were conical holes dug in the ground with stake protruding upward. They were then covered and served as traps for attacking infantry. See Jackson, *Pennsylvania Navy*, p. 211.

[36] Ibid, p. 227.

[37] Ibid.

[38] Ibid, p. 201.

[39] Ibid.

[40] Colone Smith to George Washington, Fort Mifflin, October 26, 1777, quoted in *NDAR*, vol. 10, p. 302.

[41] Ibid.

[42] Commodore John Hazelwood to George Washington, Chatham Galley, October 26, 1777, quoted in *NDAR*, vol. 10, p. 307.

[43] Commodore John Hazelwood to George Washington, October 26, 1777, quoted in *Washington, Rev. War*, vol. 12, pp. 18-19.

[44] Jackson, *Pennsylvania Navy*, pp. 206-7.

[45] Ibid, p. 208.

[46] Ibid, pp. 207-8.

[47] Minutes of the Pennsylvania Supreme Executive Council, October 27, 1777, quoted in *NDAR*, vol. 10, p. 320.

[48] Captain Henry Bellew to Captain William Cornwallis, aboard the HMS *Liverpool* of Billingsport, October 27, 1777, quoted in *NDAR*, vol. 10, p. 323.

[49] Cornwallis to Bellew, HMS *Isis* off Billingport, October 27, 1777, quoted in Ibid, pp. 323-4.

[50] Smith, *Fight for the Delaware*, p. 27.

[51] Jackson, *Pennsylvania Navy*, p. 209. The men were taken from the regiments of Muhlenberg, Weedon, Woodford, Scott, Smallwood and McDougal.

[52] Hazelwood to Wharton, Chatham Galley, October 29, 1777, quoted in *NDAR*, vol. p. 10,

[53] Jackson, *Pennsylvania Navy*, p. 216.

[54] Washington to Hazelwood, Whitpain, PA, October 28, 1777, quoted in Ibid, p. 333.

[55] Ibid.

[56] The first phrase relating to Hazelwood's response to a request for aid from d'Arendt and Smith, which they had forwarded to Washington, see above. Washington to Lt. Col. Smith, quoted in Ibid, p. 334.

[57] Captain to Cornwallis to Admiral Howe, HMS *Isis* of Billingsport, October 26, 1777, quoted in Ibid, p. 306.

[58] Montresor, *Journal*, October 29, 1777, p. 471.

[59] Ibid.

[60] Jackson, *Pennsylvania Navy*, pp. 212-13.

[61] Feilitzsch, *Diary*, October 30, 1777 quoted in Burgoyne, trans., *Diaries of Two Ansbach Jaegers*, p. 24.

[62] Anonymous, Letter from Continental Army Camp 13 Miles from Philadelphia, October 29, 1777, quoted in *NDAR*, vol. 10, p. 342.

[63] Smith, *Fight for the Delaware*, p. 27.

[64] Ibid.

[65] Captain Henry Lee to Washington, October 31, 1777 Chester, PA, quoted in *NDAR*, vol, 10, p. 364.

[66] Smith, *Fight for the Delaware*, p. 27.

[67] Washington to James Mitchel Varnum, Whitpain, PA, November 1, 1777, quoted in *NDAR*, vol. 10, p. 369.

[68] Ibid.

[69] See captain Linzee to Cornwallis and Cornwallis to Linzee, Delaware River, November 1, 1777, quoted in Ibid, p. 370.

[70] Washington's proclivity to focus on minutiae at times of great stress is documented in *Edward G. Lengel General Washington: A Military Life.* (New York: random House, 2005), pp. 273-4 Robert Middlekauff, *Washington's Revolution: The Making of America's First Leader* (New York: Alfred Knopf, 2015), pp. 5-6. This topic will receive further attention in the section discussing the Conway Cabal below.

[71] Washington to Hazelwood, Whitpain, PA, November 2, 1777, quoted in Ibid, pp. 377-78.

[72] Ibid.

[73] Ibid.

[74] Continental Navy Board of the Middle Department to John Barry, Borden Town, November 2, 1777, quoted in Ibid, vol. 10, p. 377.

[75] Smith, *Fight for the Delaware*, p. 27.

[76] Jackson, *Pennsylvania Navy*, pp. 216-7.

[77] Brigadier General James Potter to George Washington, n. l. November 3, 1777, quoted in NDAR, vol. 10, p. 384.

[78] Lieutenant Colonel Samuel Smith to George Washington, Fort Mifflin, November 3, 1777, quoted in Ibid, p. 385.

[79] Fleury, *Journal*, Fort Mifflin, November 3, 1777, quoted in Ibid, p. 385

[80] Jackson, *Pennsylvania Navy*, p. 222.

[81] Fleury, *Journal*, Fort Mifflin, November 3, 1777, quoted in NDAR, vol. 10, p. 385.

[82] Journal of the HMS Pearl, Captain John Linzee, Billingsport, November 3, 1777, quoted in Ibid, p. 386.

[83] Washington received a report on this traffic in a letter from Lieutenant Colonel Samuel Smith at Fort Mifflin dated the same day, see Colonel Samuel Smith to George Washington, Fort Mifflin, November 4, 1777, quoted in Ibid, pp. 396-7.

[84] George Washington to Commodore John Hazelwood, Whitemarsh, PA, November 4, 1777, quoted in Ibid, vol. 10, p. 394.

[85] Ibid, pp. 394-5.

[86] Montresor, *Journal*, p. 173.

[87] Journal of the HMS Liverpool, Captain Henry Bellew, in the Delaware River, November 4, 1777, quoted in NDAR, vol. 10, p. 396.

[88] Henry Lee to George Washington, Near Grubb's Landing, Delaware, November 3, 1777, quoted in Ibid, p. 388. On Henry Lee, see Michael Cecere, *Wedded to my Sword: The Revolutionary War Service of Light Horse Harry Lee.* (Westminster, MD: Heritage Books, 2012) and Charles Royster, *Light Horse Harry Lee and the Legacy of the American Revolution.* (Baton Rouge: Louisiana State University

Press), 1981.

[89] Brigadier James Mitchell Varnum to George Washington, Woodbury, New Jersey, November 3, 1777, quoted in Ibid.

[90] Jackson, *Pennsylvania Navy*, p. 218.

[91] Journal of the Continental Congress, November 4, 1777, quoted in *JCC*, vol 9, pp. 862-4.

[92] Jackson, *Pennsylvania Navy*, p. 216.

[93] Lieutenant's Journal of the HMS *Isis*, Captain William Cornwallis, anchored off Billingsport, November 5, 1777, quoted in *NDAR*, vol. 10, p. 405.

[94] Montressor, *Journal*, p. 56.

[95] Downman, *Journal*, p. 49.

[96] Lieutenant's Journal of the HMS *Isis*, November 5, 1777, quoted in *NDAR*, vol. 10, p. 405.

[97] Journal of the HMS Pearl, Captain John Linzee, off Billingsport, November 5, 1777, quoted in Ibid.

[98] An Officer at Fort Mercer to Colonel Hugh Hughes, Fort Mercer, Red Bank, November 6, 1777, quoted in Ibid, p. 421.

[99] Captain William Cornwallis to Viscount Howe, *Isis* off Billingsport, November 6, 1777, quoted in Ibid, p. 421.

[100] See Master's Journal HMS *Roebuck* and Journal of HMS *Pearl* respectively quoted in Ibid, pp. 405-6.

[101] Downman, *Journal*, p. 49.

[102] Varnum to Washington, Woodbury, N.J., November 6, 1777, quoted in *Papers of George Washington*. Vol. 12, p. 146.

[103] Captain John Linzee to Captain William Cornwallis, *Pearl*, off Billingsport, November 5, 1777, quoted in *NDAR*, vol. 10, p. 407.

[104] Smith, *Fight of the Delaware*, p. 28.

[105] Ibid.

[106] Montresor, *Journal*, November 5, 1777, p. 473.

[107] Ibid.

[108] Jackson, *Pennsylvania Navy*, p. 216.

[109] Varnum to Washington, Woodbury, N.J., November 6, 1777, quoted in *Washington, Rev. War*. vol. 12, p. 146.

[110] Downman, *Journal*, p. 49.

[111] Varnum to Washington, Woodbury, N.J., November 6, 1777, quoted in *Washington, Rev. War*. Vol. 12, p. 146.

[112] Ibid.

[113] Admiral Howe to Captain Cornwallis, *Eagle*, November 6, 1777, quoted in *NDAR*, vol. 10, p. 425.

[114] Admiral Howe to Captain Cornwallis *Eagle*, off Chester, November 7, 1777, quoted in Ibid, p. 429.

[115] Varnum to Washington, Woodberry, November 8, 1777, quoted in Ibid.

[116] Biographical information on Isaiah Robinson is derived from Tim McGrath, Give Me a Fast Ship: The Continental Navy and American Revolution at Sea. (New York: Penguin Books, 2014), p. 99, p. 105. See also Jackson, *Pennsylvania Navy*, p. 102.

[117] Washington to Varnum, November 7, 1777, quoted in Washington, Rev. War, vol. 12, p. 161.

[118] Ibid.

[119] Ibid.

[120] Ibid.

[121] Council of War, November 8, 1777, in Ibid, p. 163.

[122] Lee to Washington, no location, November 8, 1777, quoted in Ibid. The British method of moving supplies consisted in landing, "Their provisions, above Jone's wharf, near a branch of Eagle-creek, they are carried from hence by water to Guiers dam, where they again put them in boats and ready convey them down another creek to the Schuylkill." Lee continued, "There is no way of interrupting them in this business but by taking Carpenters island."

[123] Smith, *Fight for the Delaware*, 28.

[124] Downman, *Journal*, November 7, 1777, p. 49.

[125] Ibid.

[126] Jackson, *Pennsylvania Navy*, p. 222.

[127] Mark E. Lender, *River War*, p. 31.

[128] Smith to Washington, November 9, 1777, quoted in Ford, *Defenses of Philadelphia, p. 80.

[129] Master's Journal of the HMS *Roebuck*, November 9, 1777, quoted in *NDAR*, vol. 10, p. 448.

[130] Fluery Journal, quoted in Ford, *Defenses of Philadelphia in 1777*, pp. 80-81.

[131] Colonel Samuel Smith to George Washington, November 9, 1777 quoted in Ford, *Defenses of Philadelphia, p. 80.

[132] George Washington to the Continental Navy Board of the Middle Department, Whitemarsh, PA, November 9, 1777, quoted in *NDAR*, vol. 10, pp.447-8.

Chapter Seven
The Siege of Fort Mifflin

On November 10, the British planned to launch their much-anticipated bid to crush the defenses Fort Mifflin and break through the last layer of the American river defenses. Prior to describing the final siege of Fort Mifflin, it is useful to summarize the status of forces on both sides prior to the initiation of the final push.

On the British side, the assault would be supported by a battery on Providence Island, consisting of two thirty-two-pounders and one eighteen-pounder, a second battery on Province Island mounting a single thirty-two-pounder would join the bombardment. In addition, there would be a battery on Carpenters Island composed of six twenty-four-pounders, an eight-inch howitzer, and an eight-inch mortar. The twenty-four-pounders had been removed from Lord Howe's flagship, HMS *Eagle*. A second battery on Carpenters Island consisted of one eight-inch howitzer, and one seven-inch mortar. A third battery on the same island included a single 13-inch mortar. Finally, a battery situated on the mainland containing two twelve-pounders and one eighteen-pounder contributed their weight to the bombardment as well. These land batteries were to be supplemented by ships' guns from Lord Howe's naval squadron in Delaware. Forces were even being drawn in from the encampment at Germantown to lend support the attack and potentially storm Mud Island once the works were sufficiently weakened by the bombardment.[1] However, winds and high tides in the river prevented the British ships in the river from throwing the full weight of their guns into the bombardment until the 14th.[2]

For the Americans, in addition to improvements listed above, Maj. Fleury had the men build traverses in the main battery and excavate ditches fronted with a fraised earthen rampart on the southeast corner of the fort. This work offered the gunners a modicum protection from enfilade and ricochet fire. A double chain was stretched at the water's edge to provide some security, especially against an amphibious landing, to the right of the battery. Likewise, the earthen ramparts of the north and west sides of the fort in front of the main battery were augmented with fraised works. These, in addition to the wolf pits already added by d'Arendt, would offer some security to the garrison in the event the British did attempt to take the works by storm. Additionally, Fluery constructed a demilune battery which gave riflemen stationed within the post a position from which they could rake the flanks of the northern rampart.[3]

A banquette along the stone wall on the east side of the fort allowed the riflemen of the garrison a clear field of fire to defend against attacks in that quarter as well. The ramparts on the north and west sides of the fort were poorly situated, however, making it impossible for any men acting as infantry to defend against ground assault in those quarters. Still, if the British made a breach in the outer defenses, the garrison could fall back on parapets of a reunion which Fleury ordered constructed between the northern and western barracks. The fall back of last resort encompassed a redoubt which resembled a Greek cross in the middle of the parade ground.[4]

Clearly, Maj. Fleury had done his utmost with the materials available to him to elaborate the defenses of Fort Mifflin and make it capable of withstanding the British assault for a time. The looming question was how long? Weather delayed the onslaught, permitting the French engineer time to shore up these modifications as best he could. The inclement weather served the American objective as well. The longer the assault was delayed, the greater the chance the river would freeze, and the British be forced to abandon their prize.

One of the great sources for the conditions the garrison endured at Fort Mifflin was Joseph Plumb Martin of Connecticut. As a teen Martin served through much of the War for Independence in various capacities. In April 1777, he enlisted as a Continental for the duration of the war. Martin served in the fort during the bombardment. Years later, when he composed his memoir of his military services, the memories of the siege remained vivid. Martin opens his account of his time at Fort Mifflin with the statement, "Here I endured hardships sufficient to kill half a dozen horses."[5] He continued with a description of the fort itself,

> *Well, the island, as it is called, is nothing more than a mud flat in the Delaware, lying upon the west side of the channel. It is diked around the fort, with sluices so constructed that the fort can be laid under water at pleasure, (at least it was so when I was there, and I presume it has not grown much higher since.) On the eastern side next to the main river, was a zigzag wall built of hewn stone, built as I was informed, before the Revolution at the king's cost. At the southeastern part of the fortification (for fort it could not*

properly be called) was a battery of several long eigh-
teen-pounders. At the southwestern angle was another
battery with four or five twelve- and eighteen-pound-
ers and one thirty-two-pounder. At the northwest-
ern corner was another small battery with three
twelve-pounders. There were also three blockhouses in
different parts of the enclosure, but no canon mounted
upon them, nor were they of any use whatever to us
while I was there. On the western side, between the
batteries, was a high embankment, within which was
a tier of palisades. In front of the stone wall, for about
half its length, was another embankment, with pali-
sades on the inside of it, and a narrow ditch between
them and the stone wall.[6]

Martin's account is impressive in its detail, all the more so considering it was written so long after the event. For many at the time, the defenses of Fort Mifflin were nowhere near capable of withstanding the British onslaught. The surgeon Albigence Waldo referred to the post as "A Burlesque upon the art of Fortification."[7] As the siege progressed, conditions in the fort deteriorated substantially, as will be described below.

The British unleashed their initial bombardment of Fort Mifflin on November 10 at 7:30 A.M. a day that began overcast with some rain. The British positions consisted of the batteries described above. Each battery had been instructed to fire eighty rounds per gun during the day. These could be round shot, shell or carcasses. Based on the number of guns in the British batteries, this would amount to 1,120 rounds, if all of the guns actually fired their allotted rounds.[8] The Americans returned fire from five guns, which according to Capt. Montressor, were all silenced by noon save one. Certainly, the British gunners silenced the fort's two flanking batteries by then. The British raked the western ramparts, destroying the palisades. As a result, the guns in the fort were either dismounted or expended their supply of ammunition.[9]

Writing Washington on the 10th, Lt. Col. Smith suggested that the British could be held below the second line of chevaux de frise by the Mantua Creek battery, if it were supplemented by a two-gun battery on Bush Island and supported by Hazelwood's ships. Smith further indicated that it was his "Opinion and the Opinion of the Officers in this Garrison...that unless the Siege can be rais'd the enemy in a short time must reduce this place," After floating this possibility to Washington, Smith then reassured his commander "we are determined to defend it [Fort Mifflin] to the last extremity..." Then Smith proceeded to advise Washington that it was his opinion and that of the other officers in the fort that it would be best to destroy the post and retreat with the guns to the New Jersey side and use them to mount an attack on Billingsport.[10] The strain of command was obviously weighing heavily on the young officer.

Some relief for this stress came for Smith, albeit unpleasantly, when later that day Smith "received a contusion from the shattered walls of the fort," which obliged him to be evacuated to the New Jersey side.[11] The injury occurred when Smith had "imprudently went into my Barracks," in order to respond to a note he received from Varnum.[12] At that point a spent canon ball which had gone through "the stockade, the barracks and two stacks of chimneys," struck him on the left hip.[13] Command of the beleaguered post then devolved on a Lt. Col. Simms. Simms continued to hold the post "with unyielding firmness, until he was relieved by Col. Russell of Massachusetts..."[14] The rapid changes in command further support the horrific conditions under which the garrison held out against the onslaught of the British forces arrayed against them. Not only was there the ever-present bombardment of the post. Add to this the fact that the men labored under the constant threat of a ground attack by the besiegers.

The damage wrought by the British cannonade was extensive. Two blockhouses were essentially out of action, with only one canon still serviceable between both structures. Likewise, the batteries erected outside the fort had been disabled and the palisades pulverized. Furthermore, the British gunners had done their work quite effectively against the western ramparts, with each shot taking out four to five palisades. Consequently, by the afternoon a large section of the wall as well as the barracks paralleling the wall had been destroyed. The northeast and northwest blockhouses had been subjected to punishing fire by the two thirty-two pounders in the hospital battery, which had dismounted three eight-pounders from their carriages. Likewise, the northern palisades and barracks sustained significant punishment.[15]

As "Lighthorse" Harry Lee noted in his account for November 10, "The enemy from his ships below, and from his batteries in Province Island, and the heights above Schuylkill, continued to press his attack with renewed vigor and increased effect."[16]

The Americans could now oppose the British batteries on Carpenters and Province Islands with only two four-pounders at the ferry wharf on Mud Island, and a battery of two eighteen-pounders near the northwest blockhouse of the fort. Fleury had ordered these last two guns moved from the fort and placed in the external battery. Still, it should be evident that the American defenses against a landward bombardment were much weaker than what the British were bringing to bear upon them.[17]

The weather turned in the afternoon, with rain and gusts of wind from the southwest. The rain continued through the night.[18] The rain hampered British efforts at continuing their cannonade and thus served as something of a blessing for the Americans as the fort sustained significant damage due to the British bombardment. Most of the destruction inflicted on the American works should be attributed by the British main battery of six twenty-four pounders and the hospital battery of two thirty-two pounders.[19]

Observing the bombardment from across the Delaware in Fort Mercer, Israel Angell of the Second Rhode Island reported, "This day the enemy Opened five new Batteries on fort Mifflin, which play'd briskly. During the whole day, and the Evening until nine o'clock, but did no great Dammage."[20] While it appeared that the damage to Fort Mifflin was minor from a distance, within the fort the story was quite different.

Inside Fort Mifflin, Fleury remained confident in the ability of the post to hold out while he struggled to repair the damage through the night with whatever supplies he had on hand or could salvage from the devastation. He supervised this work through the night of November 10, during a storm that saw increasingly heavy rains and west-northwesterly winds develop.[21] A pattern thus emerged between the two sides under which the British would fire on the fort during the day, with the Americans responding as best they were able, and Fluery effecting repairs on the fort through the night. As a result, the garrison had very little opportunity for sleep for the duration of the siege. To compound the suffering of the defenders, British maintained a regular bombardment of the fort through the night, thereby exacerbating the defenders' exhaustion.[22]

The British did not pass through the first day of the bombardment unscathed, though their casualties were minor. They lost an artillery sergeant killed and two wounded and one corporal killed.[23]

Privately, Fleury worried in his diary that the British would attempt to take the post by storm. He admitted, "I should not fear them if we could fix the float Chain described in the Figure;"[24] [see above map] He believed the obstruction would have the effect of channeling the British assault and allowing the defenders to concentrate their efforts to block it. Several lines later, the engineer stated his preference for the placement of the chain in question, and, echoing what was by now a common refrain among the leadership of the defenders, blamed what he saw as its poor placement on Cmdre. Hazelwood, whom he termed, "Master of the incomparable Chain."[25] Hazelwood and Varnum had previously met and discussed the deployment of the chain and agreed that it would be best if it were located between Hog and Province Islands. The reasons for its not being placed in that location remain unknown, though the weather could certainly have prevented the galleys from placing it. With a storm and high winds, the small galleys and guard boats could easily sink in the river, especially if weighted down with a heavy chain. In addition, Hazelwood was to place fourteen of his guard boats in a line behind the chain, though, as one historian of the fighting observed, such a gamble with boats that were easily capsized would have been very out of character for the commodore.[26]

On the British side, Capt. Andrew Snape Hamond then aboard the HMS *Somerset*, received word from an American deserter of plans to erect an additional battery on the Jersey side. He dutifully passed the information on Capt. Cornwallis in the *Isis*. The latter thanked Hamond for the information, and while he promised to reposition his ship for security, added the additional comment, "But for my part I think there's more danger to be apprehended in moving in the night than there would be from Rebel Hot Shot."[27] Clearly, the Royal Navy captain was not impressed by his foes' gunnery. At the same time, the comment could simply refer to the small size of battery facing them. The site of the second battery was about 800 yards north of the Mantua Creek, just below the Little Mantua Creek.

To the people in Philadelphia, the bombardment presented something of a spectacle. Young Robert Morton recorded in his diary for November 11, "Went to the Mouth of the Schuylkill to see the firing between the Mud Island Fort and the British Batteries upon Province Island."[28] At the same time, the British continued to expand the flow of supplies into Philadelphia. As John Montressor recorded in his Journal on the same day, "This night at high water at 10 arrived two brigs and 2 sloops loaded with Provisions and ammunition which supplies the army with provisions 3 weeks to come." Robert Morton recorded the passage of these vessels as well.[29]

The morning of the 11th dawned clear but much colder, leading to a heavy frost with ice as much as a half-inch thick in areas. The change in temperature adversely effected both the attackers

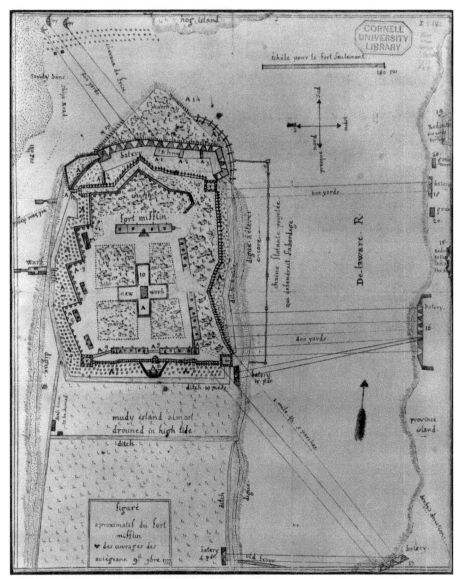

Figure 18 Francois Fleury, Map of Fort Mifflin on the Delaware River near Philadelphia PA, November 9, 1777.

and the besieged, though the garrison of Fort Mifflin felt the strain more so as many of their uniforms were mere rags.[30]

With the rising sun came a return of the British cannonade, the bombardment growing even heavier than the previous day. The bombardment intensified despite the fact that the Americans managed to disable two eight-inch howitzers in the previous day's fighting. Likewise, the British batteries in the meadow required extensive repair efforts during the night of the 10th-11th.[31] Fleury noted in his journal, "The firing increases but not the effect—our barracks only suffer."[32] The barracks became a prime target for British gunners. Any soldiers of the garrison desperate enough for rest to seek shelter there did so at the risk of life and limb.

Later in the morning of the 11th, the HMS *Cornwallis* and the tender *Elk* warped over the lower chevaux de frise. The two ships moved into position and began to shell the new battery under construction above Mantua Creek. These works were as yet unarmed, so they were unable to return fire. Given that reality, the casualties were surprisingly light with a sergeant being killed and another man wounded.

For their part, the British, or more specifically John Montresor, altered the direction of the embrasures of the main British battery and the hospital battery. Now, instead of pummeling the palisades of the fort, they were firing obliquely and inflicting significant casualties on the garrison. The new angle of canon fire wrought major damage to the northeast blockhouse as well. The guns in the structure were blasted from their carriages and the heavy fire made the building untenable for their crews. Fleury recorded the results of this new angle of fire, "At 2 o'clock. The Direction of the fire is changed - our Palisades suffer - a dozen of them are broken down - one of our Cannon is damaged near the Muzzle - I am afraid it will not fire straight."[33]As well as the damage Fleury described, the intensified bombardment brought the first fatality of the siege in the fort. Capt. Treat of the Virginia artillery died when a 32-pound solid shot passed close by him and winded him. Lt. Col. Smith stood next to the captain when he expired and observed no visible wounds on the latter's person.[34]

During the fighting on November 11, the batteries at Fort Mercer attempted to come to the aid of Fort Mifflin. However, the batteries at the former were too distant for their shot to exert any effect. By the same token, an eighteen-pounder that may have come from the *Augusta* burst, killing one and wounding several others.[35]

In addition, signals were given to the Pennsylvania Navy to come to the aid of the fort. The conditions in the river mitigated against such efforts. After the heavy rains and winds of the preceding night, the waves in the river were choppy and rendered is difficult, if not impossible for Hazelwood's small vessels to lend much support to the beleaguered fort. The lack of naval support further exacerbated the tensions building between Smith and Hazelwood already mentioned. It provided Smith with more fuel to feed his resentment against the state navy and its commander.

Varnum reported the effects of the days cannonade to Washington,

> *The enemy had battered down a great part of the Stone Wall. The Pallisades and Barracks are prodigiously shattered. The Enemy fire with Twenty-four and thirty-two Pounders. Upon these, and the other Considerations, Colonel Smith is of the Opinion that the Fort must be evacuated. A storm should not be dreaded; But it appears impossible for the Garrison to withstand point blank shot. I am going to consult the Baron [d'Arendt] and Col. Greene. I expect we shall cause an evacuation this Night.*[36]

As implied above, in consequence of the punishment meted out to the fort that day by the British batteries, Brig. James Varnum held a council of war. This council included Col. Greene, still in command at Fort Mercer, and Baron d'Arendt, still the official commander of Fort Mifflin. Not included in the council was Cmdre. Hazelwood.[37] Therefore, as these men debated the fate of Fort Mifflin, they had no idea as to the navy's ability to support the garrison, a critical omission in what was after all a joint operation. The members of the council felt certain that the fort could not continue to withstand any further British efforts. Still, the council determined to hold the fort, and selected a new commander. Lt. Col. Giles Russell of the Fourth Connecticut Regiment assumed command of Fort Mifflin late in the day on November 11. He was a veteran of the French and Indian War and described by Varnum as a "sensible and excellent officer," though by the time he assumed his latest post his services had seriously weakened both his physical and mental capacities.[38]

One of Russell's fellow New Englanders provided some insights on the progress of the bombardment from the perspective of the garrison at Fort Mercer. Writing to Nicholas Brown on the 11th, Ebenezer David, the Chaplain of the Second Rhode Island Regiment began by describing the conduct of the siege thus far, "the Enemy opened several Batteries upon us from Province Island and have by day cannonaded an heave shells ever since - not by Night so constant - " He then passed along what he knew of conditions in Fort Mifflin, "We have lost but few men - But the works Barracks ...are near cut all the peaces [sic]...I find that it is in agitation to abandon them."[39] The chaplain continued, eluding to the problems between Cmdre. Hazelwood and the leadership at the fort and reflecting, "I weep for the Consequences." David concluded with a prediction regarding the fate of both forts,

> *I expect that the Enemy will get a superior force upon the Water above our Chevaux de frize and the Consequences are evident...We still think we can hold this Post [Fort Mercer] as long as it shall be thought necessary and Both officer and Men are Firm and unshaken...*[40]

Through the night of November 11-12, the same cycle repeated wherein the British continued their cannonade, through somewhat less aggressively. At the same time, Maj. Fleury tried to repair what he could of the damaged works.

Due to gales on November 12, which blew down a mix of snow and rain, the British ships were unable to maneuver upriver and aid in the bombardment that day, thus there occurred some respite for the defenders the fort. Even with dangerous weather on the river, Hazelwood ordered his galleys down the eastern side of the to try and drive the British ships below the first line of chevaux-de-frise. At this time, the *Isis*, the *Cornwallis*, and two tenders were shelling the American battery at Mantua Creek. During the fighting on the river, one of the Pennsylvania guard boats deserted to the British.[41]

Even with the Royal Navy vessels out of the main action, the bombardment on November 12 resumed with great ferocity. Robert Morton recorded in his diary on November 12, "This day severe firing by which the American Barracks was several times set on fire, but soon extinguished."[42]

At the fort, after serving as commander of Fort Mifflin for one day, Russell asked for relief. A call for volunteers among the officers of Varnum's brigade produced Maj. Simeon Thayer, who assumed the command over Fort Mifflin on November 13 and remained in that position for the duration of the siege.[43]

Thayer was born in Mendon, Massachusetts on April 28, 1738. He began his military service in the Army of Observation outside of Boston in April 1775, as a lieutenant in one of the Massachusetts militia companies that came out for the Lexington alarm. He took part in the ill-fated march on Quebec under Arnold and was captured during the unsuccessful attempt to storm the city on December 31, 1775. The British formally exchanged Thayer on July

1, 1777, at which point he received a major's commission in the Second Rhode Island Regiment. Following his service at Fort Mifflin, he took part in the battle of Monmouth, where he lost an eye. He retired from the Continental Army on January 1, 1781.[44] Probably his most important contribution to the cause was his determined leadership during the last stages of the siege of Fort Mifflin.

Writing directly to Washington from the fort at 10 PM on the 12th, Maj. Fleury presented a hopeful but realistic appraisal of the situation of the post as well as its garrison. He noted that the bombardment that day inflicted further damage on the block houses, dismounting all the canon in them save two. This despite the fact that the walls of the blockhouses had been reinforced with logs. Rounding out his report on the condition of the position, "in all the fort is certainly yet in a state to be defended," the real concern for the major was that "the garrison is so dispirited that if the enemy will attempt to storm us, I am afraid they will succeed."[45] Fleury blamed the cold, rain, and fatigue for the slackening morale of the garrison. Bolstering his assessment, he explained to Washington that in the last alarm one half the garrison were unfit for duty.

Meanwhile additional British vessels, such as the HMS *Experiment* under Capt. Sir James Wallace, a fifty-gun fourth rate launched in 1774, continued to make their way up the Delaware in anticipation of the river's opening to traffic.[46] Even with additional ships moving upriver, for the British, the siege was not going as planned. The American defenders proved more resilient than expected, holding out longer and inflicting more casualties than the Howe brothers anticipated. At the same time, the British held off launching any land assault on the works until they could bring the HMS *Vigilant* into play.

The HMS *Vigilant* was formerly an East Indiaman named the *Grand Duchess of Russia*. For this mission, she had her regular compliment of guns removed, and replaced with one twenty-four pounder, nine two-pounders, and six four-pounders, all mounted on a single side. As a result of these modifications, she drew only eleven and a half feet of water.[47] This would allow her to get into the back channel that separated Fort Mifflin from Province and Carpenters Islands. As Capt. Downman recorded in his journal, "The Vigilant is to come up as soon as the tide will admit her. She is not to come over any part of the *chevaux-de-frise*, but up a creek between Province Island and another small isle." Downman further noted "Her station is to be on the angle of the rebel ground battery and on the right of our batteries."[48] In essence, she constituted a floating gunnery platform capable of coming close-in to Fort Mifflin and thereby depriving the defenders of any cover. Men in the masts of the *Vigilant* could easily observe the whereabouts of the garrison and direct the fire of the ship's guns on them. Likewise, a contingent of Royal Marines was attached to the ship to add their small arms fire the assault. The weather thus far interdicted the placement of the *Vigilant*. In fact, she grounded near Tinicum Creek on the night of November 11-12 and was only freed with great difficulty.[49] Augmenting the firepower of the Vigilant would be a cut-down sloop, the HMS *Fury*. She mounted only three 18-pounders along one side. The plan was for her to anchor just ahead of the Vigilant and serve as another floating battery.[50]

One additional incident occurred on the evening of November 12. The British managed to sneak two brigs and two sloops laden with supplies into Philadelphia. While American batteries successfully shot away the rigging of one sloop, forcing it aground, the British were able to salvage its cargo. Capt. Montresor believed the convoy brought up enough material to maintain the garrison for two weeks.[51] According to Maj. John André, the boats "passed between Province Island and the fort, the received very little damage either from the fort or the gallies, one only (a small sloop) having had part of her rigging shot away..."[52] The latter boat the major referred to obviously being the one that grounded. This constituted the second successful supply mission to Philadelphia in as many days. Clearly, the goal of keeping the river closed to the British supply efforts was growing increasingly untenable.

After sustaining two days of merciless bombardment, a deputation from Fort Mifflin met with Gen. Varnum to request reinforcements. Casualties from the bombardment as well as losses due to sickness and fatigue had significantly reduced the garrison. At the time of the deputation, the defenders numbered roughly 286 men, plus Capt. Lee's artillery company of about twenty. Roughly half of the infantry in the fort by then were from Gen. Varnum's consolidated Connecticut-Rhode Island brigade.[53] Varnum pledged to send what reinforcement he could.

Varnum ordered the delegation to hold the fort. Heeding their call for reinforcements, the brigadier dispatched a detachment so that when he assumed command Thayer brought with him one hundred replacements to relieve the most fatigued as well as the wounded among the garrison.[54] Joseph Martin's account of the conditions in the post demonstrates how appalling the situation was for the men. His reminiscence is especially poignant when it is considered that he was not among those relieved of duty in the garrison. He wrote,

> *Let the reader only consider for a moment and he will be satisfied if not sickened. In the cold month of November, without provisions, without clothing, not a scrap of either shoes or stocking to my feet or legs, and in this condition to endure a siege in such a place as that was appalling in the highest degree.* [55]

Keeping abreast of events on the Delaware as best he could from the Whitemarsh encampment, Washington did everything in his power to provide some relief to the fort. He fully realized that every day the post held furthered American plans of driving William Howe out of Philadelphia without a full-fledged military assault, something his army remained incapable of at the time. Since the beginning of the bombardment, Smith and Varnum wrote to Washington asking that the post be abandoned. When their communiques reached the commander in chief, he summoned a council of war to discuss the fate of Fort Mifflin. All the officers in attendance agreed the post should be held to the last.[56]

Just as Washington relayed orders to hold the fort to Varnum, he received an update from the Rhode Islander, "The Garrison hold out; tho' the Enemy continue to batter with great Success upon the Works, but few Men are killed and wounded." He continued, describing the state of the garrison and his plans to reinforce them. Varnum closed with the forecast, "Should the Enemy continue their Cannonade the Island will be lost; however, the Garrison will continue 'till your Excellency should order otherwise."[57]

On receipt of this information, Washington summoned a second council of war. Hearing the news, the council reversed their earlier decisions. Washington then directed Varnum to remove the heavy guns and all the stores possible from the fort and prepare it for demolition to prevent the works from falling into the hands of the British in any defensible state. The communique did include a reminder to Varnum that every day the fort held out furthered American designs.[58]

As noted above, Varnum sent in one hundred reinforcements to the fort with Thayer on the night of the 12th and planned to augment these the following morning with troops from Durkee's and Chandler's Regiments. Likewise, he would withdrawal the remainder of Smith's command as well as the Virginians. In essence, Varnum's intent was to rotate out the garrison and replace it with fresh troops.[59]

As November 13 dawned, the weather again intervened to complicate the efforts of both sides. Gale force winds blew from the north-northwest the entire day. The winds drove the *Vigilant* back toward Tinicum Island. As Capt. Downman noted in his journal, "The wind blows exceedingly hardly; the *Vigilant* cannot come up, nor the floating battery get down." Still, the ships of the British fleet made their way up the Delaware to join the British land batteries in shelling Fort Mifflin. Downman continued, "Our batteries keep up a constant fire with cannon and mortars."[60] The Americans responded as best they could with their single operational 18-pounder canon, which was located near the northwest blockhouse. The 4-pounder battery at the ferry wharf joined in occasionally as well, but to little effect. Still, the defenders did manage to damage one British 24-pounder during the fighting that day.[61] Downman described Fort Mifflin from his perspective, "The fort appears a perfect wreck; they return our fire but very faintly."[62] The British gain targeted the small Mantua Creek battery under construction on the New Jersey side of the river as well, with the *Isis, Cornwallis,* and *Liverpool* and as several tenders once again taking it under fire. The galleys of the Pennsylvania Navy joined in the fighting to harass the British shipping.[63]

Responding to the reports he received from Varnum concerning the state of Fort Mifflin over the preceding days, Washington wrote to Hazelwood on November 13. He informed the commodore that he thought it likely the post would have to abandoned sometime in the near future. He then enquired, "whether it will be possible for you to remain at or near your present station with the fleet, after our people have totally evacuated the Island, and the enemy have taken possession?" He further asked, "whether it will be in your power to hinder them from erecting new Works upon the Island by the Fire of your Ships, Floating Batteries and Gallies?"[64] Clearly, Washington considered attempting to hold the Delaware even after the fall of the fort. The commander in chief's goal remained preventing the British from gaining control of the river before it froze, though each additional report from the fort made this goal seem more and more fleeting. Likewise, the conditions on the Delaware were about to undergo a change that would further disconcert Washington's objective.

At the height of the siege, some discussion occurred as to taking some of the pressure off of Fort Mifflin. One possible means to this end involved launching an attack on Philadelphia, or even simply moving the main army closer to the city as a feint. Washington called a council of war to explore this very option. The overall verdict of the council was in the negative, aside from fire-eaters such as Brig. Gen. Anthony Wayne of Pennsylvania. The majority believed that such moves ran the risk of brining on a major engagement that the army was not strong enough to undertake until reinforcements, requested from Gates, arrived at camp. Furthermore, such moves ran the risk of exposing the American supply depots at Easton, Reading and Bethlehem. Washington did dispatch Nathanael Greene to tour the British defenses of Philadelphia and determine the potential for success of such an attack on the city. Greene took along generals Cadwalader and Wayne, as well as Thomas Paine, who acted as a volunteer aide, along with an escort.[65]

On the night of the 13-14th, the wind abated somewhat, allowing the *Vigilant* floating battery to take up a position to bombard the fort.[66] That same night, Maj. Fleury sat down and, possible using a wheelbarrow for a desk, recorded his latest efforts to repair the damage the British had inflicted on the fort. He noted that his efforts were made more difficult as the light of the moon exposed the workmen to fire from the British batteries. He described how he repaired the breaches in the palisades with any materials that came to hand, including planks, sentry-boxes and rafters. Finally, he expressed a note of frustration at Gen. Varnum for not sending over promised supplies, "it is impossible however, with watry [sic] mud alone to make works capable of resisting the Enemy's 32 Pounders."[67]

November 14 dawned another cloudy, windy day, standard weather for the Delaware Valley in the late autumn, then and now. In the morning the British attempted to send a floating battery with two thirty-two-pounders down the Schuylkill River towards Fort Mifflin. Observing the new threat to the garrison, Maj. Thayer ordered Fleury to construct a battery mounting two eighteen-pounders on the western side of the fort to contend with this latest threat. The guns for the new battery came from the fort's main battery, reducing the number of cannons there to a mere seven.[68]

Fleury lamented Smith's continuing to give orders from New Jersey, "...our Commanding Officer issues orders from Woodberry - if he were nearer, he would be a better judge of our Situation." Smith's attempt to exercise some level of authority from afar exacerbated an already muddled command situation. Fleury's frustration is both palpable in his writing and understandable in context. Here was a military professional, trained in the state recognized as the premier in Europe for military engineering, receiving directions from a lieutenant colonel with next to no experience in fortifications, and effectively sidelined by his injuries. Further, this raises the issue of just who exactly was in command at the fort, d'Arendt, Smith or Thayer? In the end, overall responsibility for this conundrum resides with Varnum, as Washington had vested him with the power to make decisions on the scene as he saw fit. It stands as a testament to Fleury's professionalism and dedication to the cause that he continued to work admirably with this sort of leadership dysfunction above him. Regardless of who officially commanded the fort, the threat of the British floating battery remained, and Fleury quickly set about establishing the new gun position.

Capt. Lee's guns on the lower battery of the fort silenced those of the floating battery by noon on the 14th. Fleury noted the success in his journal, uncertain of whether the guns of the fort had succeeded in dismounting those of the battery, or if its commander had decided it was too exposed.[69] The British declared this effort a failure.[70] In addition, the British again attempted to get the *Vigilant* into the back channel on the western side of Fort Mifflin, between the fort and the mainland. A group of American officers, including Nathanael Greene, observed this action. In addition to the guns enumerated above, the *Vigilant* possessed a compliment of Royal Marines who were to ascend the masts and fire into the works of the fort, targeting the men who served the batteries.[71] The *Vigilant* was supported by an additional ship, the HM sloop *Fury*, which mounted three twenty-four pounders, also all on one side. The *Fury* was commanded by Lt. John Botham of the *Eagle*.[72]

Even without the additional firepower of the two modified vessels, the fort sustained a terrific pounding. Still, Maj. Fleury remained confident in the ability of the garrison to hold out,

> *Their grand battery is in little better condition than out block-houses - We have open'd an embrasure at the Corner of the Battery and the two pieces here joined two others on the left which we have reinstated, throw the Enemy into disorder.[73]*

He continued, sounding a defiant note

> *I repeat it - their fire will kill us men, because we have no cover, but it will never take the Fort, if we have sufficient courage to keep our ground-but a*

stronger Garrison is indispensably necessary, we are
not secured against Storm, if the Enemy attempt it.[74]

The major's concern, which was shared by many of other officers concerned in the defense of Fort Mifflin lay more in the possibility of the British attempting to take the post by storm. It would seem, with the growing amount of firepower arrayed against the post, this concern was somewhat misplaced. While the British did intend to finally occupy the island with infantry, William Howe wanted the post thoroughly destroyed in the bombardment to make effective resistance impossible.

Considering the staunch efforts of the garrison to this point, some thought was given to reinforcing Fort Mifflin. Some officers of the garrison, Fleury in particular, believed the fort capable of continued resistance. Continued resistance formed the core of Washington's hope as well. On the strategic level, if the British could be prevented from reducing the fort until the river froze, an event that usually occurred in late November or early December at this time, Philadelphia might become untenable for the British. If such an eventuality materialized, Washington could retake the capital without launching an assault on the City of Brotherly Love. He would then come close to achieving the acme of skill according to the Chinese military theorist Sun Tzu and win the capital almost without fighting for it. [75]

Thus, each day that the British could be kept from Philadelphia encompassed a small victory for American arms. Likewise, morale among the leadership in the fort remained high. Writing in his journal later on the 14th, major Fleury asserted "Fort Mifflin is certainly capable of defense if the means be furnished." He continued, waxing somewhat philosophically, "- if they supply us from Red-bank with Tools, Fascines, Palisades…all which they may do in abundance - the Fire of the Enemy will never take the Fort, it may kill us men but this is the fortune of War…" He concluded these sentiments striking a defiant note, "And all their bullets will never render them masters of the Island, if we have the courage enough to remain on it."[76] Still, the major was no deluded romantic, he noted in his journal at 7 P.M. that evening that the British were still keeping up a "great Fire" on the fort.[77]

The engineer learned as well of Washington's inquiry to the possibility of removing some of the guns from the fort. There were several reasons for this line of action. One was to prevent them from falling into British hands when the fort fell. Another lay in placing the guns in batteries on the Jersey side of the river so they could continue interdicting British shipping further south in the river. The commander in chief was hedging his bets and keeping all his options open. Fleury deemed this idea useless, questioning the rationale "will they not by taking this Fort have the Channel of province Island open, for their small Sloops and other light vessels?"[78] Fleury, on the scene as it were, possessed a much keener sense of the situation than the commander in chief. Fort Mifflin stood as the key to the river defenses at this point, and the Frenchman was determined to hold the post.

Major Thayer gave some indication of his determination to hold the post as long as possible. Writing to Brig. James Varnum, Thayer declared "...I would give you to understand that the cannonade we have here we value not, nor can conceive how anyone can dream of delivering up so important a post as this at present;" [79] The major continued, with a certain sense of bravado, "from the Cannon we have nothing to fear, if there should be no sudden storm."[80] Still, Thayer requested additional reinforcements to the garrison "tonight of 100 or more men, it will certainly be a great means of salvation of the garrison."[81] He concluded by informing Varnum that the defenders of the fort managed to silence a British floating battery that morning.

As described above, following a council of war, Washington had sent a delegation from headquarters to inspect and report on the state of the river defenses. On the evening of the 14th, one of the members of the delegation, Nathanael Greene, dispatched a report to Washington. Writing at 8 o'clock P.M., the major general covered a range of topics. When he narrowed to the status of Fort Mifflin, Greene began by noting "The flag was flying at Fort Mifflin at sunset this evening..." In the same sentence, he moved to the less heartening portion of his report, "there has been a very severe cannonading today." Greene went on to note the attempted passage of the *Vigilant* and *Fury* into position in the back channel, as well as their missing guns on the side facing the Pennsylvania shore. From his vantage point, the major general could only see the side facing the shore and believed the ships to be completely disarmed. Greene advocated sinking "a vessel or two in the new channel [back channel] as soon as possible, and the fort encouraged to hold out to the last."[82] While sinking a ship to block the channel and prevent the British from getting any ships in close to Fort Mifflin seems a viable alternative in hindsight, it would require a ship larger than the small vessels under Hazelwood's command, and with the port of

Philadelphia under British control, such a vessel would have been quite difficult to acquire. Add to the difficulty of finding a suitable ship the problem of finding enough men to crew it even for the short voyage to the back channel, while under enemy fire, and the obstacles to enacting the plan grow apparent.

Still, the major-general's focus remained on the overarching goal-preventing the British from gaining control of the river before it froze. On that point, he passed along some heartening news to the commander in chief, "The enemy are greatly discouraged by the forts holding out so long, and it is the general opinion of the best of the citizens that the enemy will evacuate the city if the fort holds out until the middle of next week."[83] Stretching out the time Fort Mifflin could hold on thus remained the key to victory for the Americans.

The back channel now emerged as a decisive point in the contest for the river defenses. If the British could implement their plan and bring the *Vigilant* and *Fury* into the channel, they could rain fire into the works of the fort. The Journal of HM *Vigilant*, under Cdr. John Henry made this point abundantly clear on the 14th "employed preparing the Ship and People for Action, expecting every day to go against mud Fort." The Journal further noted that the ship was able to get over the bar at about 1:30 PM, and settle in between Hog Island and Bow Creek, fastening a hawser to a tree to stabilize the ship, as guns were only mounted on the one side.[84] The Journal of HM sloop *Zebra* elaborates on British preparations, "AM lent a hauser to the Fury Armed Ship and Warp thro Hog Island Channel against mud [sic] Isle."[85]

Commander Henry's anticipation ended the following day. On November 15th, as one historian of the fighting noted, "all plans to help the men of Fort Island became academic."[86] The reason for this was that the contrary winds which prevented the British fleet from coming in close to bombard Fort Mifflin finally abated. The ships took up firing positions to the east and west of the island and proceeded to unleash a pulverizing cannonade.[87] The British opened up from their numerous shore batteries as well. With regards to their shipping, the British were now able to take advantage of an unexpected change brought about the sinking of the chevaux-de-frise. The size of the obstructions had served to alter the depth in the channel behind the fort, making it somewhat deeper. This, combined with the change in the direction of the winds, finally allowed the *Vigilant* and *Fury* to gain access to the back channel separating the Fort from the islands on the landward side.

The total number of guns involved might have reached as

high as 350 on the British side. This number included the land batteries already described, as well as those mounted on the various
ships that took post in the river.[88] Canons thundered with the fury
of Armageddon-like proportions as the largest cannonade prior to
the battle of Gettysburg tore into the meager defenses of Fort Mifflin.

Washington received intelligence of the attack on the fort
from several sources. One of these was a Capt. Charles Craig, who
wrote to Washington from Frankford, Pennsylvania on November
15, stating that the enemy planned to attack the fort and sought to
reduce it before reinforcements could join Washington from Gates's
victorious army in New York.[89] There was little the commander in
chief could do, however, as much of his army was needed to stay in
position at Whitemarsh should the British decide to strike out of
the city and raid into the countryside for supplies. Add to this that
many of his troops were still in New York with Gates following Burgoyne's surrender at Saratoga.[90] He simply did not possess sufficient
manpower to address all the demands placed on his forces.

Major John André recorded in his journal for that day how
the *Vigilant* and *Fury* took up positions between Province and Mud
Islands, and that they, along with the shore batteries and the various ships in the river "kept up an incessant cannonade the whole
day." He further observed how the "Rebel floating Batteries fired a
good deal on the ships."[91] British Capt. James Parker, stationed on
Carpenters Island noted how the "large Ships have got as far up as
the Chevaux de frise will permit."[92] These vessels included the *Somerset, Isis, Roebuck, Pearl* and the galley *Cornwallis*. Together with
the shore batteries and the two hulks they subjected the fort on Mud
Island to a tremendous, annihilating cannonade.

Capt. Parker watched the British bombardment from "the
Embankment along the Verge of the River [which] affords fine shelter and there between the batterys [sic] with Capt. Patrick Sinclair
and several others I had a fine View of the whole scene -" From his
vantage point, Parker was able to discern that Hazelwood's galleys
came down the river to try and lend some support to the garrison,
"but the big ships soon drove them up again." Finally, Parker recorded the presence of both of the Howe brothers, Lord Cornwallis
and Gen. Grant on the island observing the bombardment as well.[93]

Now that the *Vigilant* and *Fury* were in position, nowhere
was safe in the confines of the fort. The canon could enfilade the
entire compound at will. Likewise, Royal Marines stationed in the
ships' crow's nests could add rifle fire and lob grenades into the

fort.[94] The only place of safety for the garrison was behind a low stone wall. Amidst the constant bombardment, soldiers grew inured to the dangers around them. Fatigue began to manifest as carelessness among many in the garrison. As Joseph Martin recorded, "The British knew the situation of the place as well as we did. And as their point-blank shot would not reach us behind the wall, they would throw elevated grapeshot from their mortars, and when the sentries had cried, 'a shot,' and the soldiers, seeing no shot arrive, had become careless, the grapeshot would come down like a shower of hail about our ears."[95]

Much of the men's apathy likely stemmed from pure exhaustion. Martin further related

> *It was utterly impossible to get any rest or sleep on account of the mud, if the enemy's shot would have suffered us to do so. Sometimes some of the men, when overcome with fatigue and want of sleep, would slip away into the barracks to catch a nap of sleep, but it seldom happened that they all came out again alive. I was in this place a fortnight and can say in sincerity that I never lay down to sleep a minute in all that time.*[96]

The fatigue Martin refers to in the above passage seems to have affected the judgement of the men of the garrison, or possibly his own recollections of the events he took part in which the following account describes,

> *I will here just mention one thing which will show the apathy of our people at this time. We had, as I mentioned before, a thirty-two pound cannon in the fort, but had not a single shot for it; the British also had one in their battery upon Hospital-point, which, as I said before, raked the fort; or rather it was so placed as to rake the parade in front of the barracks, the only place we could pass up and down the fort. The Artillery officers offered a gill of rum for each shot, fired from that piece, which the soldiers would procure. I have seen from twenty to fifty men standing on the parade waiting with impatience the coming of the shot, which would often be seized before its motion had fully ceased and conveyed off to our gun to be sent*

back again to its former owners. When the lucky fellow who had caught it had swallowed his rum, he would return to wait for another, exulting that he had been more lucky or more dexterous than his fellows.[97]

Martin's story seems apocryphal, or at the least greatly embellished on several counts. First, it seems unlikely that soldiers would try to intercept a shot before it was completely spent as the projectile could still inflict significant injury even while only rolling along on the ground. Likewise, the provision of the rum ration would quickly render tired, underfed men too inebriated to fight. Finally, given the intensity of the bombardment, it would seem suicidal for troops to line up in the open and expose themselves while awaiting the chance to pursue a spent or nearly spent shot, especially with the *Vigilant* and *Fury* in such close proximity.

This is not to discount Martin's testimony completely. Rather, it seems logical to suggest that the intervening years between Martin's service at Fort Mifflin and the composition of his memoire may have muddled his recollections to an extent. Likewise, he admitted to suffering extreme fatigue and overwork while serving at the fort. These factors combined with the stress of unremitting combat could certainly cloud anyone's recollection of events.

The above possibilities, combined with the weather conditions in the region suggest a possible alternative to Martin's remembrances. The compound within the fort was often quite muddy. Solid shot colliding with the mud would lose much of its velocity, becoming spent more rapidly than they would otherwise. As a result, they could be retrieved much more rapidly than if the men had to wait for them to roll to a halt on dry, solid ground. Perhaps the men simply waited for the shot to sink in the mud and come to a halt, and then retrieved it. Later, Martin, something of a raconteur, added some drama to his account either wittingly or unwittingly.

In the final analysis, it does not seem impossible that the men of the garrison attempted to retrieve spent shots from their British assailants and recycle them. Calls for additional ammunition feature as a regular portion of the correspondence from Smith, Thayer and Fleury to Varnum. Only the method might vary somewhat from what Martin recalled decades after the fact. In many other respects, Joseph Plumb Martin's description of the siege of Fort Mifflin stands as a truly valuable account. He provides a very detailed description of the fort, which is substantiated by contemporaries. The same may be said concerning his account of the damage the post sustained. Not only Martin, but other Continentals serving in the vicinity testified to the effects of the British bombardment.

The devastation at Fort Mifflin could be seen from across the Delaware at Fort Mercer. Writing to Gen. Potter of the Pennsylvania militia, Col. Christopher Greene observed,

> *Since my last the Cannonade has been very severe upon Fort Mifflin - this Day the Ships have come as near as the Chevaux de Frize would allow them. A floating Battery with 18-24 pounders came up between Fort Mifflin & Province Island, and Fire from Them together with that of their Batteries has dismounted all the Guns but two, Almost destroyed the works - and have killed and wounded a very considerable Number...*[98]

In addition to his poignant description of the devastation the British wrought on the fort, Greene mentioned that plans were being laid to evacuate the garrison, "We have sent Boats to the Brave Major Thayer, who has discretionary Orders to maintain the Post as long as he thinks practicable - that the brave Garrison may have a secure retreat when the Post is no longer tenable..."[99]

Brigadier James Potter of the Pennsylvania militia informed Washington that night, "I see myself that the Barricks [sic] are Burnt and the enemys ships Vigilint and a sloop are leying a long side of the island."[100]

Those in the Philadelphia area noted the intensity of the bombardment just from the sound it produced. John Laurens recorded, "There has been firing in the course of the day and some scatter'd guns in the evening."[101]

The firing continued during the afternoon and evening, with casualties mounting in the meager garrison. For instance, a first lieutenant Aaron Steele of the Seventh Massachusetts Regiment was severely wounded. He was evacuated from the fort that night and died of his wounds on November 24, 1777.[102] During the bombardment of November 15, the bodies of those killed lay where they fell, unless the dead interfered with the dwindling efforts of the living to maintain some sort of defense. The devastation wrought by the British attack was incredible. Considering the casualties, and the fact that the fort could no longer respond to British fire effectively, the decision was made to abandon what was left of the works.

Writing to Washington from Fort Mercer at 6 PM on November 15, Varnum reported "We have lost a great many Men today - a great many of the officers are killed and wounded - My fine Company of Artillery is almost destroy'd"[103] Still, some Continental officers, including John Laurens, who was not in the vicinity continued to maintain a fairly positive outlook on the situation at the fort. He reported that "The new commandant at Fort Mifflin [major Thayer] thinks the post tenable in spite of the enemy's land and water batteries."[104] He continued, "Engineer Fleury says if he is supplied from Red Bank with fascines, gabions, earth and fatigue-men, he will repair as much as possible each night the havoc made by day."[105] Unfortunately, Fleury was among the wounded, though his injuries were not critical.[106]

During the bombardment, British troops assembled on Province Island in preparation for a final assault on the works, scheduled to be carried out the following morning.[107] Capt. Parker noted this in his dairy as well. "The flat boats were up [blank] Creek to receive the Grenadier Guards, and the other troops that were to Storm which was to be led by Sr. George Osburn. There were many Young Gentlemen goeing [sic] Volunteers on this service..."[108] The men mentioned in Parker's entry were likely junior officers from various British regiments who volunteered for the dangerous service in the hopes of distinguishing themselves in front of their senior commanders. With the campaign season nearing an end, this appeared a last chance for them to begin to acquire a military reputation. The garrison, no longer able to maintain the post, evacuated the fort.

Most of the surviving defenders abandoned the post on the night of November 15-16th. A small force remained behind to destroy whatever materials were left in the post so as to prevent them from falling into British hands. As the last defenders evacuated the post, rowing as silently as possible across the river to Fort Mercer so as not to alert the sentries on the British warships in the river, they left the flag flying over the fort to deceive the British into thinking it was still manned. It was later in the day on the 16th that a British landing party confirmed the fort was abandoned.[109] Soon thereafter, Montresor and his men began work on a battery of four thirty-two pounders. These guns were to ward off any ships of the Pennsylvania or Continental Navies as the British continued their efforts to clear the upper row of chevaux de frise.[110]

On that same day, Brig. Gen. Varnum reported the loss of the fort to Washington,

Agreeable to what I wrote you last Evening, we were obliged to evacuate Fort Mifflin. Major Thayer returned from thence a little after two this morning. Everything was got off that possible could be.[111]

Many in the high command were impressed by the determined resistance offered by the defenders of Fort Mifflin. Maj. Gen. Henry Knox writing to Col. John Lamb expressed his admiration for the dogged stand of the garrison, "The defense of Fort Mifflin was as gallant as is to be found in history..." He continued, singling out Maj. Thayer, "The brave little garrison, then commanded by Major Thayer, of the Rhode Island Troops, had but two cannon but what were dismounted." While Knox was not present at the fort during the last bombardment, he possessed solid knowledge of the details, concerning the remaining guns, he noted, "These soon shared the fate of the others."[112] Knox continued, focusing on the plight of the garrison "Everybody who appeared on the platform was either killed or wounded, by the musketry from the tops of the ships, whose yards almost hung over the battery." His correspondence to Lamb painted a vivid picture of the final defense of the fort, remarkable for one not directly involved in the fighting, "Long before night there was not a single palisade left. All the embrasures ruined, and the whole parapet levelled. All the block houses had been battered down some days before."[113]

The garrison at Fort Mifflin withstood a remarkable onslaught for several weeks, culminating in the largest cannonade in North America prior to the battle of Gettysburg. Still, many at the time perceived the defense as a defeat in that the garrison failed to hold the post until the river froze over.

CHAPTER NOTES

[1] Strittmatter, *Campaign in the Delaware*, p. 9.

[2] Smith, *Fight for the Delaware*, pp. 10-11.

[3] Jackson, *Pennsylvania Navy*, p. 227.

[4] Ibid.

[5] Joseph Plumb Martin, *A Narrative of a Revolutionary Soldier Some of the Adventures, Dangers and Sufferings of Joseph Plumb Martin* (New York: Signet Classics, 2001), 85.

[6] Ibid.

[7] Albigence Waldo, "Valley Forge, 1777-1778. Diary of Albigence Waldo of the Connecticut Line." in *The Pennsylvania Magazine of History and Biography*. 21, 3 (1897): 301.

[8] Jackson, *Pennsylvania Navy*, p. 231.

[9] Jackson, *River Defenses*, p. 20.

[10] Smith to Washington, Fort Mifflin, November 10, 1777, quoted in *NDAR*, vol. 10, p. 456.

[11] Lee, *Revolutionary Memoirs*, p. 103.

[12] Smith to Washington, Woodbury, November 12, 1777, quoted in Ford, *Defenses of Philadelphia*, p. 121.

[13] Jackson, Pennsylvania Navy, p. 239.

[14] Lee, *Revolutionary Memoirs*, p. 103.

[15] Jackson, *Pennsylvania Navy*, p. 231.

[16] Lee, *Revolutionary Memoirs*, p. 103.

[17] Smith, *Fight for the Delaware*, p. 29.

[18] Montressor, Journal, p. 57.

[19] Jackson, *Pennsylvania Navy*, p. 231.

[20] Angell, Diary, p. 115.

[21] Jackson, *Pennsylvania Navy*, p. 238.

[22] Fleury, *Journal*, quoted in Ford, ed. *Defenses of Philadelphia*, p. 45.

[23] Jackson, Pennsylvania Navy, p. 242.

[24] Fleury, *Journal*, Fort Mifflin, November 10, 1777, quoted in *NDAR*, vol. 10, p. 456.

[25] Ibid.

[26] Jackson, *Pennsylvania Navy*, p. 219.

[27] See Captain Andrew Snape Hamond to Captain William Cornwallis, HMS *Somerset*, below Billingsport, and Captain William Cornwallis, HMS *Isis*, off Billingsport, November 10, 1777, quoted in Ibid, p. 458.

[28] Robert Morton, *Diary*, November 12, 1777, p. 27

[29] Montressor, *Journal*, p. 57. See also Morton, Ibid.

[30] Jackson, *Pennsylvania Navy*, p. 218.

[31] Ibid,

[32] Fleury, *Journal*, November 11, 1777, quoted in Ford, *Defenses of Philadelphia*, p. 107.

[33] Ibid.

[34] Smith, *Fight of the Delaware*, p. 29.

[35] Ford, *Defenses of Philadelphia*, 116, See also, Jackson, *Pennsylvania Navy*, p. 242.

[36] Varnum to Washington, November 11, 1777, Woodberry, New Jersey, quoted in Ford, *Defenses of Philadelphia*, pp. 115-6.

[37] Jackson, *Pennsylvania Navy*, pp. 239.

[38] Stryker, *Forts*, p. 34.

[39] Ebeneezer David to Nicholas Brown, November 11, 1777, quoted in *NDAR*, vol. 10, p. 467. David received his B.A. from the College of Rhode Island in 1772. He joined the Ninth Continental Regiment of Foot in 1776, serving under then Colonel James Varnum. When that unit's service ended, he joined the Second Rhode Island under Colonel Israel Angel. He died in Lancaster, PA, March 19, 1778. For biographical information, see Daniel M. Popek, *They "fought bravely but were unfortunate:"*, p. 39, p. 71.

[40] David to Brown, November 11, 1777 quoted in *NDAR*, vol. 10, p. 467.

[41] Jackson, *Pennsylvania Navy*, p. 244. See also Smith *Fight of the Delaware*, p. 32. On the weather conditions on November 12, see Stryker, *Forts*, p. 34.

[42] Morton, *Diary*, November 12, 1777, p. 27.

[43] Jackson, *Pennsylvania Navy*, 244. See also Smith, *Fight of the Delaware*, p. 32.

[44] The biographical information on Simeon Thayer is taken from Stryker, Forts on the Delaware, p. 34, and Henry Lee, *Revolutionary War Memoirs*, pp. 578-9.

[45] Fleury to Washington, Fort Mifflin, November 12, 1777, quoted in Ford, *Defenses of Philadelphia in 1777*, p. 120.

[46] Journal of HMS Experiment quoted in NDAR, vol. 10, p. 468.

[47] Smith, *Fight for the Delaware*, pp. 33-34.

[48] Downman, *Journal*, p. 50.

[49] Jackson, pp. 242-43. On the grounding of the *Vigilant*, see Smith, p. 32.

[50] Downman, *Journal*, p. 50.

[51] Jackson, *Pennsylvania Navy*, p. 241.

[52] John Andre, *Major Andre's Journal: Operations of the British Army under General Sir William Howe and Sire Henry Clinton, June 1777, to November, 1778.* (William Abbatt, ed. New York: 1930), p. 63.

[53] Smith, *Fight for the Delaware*, p. 32

[54] Ibid.

[55] Martin, *Narrative*, p. 86.

[56] Jackson, *Pennsylvania Navy*, p. 243.

[57] Varnum to Washington, Woodberry, November 12, 1777 quoted in Ford, *Defenses of Philadelphia*, p. 121.

[58] Jackson, *Pennsylvania Navy*, p. 243.

[59] Downman, *Journal*, p. 50.

[60] Ibid.

[61] Jackson, *Pennsylvania Navy*, p. 244.

[62] Downman, *Journal*, p. 50.

[63] Jackson, *Pennsylvania Navy*, p. 244.

[64] Washington to Hazelwood, November 13, 1777, Whitemarsh, PA, quoted in *NDAR*, vol. 10, pp. 477-8.

[65] Jackson, *Pennsylvania Navy*, pp. 245-6.

[66] Downman, *Journal*, p. 50.

[67] Fleury, Jounral, November 13, 1777, quoted in Ford, *Defenses of Philadelphia*, p. 123. On Fleury's use of a wheelbarrow as a desk, see Jackson, *Pennsylvania Navy*, p. 247.

[68] Jackson, *Pennsylvania Navy*, p. 248.

[69] Fleury, Journal, November 14, 1777, quoted in Ford, *Defenses of Philadelphia*, p. 125.

[70] Stryker, *Forts*, p. 35.

[71] Ibid.

[72] Ibid, p. 34.

[73] Fleury, *Journal*, November 14, 1777, quoted in Ford, *Defenses of Philadelphia*, p. 125.

[74] Ibid.

[75] The actual quote is: "For to win one hundred victories in one hundred battle is not the acme of skill. To subdue the enemy without fighting is the acme of skill." See Sun Tzu, The Art of War. Samuel B. Griffith, trans. (London: Oxford University Press, 1963), p. 77.

[76] Fleury, *Journal*, November 14, 1777, quoted in *NDAR*, vol. 10, pp. 489-90.

[77] Ibid.

[78] Ibid, p. 490.

[79] Thayer to Varnum, November 14, 1777, quoted in Ford, *Defenses of Philadelphia*, p. 127.

[80] Ibid.

[81] Ibid.

[82] Greene to Washington, at Morris, November 14, 1777, quoted in Ford, *Defenses of Philadelphia*, p. 128.

[83] Ibid.

[84] Journal of the HM *Vigilant*, November 14, 1777, commander John Henry off Billingsport, quoted in *NDAR*, vol. 10, p. 492. This seems to be a derivation of haw-

ser, a large rope utilized in mooring or towing a vessel. Using a rope like this to anchor the ships to some static object would be necessary as they were unbalanced due to their armament being on only one side.

[85] Journal of HM Sloop *Zebra*, November 14, 1777, commander John Orde off Tinicum Island, quoted in *NDAR*, vol. 10, p. 493.

[86] Lender, *River War*, p. 32.

[87] Ibid, pp. 32-3.

[88] Smith, *Fight for the Delaware*, p. 37.

[89] Captain Charles Craig to George Washington, November 15, 1777, *Washington, Rev. War*, vol. 12, p. 266.

[90] On the Saratoga campaign, see John F. Luzader, *Saratoga: A Military History of the Decisive Campaign of the American Revolution.* (New York: Savas Beatie, 2008); Max M. Mintz, *The Generals of Saratoga.* (New Haven, CT: Yale University Press, 1990); Dean Snow, *1777: Tipping Point at Saratoga.* (New York: Oxford University press, 2016). For an alternate take on the entire campaign, see Theodore Corbett, *No Turning Point: The Saratoga Campaign in Perspective.* (Norman: University of Oklahoma Press, 2012).

[91] John Andre, *Journal*, November 15, 1777, p. 64.

[92] Parker, *Journal*, November 15, 1777, quoted in *NDAR*, vol. 10, pp. 500-1.

[93] Ibid, p. 501.

[94] Journal of H.M. Armed Ship *Vigilant*, Commander John Henry, November 15, 1777, quoted in Ibid, p. 508. On the British use of rifles, see DeWitt Bailey, *British Military Flintlock Rifles 1740-1840* (Lincoln, RI: Andrew Mowbray Publishers,2002), pp. 21-30.

[95] Martin, *Private Yankee Doodle*, p. 89.

[96] Ibid, p. 89.

[97] Ibid, p. 78.

[98] Colonel Christopher Greene to General Brigadier General James Potter, November 15, 1777, quoted in Ford, *Defenses of Philadelphia*, pp. 139-40.

[99] Ibid.

[100] Brigadier James Potter to George Washington, November 16, 1777, quoted in Ford, *Defenses of Philadelphia*, p. 140.

[101] Laurens, *Army Correspondence*, p. 77.

[102] Stryker, *Forts on the Delaware*, p. 35.

[103] Varnum to Washington, November 15, 1777, quoted in Ford, *Defenses of Philadelphia*, p. 132

[104] John Laurens, *The Army Correspondence of Colonel John Laurens in the Years 1777-8.* (New York: The New York Times and Arno Press, 1969), pp. 76-77.

[105] Ibid.

[106] Varnum to Washington, November 15, 1777, quoted in Ford, *Defenses of Philadelphia*, p. 132

[107] Lender, *River War*, p. 33.

[108] Parker, *Journal*, November 15, 1777, quoted in *NDAR*, vol. 10, p. 501.

[109] Smith, *Fight for the Delaware*, p. 37.

[110] Browne, "Mifflin and Mercer," p. 156.

[111] Brigadier James Mitchell Varnum to George Washington, November 16, 1777 quoted in Ford, *Defenses of Philadelphia*, p. 140.

[112] Henry Knox to John Lamb, n.d,, quoted in Edwin Martin Stone, *The Invasion of Canada in 1775 including the Journal of Captain Simeon Thayer describing the Perils and Sufferings of the Army under Benedict Arnold*. Providence, RI; Knowles, Anthony and Company, Printer, 1867, p. 77.

[113] Ibid.

Chapter Eight

The Evacuation of the Forts and the End of the Navy

I am sorey to be the messenger of Bad news last
night at Ten oClock our Breve Garreson at fort Mifflin
set fier to the Barrecks and set off to Rid bank—this
Intiligance I have by express that Brought me the in
Closed—I see my self that our Barricks are Burnt and
the enemys ships Veglint and a sloop are leying a long
side of the Island.[1]

The above message from Brig. Gen. James Potter of the Pennsylvania militia stood among the first reports Washington received on the evacuation of Fort Mifflin. Lt. Col. Samuel Smith's account followed soon thereafter. Writing from Woodbury, New Jersey. The young officer stated simply, "Gen. Varnum will have inform'd your Excelly of the Evacuation of fort Mifflin. I am extremely Sorry for the Circumstance. Major Thayer defended it too bravely."[2] Smith recommended several of his subordinates to Washington for their conduct during the final hours of the siege. Those singled out for praise in the final defense of the fort included the engineer Maj. Fleury, whom Smith described as "a Treasure that ought not to be lost," as well as Capt. Dickinson of the Virginia Regiment who stayed on assisting Fleury until the end of the fighting.[3] Several other officers recommended Thayer for his role in the final defense of the post as well.[4] According to some accounts, the British took possession of the remains of Fort Mifflin within a half hour after the last survivors of the garrison pushed off from the shores of the devastated post.[5] For instance, the Lieutenant's Journal of the HMS *Isis* which noted on November 16, "At 1 AM Observ'd Mud Fort with Barracks on fire and an English flag hoisted."[6] The most detailed account on the British occupation of the fort derives from the Journal of HM Armed Ship *Vigilant*, which remained in close proximity to the devastated post,

at One [the Rebels] abandoned it [Mud Fort],
during which time we kept a fire on them of Grape, at
6 AM sent the Marines on shore to take Possession of
the Fort, hauled down the Rebel Flag and hoisted an

*English Jack, at 8 a Party of the Guards came and
took charge of the Fort and our Marines returned on
Board.*[7]

Since the Vigilant still lay close to the fort, its crew possessed
an excellent vantage point for any activities transpiring in the post.
Francis Downman's account reinforces the Journal of the *Vigilant*
as well as providing a poignant description of the conditions the
British encountered when they occupied the fort,

> *At break of day we discovered the rebel colours
> still flying and the fort almost totally destroyed but
> no appearance of any person. In a little time the Vigi-
> lant sent her boat well manned ashore; one of the jacks
> mounted the flagstaff and tore down the rebel and
> hoisted in their stead the English colours.*[8]

Changing the flags was significant as it signaled to the various British contingents that they now controlled the fort. Soon
after the sailors from the Vigilant took possession of Mud Island,
Downman secured a boat and crossed to the island himself. On his
arrival, he learned that initial occupation force had discovered one
American who had not abandoned the post. From him the British
learned that the garrison had lost "about 50 men killed and between
70 and 80 wounded."[9]

Downman continued, making a personal inspection of what
remained of the American works. The captain was clearly impressed
with what he found, "The fort is strong and had it been stormed a
very considerable loss would have been the consequence." He added,
"Nothing that could add to its strength was left undone."

Still, the damage inflicted by the bombardment was significant. The artillerist described how "The blockhouses were entirely
knocked to pieces, a great number of their guns and carriages were
rendered useless by the shot they have received, in short it is such
a battered situation that it is past describing." Downman noted the
damage inflicted on the post's defenders as well, "In almost every
place you see blood and brains dashed about and hardly a spot in
the hole place that was not a shot."[10]

As the dust settled on the still-smoldering remains of Fort
Mifflin, both sides sought to ascertain the status of the fort and plan
their subsequent moves accordingly. For George Washington, forming a picture of the current state of the river defenses entailed rapid

the exchange of a series of letters between himself and his subordinates. For instance, writing Brig. Gen. James Varnum on November
16, 1777, from his headquarters in Whitemarsh, the commander in
chief inquired, "I imagine from yours of the last Evening by Maj.
Ballard that the fort was totally evacuated last night." [11] While presented as a statement, the preceding clearly contains an interroga-
tive quality. It seems Washington desired confirmation of what he
already suspected to be true. It is further likely Washington had not
yet received the missive from Varnum quoted in the previous chapter when he made the inquiry of his subordinate.

Meanwhile, the word of the fort's loss began to disseminate
to the civil authorities. William Bradford of the Pennsylvania militia reported the loss of the fort to Thomas Wharton, Jr. from the
sloop *Speedwell* in the Delaware River. Bradford noted the role of
the *Vigilant* and describing how "She with the five Batteries tore
the Fort all to pieces and knocked down all the Ambrusers, [embra-
sures] killed many of our People and wounded more." He further
explained how "About 12 o'Clock at Night, the Officers finding it impossible to Stand it any longer, set fire to the Barracks and brought
off the People."[12] Bradford reported on the status of the ships in the
river as well, observing that the recent weather had destroyed most
of the fire rafts and that the men stood in great want of clothes and
shoes. Significantly, he reported that "In the Engagement the Galleys had several Men killed and 10 or 12 wounded."[13]

In addition to the flurry of communications, the fall of Fort
Mifflin triggered a series of councils of war on the American side. At
issue stood the fate of the remaining river defenses as well as the
troops in New Jersey. The councils were attended by Brig. James
Varnum, Cmdre. Hazelwood, Cols. Smith and Greene, and in all
likelihood several other officers as well. Washington dispatched
three additional general officers from the main army to consult with
the leaders on the scene, Henry Knox, Arthur St. Clair, and Johann
DeKalb.[14]

Knox stood as a logical choice as he commanded the Continental Artillery. The Boston bookseller turned artillerists was
one of the commander in chief's most trusted subordinates as well.
While he had recently blundered at the battle of Germantown, he
was a generally solid and, importantly, loyal, officer.

St. Clair, a former British officer, served in the French and
Indian War and participated in the British expedition against Louisburg in 1758. He therefore enjoyed some experience in amphibious
operations against fortified places.[15] Johann de Kalb's military ca-

reer stretched back to the War of the Austrian Succession (1740-1748) in Europe.[16] It is likely, then, that Washington dispatched these two officers over to New Jersey to act as advisers and bring their substantial military experience to the council tables. The three generals were tasked with ascertaining the overall situation, determining if the chevaux de frise could be maintained following the loss of Fort Mifflin, and if the channel between Mud and Providence Islands could be blocked with a hulk.[17]

The delegation learned of the fort's fall on their way to confer with Varnum. Arthur St. Clair wrote to Washington from Dunks Ferry on November 17, explaining:

> *Two Gentlemen, one from General Varnum and the other from the Fleet with Dispatches for your Excellency having this Moment arrived, we took the Liberty to open them—from their Contents I fear that out Journey will be to no great Purpose, but it the general Sentiment that we proceed; and we shall endeavor to take such Measures as may be most conducive to the public Good, and return as soon as possible.[18]*

When DeKalb, Knox, and St. Clair arrived at Fort Mercer, they immediately called a council of war to cull information from the officers on the scene. On November 18 at 9:30 p.m., they rendered a report on their deliberations. It was the unanimous opinion of the officer's present that the Pennsylvania fleet could offer no further assistance if the British occupied and fortified Fort Island. Instead, the generals suggested that Hazelwood withdraw up the Delaware with his remaining vessels and attempt to destroy the captured frigate *Delaware* with fire ships as he passed by Philadelphia. [19]

Prior to the arrival of the triumvirate of major generals, Varnum replied to Washington with the time included, 11:15 a.m. In it, the brigadier relayed a more thorough report on the situation as it appeared on the scene. His report is therefore worth reviewing at some length as it provided the first clear intelligence Washington received concerning the fall of Fort Mifflin,

> *Agreeable to what I wrote you last Evening, we were obliged to evacuate Fort Mifflin. Major Thayer returned from thence a little after two this Morning. Every Thing was got off, that possibly could be. The Cannon could not be removed without making too*

> *great a Sacrifice of Men, as the Empress of Russia,*
> *alias Vigilant, lay within one hundred yards of the*
> *Southwest part of the Works, and with her incessant*
> *Fire, Hand Grenades and M   usketry from the*
> *Round Top, killed every Man that appeared upon the*
> *Platforms. The Commodore gave positive Order to Six*
> *Gallies to attack, and take that Ship. They warp'd*
> *over to the Island & there held a Council, lost a few*
> *of their Men, and then returned, without attempting*
> *any Thing. I left the Commodore since one this Morn-*
> *ing; He had positive ordered Six Gallies, well manned,*
> *to attack the same Vessel; how they succeeded I am*
> *not inform'd; but, according to Major Thayer's Sen-*
> *timents, we could have held the Island, had the Ship*
> *been destroy'd.*[20]

In the above description of the loss of Fort Mifflin lay additional fuel for the fires of a controversy which raged among contemporaries and would later find its way into the work of historians of
the fighting in the Delaware. The essential question was whether
the Pennsylvania Navy performed its due diligence in lending aid
to the garrison of Fort Mifflin. This controversy will receive attention in due course. Suffice it to say currently, that the above as-
sumes that the vessels of the Pennsylvania navy, with the support
of the Continental ships in the area, would be enough to successfully
attack the *Vigilant*, which itself received coverage from the other
Royal Navy warships in the Delaware. This seems a very difficult
premise to sustain, especially given the fact that the *Vigilant* was
not the only vessel in the back channel, the HMS *Fury* took part in
this phase of the assault as well. Both ships enjoyed the support of
various land batteries on the Pennsylvania side as well. Still, the
failure of Hazelwood's ships to render necessary aid stood as an assertion maintained by the commanders of the ground forces in the
area, Smith chief among them.

Varnum continued his report elaborating on the status of
the river defenses,

> *I don't think the Shipping can pass the Che-*
> *vaux de Frize while we keep this Shore - The two Gun*
> *Battery, near Manto Creek, annoy'd them very Much*
> *Yesterday. It is still firing slowly; but, the Shipping*
> *having remov'd out of direct distance too much firing*

would be Profusion. We are erecting a Battery between
Red Bank and Manto Creek Battery directly opposite
the Frizes, w'ch I believe will be finished to day. [21]

Clearly, Varnum sought to continue harassing the British shipping as they attempted to penetrate the obstructions the Americans placed in the river. For the Rhode Islander, the campaign was far from over. The desire for continued action along the banks of the Delaware leads to an additional point. Those on the ground did not consider the fall of Fort Mifflin as marking any sort of culminating point to the fighting. Instead, they hoped to continue the attritional struggle against the British flotilla as it closed in on Philadelphia using whatever means still available. The desire to continue the fight is evidenced in the creation of a new battery to attempt to further stymie British efforts at removing the obstructions.

Varnum remained optimistic concerning the Americans' ability to maintain the river defenses. He continued his report to Washington reflecting on Mud Island, "I am not of the opinion that the Enemy can possess themselves of the Island, without too great a Loss."[22] He continued, "Whither we shall keep a Guard upon it or not, I cannot determine 'till, from an actual Observation, I shall be furnished with new Circumstances."[23] Varnum hit upon one important reality in his report to the commander in chief, "While we keep the Shipping down, our Navy will be safe; but, should our Defenses prove ineffectual, we shall take out a part of their Guns & let the others attempt passing the City."[24]

While Varnum possessed a workable plan to continue keeping the river closed to British, the forces he had at his command were feeling the effects of their recent service. Joseph Plumb Martin recalled that when he made it to New Jersey he "had the first sound sleep I had had for a fortnight."[25] For Martin and the other weary survivors, the evacuation of Fort Mifflin meant a respite and some greater level of safety following the pummeling they had recently endured. Likewise, Varnum provided Washington with a realistic assessment of the troops at his disposal, as well as the merging operational situation,

Out troops are so extremely fatigued that no
time will be lost in knowing your Excellency's Orders,
whether the Troops commanded by Colo. Smith shall
remain here or return to Camp. The Officers seem anx-
ious to join the Army as their Men are much harass'd.

> *However, they have had two Nights Rest, & are nec-*
> *essary here, should we attack Billingsport. As a great*
> *part of my own Brigade have been lost at Fort Mifflin*
> *I shall not be able to make any hostile attempt this*
> *Night; but am of the Opinion that the Enemy should*
> *at all hazards be dispossessed of this Shore...*[26]

Fighting in the river continued even as Varnum made out his report to Washington. So much is evidence in the following lines, "I am just told that the Gallies last ordered to attack the *Vigilant,* did nothing; That misfortune will prevent us from keeping men upon the Island."[27] Here, Varnum was referring to a squadron of six galleys that sailed down to offer assistance to the fort on the afternoon of the fifteenth. The vessels refrained from entering the back channel. Such a refusal is understandable, considering that each galley mounted one cannon in the bow and several swivels. They would be going up against the *Vigilant* and the *Fury*, as well as the supporting British land batteries. Furthermore, they could expect no support from Fort Mifflin as the defenses were by then already falling apart. Again, the aspersion of the land commanders served to further implicate the Pennsylvania Navy for failing to perform its vital role in holding the river. Likewise, Varnum charged that Hazelwood had failed to supply the fort with sufficient shot to maintain the defense.[28]

Varnum closed his account to Washington on an optimistic note, "P.S. Colo. Greene offered to Officer and Man three Gallies, that would destroy he Empress of Russia, or perish to a Man..."[29] A brave gesture, certainly, however, the dawning reality was that the defensive net constructed at such great effort and expense by the Pennsylvania government and the Continental Congress, now without a lynchpin, was collapsing.

At the same time, Varnum's final two statements served to further sew the clouds what would be a storm of controversy as to which service was most at fault for the loss of the fort, especially when he added that, "Capt. Robin<son> of the Continental Fleet, offered to go himself & the Commodore possesses a fine Disposition, but cannot command his Fleet."[30] It is likely that Varnum gained some of his dislike of Hazelwood through Lt. Col. Smith. One of the first historians to study the siege in some depth, William Stryker, noted that "Smith had a contempt for Hazelwood because he said he did so little to aid his garrison." [31]

Others were implicated in the loss of the forts as well. Writing on October 29, even as the British were closing in on Fort Mifflin, Brig. Gen. David Forman of the New Jersey militia wrote to inform Washington concerning the conduct of Gen. Silas Newcomb of New Jersey. He observed, "from the best information I can Collect he has at no time given any assistance to the Garrisons or the fleet - particularly in the late Attack on Red Bank he neither harassed the Enemy in Their Advance, During the Assault or in Their retreat."[32] It will be remembered that Newcomb previously retreated from the British advance on Billingsport as well.

While the Americans sought to ascribe blame for the loss of the river forts, the British leadership exchanged congratulatory letters on the successful penetration of the American defenses. Writing from his flagship, the HMS *Eagle* on November 16, Adm. Sir Richard Howe singled out the officers of the HMS *Isis* and Capt. William Cornwallis for special praise for their efforts in the reduction of Fort Mifflin.[33]

The following day, Gen. William Howe dispatched a note to his brother thanking the navy for their support of the army. On this occasion, the general's praise was effusive, he opened the missive by stating, "I cannot too highly acknowledge the signal Services the Army has received from the Perseverance and Activity of the Officers and Seamen under your Lordship's Command since the King's Troops entered Philadelphia." Howe continued, singling out Capt. Henry and Lt. Botham "for the Gallantry they displayed on the 15th Instant in the Reduction of the Enemy's Works on Mud-Island."[34]

Quickly, on the American side, bitterness over the loss of Fort Mifflin gave way, at least in some measure, to concern for subsequent actions. Mauduit Du Plessis, the French engineer who rendered such great services at Fort Mercer offered his opinions to Washington in a letter of November 17. He took an aggressive stance, observing that if Washington wanted to attack the British post at Providence Island, then Fort Mercer should be retained as a staging area for such a stroke.[35] He went on to voice his opinion that if the garrison of Red Bank were reinforced with some five hundred additional troops, they could hold the fort.[36] He sounded a confident note, in his broken English, observing, "if every body make well Their duty, we are in the situation to hope, we have seen, the rhode island's troops in the action of the 22d."[37] Du Plessis continued, informing Washington as to the particular of the condition of Fort Mercer at the moment. In doing so, the Frenchman underscored his belief that the post could withstand another land assault, if properly reinforced.

Later that same day, Col. Christopher Greene dispatched his report to Washington. The tone of his letter is that of a subordinate who has failed in a mission that was not his, but one which he accepted responsibility for just the same:

> *Your Excellency I dare say has been inform'd of the evacuation of Fort Mifflin, and the Gallant defense there made by Major Thayer. The evacuation of that Fort. The removal of Our Navy. The movements of the British Fleet, and our own situation at present has put it wholly out of my Power to answer those important purposes for which your Excellency was pleased to order me to this Command.*[38]

Next, the young colonel apprised Washington of the conditions in the river, "Our Fleet here are now going as fast as possible to Timber Creek." The fleet Greene referred to included the remaining elements of the Pennsylvania Navy making a run up the river to the above location. He went on to inform his commander that, "The River is so open to the Enemys Shipping that Topsail & other Vessels are now passing between Mud Island and Province Island to Schuylkill unmolested."[39] This last may have been something of an exaggeration, as it took the British several days to clear a channel for their larger vessels to begin making their way to Philadelphia.[40] Still, smaller vessels could now make the run up the western side of the river without fear of the guns of Fort Mifflin or the American ships in the river. The ships Greene mentioned had waited waiting below the chevaux de frise for the opening of the river.

Greene then turned to the situation at Fort Mercer,

> *Fort Mercer is tolerable secure against a Storm only. A Bomproof [sic] Magazine is nearly finish'd, no other security in the Fort against Shells. A strong Brest work partly finish'd on the Bank which takes up a considerable part of the Floor of the Fort, & the Magazine takes up so much, that the remainder of the Floor is insufficient to spring Tents on for more than One third of the Garrison - The proposal for building a Bomproof under the Bank is now at an end, since Fort Mifflin is lost - The communication to Red Bank by Water is nearly interrupted, And should a part of*

the Enemy invest this Fort by Land our whole supply, would be cut off, and should they erect Bombattere on the Land side would be able to throw shells to us on all sides - from all of which I conclude that an Army investing us sufficient to keep the Field will reduce the Garrison, and make the survivors Prisoners as we could have no retreat.[41]

Greene's appraisal of the situation of the troops along the Jersey side of the river clearly conflicts with that of du Plessis. The Continental colonel based his assessment on the state of the works he would have to defend as opposed to the perceived morale of his men. His testimony therefore carries more weight in the sense that morale can fluctuate fairly rapidly and be affected by other factors which a commanding officer has little to no control over such as supply, and even the weather. In the end, however, the decision as to the next moves for the troops in New Jersey belonged to Washington.

For his part, now that he had confirmation of the situation along the Delaware, Washington reported the fall of Fort Mifflin to Henry Laurens, the recently seated president of Congress. His statement warrants examination at some length as Washington was working both to report on recent events but to undermine any criticisms of his command by various members of Congress, a situation which will be addressed below.

I am sorry to inform you that Fort Mifflin was evacuated the night before last, after a defense which does credit to the American Arms, and will ever reflect the higher honor upon the Officers and Men of the Garrison. The Works were intirely beat down, every piece of Cannon dismounted and one of the Enemy's Ships so near, that she threw Grenades into the fort, and killed the men upon the platforms, from her tops, before they quitted the Island. The Ship had been cut down for the purpose, and so constructed, that she made but a small draft of Water, and, by these means, warped in between Fort Mifflin and the province Island.[42]

Following the defeats at Brandywine and Germantown, it was important to present the defense of Fort Mifflin in the most positive light. To justify abandoning the post, Washington had to give the impression that its continued defense stood as an impossible task. In reality, this was the case. At this juncture, it is important to recall that the goal was not to hold the fort indefinitely, but only until the Delaware froze preventing further ship traffic on the river. The defenders failed in achieving the above goal, and so a convincing reason had to be provided. It is no exaggeration to state that in some respects, Washington's continued command of the Continental Army depended on it.[43] Making certain that his version of events reached Congress first stood as an important objective as there were critics of Washington in that body, one of the chief among them being John Adams.[44] Likewise, there were critics of the general's leadership within the officer corps as well. All of this would coalesced into what historians have dubbed the Conway Cabal, which will be discussed in below. The salient point in the current discussion is that Washington clearly believed by late 1777 that something was afoot. Therefore, any report to Congress required careful wording.

After reporting on the loss of the fort, Washington sought to remain above the controversy already brewing over the efforts of the Pennsylvania Navy during the fighting. He stated simply, "Some complaints are made, that the Captains of the Galleys did not sufficiently exert themselves to drive this Vessell from her Station, but I shall not determine any thing upon the matter, till a proper inquiry is made."[45] The particular vessel Washington referred to in the above was, of course, the *Vigilant*, which warped in behind Fort Mifflin. As noted in the above, the fire of the men in the *Vigilant* and her companion the HMS *Fury* combined to make holding Fort Mifflin untenable for the defenders. The commander in chief then sought to preempt any criticism of his own conduct concerning the defense of the river forts by informing the president of the overall military situation and the reasons underlying his decisions.

First, he observed, "Nothing in the Course of this Campaign has taken up so much of the attention and consideration of myself and all the General Officers, as the possibility of giving further relief to Fort Mifflin, than what we had already afforded."[46] Here, Washington sought to defuse any claims that he had not given enough support to the garrison, or that with more men the fort could have been held. Certainly, this was true. Given the construction of the fort and the forces arrayed against it, there was no way the post could have withstood further bombardment. He continued, "Such a Garrison was thrown into it, as has been found by experience, capable of defending it to the last extremity, and Red Bank, which was deemed essentially necessary not only for the purpose of keeping open communication, but of annoying the Enemy's Ships and covering our own Fleet, has been possessed by a considerable detachment from the Army."[47]

Washington continued his explanation of the situation of Fort Mifflin,

> *The only remaining and practicable mode, of giving relief to the Fort, was by dislodging the Enemy from province Island, from whence they kept up incessant fire. But this, from the Situation of the Ground, was not to be attempted with any degree of safety to the attacking party, without the whole or a considerable part of the Army should be removed to the West side of the Schuylkill, to support and cover it.*[48]

Driving home his point, the commander launched into a detailed description of the terrain. In this section, it is likely that Washington was not so much writing to Laurens, who had been to Philadelphia and seen some of the terrain around the city, as he was providing the president with ammunition to challenge likely critics in Congress.

> *To account for this, you must be made acquainted with the nature of the ground. In order to have made the attack on province Island, the party destined for that Service (which should have been at least 1500) must have marched down the Chester Road as far as the Bell Inn, near Derby, and thence, turning towards Delaware, must have proceeded about four Miles further, thro' a neck of land, to the Island. The enemy has a Bridge at the middle ferry upon Schuylkill, which is but four Miles from the Bell Inn, consequently by throwing a Body of Men over that Bridge, upon the first discovery of our design, and marching down to the Bell, they would effectually cut off our detachment upon their return. It is true, the covering party might have consisted of a less number than the whole Army, but then these remaining upon this side of the River would have been too few, to have been intrusted with all the Artillery and Stores of the Army, within twelve*

Miles of the Enemy.[49]

Continuing, Washington peremptorily addressed another possible line of criticism concerning his conduct of the campaign along the river.

> *There were many and very forcible Reasons against a total remove to the West Side of the Schuylkill. Leaving all our Stores at Easton, Bethlehem, and Allen Town uncovered, and abandoning several of our Hospitals within reach of the Enemy first presented themselves - Another was the importance of supporting the post at Read [Red] Bank, upon which that of Fort Mifflin in a great measure depended, as thro' it, we sent in Supplies of Men provision and Ammunition. The Enemy, sensible of this, endeavoured to dislodge us from Red Bank on the 22nd last month, which, as Congress have been informed, cost them 400 Men. Now, had our Army been upon the West Side of the Schuylkill, they might, without any danger of an attack upon their lines, have thrown over so considerable a force into Jersey, that they might have overpowered the Garrison, and by making themselves masters of it, have reduced Fort Mifflin by famine or want of ammunition. Thus we should in all probability have lost both posts by one Stroke.*[50]

The Continental Army commander broached another possibility with the president of Congress,

> *They might also, by taking possession of the fords upon Schuylkill, have rendered the Junction of our northern reinforcements with us a very difficult if not impractical matter, and should any accident have happened to them, we should have stood a very poor chance of looking Genl. Howe in the face thro' the Winter with an inferior Army.*[51]

In the preceding section of his report Washington is referring to the units of the Continental Army which were then in the process of making their way south following their service under Maj. Gen. Horatio Gates in the Saratoga campaign. Washington had requested these troops in order to supplement his own forces which suffered significant losses in the preceding campaign.[52] As the commander in chief went on to observe, if Howe managed to prevent the junction of Washington's main Continental Army with these reinforcements, he would possibly have been able to defeat at least one, or possibly both forces in detail.

> *We should finally, have thrown the Army into such a situation that we must inevitably have drawn on a general Engagement before our Reinforcements arrived, which, considering our disparity of Numbers, would probably have ended with the most disagreeable Consequences.*[53]

Further defending his decisions, Washington noted that "It was therefore determined, a few days ago to wait the arrival of the Reinforcements from the Northward, before any alteration could safely be made in the disposition of the Army, and I was not without hopes, that the Fort would have held out till that time."[54] Here, Washington discloses the hope that the forts could buy more time for his army to regroup and concentrate. Building on that theme, the Continental Army commander in chief noted, "That we might then have moved without endangering the Stores, I had given orders for the removal of them from the places in Lancaster Country, which is, at any rate, more safe and convenient than they were." [55]

Washington then returned to the current situation facing the American forces and some of the possibilities they offered. He observed,

> *As the keeping possession of Red Bank, and thereby still preventing the Enemy from weighing the Chevaux de frize before the frost obliges their Ships to quit the River, has become a matter of the greatest importance, I have determined to send down Genl. St. Clair, Genl. Knox and Baron Kalb to take a view of the Ground, and to endeavor to form a Judgment of the most probable means of securing it. They will at the same time, see how far it is possible for our fleet to keep their station since the loss of Fort Mifflin, and also make the proper inquiry into the Conduct of the Captains of the Galleys, mentioned in the former part of the letter.*[56]

Clearly, the preceding long communique to Henry Laurens was designed to establish the overall operational situation as it then existed and at the same time blunt any potential criticisms of

Washington's leadership while reporting the current military situation. He may have followed the adage that the best defense is a strong offense in that Gates was clearly in favor with much of the political leadership for his success at Saratoga. On the other hand, Washington seemed to have nothing to report but one failure after another. By explaining the practical necessity of each decision as he went, he in effect led his readers along to the same conclusion, or at least attempted to do so.

Initially, the Continental Congress, meeting in York, Pennsylvania, received the news of the loss of Fort Mifflin somewhat stoically. For instance, James Duane of New York, writing to the state's Council of Safety around November 19, he observed of Fort Mifflin, "A report prevails that it is evacuated; we have no authentic intelligence, but it is more than probable."[57] Many in the body praised the conduct of the garrison. Duane wrote later that same day to Philip Schuyler, observing, "The Garrison have already immortalized themselves by uncommon Valour and Perseverance."[58] Likewise, Cornelius Hartnett of North Carolina wrote to William Wilkinson, "Our Little fleet & forts on the Delaware have behaved nobly."[59] The following day he wrote the governor of North Carolina, Thomas Burke, "The River has been as well defended as could possibly be expected..." He continued, observing the "Bob Morris still thinks the Enemys Ships will not be able to get to Philadelphia this winter; others are very doubtful; for my part I anxiously look for the time of the river being froze over; this seldom happens before Christmas."[60] Richard Henry Lee of Virginia was effusive in his praise of the defenders to Samuel Adams. The Virginian informed the New Englander, "...we have lost Fort Mifflin, which out brave garrison was obliged to abandon after a most gallant defence[sic], in which all their guns were dismounted but two, and all the works beaten away about a rod and a half."[61]

James Lovell of Massachusetts praised the defenders as well, though his letter to Joseph Whipple of New Hampshire belies some criticism directed at other quarters,

> *Fort Mifflin is lost after the bravest defense. The naval part of our forces behaves well. They tell us from the* grand army *that our Gallies still maintain their Places of Command over the Chevaux de Frize.*[62]

There is something of a critical tone in Lovell's note, especially in his italicizing of grand army. This implied criticism grows more pronounced in a letter of Elbridge Gerry to Joseph Trumbull. The former observed, "The Enemy have obtained possession of Delaware River, from the Delay of the Army to support Fort Mifflin & Red Bank;" Such an expedition had never been serious planned, as the main army under Washington was at that time too weak to offer assistance, between the defeats suffered at Brandywine and Germanton, and the detachments sent to support Gates. Still, Gerry continued, "I think that an Enquiry into this affair...will necessarily take place."[63] The above is an early rumbling of the storm historians have dubbed the Conway Cabal.

As generally understood, the cabal, then, comprised an attempt, centered around the Inspector General, the Irish-born Thomas Conway, and Horatio Gates, the recent "victor of Saratoga" as well as Thomas Mifflin, the army's quartermaster general, to remove Washington from command of the army and replace him with Gates. Controversy swirled around whether any such an attempt even occurred almost since the events were said to have transpired. Contemporaries such as Marcy Otis Warren and George Bancroft believed a conspiracy to unseat Washington existed. In the nineteenth century, the notion gained support from a number of historians. Jared Sparks, one of the earliest to collect and categorize a number of Washington's writings, while he could not find evidence of the plot, accepted that something happened. There matters remained until the mid-twentieth century, when in 1941, Bernhardt Knollenberg challenged the entire existence of any conspiracy against Washington for lack of firm evidence.[64]

The more recent scholarship remains divided. John Buchanan supports the notion that some sort of conspiracy seemed to exist and takes the challenge to Washington's authority quite seriously. Buchanan connects the criticism of Washington to the notion held by many Patriot leaders that the war would be a short one. When the conflict protracted, they sought a concrete reason for why, and placed the blame on Washington's military leadership.[65]

Conversely, John Ferling interprets the cabal as the result of Washington's own insecurity and asserts that "In all likelihood, the supposed intrigue never amounted to more than a handful of disgruntled individuals who grumbled to one another about Washington's shortcomings."[66] The most recent and in-depth study of the Conway Cabal, by historian Mark E. Lender asserts that a real challenge to Washington's authority did, in fact, take place. The effort, however, was something different from what is usually described. Consequently, he discusses two different narratives. Since recent scholarship has revealed that a challenge to Washington's authority did in fact occur during the end of 1777 and early 1778, it is worth a digression to establish what Lender dubs the "Classic Cabal" and the "Real Cabal."[67] First, however, it is important to describe some of the key players in what Lender describes as the "Classic Cabal."

The central figure in the cabal, Thomas Conway (1733-1800?) was born in Ireland to a Catholic family and sailed for France at age six. There he received an education and joined the French Army in 1747 as a *lieutenant en second*. His first combat experiences were during the War of the Austrian Succession (1740-1748). In 1772, he rose to the rank of colonel. When the fighting broke out in the colonies, Conway sought and received royal permission to sail for America, embarking on December 14, 1776. The long-time professional soldier initially impressed Washington, who forwarded Conway to the Continental Congress with a commendatory letter. The body presented Conway with the rank of brigadier general and he served with some distinction at the battles of Brandywine and Germantown.[68]

Fig.19 - Brigadier General Thomas Conway *Unknown author - 18th century portrait.*

Very soon, however, the relationship between the commander and his subordinate began to sour. Numerous historians have speculated on the reasons for the change. Some see it as Conway, a professional, looking with disdain on Washington the amateur, while others see him believing replacing Washington with a more capable commander stood as the only means of rescuing the Continental Army from its deteriorating fortunes.[69] Conway was not the only European professional to find Washington's leadership wanting in late 1777.

Horatio Gates (1728-1806) was a British born professional officer. He entered the British army in 1745, and so gained his first military experience during the War of the Austrian Succession as well. He served in North America during the Seven Years' War as well. During the latter conflict served in the ill-fated Braddock campaign against Fort Duquesne in which he met George Washington. Following the end of the Seven Years' War, Gates retired from the British army and took advantage of a land grant in Virginia to establish himself as a farmer. As the colonial relationship deteriorated, he joined the Patriot movement. Congress took advantage of his previous military experience and commissioned him a brigadier general. Washington, in turn, appointed Gates as Adjutant General for the Continental army.

Figure 20 Thomas Mifflin and his wife, Sarah Morris. *John Singleton Copley, 1773.*

Gates was very much a political player and sought to enhance his reputation. His first major action in this line was to jockey to supplant the command of Philip Schuyler in the Northern Department. In this role of commander, which Gates saw as an independent command, he oversaw the defense against Lt. Gen. John Burgoyne's invasion. Gates took full credit for defeating the invasion, though many contemporaries saw Benedict Arnold and Daniel Morgan as key figures in winning the critical tactical engagements of the campaign. In late 1777, Gates military reputation waxed as Washington's seemed to wane.[70]

The third proposed conspirator was Thomas Mifflin, then serving as the head of the Quartermaster General's department. A successful Philadelphia merchant and an early supporter of resistance against Crown policy, he held a strong reputation in Patriot circles. The son of Quakers, he graduated the College of Philadelphia in 1760. As war with the mother country became more and more a possibility, Mifflin embraced greater involvement in military affairs, despite his Quaker background. Once the fighting did begin, he quickly rose in the Continental ranks and became an aide-de-camp to Washington. He received promotion to colonel on December 22, 1775, brigadier general on May 16, 1776, and major general on February 19, 1777. Mifflin's background as a successful merchant led to his being assigned as Quartermaster General. Initially, he did well in this position, and the army benefited from his attention. Beginning early in the summer of 1777, however, there appeared a significant decline in his efforts.[71]

The decline in Mifflin's performance as quartermaster coincided with a growing chasm in his relationship with Washington. Once a close subordinate to the commander in chief, Mifflin grew more distant over time as well. There were several reasons for the breakdown of their relationship according to Lender. One, Mifflin, an ardent Whig, placed much greater faith in the institution of the militia as opposed to a standing army. Second, as the 1777 campaign progressed in the Philadelphia region, with failure after failure, Mifflin grew disenchanted with Washington's leadership. Finally, Mifflin's close relationship with the commander in chief was eclipsed by the latter's growing affinity for Nathanael Greene.[72]

The main effort of the Cabal, according to Lender, encompassed an attempt by the three men just described to significantly curtail Washington's authority as commander of the Continental army. Their vehicle for enacting the change was the revamped Board of War. The new and stronger body possessed a broader scope than its predecessor. Ironically, the reformed institution constituted something many in the officer corps desired. In essence, these three sought to expand the scope of the Board's oversight even further, from areas such as logistics to the planning and implementation of strategy as well. At the time of their initial moves, just after the evacuation of Fort Mifflin, they received significant backing from members of the Continental Congress as well.[73] Many of the above correspondents believed it was time for a change, if not in the person of the commander, then in the manner in which the army was run.

Regardless of whether one fully accepts his argument, Lender's thorough examination of the Conway Cabal demonstrates that the activities of some both in the army and in Congress amounted to much more than mere grumbling. Likewise, one thing all the historians surveyed agreed on was that Washington not only weathered the storm but managed to come out of it with his authority strengthened. In fact, Ferling goes so far as to assert that Washington may almost have "welcomed or even fostered, the impression of a conspiracy, as it afforded an opportunity to at least plant seeds of malice against Gates, his latest antagonist."[74] Simply put, it gave the commander a chance to clean house once his political opponents revealed themselves. While this seems an extreme assessment, the demonstrative fall of the cabal, if there were one, cowed any further descent directed against Washington personally. Throughout the remainder of the conflict, there were no murmurs deriding Washington's leadership of the army.[75]

Beyond the possible political repercussions of the loss of the river forts within the American ranks, in the immediate aftermath of the evacuation of Fort Mifflin, the question remained of what steps to take next? Should the Pennsylvania Navy, outnumbered and out-gunned as it certainly was, sacrifice itself in an attempt to further prevent the British from moving up the Delaware, or should they make a run up the Delaware past Philadelphia to the relative safety of Bristol? Should additional troops be sent into New Jersey to reinforce those already there? If Fort Mercer could be retained, then the job of controlling the Delaware remained incomplete for the British.[76]

William Howe's next steps were clear, and he embarked on them with the vigor he displayed on such occasions. While William Howe is often portrayed as lethargic if not downright slothful in his execution of operations, a careful examination of his approach demonstrates something different. Following the costly success at Bunker Hill on June 17, 1775, which he not only planned but led, Howe demonstrated a much more methodical streak. He would wait for his enemy to make a mistake or offer an opportunity. Then he would organize his forces accordingly, and act. The British commander clearly understood that with the evacuation of Fort Mifflin, Fort Mercer now stood as the key obstacle in securing free navigation of the Delaware. If it were reduced, Lord Howe's ships could work on removing the chevaux de frise unmolested and gain access to the port of Philadelphia. Howe settled on Fort Mercer as his target and set forces in motion accordingly.

Under orders from Howe, Earl Charles Cornwallis, always an aggressive commander, crossed the Schuylkill with roughly two thousand troops in the evening of November 17th. The troops marched to Chester, where they were reinforced by additional forces under Maj. Gen. Sir Thomas Wilson to the number of about 5,500, some sources give a figure as high as 6,000, many of them experienced veterans who took part in the storming of Forts Clinton and Montgomery in New York. [77] Cornwallis then crossed the Delaware to Billingsport. His strike force included the 5th, 15th, 26th, 27th,33rd, 45th, 56th, and 63rd Regiments along with the 17th Light Dragoons, the 7th Royal Fusiliers, the 1st Light Infantry, two battalions of Anspach Grenadiers, 500 Hessian Jägers, twelve cannon and several howitzers. Once across the river, Cornwallis began moving on Billingsport.[78] In order to bolster this force, Howe dispatched the 42nd regiment to Cooper's Ferry.[79] The artillery component of his force led Varnum to believe the British general planned to besiege Fort Mercer.[80] Francis Downman aptly observed that "The junction of the parties will be the decisive stroke against that place, for the very idea of being surrounded is what they cannot bear."[81]

At this time, the garrison at Fort Mercer mustered some 565 men. There were 211 from Greene's regiment, another 215 from Angell's and perhaps sixty-five from Forman's New Jersey militia brigade. There were roughly seventy-four officers and men attached to the artillery. There were vessels of both the Continental and Pennsylvania Navies as well, though the crews of both were depleted and in need of rest and resupply. Likewise, many of the galleys as well as the floating batteries were in need of immediate repair.[82] Clearly the British forces, both on land and in the river were superior to those of the Americans, both quantitatively and qualitatively.

Once again, Washington's spy network kept him well informed of the British movements, writing from Frankfort on November 18, at 11:30 AM, Capt. James Craig informed Washington, "I have this moment received information of Lord Cornwallace [sic] crossing in Jersey last night with for thousand men."[83]

Craig followed up his initial communique to Washington with another missive the same day at 3:30 PM,

> *Since my last I have had I believe a True Acct of Lord Cornwalls [sic] rout. Last night about 12 o'Clock his Lordship Marchd from the City with Two thousand Granadiers, & light Infantry, he intends his march for Willington where he is to Cross the river and march up the other side and make an Attack on Red Bank Fort.*[84]

While clearly erring in the particulars, Craig did pass along to Washington the salient details: that Cornwallis was on the move with a significant force composed of shock troops, and that their intended target was Fort Mercer.

Washington received additional intelligence from Joseph Reed of Pennsylvania. Writing from Lewis Davis's near Springfield Meeting House (likely modern Springfield, Delaware County) on November 18, the Pennsylvanian described a force of British troops making their way to Chester under the command of Lord Cornwallis. Reed indicated that their objective was Red Bank and that according to his source "they would storm it tonight if practicable but they were so late the Informant thinks they could not effect it tonight."[85]

Washington responded to the various reports on British actions in several ways. First, he passed the information on British movements on to Varnum, alerting him that "A Body of the Enemy marched last Night from Philadelphia, across the Bridge at the Middle Ferry and proceeded to Chester."[86] He further informed his subordinate, that he believed, "they intend to cross over to Jersey and pay you a visit." Further, he advised Varnum, "Therefore keep a good look-out below; if you do this, they cannot surprise you..."[87] Finally, he instructed Varnum to defer,

> *To all matters contained in yours of yesterday I refer you to the Generals St. Clair, Knox and Kalb, who went down to consult with you and the Commodore. I expect a report from them to government in my operations towards assisting you.*[88]

Washington, in effect, decentralized decision-making authority to his subordinates on the scene, placing himself in more of a supporting role. Given the overall situation, there was little else Washington could do. By the same token, Washington moved to Crooked Billet, Pennsylvania (modern Hatboro) in order to be closer to the developing action. Thus, it seems that this delegation of authority was meant to be only temporary. Beyond advising Varnum, Washington took steps to reinforce the troops in New Jersey as well. At 11 PM that night, Washington sent orders to Brig. Gen. John Glover explaining that

> *The Enemy having thrown a considerable part of their force over the Delaware, with an Intention as I suppose of making an attack upon our Fort at Red Bank, occasions me to Reinforce the Garrison and Troops already there with a large Detachment from this Army - in addition to which it is my desire & you are hereby order'd to March by the most convenient Route after receipt of this to Join the Continental Army which may be in the Neighborhood of Red Bank under the command of Major Genl. Greene...* [89]

Washington further advised Glover that "Your first Route should be directed to Haddonfield and from thence as Circumstances will require." [90] Glover's unit, as well as Daniel Morgan's riflemen had just marched southwards from their triumph over Burgoyne. Washington repeatedly called on Gates to dispatch additional troops to the Philadelphia theater to aid in operations there. The latter's dalliance in the matter served as another source of friction within in the Continental army command.

Shortly after ordering Glover and his reinforcements into New Jersey, Washington wrote Varnum, informing the latter of his moves. In addition, Washington instructed, "You will please to direct the detachment that went first down to Fort Mifflin under the command of Colonel Smith to return to camp, they are in so much want of Necessaries that it is impossible for them to remain longer." [91] Finally, the men of the remnants of the garrison could look forward to some well-deserved rest.

While both sides prepared for a final showdown in New Jersey, the British continued their efforts on the newly occupied Mud Island. On November 18, Francis Downman recorded that he went down to Mud Island where "I got two 18-prs. Mounted on our new battery." He further noted "Two 32-prs. Are to be put on this battery also." The new battery would, when complete, be capable of defending the efforts of the Royal Navy to remove the chevaux de frise. Likewise, they would provide additional cover for British supply ships bringing much needed provisions to the main army in Philadelphia.

As the new realities of the operational situation emerged, another council of war was hastily convened under Varnum to determine if an attempt should be made to hold Fort Mercer, and what role the fleet would play in upcoming operations. Hazelwood, Col. Christopher Greene and their subordinates attended the conference. Here it was determined that the remaining vessels of the Continental should try and make their way up the Delaware past Philadelphia.[92] Capt. Downman observed some of the preparations for the move, noting on the 18th, "The galleys this afternoon were in motion; we expected them down to the fort."[93] What the artillerist thought were preparations for an attack were actually arrangements for a withdrawal.

Early in the morning on November 19, Cmdre. Hazelwood received a report that Col. Greene and his forces were in the process of abandoning Fort Mercer. Hazelwood determined to lead the fleet to Ladd's Cove, at the mouth of Big Timber Creek in New Jersey, just above Fort Mercer. There, they would await a favorable wind to make the dangerous run past Philadelphia.[94]

As the naval commanders plotted their escape, Washington continued to receive updates from his information network concerning British movements into New Jersey. On November 19, for instance, he received several messages from Capt. Craig informing him of additional units being dispatched into New Jersey.[95]

Varnum reported to Washington on the 19th as well. He established his new headquarters at Haddonfield, which he perceived to be "a more fit situation for benefiting Red Bank."[96] The reason underlying the general's choice of location revolved around the fact that it allowed him to stand between any junction of the British forces moving north from Billingsport and those reportedly on the march south from Cooper's Ferry. As Varnum informed his commander, his position would allow him to attack the two forces in detail. He further explained that he planned to go to Red Bank himself and consult with Col. Greene on the likelihood of a successful defense should the British forces mount another attack on that location.

The reason he gave Washington for the personal reconnaissance was that "I shall not suffer the Garrison to be sacrificed on Conjecture; but continue them as long as I can cover them..."[97]

Based on this information, it seems Washington now perceived that Fort Mercer and the deployment of Varnum's troops in the vicinity might yield one last chance of giving a check to the British forces before the end of the campaign season. The delegation of Maj. Gens. Washington dispatched to support Varnum was the source of his estimate, and they made their recommendations clear on their return to headquarters. The Continental commander wrote Varnum on November 19, "The Generals St. Clair, Knox and Kalb returned to Camp this Evening - they are all clear in their opinion that keeping possession of Red Bank is of the last importance." Based on this assessment, Washington continued, "I have therefore determined to make such an addition to the Reinforcement that marched this morning under Genl. Huntington that I am in hopes that you will be able to give an effectual Check to the force which the Enemy at present have in Jersey." Given that this force now amounted to a significant portion of the army, Huntington's brigade being roughly 1,200 strong, Washington placed Maj. Gen. Nathanael Greene in overall command.[98] Still, he advised Varnum, "Very much will depend upon keeping possession of Fort Mercer as to reduce it the Enemy will be obliged to put themselves in a very disagreeable situation to them and advantageous to us, upon a narrow neck of land between two Creeks, with our whole force pressing upon their Rear." [99] Washington continued, giving his subordinate precise directions as to his intentions,

> *Therefore desire Colonel Green[sic] to hold it [Fort Mercer] if possible till the relief arrives. All superfluous Stores may be removed if it can be done after this reaches you; that in Case of Accident as little may fall into the hands of the Enemy as possible.*[100]

Here, Washington may have been concerned with avoiding a debacle such as occurred at Fort Washington in New York the previous year. On that occasion, the British captured the entire garrison as well as substantial supplies following only a brief resistance by a post which his subordinates had assured Washington was difficult to assail and that the garrison could be ferried off if an assault seemed like it would succeed. In the end, the capture of Fort Washington occurred after only a brief, but extremely violent assault. The remaining members of the garrison were made prisoners and substantial quantities of supplies taken by the British. [101]

Washington has often been noted for being, by nature, an aggressive commander. He possessed a disdain for inactivity. As

Edward Lengel has noted, Washington's impatience and hatred of inactivity left him with little tolerance for any kind of delay or obstruction." He further observed, "When frustration or boredom led him into a funk, therefore, the prospect of battle ...could throw him instantaneously into a more optimistic frame of mind." [102] Likewise, Robert Middlekauff notes that he "possessed a desire, a forceful impulse, to force action and not give way when resisted."[103] He further observes,

> *In many men, such a will is often violent, at least in verbal expression and sometimes in physical aggression. Countering, or holding down, even controlling, Washington's will was a sense of restraint - a brake on unrestrained impulse that could yield to self-defeating action.*[104]

Perhaps in this instance, his normal predisposition to activity received a further boost from the perceived threat to his command. At the same time, it appears that the general's omni-present self-control intervened to keep him from authorizing his subordinate to engage in self-defeating action.

By this point in the war, moreover, Washington had clearly come to grasp the significance of the Continental army to the continued existence of the Revolution. From that realization sprung the Fabian strategy as contemporaries and later historians described it. Named for the Roman dictator Quintus Fabius Maximus, it entailed the notion that Washington would no longer hazard his entire force on the outcome of a single clash. He had first begun to adopt this approach during the autumn of 1776.[105]

Washington continued to follow the Fabian approach in 1777, and it is clearly evident in his instructions to Varnum. After outlining his hopes that the British could be drawn into a clash on favorable terms for the Continental army, he went on to add a caveat in a post-script: "Altho I am anxious to have the fort kept, I do not mean that it should be done at all events so as to endanger the safety of the Men without any probability of success."[106] Essentially, Washington, while encouraging his subordinate to act aggressively desired Varnum to temper any risks with the probability of success.

On the same day, the French engineer, Louis Duportail wrote to the French foreign minister St. Germain, informing him of the progress of the fighting in North America. His account of the campaign around Philadelphia, which included a map, was quite positive in its tone. It further demonstrates how the fighting for control of the Delaware river helped to shape the international situation and combined with the victory at Saratoga, helped push the kingdom of France into making an open pact with the Americans. Duportail began by noting that:

> *Up to the present, General Howe has not taken the forts on the river which prevent vessels from reaching the city and which compel him to communicate only by the little road which I marked on the map and which we could easily cut this winter when we have received a reinforcement of victorious troops from the north.*[107]

Duportail had not yet learned of the evacuation of Fort Mifflin. He did, however, present the American position as one poised to take the offensive, "We expect to strike a blow on the other side of Schuylkill;" Further bolstering this claim, he observed, "there are already some troops in the Jerseys, on the bank of the Delaware river; so Gen. Howe will be obliged to remain in Philadelphia and run great risk of famine."[108] Duportail then qualified the preceding with, "But in truth, we do not expect very much."[109]

The French engineer then turned to the fighting then going on in the river. He observed of Gen. William Howe, "He will surely take the forts if he makes a determined attack, and then he will have a sure communication with his fleet."[110] Summing up the American position, Duportail noted, "You see, Monseigneur, that for men who have suffered two defeats, we are not in too bad a position, which we owe to the fact that the English have few cavalry and cannot follow up their victories, and still more to our forests, and to obstacles of all kinds by which this country is defended."[111] The generally positive description of the American position outside of Philadelphia should be placed in the context of the news of the victory at Saratoga then on its way to France as well. The image it provided is one of American success in one sector combined with stalemate in another. Granted, Duportail does not credit Washington or his troops with blunting the British offensive in the Delaware Valley, instead referring to the British lack of cavalry and the terrain. Still, his talk of offensive plans does not give the impression of a defeat and beleaguered force either.

He the downplayed the achievement of the Americans in New York, stating that "It is not the good conduct of the Americans which won for them the campaign which on the whole has been so happy; it is rather the mistakes of the English."[112] The preceding could be viewed as an indirect snub at the leadership of Horatio Gates. Why he would include such a line in a communication to his own foreign minister, and outside the loop of the Conway Cabal remains unclear. When it came to criticizing leadership, Duportail was much less veiled in his criticisms of the British command. Concerning Gen. William Howe, he wrote,

> *If we consider next the conduct of General Howe, we shall see that he has not done that which he could have done, as I had the honor of informing you after the battle of Brandywine. If the English followed up their advantage, there would no longer be any question of the army of Washington and since then, General Howe has conducted all his operations with a sluggishness, a timidity, which astonishes me every day. But it is necessary to bethink oneself—they can send another general, and then we shall not find ourselves so well off.*[113]

The above description of Howe's overall demeanor presents him as something bordering on a strategic asset to the Americans. This contemporary view has been taken up by later historians as well who have interpreted Howe's conduct of the campaign as one of restraint based either on his own laziness, or the conflict between his dual roles as commander of British forces in North America and peace commissioner.[114] As Michael Harris has pointed out, however, at least in connection with his conduct immediately following the battle of Brandywine, Howe was not really in a position to offer and immediate pursuit of Washington as his own force sustained significant damage in the fighting.[115]

Finally, Duportail presented a damning judgement on the morale of most Americans for the war effort in late 1777, "There is a hundred times more enthusiasm for this revolution in a single café in Paris than in all the united colonies."[116] By late 1777, many ardent supporters of the revolt at the outset had lost much of their zeal. The halcyon days of the *rage militaire* were definitely a thing of the past.[117]

Return to developments in the campaign, Varnum replied to Washington's instructions at 5PM the same day. First, he informed Washington that he had relocated, with his troops which he now styled a flying camp, to Haddonfield. He gave as his "principal Inducement" the various reports that British troops "from Philadelphia were to form a Junction with those from Billingsport."[118] Adopting this new position would allow Varnum to attack any column moving south from Philadelphia, which would help to keep open the line of retreat for the garrison at Red Bank.

As Varnum explained his motives for the change in position to Washington, he incorporated new intelligence which underscored the fluid nature of the tactical situation,

> *My Videts [sic] have just informed me from Manto Creek Bridge, Sunton, that the Enemy moved, three Hours since with about one Thousand towards that Bridge, but as it was taken up, which they could not fail knowing, I imagine their Principal Maneuver was filing off from their Rear to their Right, in Order to cross five Miles above, where the Creek is easily fordible.*[119]

Varnum feared that if the British made the move he described to Washington, then Fort Mercer would become untenable. Varnum determined to find out for himself the precise nature of the situation. "I am at this Moment going to Red Bank, & its Vicinity to satisfy myself more fully, & consult with Col. Greene."[120] There was significant skirmishing between British and Continental forces that day, and Washington ordered Varnum to the upper side of Big Timber Creek in order to avoid being trapped by the British forces in the area.[121]

Dr. Albigence Waldo, summarized the situation writing in his diary on November 19, he observed, "This Day Huntington's Brigade ... march'd for Red Bank, which the Garrison Evacuated before we arrived."[122] The main camp for the Continental Army at this time was located at Whitemarsh. Waldo further observed how this force was joined with Nathanael Greene's division and Varnum's brigade at Mount Holly, where they remained until November 25.[123]

Not only were the land forces in motion. On November 19th, Downman noted from Mud Island that "Early this morning I observed the galleys in motion and prepared everything to receive them, but instead of paying us a visit they went and joined the fleet at Gloucester Point;"[124] What Downman observed was in fact the first stage of the evacuation of the American naval forces from the vicinity of Fort Mifflin to Ladd's Cove.

Shortly after the arrival of the remnants of the fleet at Ladd's Cove, Hazelwood and Robinson held a brief council of war during which they decided to attempt to move their ships further up the Delaware on the 20th. They divided their force into two squadrons. The Continental ships, and the larger vessels of the State Navy would be compelled to take the main channel up the Delaware. This route would take them perilously close to the British batteries in Philadelphia, as well as under the guns of the *Delaware* frigate. Each ship was to take on a supply of combustibles so that if it were damaged, or the wind turned unfavorable, the crew could abandon the ships and fire them rather than allow them to fall into British hands.[125]

The galleys and other smaller vessels of the Pennsylvania Navy, on the other hand, were designated to follow the eastern channel in the river, hugging the New Jersey coast until they were north of Cooper's Ferry. These vessels, as well, were prepared for self-destruction if necessary.

At three o'clock in the morning of the 20th, they put the plan into action. The thirteen galleys and nine guard boats made their way northward, hugging the Jersey coast and passed by the British batteries undetected, making their way to Bristol by roughly ten in the morning. [126] The winds were not favorable at that time for the larger ships to make their escape.[127]

Once Hazelwood was certain the galleys were safely on their way, he turned his attention to getting the remaining ships of his command off. At this point, his subordinates informed him of a large quantity of stores still at Ladd's Cove and on the Continental vessels. If these supplies were not moved or destroyed, they would certainly fall into British hands. The commodore then borrowed a horse and road to Bristol, hoping to secure enough wagons to relocate the material. Failing that, he planned to return with some of the galleys.

As Hazelwood worked to secure the supplies left behind at Ladd's Cove, Continental Navy Capt. Isaiah Robinson met with Varnum. The Continental general said he could not provide any protection for the ships on the landward side until they reached Rancocas Creek above Philadelphia. It seems clear that Varnum planned at this time to fall back on Mount Holly.[128] Given the size of the force Cornwallis brought with him into New Jersey, Varnum's move made sense. His forces were numerically inferior.

Varnum followed up his previous communication to Washington on the 20th. At 11 AM, he notified the commander in chief that when he rendezvoused with Col. Greene, the latter had received intelligence that the British had crossed the ford of Manto Creek. Furthermore, "In Consequence he [Greene] had given Orders for an Evacuation."[129] To deny the British the post intact, Col. Greene and Maj. Duplessis had prepared Fort Mercer for demolition by spreading powder from the magazine over the works. They seemed concerned with being caught in a pincer movement between the troops traveling from Philadelphia and those moving up from Billingsport as well.

Varnum continued, "However, upon an Apprehension that your Excellency might make a great Effort to save it, the Garrison agreed to remain; Hoping to take up the scattered Powder in the Day Light."[130] Both the decision to remain at the fort through the rest of the night, with the powder strewn across the work, and the plan to pick it up again in the morning exposed the garrison to great risk. As John W. Jackson aptly summarized, the garrison forgot "that the very presence of this powder made their position untenable; the discharge of a musket or the bursting of a shell would ignite the powder and destroy the fort and a large segment of the garrison with it." [131]

The sound of oars nearby seemed to temporarily unnerve Col. Greene and Brig. Gen. Varnum, and they beat a hasty retreat from Fort Mercer, leaving behind a strong guard to fire on the boats should a British attack materialize. Since there is no evidence to suggest that any British vessels were near Fort Mercer that night, what the commanders heard was most likely the sound of the galleys making their way northward up the Delaware, a maneuver which will be described below.[132]

The sound of the oars in the water grew fainter, and the garrison regained its composure, and the bulk of the garrison returned to the fort. The commanders still worried that Cornwallis might launch a strike at them that night or the following morning.[133]

As the defenders returned to finish a nerve-wracking vigil through the night at Fort Mercer, the remnants of the Pennsylvania Navy moved up the Delaware past Philadelphia. Capt. Robinson assisted in the maneuver. Moving up the middle channel of the Delaware, they were soon observed by British sentries, and they came under heavy fire from the batteries in the city. The British batteries in the city let loose a heavy bombardment on the passing ships, which drove two small sloops on to the Pennsylvania shore. The schooner *Delaware* (not to be confused with the frigate now in the British service) and another small vessel were forced to beach themselves and were set on fire by their crews. The Continental brig *Andrea Doria*, the xebecks *Repulse* and *Champion*, the sloops *Racehorse* and *Fly*, the state ship *Montgomery*, and two floating batteries were all set on fire. Only the brig *Convention* and four shallops successfully ran the gauntlet up the river to safety. [134] Two shallops and a few guard boats remained at Ladd's Cove transferring their supplies to wagons. Three and possibly more of the surviving guard boats eventually made their way north to Bristol, Pennsylvania.[135]

A group of volunteers from Greene and Angell's regiments returned to Fort Mercer to hold the works and destroy them should the British return. The detachment first marched to Gloucester Point in New Jersey where they boarded boats and completed the return to Fort Mercer. These same boats were retained at the fort as a means of escape should the British cut the composite force off from the landward side. The detachment blew up the fort on the afternoon of November 20.[136]

As previously noted, Varnum returned to his headquarters on the 20th and quickly relocated to Mount Holly where he was joined by Cols. Greene and Angell late on the same day or early on the 21st. Varnum sent a note to Washington informing the latter of his move and his reasoning, explaining that he did not want to be trapped between the two creeks should the British advance. By now, Varnum had been reinforced by Huntington's brigade, and the former received information that Maj. Gen. Nathanael Greene was at Burlington.[137]

Even with the forts reduced and ships capable of sailing up the Delaware, conditions did not immediately improve in Philadelphia. An anonymous letter sent to Washington containing intelligence on conditions in the city noted that rum was being brought in via the Schuylkill and selling at a Guiney per gallon. Pork was available, but beef and butter were not. Likewise, the flour available in the city was very "musty."[138] The anonymous informant further passed along rumors to the effect that "they say Cornwallis is to scower the Jerseys whilst How[sic] is to maintain this city with about 3000 men..." The same source further informed Washington that "Their different preparations plainly denote their determination of wintering here." Concerning the state of the British forces in Philadelphia, the anonymous correspondent described them as "healthy & very saucy, say they have men enough to defend their Lines whilst Cornwallis clears the Country." They added a final note, "I hope His Excellency General Washington will soon convince them to the contrary."[139]

Washington had dispatched Greene into New Jersey to assume overall command of the various detachments already dispatched there. As noted, the Rhode Islander established a temporary headquarters in Burlington, and waited for his division, which was ferried across on November 21, with his baggage and artillery joining the following night. While at Burlington, Greene met with Hazelwood, who expressed the resentment of commanders in the fleet at the aspersions cast on them by Smith and others. [140]

Writing to Washington from Burlington, New Jersey on November 21, Nathanael Greene passed on Hazelwood's report. Hazelwood had told Greene, "that the greater part, if not all the fleet except thirteen Gallies were burnt this morning; one or two of the smallest vessels attempted to pass and could not effect it..."[141] Greene further informed the commander in chief that "one was set on fire and one other fell into the enemies hands owing to the match going out - the People made their escape."[142] Many of the larger ships of the Pennsylvania Navy were set on fire to prevent their falling into British hands as the *Delaware* had. In a postscript, Greene informed Washington of additional intelligence from Cmdre. Hazelwood to the effect that three sloops and a brig had succeeded in getting past Philadelphia on the Jersey side.[143] The smaller vessels, such as the gallies and guard boats were often concealed in smaller creeks along the river north of Philadelphia and sunk there. Many of these vessels were later raised following the British evacuation of Philadelphia the following year.[144]

On the same day, Varnum wrote Washington from Mount Holly, updating him on the situation. His letter warrants quoting at length as he sets out the situation of the Patriot forces then deployed in western new Jersey:

> *Last Evening Fort Mercer was evacuated. Some of the Shipping burnt this Morning. Most of the Stores bro't safely off. The enemy, part at Billingsport, part between Manto & Timber Creeks, and some at Fort Mercer. We have moved to this Place as the first safe Position on Account of the Creeks. From hence, we can move by the Head of the Creeks, go down upon the Enemy, secure both our flanks, by the Creeks, and by the same means, secure a Retreat in Case of Disaster. It is a fit Situation of making a Junction of the Respective Corps; Genl Huntington has already joined me. Genl Greene is at Burlington. The Militia amount*

to Twelve Hundred. Three hundred here, Seven Hundred at Haddonfield: I have ordered them here, but am just told they don't like the Manouevre. Two Hundred at Coopers Ferry & Gloucester; They are to join. With the Great Force you have ordered, we shall be superior, I believe, to the Enemy in the Field. We have the Advantage by being at the Head of the Creeks; & it is my firm Sentiment, we ought & shall attack them to Advantage. The Success of that Manoeuvre, as I mention before, will determine the Possession of the Forts.
145

Varnum does not present the impression of a beaten commander in full retreat. Quite the contrary, he was spoiling for a fight, and held out the hope of regaining the American forts long the Delaware and depriving the British of their hopes of access to the port of Philadelphia.

Nathanael Greene continued updating his chief on the developing situation the following day, this time writing from Mount Holly, New Jersey. He first informed the commander of his difficulties in getting his baggage over the river, noting "the Boats & Scows at Burlington are under very bad Regulations." He went to inform his commander that "Gen. Varnum had retreated as I wrote your Excellency before to this place. He left a Party of Militia at Haddonfield. I am afraid there has a very considerable Quantity of Stores fallen into the Enemies Hands, but principally belonging to the Fleet."[146]

In addition to overseeing the various units in New Jersey, the major general, by now one of his commander's most trusted subordinates, Possessed the operational freedom to potentially engage the British should a favorable opportunity present itself. Greene therefore set out for Mount Holly to rendezvous with Varnum and Huntington.

On establishing his headquarters Mount Holly, Greene planned to intercept the British advanced guard somewhere beyond Haddonfield. At the same time, Cornwallis lack of aggressive actions towards the Continental troops in the area confused the Rhode Islander. Still, he set up a defensive line along Rancocas Creek and threw out patrols as far as Haddonfield and Little Timber Creek.

Cornwallis had specific objectives, which included the destruction of Fort Mercer and the other American batteries, and to force the surrender of the remainder of the American feet. Cornwallis planned to remain in the region until he met these objectives. He would then evacuate his men to Philadelphia by way of Gloucester Point.[147]

Problems of supply as well as a general lack of support from the local militia plagued Greene in his position along Rancocas Creek, though Washington urged him to attack the British if the opportunity arose. Writing to Greene on November 23, Washington noted that it appeared the British were still operating in New Jersey, "I am inclined therefore to wish that you would advance to meet it as much in force as possible - and that for this purpose you would use every means to hasten the junction of Glover's Brigade."[148] The commander in chief further informed his subordinate that he was working to send him further reinforcements in the form of Lee's Legion.[149] It appears that Washington hoped for an additional engagement with a part of the British army which might result in a tactical win for the Continentals. This would serve several purposes. Most importantly, it could prevent the enemy from clearing the river obstructions before it froze, and thus make their continued occupation of Philadelphia extremely difficult if not impossible. Further, it would demonstrate that his forces remained a threat to the British, and it might serve to raise his sullied reputation in the eyes of the Congress and reduce the aura of success then surrounding Gates.

The possibility of an engagement was very real as Greene had by now amassed a significant force under his command. It included his own division, Varnum's forces, composed of the Rhode Island regiments of Cols. Greene and Angell, and the Connecticut regiments of Cols. Chandler and Durkee. On the 23rd, Col. Daniel Morgan arrived with 170 of his riflemen who had marched south following the defeat of Burgoyne in October. Finally, Gen. John Glover's brigade arrived on November 25. These last troops made a very rapid march, leaving the Hudson Highlands on the 10th.[150]

As far as the fate of the fleet was concerned, two members of the Navy Board, a Mr. Hopkinson and John Wharton, informed Washington on the same day Morgan's contingent arrived in New Jersey,

> *It is with the greatest Concern we inform you of the total Destruction of the Continental Fleet at Red Bank; having been burned by our own Officers in Consequence of a Determination of a Council of War. We have not yet had an Opportunity of making a regular Enquiry into the Reasons of so desparate [sic] a Measure. As far as we can collect from the Officers and*

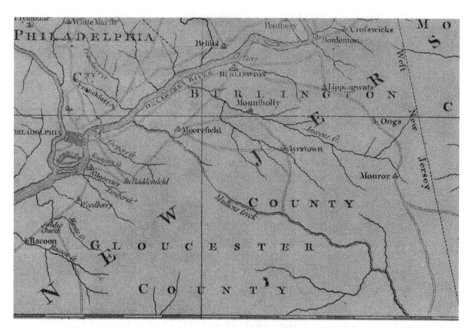

Fig. 21 - Contemporary map of the area of operations of Greene and Cornwallis in New Jersey, November-December 1777. *Taken from A New and accurate map of the present seat of war in North America, comprehending New Jersey, Phila- delphia, Pensylvania, New-York, &c. London, 1777. Library of Congress Library of Congress Online Catalog (1,124,204)*

> *Crews here it was occasioned by the Assurances of the Commander of the Land Forces, that they must expect no further Protection from his Army; not even to secure a Retreat in Case of Emergency.*[151]

The men continued, "But this must be the Subject of future Enquiry. Be the Cause what it may, the Loss seems at present, to be irreparable."[152]

That same day, Washington composed another long letter to Henry Laurens, the president of the Continental Congress,

> *I am sorry to inform Congress that the Enemy are now in possession of All the Water defenses. Fort Mifflin and that at Red Bank mutually depended on each Other for support, and the reduction of the for- mer made the tenure of the latter extremely precari- ous if not impracticable. After the loss of Fort Mifflin, it was found, Red Bank could derive no advantages from the Gallies and Armed Vessels—(they could not maintain their Station) and in the case of Investiture,*

the Garrison could have no Supplies - not retreat - nor any hope of relief, but such as might arise from a Superior force acting without on the rear of the Enemy and dislodging them. Under these circumstances, the Garrison was obliged to evacuate it on the night of the 20th Int., on the approach of Lord Cornwallis, who had crossed the River from Chester, with a Detachment, supposed to be about Two Thousand Men, and formed a junction with the Troops, lately arrived from New York and those that had been landed before at Billingsport.[153]

The commander in chief continued,

> *From Genl Varnum's Account, I have reason, to hope, that we saved most of the Stores, except a few Heavy Cannon - however I cannot be particular in this instance. I am also to add, from the intelligence, I have received, that most, if not All of the Armed Vessels have been burnt by our own people, except the Gallies - One Bring and Two Sloops, which are said to have run by the City. How far this might have been founded in necessity, I am not able to determine - but I suppose it was done under the Idea and an apprehension of their falling into the Enemy's hands, if they attempted to pass up the River.*[154]

Washington further explained the measures he took to engage the British and detailed for the president the units he dispatched into New Jersey. He noted that his goal in making the deployment and calling out the New Jersey militia was holding Fort Mercer, "But they [the British] were so rapid in their advances, that our troops could not form a junction & arrive in time to succour the Garrison which obliged them to withdrawal." [155] The commander continued, expressing his hopes for further opportunities to bring the British to battle, "Genl Greene is still in Jersey, and when Glovers Brigade joins him, if an Attack can be made on Lord Cornwallis with a prospect of success, I am confident it will be done." Washington concluded, noting that "About a Hundred & Seventy of Morgan's Corps are also gone to reinforce him."[156] Again, Washington seemed to be both reporting to his civilian superior and providing the latter with ammunition to fend off any attacks by the commander's critics. Washington was preparing his superior for more bad news as well.

As more missives arrived from Nathanael Greene, the American position in New Jersey appeared nothing if not gloomy.

As he surveyed the overall situation in western New Jersey, Nathanael Greene updated Washington on situation as he perceived it. While he had little new to report on the movements of the enemy, Greene sought clarification on his superior's expectations. First, he laid out that the New Jersey militia were dwindling in numbers as time went on. He further informed the commander in chief of the efforts of local leaders to draw some back into the field.[157] Greene then asked Washington for additional troops, especially cavalry and noted that he had thus far received no word from John Glover.[158] Finally, the major general laid out the crux of his concern to his superior, should he attack the British or not?

Considering that "Your Excellency observes in your last, you must leave the Propriety of attacking the Enemy to me. Would you advise me to fight them with very unequal numbers?"[159] Greene went on to note that the British outnumbered him by about two thousand men. It seemed that the subordinate was searching for permission not to engage the enemy. By the same token, some have pointed out that given the criticisms then being leveled at Washington, Greene, as well as other subordinates, may have feared a failed attack would only generate greater condemnation of the Continental commander.[160]

Washington continued to reinforce Greene, and this did generate some skirmishing. On November 24, the Marquis de Lafayette led a composite force of about one hundred and fifty of Morgan's riflemen and an equal number of Gloucester County militia under a Colonel Ellis into New Jersey. They collided with a Hessian force on the Gloucester Road between Big and Little Timber Creeks. In the resultant skirmish some fourteen Hessians were captured, and between twenty-five and thirty were killed and wounded. The American loss was two militia officers killed and five privates wounded.[161] The skirmish, though small and often overlooked in the secondary sources fueled a movement by Washington, already seemingly underway, to give Lafayette the command of a division in the Continental army. Congress supported the appointment on December 1. [162]

Soon after dispatching the above message to his commander, Greene shifted his position. On November 25, the Continentals concentrated at Mount Holly marched for Haddonfield, which they reached on the following morning. Surgeon Albigence Waldo noted in his diary for the 26th, "Lay in the Forrest of Haddonfield, cold and uncomfortable."[163]

As for Greene's antagonist, following the destruction of Fort Mercer, Cornwallis perceived his task in New Jersey as finished and began marching for Gloucester and from there rejoining the main British army in Philadelphia. As he withdrew his troops, Cornwallis conducted a foraging operation designed to gather desperately needed foodstuffs for the city. The earl began embarking his forces on November 23rd. Some assert that Washington wanted Hazelwood to break the dikes and flood the low-lying areas along the river in order to further interdict British progress during these operations.[164] Cornwallis completed his withdrawal from New Jersey two days later.[165]

Also on the 23rd, the John André noted in his *Journal*, "The first vessel came to Philadelphia. The ships were obliged to pass singly through an opening left by the Rebels for their own shipping;" He further commented that "the weighing of the chevaux-de-fries was said to be a work of great labor and perhaps not to be effected."[166] In some respects, André was quite correct as the remnants of many of the frames lay in the river for some time after the war, some into the nineteenth and twentieth centuries.

Greene led his forces out of New Jersey to rejoin the main army at Whitemarsh on November 28.[167] That same day, the members of the Continental Congress, by then meeting in York, Pennsylvania, grew concerned over the loss of the Delaware River forts. On November 28, the resolved, "That an enquiry be made into the loss of ...Fort Mifflin on the river Delaware, in the State of Pennsylvania, and into the conduct of the principal officers commanding the forts;"[168] The body further ordered "that General Washington be directed to cause the enquiry to be made, and to transmit the proceedings of the court to Congress with all possible dispatch." Washington then spent the next few weeks trying to determine where to encamp the army.

William Howe made one final lunge at Washington, marching a substantial part of his army out of Philadelphia in early December. They made their way towards the main Continental Army encampment. This move resulted in some desultory skirmishing between December 5-8 known collectively as the battle of Whitemarsh or Edge Hill.[169]

While the river was opened and some supplies were getting into the city, it was still not enough to make living comfortable by any means. Certainly, this led to tensions within the city, and at times, the soldiers vented their frustrations on the property of Whig-leaning civilians who had left the city.

Some feeling for conditions in Philadelphia was given by the chaplain of the Anspach Jägers. Writing on December 20, 1777, he noted,

> *Despite the most strict orders, many of the inhabitants' house were burned down over their heads and others were plundered and everything taken. Even if these unfortunate persons at the same time have earned this treatment, through previous life style or by their present conduct, I still do not wish to be considered an instrument in punishing them, nor even to be witness thereto. If there are those who take pleasure in such cruelties, they may take satisfaction to their fullest, us there are ample opportunities to do so.*[170]

Clearly, conditions in the city were still tense. Those who backed the Patriot side in the civil war were paying for it with their property. By the same token, it is very likely that at least some of the plunder of the civilian populace arose out of necessity. Still, this practice worked against the greater goal of Gen. William Howe, that of restoring the colonies to British rule.

Howe now possessed uncontested control of Philadelphia, but he had not destroyed Washington's main army, nor had he captured the Continental Congress.

CHAPTER NOTES

[1] Brigadier General James Potter to General George Washington, November 16, 1777, quoted in *Washington, Rev. War.*, vol. 12, p. 280.

[2] Lt. Col. Samuel Smith to George Washington, November 16, 1777, Woodbury, New Jersey. Quoted in Ibid, pp. 281-2.

[3] Ibid.

[4] These included Varnum himself.

[5] Brackenridge, "Siege of Fort Mifflin," p. 88.

[6] Lieutenant's Journal of HMS *Isis*, Captain William Cornwallis, November 16, 1777 quoted in *NDAR*, vol. 10, p. 512.

[7] Journal of HM Armed Ship *Vigilant*, Commander John Henry, November 16, 1777 Fireing [sic] on Mud Fort, quoted in Ibid, p. 513.

[8] Downman, *Services*, p. 51. The jack Downman refers was short for "Jack Tar," the contemporary slang for British sailors.

[9] Ibid.

[10] Ibid.

[11] Washington to Brigadier General James Mitchell Varnum, November 16, 1777 in *Washington, Rev. War*, vol. 12, p. 282.

[12] William Bradford to Thomas Wharton, Jr, November 16, 1777, Sloop *Speedwell* n the Delaware River, quoted in *NDAR*, pp. 513-14.

[13] Ibid, p. 514.

[14] Jackson, *Fort Mercer*, p. 27

[15] Kevin Patrick Kopper, "Artur St. Clair and the Struggle for Power in the Old Northwest, 1763-1803." (Phd. diss.: Kent State University, 2005), pp. 22-3.

[16] John Beakes, *De Kalb: One of the Revolutionary War's Bravest Generals*. (Berwyn Heights, MD: Heritage Books, Inc. 2019), pp. 1-38.

[17] Jackson, *Pennsylvania Navy*, p. 271.

[18] Major General Arthur St. Clair to George Washington, Dunks Ferry, November 17, 1777 quoted in *Washington, Rev. War*, vol. 12, p. 299.

[19] Ibid.

[20] Brigadier General James Varnum to George Washington, Woodbury, NJ, November 16, 1777. in *Washington, Rev. War*, vol. 12, p. 283.

[21] Ibid.

[22] Ibid.

[23] Ibid.

[24] Ibid.

[25] Martin, *Narrative*, p. 82.

[26] Varnum to George Washington, Woodbury, NJ, November 16, 1777. in *Washington, Rev. War*, vol. 12, p. 283.

[27] Ibid, pp. 283-4.

[28] Jackson, *Pennsylvania Navy*, p. 261.

[29]Varnum to George Washington, Woodbury, NJ, November 16, 1777. in *Washington, Rev. War*, vol. 12, p. 284.

[30] Ibid.

[31] Stryker, *Forts*, pp. 30-1.

[32] Brigadier General David Forman to General George Washington, Mr. Ladds Near Red Bank, October 29, 1777 quoted in *Washington, Rev. War*, vol. 12, pp. 49-50.

[33] Vice Admiral Viscount Howe to Captain William Cornwallis, *Eagle* off Chester, November 16, 1777, quoted in *NDAR*, vol. 10, p. 515.

[34] General Sir William Howe to Vice Admiral Viscount Howe, Philadelphia, November 17, 1777, quoted in Ibid, p. 519.

[35] Captain Mauduit Du Plessis to George Washington, November 17, 1777 Fort Mercer, NJ quoted in *Washington, Rev. War*, vol. 12, p. 287.

[36] Ibid.

[37] Ibid.

[38] Col. Christopher Greene to George Washington, Fort Mercer, November 17, 1777, quoted in Ibid, pp. 288.

[39] Ibid.

[40] Jackson, *Pennsylvania Navy*, p. 265.

[41] Col. Christopher Greene to George Washington, Fort Mercer, November 17, 1777, quoted in *Washington, Rev. War*, vol. 12, p. 287, p. 288

[42]George Washington to Henry Laurens, Whitemarsh, November 17-18, 1777, quoted in *Washington, Rev. War* vol. 12, p.292.

[43] On the significance of the fall of Fort Mifflin to the growing criticisms of Washington, see Mark Edward Lender, *Cabal! The Plot against General Washington.* (Yardley, PA: Westholme Publishing, 2019), pp. 30-3

[44] Buchanan, *Road to Valley Forge*, p. 291.

[45] George Washington to Henry Laurens, Whitemarsh, November 17-18, 1777, quoted in *Washington, Rev. War*, vol. 12, p. 292.

[46] George Washington to Henry Laurens, Whitemarsh, November 17-18, 1777, quoted in *Washington, Rev. War*, vol. 12, pp. 292-3.

[47] Ibid, pp. 293-4.

[48] Ibid, p. 294

[49] Ibid.

[50] Ibid, pp. 294-5.

[51] Ibid, p. 295

[52] On the losses sustained by Washington's main army over the course of the 1777 campaign, see Harris, *Germantown*,

[53]Washington to Laurens, quoted in *Washington, Rev. War* vol. 12, p. 295.

[54] Ibid.

[55] Ibid.

[56] Ibid.

[57] James Duane to the New York Council of Safety, York, PA, November 19, 1777, quoted in Smith, ed. *LoD*, vol. 8, 281. The letter is actually dated November 3, however, a note from the editor explains that this is probably a mistake as the letter contains much information on events that transpired after that date. See Ibid, p. 282.

[58] Duane to Philip Schuyler, York, PA, November 19, 1777, quoted in Ibid, p. 282.

[59] Cornelius Hartnett to William Wilkinson, York, PA, November 19, 1777, quoted in Ibid, p. 284.

[60] Cornelius Hartnett to Thomas Burk, York, PA, November 21, 1777, quoted in Ibid, pp. 289-90.

[61] Richard Henry Lee to Samuel Adams, York, PA, November 23, 1777, quoted in Ibid, p. 310-11.

[62] James Lovell to Joseph Whipple, York, PA, November 21, 1777, quoted in Ibid, p. 302.

[63] Elbridge Gerry to Joseph Trumbull, York, Pa, November 27, 1777, quoted in Ibid, p. 327.

[64] Ibid, pp. x-xii.

[65] Buchanan, *Road to Valley Forge*, pp. 292-3. Robert Middlekauff discusses the perceived threat in very hesitant terms. See Robert Middlekauff, *Washington's Revolution: The Making of America's First Leader*. (New York: Alfred A. Knopf, 2015), pp. 176-7. The most recent and thorough examination of the cabal at the time of this writing is Lender, *Cabal!*, which makes the case that there indeed was some threat to Washington's authority at this time.

[66] John Ferling, *Almost a Miracle: The American Victory in the War of Independence*. (Oxford: Oxford University Press, 2007), p. 282.

[67] Lender, *Cabal*, pp. xvi-ii.

[68] Boatner, *Encyclopedia*, pp. 276-7.

[69] For these opposing points, see Ferling, *Almost a Miracle*, 282 and Lender, *Cabal!* pp. 34-5.

[70] For biographical information on Gates, see Paul David Nelson, General Horatio Gates: A Biography. (Baton Rouge: Louisiana State University, 1976). See also Boatner, *Encyclopedia*, pp. 412-3.

[71] Biographical information on Mifflin is derived from Boatner, *Encyclopedia*, pp. 704-5.

[72] Lender, *Cabal*, pp. 33-7, pp. 73-81.

[73] Ibid, p. 28.

[74] Ferling, *Almost a Miracle*, p. 283.

[75] See Buchanan, *Road to Valley Forge*, 301, and Ferling, *Almost a Miracle*, p. 284.

[76] Browne, "Mercer and Mifflin," p. 156.

[77] On the number of troops in the detachment, see Jackson, *Pennsylvania Navy*,

p. 271. Concerning their previous military experience, see Browne, "Mercer and Mifflin," p. 157.

[78] Jackson, *Pennsylvania Navy*, pp. 271-2.

[79] Browne, "Mercer and Mifflin," p. 157

[80] Jackson, *Pennsylvania Navy*, p. 272.

[81] Downman, *Services*, p. 52.

[82] Jackson, *Pennsylvania Navy*, p. 269. Smith, in an undocumented estimate, places the American forces in New Jersey at between 1800 and 2000. Smith, *Fight for the Delaware*, p. 38. Jackson's figures are the more verifiable and thus more reliable.

[83] Captain James Craig to George Washington, November 18, 1777 quoted in Ford, *Defenses of Philadelphia*, pp. 145-6

[84] Ibid, p. 146.

[85] Joseph Reed to George Washington, Lewis Davis's, November 18, 1777 quoted in Ford, *Defenses of Philadelphia*, p. 147.

[86] Washington to Varnum, November 18, 1777, quoted in Ibid, p. 148.

[87] Ibid.

[88] Ibid.

[89] Washington to Glover, November 19, 1777, quoted in Ford, *Defenses of Philadelphia*, p. 149. John Glover (1732-1797) of Marblehead, Massachusetts was born in Salem. In his youth, he moved to Marblehead where he became a successful merchant and sea captain. At the beginning of hostilities, Glover raised a unit of local fishermen known as the Marbelehead Mariners. These troops oversaw the evacuation of Washington's army from Long Island on August 29-50, 1776, as well as transporting them across the Delaware for the surprise at Trenton on December 25 of that year. The Marblehead Mariners ended their career in 1776, as their enlistments were ended. Glover continued to serve being promoted to Brigadier General on February 21, 1777. He served in Saratoga campaign in 1777, then returned to the main army under Washington. He later served in the abortive attack on Newport, RI in 1778, later rejoining the main army. Failing health forced his retirement from active duty in 1782. He was brevetted to Major General on September 30, 1783. See Boatner, *Encyclopedia*, pp. 438-9. The most recent biography of Glover is Richard A. Brayall, *Washington's Savior: General John Glover and the American Revolution*. Berwyn Heights, MD: Heritage Books, 2013, however, it contains some significant flaws.

[90] Ford, Defenses of Philadelphia, p. 149

[91] Ibid, p. 150.

[92] Jackson, *Pennsylvania Navy*, p. 272.

[93] Downman, *Services*, p. 52.

[94] Jackson, *Pennsylvania Navy*, p. 272 .

[95] Craig to Washington, Frankfort, PA, November 19, 1777, quoted in Ibid, p. 152.

[96] Nathanael Greene to Washington, Haddonfield, New Jersey, November 19 1777 quoted in Ford, *Defenses of Philadelphia*, p. 163.

[97] Ibid.

[98] Browne, "Fort Mercer and Fort Mifflin," p. 157.

[99] Washington to Varnum, November 19, 1777, quoted in Ford, *Defenses of Philadelphia*, p. 151.

[100] Ibid.

[101] On the loss of Fort Washington, see Fischer, *Washington's Crossing*, pp. 111-4.

[102] On Washington's character in this regard, see Edward G. Lengel, *General George Washington, A Military Life*. (New York: Random House, 2005), p. 78.

[103] Middlekauff, *Washington's Revolution*, p. 5.

[104] Ibid.

[105] On the Fabian Strategy, see Lengel, *George Washington*, 149-50. See also Buchanan, *Road to Valley Forge*, pp. 214-16.

[106] Washington to Varnum, November 19, 1777 quoted in Ford, *Defenses of Philadelphia*, p. 151.

[107] Duprotail to St. Germain, November 17, 1777, quoted in Ibid, p. 103.

[108] Ibid.

[109] Ibid.

[110] Ibid.

[111] Ibid.

[112] Ibid.

[113] Ibid.

[114] On the criticisms of William's Howe's conduct of the 1777 campaign, see Gruber, *Howe Brothers*, pp. 252-6, and O'Schaughnessy, *Men Who Lost America*, pp. 118-9.

[115] Harris, *Brandywine*,

[116] Duportail to St. Germain, November 17, 1777, quoted in Ford, *Defenses of Phialdelphia*, p. 105.

[117] On the concept of the *rage militaire*, see chapter one, n. 101.

[118] Varnum to Washington, from Haddonfield, NJ, November 20, 1777, quotes in Ford, *Defenses of Philadelphia*, p. 153.

[119] Ibid.

[120] Ibid.

[121] Jackson, *Pennsylvania Navy*, p. 275.

[122] Waldo, *Diary*, p. 301.

[123] Ibid.

[124] Downman, *Services*, p. 52.

[125] Jackson, *Pennsylvania Navy*, p. 275

[126] Ibid, p. 273.

[127] Browne, "Fort Mercer and Fort Mifflin," p. 156.

[128] Ibid.

[129] Varnum to Washington, Haddonfield, NJ, November 20, 1777quoted in Ford,

Defenses of Philadelphia, p. 156.

[130] Ibid.

[131] Jackson, *Pennsylvania Navy*, p. 276

[132] Ibid.

[133] Ibid.

[134] Browne, Mercer and Mifflin," p. 160.

[135] Ibid, p. 273.

[136] Ibid, p. 276.

[137] Ibid, pp. 276-7.

[138] Anonymous, "Intelligence" sent to George Washington, November 21, 1777, quoted in Ford, *Defenses of Philadelphia*, p. 160.

[139] Ibid, pp. 160-1.

[140] Ibid, p. 277.

[141] Nathanael Greene to George Washington, Burlington, New Jersey, November 21, 1777, quoted in Ford, *Defenses of Philadelphia*, p. 158.

[142] Ibid.

[143] Ibid.

[144] Jackson, *Pennsylvania Navy*, pp. 283-4.

[145] Brigadier General James Mitchell Varnum to George Washington, Mount Holly, NJ, November 21, 1777, quoted in *Washington, Rev. War* vol. 12, p. 343.

[146] Nathanael Greene to Washington, Mount Holly, New Jersey, November 22, 1777 quoted in Ford, *Defenses of Philadelphia*, p. 161.

[147] Ibid, p. 278.

[148] Washington to Greene, Headquarters Whitemarsh, November 22, 1777, quoted in Ford, *Defenses of Philadelphia*, p. 164

[149] Ibid.

[150] Browne, "Fort Mercer and Fort Mifflin," pp. 160-61.

[151] The Navy Board to George Washington from Borden Town, November 23, 1777 quoted in Ford, *Defenses of Philadelphia*, pp. 164-5.

[152] Ibid, p. 165.

[153] George Washington to Henry Laurens, White Marsh, PA, November 23, 1777, quoted in *Washington, Rev. War*, vol. 12, pp. 364-5.

[154] Ibid, p. 365.

[155] Ibid.

[156] Ibid.

[157] Greene to Washington, Mount Holly, New Jersey, November 24, 1777 quoted in Ford, *Defenses of Philadelphia*, pp. 165-6.

[158] Ibid, p. 166.

[159] Ibid.

[160] Jackson, *Pennsylvania Navy*, p. 279

[161] Stewart, *History of the Battle of Red Bank*, p. 22.

[162] Ibid. See also Browne, "Fort Mercer and Fort Mifflin," p. 161.

[163] Waldo, *Diary*, p. 302.

[164] Reed, *Campaign to Valley Forge*, p. 279

[165] Browne, "Mercer and Mifflin," p. 161.

[166] Andre, *Journal*, p. 66.

[167] Browne, "Mercer and Mifflin," p. 161

[168] *Journals of the Continental Congress*, November 28, 1777, pp. 975-6.

[169] On the battle of Whitemarsh, see John W. Jackson, *Whitemarsch 1777: Impregnable Stronghold*. (Fort Washington, PA: Historical Society of Fort Washington, 1984). Concerning the battle overall, see McGuire, Philadelphia Campaign, vol 2, pp. 238-254 and Ward, *War of the Revolution*, vol. 1, pp. 377-81.

[170] Feiltizsch Diary in Burgoyne, *Anspach Jägers*, p. 30.

Conclusion

"This then cannot be called an Inglorious Campaign."[1]

Surgeon Albigence Waldo penned the above comment concerning the 1777 campaign overall, however it seems particularly applicable to the defense of the river forts. The scope and commitment of effort by both belligerents, the leadership of the Howe brothers, Washington's handling of the competing demands on him for scarce troops and resources and joint nature of operations in and around the Delaware River can now be discussed in some detail.

The fight for control of the Delaware River could be seen as a subsidiary campaign to that for Philadelphia in that the objective shifted from gaining control of the Continental capital to securing the riverine lines of communication. In this sense, the contest fits more with Sir Julian Corbett's concept of control of the seas, or in this case, maritime lines of communication. As the theorist noted in his now-classic, *Some Principles of Maritime Strategy*, "Since men live upon the land and not upon the sea, great issues between nations at war have always been decided - except in the rarest cases - either by what your army can do against the enemy's territory and national life, or else by the fear of what the fleet makes it possible for your army to do."[2] In this case, control of Delaware by the Royal Navy would allow the British to maintain themselves in Philadelphia, and possibly launch new drives into the Pennsylvania interior at the logistical hubs of the Continental army. The latter possibility stood as a real concern for Washington and the Continental Congress, as evidenced above. In addition, the strategic context of the struggle for control of the Delaware demonstrates Clausewitz first case of interaction, that each side draws the other to new extremes in the use of force.[3] Recall that both sides drew in additional troops as the fighting continued. Washington repeatedly requested the return of detachments he had previously sent north to aid Gates following Burgoyne's surrender. Likewise, Howe called on additional troops from the New York garrison under Sir Henry Clinton. Clearly, then, there is much more to the fighting in and around the Delaware than is revealed by the cursory treatment it is usually accorded.

The fight for control of the Delaware River, while often overlooked, consumed large quantities of men and materials as well. One recent historian of the War of Independence observed that "Howe suffered losses equal to half the number that he had lost at Brandywine and Germantown combined," in his efforts to reduce the river forts and open the Delaware to British shipping.[4] Certainly, both sides committed major resources to the fight. Likewise, it contributed to the turning point that was 1777.

According to Stephen R. Taaffe, "For the British, the Philadelphia campaign was their last chance to focus their undivided attention on suppressing the American revolt."[5] Howe's inability to launch subsequent operations contributed to the strategic effects of the outcome of 1777 as well. It is often noted that the defeat of Gen. John Burgoyne's invasion of the Hudson Valley in New York and the subsequent surrender of his army emboldened France to a more active role in the conflict. By the same token, it can be asserted that Howe's failure to produce a victory larger than the capture of Philadelphia compounded the effect of Burgoyne's defeat. If Howe had broken Washington's main army, or managed to capture the Continental Congress, would France have still hazarded war in support of Britain's foe? The lack of any clear material advantage coming out of the campaign was, in itself, damning. So it was, with the loss of Burgoyne's army in the Hudson Valley, and no counterbalancing win by William Howe, it appeared to many European states, France chief among them, that there existed a chance to strike a blow at Great Britain and reduce her power. The tenacity of the American defense, in the aftermath of the defeats at Brandywine and Germantown demonstrated a determination to soldier on in the face of adversity.

Still, as noted at the outset, "the Delaware River engagements have been dismissed as unimportant except for a few studies by local historians."[6] The standard interpretation of the 1777 campaign for Philadelphia is captured in the words of Charles Royster,

> *The victory at Saratoga and the loss of Philadelphia gave with one hand and took with the other: the first promised American victory but the second promised a longer war that patriotic zeal might not be able to win. Some of the most active and ardent revolutionaries faced the prospect of a decrease in public effort and zeal - though not in public desire for independence - coupled with greater reliance on Washington and the Continental Army for the success of the*

revolution.[7]

The above does not even consider the fighting along the river. Contemporaries held a very different view of the fighting, however. For many on the Philadelphia area, including members of the Continental Congress, the successful defense at Red Bank served as an important tonic for flagging spirits. Likewise, its effect was only enhanced by the destruction of the *Augusta* and the *Merlin*.

From the outset, the reason for the British attention to the Delaware River should be clear - logistics. As Piers Mackesy noted, the British never seized sufficient forage to supply their needs while operating in North America. Instead, "the British army rested on lines of communication which were strained to the uttermost."[8] As the campaign in the Delaware River demonstrates, these lines of communication proved at times a significant vulnerability. In fact, the British fleet allowed the army a great deal of mobility and operational initiative, but at substantial risk.

In the end, the British won the campaign on the Delaware due to their more refined approach to jointness. Simply put, they possessed a more mature conception of the army and navy working together to achieve a common goal. While the British did not possess any formal institutional organization to facilitate amphibious or joint operations. At first glance, this appears to make efforts in this realm appear ad hoc in nature. The appearance is misleading, in that the British possessed a fair amount of institutional as well as personal experience in performing just these sorts of operations. Consider that in the final bombardment of Fort Mifflin, the Royal Navy vessels in the river, including Royal Marines on the *Vigilant* and the *Fury* combined their efforts with those of artillerymen stationed in the various shore batteries to inflict a devastating attack on the post. In addition, it should be recalled that the plan called for a final infantry assault to take the post, and that this was only prevented by the American withdrawal. Coordination of forces such as this requires a number of factors such as solid communication between the commanders of the various forces, a clear understanding of the operation goal and willingness of the commanders to dedicate the means necessary to achieve these goals.

The British success in breaking through the Delaware defenses, beyond simple material and numerical superiority, should be attributed to the command relationship between the ground and maritime forces. The Howe brothers communicated well and planned their operations to work in tandem. The familial relationship was a clear bonus. At the same time, the commanders were in regular communication, and shared many of the same views concerning he necessity of opening the river. It is worth noting, as well, that both had seen service in the Seven Years War, William Howe taking part in such joint operations at the attack on Quebec in 1759. The British leadership possessed previous experience in waging the type of campaign they were now embarked on, and it served them well in taking and holding the Continental capital.

By the same token, it needs to be recognized that capturing and holding Philadelphia was essentially all that William Howe did. Many attribute Howe's lethargy to a variety of sources, from a sense of caution bordering on cowardice to the preference for the comforts of urban life, including Elizabeth Loring.[9] Ira Gruber offers a damning assessment of Howe's behavior in general, "Under the pressure of command, he betrayed a fundamental lack of confidence; he was reluctant to surround himself with able subordinates, rarely asked advice, and avidly sought approbation. Nor did he exhibit and special sense of responsibility."[10] It could be argued, however, that Howe's experience leading the assault on Breed's Hill on June 17, 1775, profoundly influenced the manner in which he approached risk. Clearly, after experience outside Boston, Howe exhibited a tendency to prefer flanking movements to direct assaults. In addition, an analysis of William Howe's tactics demonstrates that he often prepared his movements thoroughly before initiating any actions. In this case, Howe could not even begin to formulate future actions until he had opened the Delaware River to the vital stores carried on the ships of his brother's fleet. Therefore, the defense of the Delaware River prohibited any additional actions by Howe during the 1777 campaign season. At least this seemed to be Howe's perception of his position. Not all those involved in the Philadelphia campaign shared that view. Howe's critics followed the general on his return to the Home Islands.

Following his return to England. William Howe eventually called for a Parliamentary inquiry into his conduct of the 1777 campaign, in part to blunt the criticisms then being leveled at him and his brother. Howe initially noted the issue of reinforcements and how the lack thereof effected his options for the coming campaign. Taking this further, the general noted that it forced him to make an amphibious invasion of Pennsylvania as opposed to taking an overland route "The communication for provisions through such an extent of country could not be maintained with the force then at my command."[11] Throughout his testimony, Howe repeatedly pointed to the lack of sufficient troops as the reason for the failure of his campaign. In doing so, he implicitly held Lord George Germain up as a scapegoat. While much of the general's testimony is self-serving, some portions do reveal his strategic conception of the conflict in North America. For instance, in one telling passage, he observed,

> *It was not one province but three, that I conceived we had reason to take possession of at the end of the year 1777. The first object was Philadelphia, a city from where, by means of the River Delaware the rebels drew the greater part of their supplies—the capital of Pennsylvania - the capital, as it were, and residence of the Congress in North America, situated in one of the most fertile provinces of that Continent, and in which I include the three lower counties on Delaware. Added to Pennsylvania I concluded that the arrival of the northern army at Albany, would have given us the province of New-York and the Jerseys; all of which events I was confident would lead to a prosperous conclusion of the war.*[12]

In the event, as William Howe's contemporary, Henry Lee, aptly noted,

> *The possession of Philadelphia, however anxiously desired and highly rated by the British ministry, did not produce any of those advantageous results so confidently expected; nor indeed could the discriminating statesman have justly calculated upon expensive benefit from the achievement.* [13]

Clearly, in Lee's estimation, the occupation of the city did not justify the effort expended to capture it. Likewise, the occupation of Philadelphia only lasted from September 26, 1777 to June 18, 1778, not quite nine months.

As a consequence of the British gaining control of the Delaware River, the defense of Fort Mifflin is usually depicted as something of a failure, or at best a draw. When depicted as a failure, historians focus on the idea of the abandonment of the fort following the heavy bombardment of November 15, though it should be clear that with the back channel breached by the *Vigilant* and *Fury*, the fort became untenable.[14] Various reasons are given for this supposed failure. The most common among contemporaries asserted that that the Pennsylvania Navy and specifically Cmdre. Hazelwood failed to provide adequate naval support tot eh garrison at Fort Mifflin. As shown in the preceding chapters, this view developed out of ideas generated by Lt. Col. Samuel Smith even before the major operations against Fort Mifflin got underway. Smith believed that the Pennsylvania Navy was not living up to its role in the defense. Again, Henry Lee offers some intriguing observations on the breakdown in their command relationship,

> *Smith felt the high responsibility devolved upon him, and was well apprised of the vast odds which he had to contend. Unhappily the commodore and himself soon disagreed; an event, likely productive of injurious effects to the service.*[15]

The portrait given by Lee is one of a somewhat junior officers, perhaps promoted above his current abilities. Consider, he was only twenty-five years old at the time, and possessed only two years of military command experience. Smith's resentment towards Hazelwood is understandable in ways. The lieutenant colonel was young, directing the defense of the fort on Mud Island constituted his first independent command. He therefore sought to prove himself in the eyes of Washington and other senior leadership. While he possessed significant maritime experience as a merchant, this was really commanding a single vessel, and not a fleet. Likewise, it was not coordinating the work of the fleet with another maritime force, the Continental Navy, and land troops. Smith was much concerned with establishing a military reputation, and the loss of a post, even if inevitable in the grand scheme of the campaign, could easily develop into a stain on the young man's reputation, and, importantly, his honor. Add to this the fact that Smith seemed to perceive himself as something of Hazelwood's social better and the sources of his dislike become clear. Still, as historian John Jackson noted, "Varnum and Smith, instead of placing the responsibility for the fall of the fort on one act of the galleys on the afternoon of November 15, might well have referred to their own prophecies of doom."[16]

By the same token, the Pennsylvania Navy constituted an easy target in that there was rampant desertion. Much of this derived from the poor conditions serving on board the ships. This situation was, in turn, exacerbated by the men's pay, which was low when compared with the Continental Navy or privateering, and even then, often in arrears.

In defense of the navy, there are the words of Joseph Reed

of Pennsylvania, written shortly after the defeat of von Donop's column and the sinking of *Augusta* and *Merlin*. Writing from Norriton on October 27, he observed to Thomas Wharton, Jr., Reed observed

> *The gallantry of the brave fellows in the fort*
> *has been emulated by the row galleys. Every mouth*
> *is open in their praise; and I can assure you from the*
> *best intelligence, that they will come in for a full share*
> *of the honour acquired in the defence of the river. I am*
> *well informed that none of them lay further than half*
> *a mile from the enemy, and many much nearer.*[17]

These same sentiments are echoed in numerous writings cited above. The small ships of the Pennsylvania Navy performed admirably with what they had, unfortunately, they did not have much. Likewise, the defense of Fort Mercer was not going to lead to an American victory in the sense of driving off the British. Eventually, the post would fall, and any thinking to the contrary is unrealistic. The real purpose of the post was to gain time. Time for Washington to reorganize in the aftermath of Germantown, and time to make life in the city of Philadelphia exceedingly difficult for its British occupiers, thus depriving them of the possibility of further operations. Those who adhere to the preceding interpretation of events tend to see the defense of the posts as constituting a draw.[18] In their understanding, the fact that the forts held out can be considered as a qualified victory. They point to the idea that the efforts along the Delaware were designed to be a delaying action from the outset. To see them any differently is to fall into the same error as Elbridge Gerry.[19] Not only was the overall objective of the defenders misunderstood, but also the part played by the various forces in the defense has often suffered from erroneous interpretation.

This is especially true concerning the role of the Pennsylvania Navy in the defense of the forts stood as something controversial even among contemporaries. Later historians have continued the debate. Much of John W. Jackson's *Pennsylvania Navy* can be considered an extended defense of the Pennsylvania Navy in general and Cmdre John Hazelwood in particular. Much of his effort was aimed at vindicating the efforts of Hazelwood and his sailors from the criticisms leveled at them before and during the campaign by Lt. Col. Smith. The men and ships of his mosquito fleet did the best with what they had, which certainly was not much in comparison to the massive fire power the Royal Navy ranged against them. The observations of a recent historian of American naval strategy in war of independence concerning the various state navies seem particularly applicable in this instance to the Pennsylvania Navy, "The purpose of a state's navy in the American War of Independence, was the coastal defense of that state, yet no state possessed enough resources to construct a force that could survive an encounter with even a small squadron of the Royal Navy."[20] In short, stopping the Royal Navy constituted an objective beyond the capabilities of the Pennsylvania Navy. Given the disparity of firepower between the two forces, the fact that through October and until the collapse of Forts Mercer and Mifflin in November, the American fleet engaged British vessels on the Delaware and supported the river forts."[21] Furthermore, Cmdre John Hazelwood had maintained the ships of the Pennsylvania Navy in a constant patrol along the river defenses between October 2 and November 9, 1777.[22] Put in this context, the accomplishments of the force seem more impressive than not meeting expectations. Such an assessment begs the question of who placed such high expectations on the state navy? This is not easy to determine. Lt. Col. Smith's possible motives have already been explored. It is possible, as well, that at least some of the delegates in Congress misunderstood the attritional nature of the defense of the Delaware. After all, they were caught up in the tumult of events as well, driven out of Philadelphia and eventually forced to relocate in York. Likewise, they were regularly confronted with a myriad of issues, all of which took on an urgency all their own. In this sort of an environment, and with the real possibility that a British thrust could, at the very least, capture some of them, it would not be surprising to have some delegates find their hope for preservation in the navy and the forts.

Between Congress and the defenses stood George Washington. In overseeing the river defenses, this stands as a point where the commander in chief's abilities as an administrator shone. This fact is often overlooked in the focus on his tactical handling of Brandywine and Germantown, and the resultant criticisms of and possible challenge to his leadership. Consider, however, that Washington worked to coordinate troop movements from the Hudson Valley, while trying to maintain his own force at a level capable of opposing any British strikes, rebuilding it after several field engagements, and working to smooth over dysfunctional relations between the army and navy commanders during the fighting. The remarkable fact is that with managing all of these efforts, Washington did not become bogged down or drawn into any single facet to the exclusion of all others. True, there was the fixation on the Continental ships north of Philadelphia, however, this went by the wayside as the crucial period of the contest for control of the Delaware dawned. Likewise, he wisely delegated authority to his subordinates in the theater and sent additional advisers when he thought it necessary. While Washington certainly micromanaged on occasion, he did authorize significant operational latitude to Varnum and Greene. Vesting his subordinates with the power necessary to act in accordance with the local conditions gave them the freedom to act as circumstances warranted.

It could be claimed that Washington was slow to recognize the importance of the river defenses, and this is true. He paid scant attention to the forts until after the battle of Germantown. An additional criticism would be that once he began to see the significance of the forts, he should have dispatched a more senior commander to oversee their defense. Such a criticism is invalidated by two facts. First, that the initial choice for command of Fort Mifflin, Baron d'Arendt, seemingly possessed significant combat experience in Europe. Smith was only ever meant to be a subordinate. Second, as the contest intensified, Washington sent more senior commanders, including Varnum and eventually Maj. Gen. Nathanael Greene. As the intensity of the campaign grew, the level of leadership committed did commensurately.

Finally, even with the controversy surrounding the defense of the river forts, some contemporaries found reason to praise the campaign in the Delaware. Writing to Washington from Williamsburg Virginia, Brig. Gen. Thomas Nelson, Jr. clearly saw victory in the fighting on the river,

> *The Noble opposition made by our Forts, upon the Delaware, will astonish the whole World. Destroying a British 64 Gun Ship and repulsing a large Body of Hessians with a few Men from a small Fort will have a powerful effect in Europe, particularly at White Hall. Pray inform me who commands at Red Bank & Fort Mifflin. I toast them daily as Commandants without knowing their names.*[23]

If anything, the British strategic situation appeared bleaker in November 1777 than it had a year previous. To make matters worse, it was clear in London that France was prepared to intervene more actively in the conflict than it had to date.[24]

In contrast, American resiliency in the Philadelphia campaign in general, and the fight for control of the Delaware River in particular helped to undermine popular support for the war in Britain. The dogged defiance of Maj. Thayer and enlisted men like Joseph Plumb Martin during the final bombardment of Fort Mifflin demonstrated that the rebels were not a weak group of malcontents whose resolve could be easily broken by the assault of determined, professional troops. At Fort Mifflin, the defenders withstood an incredible pounding and only abandoned their post when there was nothing left to defend. Such determination sent messages all its own.

At the current juncture, it may seem odd that fighting of such significance, that consumed so much manpower and supplies and swallowed the greater part of two months is generally glossed over in accounts of the War of Independence. The answer is straightforward and springs from the pen of Joseph Plumb Martin, "the reason of which is, there was no Washington, Putnam, or Wayne there."[25]

CHAPTER NOTES

[1] Waldo, *Diary*, December 26, 1777, quoted in Ibid, p. 313.

[2] Corbett, *Principles of Maritime Strategy*, p. 16.

[3] Clausewitz, *On War*, 77. The actual quote reads in full, "The thesis, then, must be repeated: war is an act of force, and there is no logical limit to the application of force. Each side, therefore, compels its opponent to follow suit; a reciprocal action is started, which must lead, in theory, to extremes. This is the *first case of interaction and the first 'extreme'* we meet with." Italics in original.

[4] Ferling, *Almost a Miracle*, p. 257.

[5] Taaffe, *Year of the Hangman*, p. 2.

[6] Jackson, *Pennsylvania Navy*, p. vii.

[7] Lee, *Revolutionary War Memoirs*, p. 181.

[8] Mackesy, War for America, p.65.

[9] On Howe's dalliances with Elizabeth Loring, see Jackson, *With the British Army in Philadelphia*, p. 209.

[10] Gruber, Howe Brothers, p. 57.

[11] William Howe, *The Narrative of Lt. Gen. Sir William Howe to a Committee in the House of Commons on the 29th of April, 1779*. London: H. Baldwin, 1779, p. 16

[12] Ibid, p. 21.

[13] Charles Royster, *A Revolutionary People at War*, p. 92

[14] The historians who see the defense of Fort Mifflin as a failure include: Anderson, *Forty Minutes*. Lender, *River War*. Royster, *A Revolutionary People at War*. Stewart, *History of the Battle of Red Bank* and Stryker, *The Forts on the Delaware*.

[15] Lee, *Revolutionary War Memoirs*, p. 102

[16] Jackson, *Pennsylvania Navy*, p. 265.

[17] Joseph Reed to Thomas Wharton, Jr. Norriton, PA, October 27, 1777, quoted in *NDAR*, vol. 10, p. 322.

[18] The historians who see the defense of Fort Mifflin as a draw include: Hugh M. Brackenridge, ed. "The Siege of Fort Mifflin." in *PMHB* 11(1887): 82-88; Browne, "Fort Mercer and Fort Mifflin"; John W. Jackson, *The Pennsylvania Navy*. See also *With the British Army in Philadelphia* by the same author, and Reed, *Campaign to Valley Forge*.

[19] Elbridge Gerry to Joseph Trumbull, York, Pa, November 27, 1777, quoted in Smith, *LoD*, p. 327.

[20] Kenneth J. Hagan, "The Birth of American Naval Strategy," in Stoker, et al, Strategy, p. 44.

[21] Dunavent, "Muddy Waters," p. 35.

[22] Jackson, *River Defenses*, p. 18.

[23] Brigadier Thomas Nelson, Jr. to George Washington from Williamsburg, Virginia, November 21-2, 1777, quoted in *Writings of George Washington*, Revolutionary War series, vol. 12, p. 342.

[24] Ibid.

[25] Martin, *Narrative*, pp. 82-3.

Bibliography

Primary Sources:

Published Primary Sources:

Abbot, W.W. and Dorothy Twohig, eds. *The Papers of George Washington, Revolutionary War Series.* 16 volumes. Charlottesville, VA; University of Virginia Press, 1985-2006.

Andre, John *Major Andre's Journal: Operations of the British Army under General Sir William Howe and Sire Henry Clinton, June 1777, to November, 1778.* William Abbatt, ed. New York: 1930.

Angell, Israel "The Israel Angell Diary, 1 October 1777- 28 February 1778." Joseph LaBoyle, ed. in *Rhode Island History* 58 (2000)

Anon. "Report of Actions in the Delaware, October and November, 1777." *The Annual Register, or a View of the History, Politics, and Literature for the Year 1777.* London, 1778.

Bell, Helen "The Hessians in Philadelphia." in *PMHB*, 1 (1877): 40-3.

Bloomfield, Joseph *Citizen Soldier: The Revolutionary War Journal of Joseph Bloomfield.* Mark Edward Lender and James Kirby Martin, eds. Yardley, PA: Westholme Press, 2018, reprint of 1982 original.

Burgoyne, Bruce E. ed. Trans. *Diaries of Two Ansbach Jaegers.* Bowie, MD: Heritage Books, 1997.

Clark, Joseph "Diary of Joseph Clark" *Proceedings of the New Jersey Historical Society.* 7 1853-56,95-110.

Collin, Nicholas *The Journal and Biography of Nicholas Collin, 1746-1831.* Amandus Johnson, ed. Philadelphia: The New Jersey Society of Pennsylvania, 1936.

D'Arendt, Henry baron "The Attack on Fort Mifflin, 1777: Two Unpublished Letters of the

Baron D'Arendt." F. Bailey Myers, trans. *Historical Magazine* 3rd Series, 1 (1872):77-79.

Drinker, Elizabeth *The Diary of Elizabeth Drinker: The Life Cycle of an Eighteenth Century Woman.* Crane, Elaine F. ed. Boston: Northeaster University Press, 1994.

Dohla, Johann Conrad *A Hessian Diary of the Revolution*. Bruce E. Burgoyne, ed. trans. Norman, OK: University of Oklahoma Press, 1990.

Donop, Carl Emil von "Letters from a German Mercenary." C.V. Easum and Hans Huth, trans. and eds. in *PMHB*62, 4 (October 1938): 488-501.

Donop, Wilhelm Gottlieb Levin von, *Des Obermarschalls und Drosten Wilhelm Gottlieb Levin von Donop zu Lüdershofen, Maspe Nachricht von dem Geschlecht der von Donop*. Paderborn 1796.

Downman, Francis *The Services of Lieut.-Colonel Francis Downman, R.A., in France, North America, and the West Indies, between 1758 and 1784*. F. A. Whinyates, ed. Woolwich: England: Royal Artillery Institution, 1898.

Du Coudray, Philippe "Observation on the Forts Intended for the Defense of the Two Passages of the River Delaware, July 1777." in *PMHB*, 24 (1900):343-347.

Egle, William H. *Pennsylvania Archives* Series 2. Vols. 10-15, Harrisburg, PA: E.K. Meyers, State Printers, 1887-

Elmer, Ebenezer "Extracts from the Journal of Ebenezer Elmer of the New Jersey Continental Line, September 11-19, 1777." John Nixon Brooks and Tobias Lear eds. In *PMHB*, 35, 1 (1911): 103-7.

Ewald, Johann *Diary of the American War*. Joseph P. Tustin, ed and trans. New Haven, CT: Yale University Press, 1979.

Force, Peter, ed. *American Archives*. Vol. 2, 1775. Washington, DC: M. St. Clair Clarke and Peter Force, 1839.

Graf, Holger Thodor, Lena Haunert and Christoph Kampmann, eds. *Aldiges Leben am Ausgang des Ancien Regime. Die Tagesbuchaufzeichnungen (1754-1798) des Georg Ernst von und zu Gilsa*. Marburg: Hessisches Landesamt fur gesscichtliche Landeskunde, 2010.

Greene, Christopher *Papers of Christopher Greene, Lieutenant Colonel of the First Regiment, Rhode Island Infantry, 1776-1781*. Microfilm. Rhode Island Historical Society, Manuscript Division, MSS 455.

Greenman, Jeremiah *Diary of a Common Soldier in the American Revolution, 1775-1783. An Annotated Edition of the Military Journal of Jeremiah Greenman*. Robert C. Bray and Paul

E. Bushnell, eds. DeKalb: Northern Illinois University Press, 1978.

Hamond, Andrew S. *The Autobiography of Captain Sir Andrew Snape Hamond, 1738-1828.* W. Hugh Moomaw, ed. MA thesis, University of Virginia, 1947.

Howe, Richard "Copy of a Letter from Vice Admiral Lord Viscount Howe to Mr. Stephens, dated on Board his Majesty's Ship *Eagle*, in the River Delaware, October 25, 1777." in *The Westminster Magazine; or The Pantheon of Taste.* 5, 2 (June 1777):653-55.

Howe, William "Copy of a Letter from General Sir William Howe to Lord George Germain, dated Philadelphia 25 October 1777." in *The Westminster Magazine; or The Pantheon of Taste.* 5, 2 (June 1777): 652-53.

_____ *The Narrative of Lt. Gen. Sir William Howe to a Committee in the House of Commons on the 29ᵗʰ of April, 1779.* London: H. Baldwin, 1779.

Laurens, John *The Army Correspondence of Colonel John Laurens in the Years 1777-8.* New York: The New York Times and Arno Press, 1969.

Lee, Henry *The Revolutionary War Memoirs of General Henry Lee.* R.E. Lee, ed. New York: DeCapo Press, 1998 reprint of 1812 original.

Londahl-Smidt, Lieutenant Colonel Donald M. ed. trans., "German and British Accounts of the Assault on Fort Mercer at Redbank, NJ in October 1777." in *The Hessians: Journal of the Johannes Schwalm Historical Association.* 16 (2013):1-33

Martin, Joseph Plumb *Private Yankee Doodle: Being a Narrative of Some of the Adventures,*

Dangers and Sufferings of a Revolutionary Soldier. George F. Scheer, ed. Boston: Little, Brown and Company, 1962.

Molyneux, Thomas More *Conjunct Expeditions, or Expeditions that have been Carried on Jointly by the Fleet and Army: with a Commentary on Littoral Warfare.* London: R and J. Dodsley, 1759.

Montressor, John *The Montressor Journals.* G. D. Scull, ed. New York: Collections of the New York Historical Society, 1881.

Morton, Robert "The Diary of Robert Morton." PMBH 1,no.1 (1877): 1-39.

Muller, John *A treatise containing the elementary part of fortification : regular and irregular: with remarks on the constructions of the most celebrated authors particularly of Marshal de Vauban and Baron Coehorn.* London: J. Nourse, 1746.

_____ *A treatise of artillery : containing I. General construc-tions of brass and iron guns used by sea and land ... To which is prefixed an introduction, with a theory of powder applied to fire-arms. The second edition, with large additions, alterations, and corrections.* London: John Millan, 1768.

_____ *The attack and defence of forthfied places. In three parts.: Containing I. The operations of an attack, from the begin-ning to the end. II. The defence of every part of a fortification. III. A treatise on mines. For the use of the Royal Military Academy, at Woolwich. By John Muller, professor of fortification and artillery, and Military preceptor to His Royal Highness William, Duke of Gloucester.* London: T. and J. Egerton, Whitehall, 1791.

Münchhausen, Friedrich von *At General Howe's Side, 1776-1778: The Diary of General William Howe's Aide de Camp, Captain Frie-drich von Muenchhausen.* E. Kipping, trans., S. Smith, ed. Mon-mouth Beach, NJ: Philip Freneau, 1974.

Nicola, Lewis *A Treatise of Military Exercise.* James R. Mc Intyre, ed. West Chester, OH: The Nafziger Collection, 2009

Paine, Thomas, "Military Operations near Philadelphia in the Cam-paign of 1777-8." PMHB, 2, no. 3 (1878): 283-296.

_____ "The American Crisis" Steve Straub, ed. in The Fed-eralist Papers Project. Internet: https://thefederalistpapers.org/wp-content/uploads/2013/08/The-American-Crisis-by-Thomas-Paine-.pdf

Peebles, John *John Peebles American War: the Diary of a Scottish Grenadier, 1776-1782.* Ira D. Gruber, ed. Strand, Gloucestershire: Published by the Sutton for the Army Records Society, 1997.

Proud, Robert "Letters of Robert Proud." in *Pennsylvania Magazine of History and Biography.* 34,1 (January 1910): 62-73.

Retzer, Henry J. trans. *The Philadelphia Campaign, 1777-1778, Let-ters and Reports from the Jungkenn Papers.* Annotated by Donald Londahl-Schmidt. In Hessians: Journal of the Johannes Schwalm Historical Association 6, 2 (1998): 1-25.

Robertson, Archibald *Archibald Robertson: His Diaries and Sketch-es in American, 1762-1780.* Edited by Harry Miller Lyndenberg. New York: Arno Press, 1971.

Serle, Ambrose *The American Journal of Ambrose Serle Secretary to Lord Howe 1776-1778.*

Tatum, Edward H. ed. New York: New York Times and Arno Press, 1969 reprint of 1940 edition.

Seybolt, Robert Francis "A Contemporary British Account of General Sir William Howe's Military Operations in 1777." *Proceedings of the American Antiquarian Society.* Vol. XL, 1931.

Showman, Richard; Dennis M. Conrad and Roger Parks eds. *The Papers of Nathanael Greene.* 13 vols. Chapel Hill: University of North Carolina Press, 1976-2005. Showman,

Smith, Jacob "Diary of Jacob Smith: American Born." Charles William Heathcote, ed. in *The Pennsylvania Magazine of History and Biography.* 56,3 (1932): 260-264.

Smith, Paul H. ed. *Letters of the Delegates to the Continental Congress, 1774-1789.* Washington, D.C.: Library of Congress, 1976-2000.

Smith, Samuel *Memoirs of Samuel Smith a Solider of the Revolution.* Charles I. Bushnell, ed. New York: Privately Printed, 1860.

_____ "The Papers of General Samuel Smith." in *The Historical Magazine and Notes and Queries, Concerning the Antiquities, History and Biography of America.* vol. 7, 2nd Series, no. 2 (February 1870): 81-92.

Stedman, Margaret "Excitement in Philadelphia on Hearing of the Defeat at Brandywine." in *PMHB*, 14, 1 (April 1890): 64-7.

Stockdale, John, ed. *The Parliamentary Register; or, History of the Proceedings and Debates of the House of Commons: Containing an Account of the most interesting Speeches and Motions; accurate Copies of the most Honourable Letters and Papers; of the most material Evidence, Petitions &c laid before and offered to the House, during the Fifth Session of the Fourteenth Parliament of Great Britain.* Vol. 10, London: Wilson and Co., 1802. 20-415.

Stone, Edwin Martin, *The Invasion of Canada in 1775 including the Journal of Captain Simeon Thayer describing the Perils and Sufferings of the Army under Benedict Arnold.* Providence, RI; Knowles, Anthony and Company, Printer, 1867.

Sullivan, Thomas *From Redcoat to Rebel: The Thomas Sullivan Journal.* Joseph Lee Boyle, ed. Bowie, MD: Heritage Books, 1997.

Waldo, Albigence "Valley Forge, 1777-1778. Diary of Albigence Waldo of the Connecticut Line." in *The Pennsylvania Magazine of History and Biography.* 21, 3 (1897): 299-323.

Webb, J. Watson ed. *Reminiscences of Gen'l Samuel B. Webb of the Revolutionary Army.* New York, Globe Stationery and Printing, 1882.

Maps:

Anon. *Plan zum Aufstieg zum Fort Redbank am 22. Oktober 1777 unter Colonel de Donop und der Angriff der Briten von Fort Mifflin oder Mud-Island am 15. November 1777.* Courtesy the Hessische Staatsarchive, Marburg, HStAM Order. WHK No. WHK 29 / 64a

Faden, William *The Course of the Delaware River from Philadelphia to Chester, Exhibiting the several Works Erected by the Rebels to Defend its Passage: with the attacks made upon them by His Majesty's Land and Sea Forces.* London: s.n.:1778.

Fleury, Francois *Map of Fort Mifflin on the Delaware River near Philadelphia PA, November 9, 1777.*

Latter, Matthais Albrecht *A Plan of the City and Environs of Philadelphia.* Augsburg, 1777.

Newspapers:

Pennsylvania Evening Post

Secondary Sources:

Reference Works:

Boatner, Mark M, III *Encyclopedia of the American Revolution.* Mechanicsburg, PA: Stackpole Books, 1994.

Bodinier, Captain Gilbert *Dictionnaire des officiers de l'armee royale qui ont combattu aux Etats-Unis pendant la guerre d'independence, 1776-1783 suivi d'un supplement a Les Francais sous le trieme etoiles du commandant Andre Lasseray.* Chateau de Vincennes, 1982.

Unpublished Secondary Sources:

Browne, Gregory M. "Fort Mercer and Fort Mifflin: The Battle for the Delaware River and the Importance of American Riverine Defenses during Washington's Siege of Philadelphia." MA Thesis: Western Illinois University, 1996.

Cahill, Matthew J. "An Unassailable Advantage: The British use of Principles of Joint Operations from 1758-1762." Fort Leavenworth, KS: United States Army Command and General Staff College, 2017.

Dunnavent, R. Blake "Muddy Waters: A History of the United States in Riverine Warfare and the Emergence of a Tactical Doctrine, 1775-1789." Texas Tech University: Phd Diss., 1998.

Ewan, N.R. "Chevaux-de-frize: military obstructions in the Delaware River during the Revolutionary War dredged up July 1941, with photographs and maps. Also, an account of the Chevaux-de-frize sunk in the Hudson River during the Revolution." Newport News, VA: Mariners Museum, 1944.

Geib, George W. "A History of Philadelphia, 1776-1789." University of Wisconsin: Phd Diss., 1969.

Kopper, Kevin Patrick "Arthur St. Clair and the Struggle for Power in the Old Northwest, 1763-1803." Kent State University: Phd Diss., 2005.

Mc Cleod, Toby "British Amphibious Operations in the American War of Independence 1775-1783." University of Birmingham: MA Thesis, 2008.

Pruett, Maj. William C. "A History of the Organizational Development of the Continental Artillery during the American Revolution." Command and General Staff College, Fort Leavenwoth, KS: MA Thesis, 2011.

Stein Roslyn "The British Occupation of Philadelphia, September 1777-June 1778." Columbia University: Phd Diss. 1937.

Books:

Allen, Thomas B. and Todd W. Braisted *The Loyalist Corps: Americans in the Service of the King*. Takoma Park, MD: Fox Acre Press, 2011.

Anderson, Fred *Crucible of War: The Seven Years War and the Fate of Empire in North America, 1754-1766*. New York: Alfred A. Knopf, 2000.

Anderson, Lee Patrick *Forty Minutes by the Delaware: The Battle for Fort Mercer*. Universal Publishers, 1999.

Anderson, Troyer Steele *The Command of the Howe Brothers during the American Revolution*. New York: Oxford University Press, 1936.

Atwood, Rodney *The Hessians: Mercenaries from Hessen-Kassel in the American Revolution.* Cambridge: Cambridge University Press, 1980.

Bailey, DeWitt *British Military Flintlock Rifles 1740-1840.* Lincoln, RI: Andrew Mowbray Publishers,2002.

Beakes, John *DeKalb: One of the Revolutionary War's Bravest Generals.* Berwyn Heights, MD: Heritage Books, Inc. 2019.

Black, Jeremy *Combined Operations: A Global History of Amphibious and Airborne Warfare.* Lanham, MD: Rowan&Littlefield, 2017.

Borick, Carl P. *A Gallant Defense: The Siege of Charleston, 1780.* Columbia, SC: University of South Carolina Press, 2003.

Borneman Walter R. *American Spring: Lexington, Concord, and the Road to Revolution.* New York: Little, Brown and Company, 2014.

Brayall, Richard A. *Washington's Savior: General John Glover and the American Revolution.* Berwyn Heights, MD: Heritage Books, 2013.

Brown, M. L. *Firearms in Colonial America, 1492-1792.* Washington, D.C.: Smithsonian Institution Press, 1980.

Buchanan, John *The Road to Valley Forge: How Washington Built the Army that Won the Revolution.* New York: John Wiley and Sons, 2004.

Carrington, Henry B. *Battles of the American Revolution 1775-1781.* New York: Promontory Press, 1877.

Cassell, Frank A. *Merchant Congressman of the Young Republic: Samuel Smith of Maryland, 1752-1839.* Madison: University of Wisconsin Press, 1971.

Catts, Wade P. et al *"It is Painful for Me to Lose so many Good People."' Report of an Archeological Survey at Red Banks Battlefield Park (Fort Mercer), National Park Gloucester County, New Jersey.* Commonwealth Heritage Group, West Chester, PA, June 2017.

Cecere, Michael *They Are Indeed a Very Useful Corps American Riflemen in the Revolutionary War.* Westminster, MD: Heritage Books, 2006.

_____ *Wedded to my Sword: The Revolutionary War Service of Light Horse Harry Lee.* Westminster, MD: Heritage Books, 2012.

Childs, John *Armies and Warfare in Europe, 1648-1789.* Manchester: Manchester University Press, 1982.

Corbett, Sir Julian *England in the Seven Years' War: A Study in Combined Strategy*. London: Longmans, Green, and Company, 1907.

Corbett, Theodore *No Turning Point: The Saratoga Campaign in Perspective*. Norman: University of Oklahoma Press, 2012.

Cox, Caroline *A Proper Sense of Honor Service and Sacrifice in George Washington's Army*. Chapel Hill: UNC Press, 2004.

Darling, Anthony D. *Red Coat and Brown Bess*. Alexandria Bay, NY: Museum Restoration Service, 1971.

Dorwart, Jeffrey M. *Fort Mifflin of Philadelphia: An Illustrated History*. Philadelphia: University of Pennsylvania Press, 1998.

_____ *Invasion and Insurrection: Security, Defense and War in the Delaware Valley, 1621-1815*. Newark, DE: University of Delaware Press, 2008.

Duffy, Christopher *Fire and Stone: The Science of Fortress warfare 1660-1860*. London: Peters Fraser & Dunlop, 1975.

_____ *Siege Warfare: the Fortress in the Early Modern world, 1494-1660*. London: Routledge, 1979.

_____ *The Military Experience in the Age of Reason, 1715-1789*. New York: Scribner, 1987.

Dunnavent, R. Blake *Brown Water Warfare: The U.S. Navy in Riverine Warfare and the Emergence of a Tactical Doctrine, 1775-1970*. Gainesville, FL: University Press of Florida, 2003.

Dwyer, William M. *The Day is Ours! An Inside View of the Battles of Trenton and Princeton, November 1776-January 1777*. New Brunswick, NJ: Rutgers University Press, 1983.

Dyke, Samuel E *The Pennsylvania Rifle*. Constantine Kermes, ill. Lancaster, PA: Bicentennial Book, 1974.

Edgar, Gregory T. *The Philadelphia Campaign 1777-1778*. Westminster, MD: Heritage Books, 2004.

Ellis, John *Cavalry The History of Mounted Warfare*. Yorkshire: Pen and Sword Books, 2004 reprint of 1978 original.

Ferling, John *Almost a Miracle: The American Victory in the War of Independence*. Oxford: Oxford University Press, 2007.

Ferling, John E. *The Loyalist Mind: Joseph Galloway and the American Revolution*. University Park, PA: Pennsylvania State University Press. 1977.

Fischer, David Hackett *Washington's Crossing*. New York: Oxford University Press, 2004.

Fleming, Thomas *The Strategy of Victory: How General George Washington Won the American Revolution*. New York: De Capo Press, 2017.

Ford, Worthington C. ed. *Defenses of Philadelphia in 1777*. Brooklyn: Historical Printing Club, 1897. Reprint, De Capo Press, 1971.

Fortescue, Sir John *The War of Independence: The British Army in North America, 1775-1783*. Mechanicsburg, PA: Stackpole Books, 2001 reprint of 1911 original.

Frey, Sylvia R. *The British Soldier in the American Revolution: A Social History of Military Life in the Revolutionary Period*. Austin: University of Texas Press, 1981.

Gallagher, John J. *The Battle of Brooklyn 1776*. Edison, NJ: Castle books, 2002.

Gluckman, Arcadi *Unites States Muskets, Rifles, and Carbines*. Buffalo, NY: Otto Ulbrich Co., 1948.

Greene, George S. *The Greene's of Rhode Island, with Historical records of English Ancestry, 1534-1902*. New York: The Knickerbocker Press, 1907.

Gross, Robert A. *The Minutemen and Their World*. New York: Hill and Wang, 1976.

Gruber, Ira D. *Books and the British Army in the Age of the American Revolution*. Chapel Hill: University of North Carolina Press, 2014.

_____*The Howe Brothers and the American Revolution*. New York, Athenaeum: 1972.

Hagist, Don N. *British Soldiers American War: Voices of the American Revolution*. Yardley, PA: Westholme Press, 2012.

Haiman, Miecislaus *Kosciuszko in the American Revolution*. New York: The Kosciuszko Foundation, 1975.

Harding, Richard *Amphibious Warfare in the Eighteenth Century: The British Expedition to the West Indies, 1740-1742*. Suffolk, UK: The Boydell Press, 1991.

Harris, Michael C. *Brandywine: A Military History of the Battle that Lost Philadelphia but Saved America, September 11. 1775*. El Dorado Hills, CA: Savas Beatie, 2014.

_____ *Germantown: A Military History of the Battle for Philadelphia, October 4, 1777.* El Dorado Hills, CA: Savas Beatie, 2020.

Hibbert, Christopher *Redcoats and Rebels: The American Revolution through British Eyes.* New York: W.W. Norton and Company, 1990.

Higginbotham, Don *The War of American Independence: Military Attitudes, Policies and Practice, 1763-1789.* Boston: Northeastern University Press, 1983.

Hoock, Holger *Scars of Independence: America's Violent Birth.* New York: Crown, 2017.

Huddleston, Joe D. *Colonial Riflemen in the American Revolution.* York, PA: George Shumway Publisher, 1978.

Hughes, B.P. *Open Fire: The Artillery Tactics from Marlborough to Wellington.* Sussex: Antony Bird Publications, 1983.

Hunt, Agnes *The Provincial Committees of Safety of the American Revolution.* New York: Haskell House Publishers, 1968.

Isaacson, Walter *Benjamin Franklin, An American Life.* New York: Simon and Schuster, 2003.

Jackson, John W. *The Pennsylvania Navy 1775-1781: The Defense of the Delaware.* New Brunswick, NJ: Rutgers University Press, 1974.

_____ *The Delaware Bay and River Defenses of Philadelphia, 1775-1777.* Philadelphia: Philadelphia Maritime Museum, 1977.

_____ *With the British Army in Philadelphia 1777-1778.* San Rafael, CA: Presidio Press, 1979.

_____ *Whitemarsch 1777: Impregnable Stronghold.* Fort Washington, PA: Historical Society of Fort Washington, 1984.

_____ *Fort Mercer, Guardian of the Delaware.* Gloucester, NJ: Gloucester County Cultural and Heritage Commission, 1986.

_____ *Fort Mifflin Valiant Defender of the Delaware.* Philadelphia: Old Fort Mifflin Historical Society Preservation Committee, 1986.

Joint Chiefs of Staff, JP3-0 *Incorporating Change*, 17 January 2017 – 22 October 2018. Washington, DC: United States Department of Defense, 2017

Kain, Henry C. *The Military and Naval Operations on the Delaware in 1777*. Philadelphia: The City History Society of Philadelphia, 1910.

Kajencki Francis Casimir *Thaddeus Kosciuszko: Military engineer of the American Revolution*. El Paso, TX: South Polonia Press, 1998.

Kapp, Freidrich *Der Soldatenhandel deutscher fürsten nach Amerika. Ein Beitrag zur Kulturgeschichte des Achtzehnten Jahrhunderts*. Berlin: Verlag von Julius J. Springer, 1874.

Lefkowitz, Arthur S. *The Long Retreat: The Calamitous American Defense of New Jersey in 1776*. New Brunswick, NJ: Rutgers University Press, 1999.

_____ *Benedict Arnold's Army: The 1775 American Invasion of Canada during the Revolutionary War*. New York: Savas Beatie, 2008.

Lender, Mark E. *The River War*. Trenton, NJ: New Jersey Historical Commission, 1979.

_____ *Cabal! The Plot against General Washington*. Yardley, PA: Westholme Publishing, 2019.

Lengel, Edward G. *General George Washington, A Military Life*. New York: Random House, 2005.

_____ ed. *A Companion to George Washington*. Malden, MA: Wilely-Blackwell, 2012.

Losch, Philipp *Soldatenhandel mit einem Berzeidnis der Hessen-Kasselischen Gubdfidienvertrage und einer Bibliographie*. Berlag zu Kassel: Barenreiter, 1933.

Luzader, John F. *Saratoga: A Military History of the Decisive Campaign of the American Revolution*. New York: SavasBeatie, 2008.

Lyon, David *The Sailing Navy List: all the Ships of the Royal Navy Built Purchased and Captured, 1688-1860*. London: Conway Maritime Press, 1993.

Mackey, Harry D. *The Gallant Men of the Delaware River Forts 1777*. Philadelphia: Dorrance & Company, 1973.

Mackesy, Piers *The Coward of Minden: The Affair of Lord George Sackville*. New York: St. Martins Press, 1979.

_____ *The War for America, 1775-1783*. Lincoln, NE: University of Nebraska Press, 1992 reprint of 1964 original.

Mahan, Alfred Thayer *The Influence of Sea Power upon History, 1660-1783*. Boston: Little, Brown and Company, 1890.

Maier, Pauline *From Resistance to Revolution: Colonial Radicals and the Development of American Opposition to Britain, 1765-1776*. New York: W.W. Norton and Company, 1972.

Martin, David G. *The Philadelphia Campaign June 1777-July 1778*. Conshohocken, PA: Combined Books, 1993.

Martin, James Kirby and Mark E. Lender *A Respectable Army: the Military Origins of the Republic, 1763-1789*. Wheeling, IL: Harlan-Davidson, Inc. 1982.

McCurdy, John Gilbert *Quarters: The Accommodation of the British Army and the Coming of the American Revolution*. Ithaca: Cornell University Press, 2019.

McGrath, Tim *Give Me a Fast Ship: The Continental Navy and America's Revolution at Sea*. New York: NAL Caliber, 2014.

McGuire, Thomas *The Philadelphia Campaign*. 2 vols. Mechanicsburg, PA: Stackpole Books, 2006-7.

_____ *The Battle of Paoli*. Mechanicsburg, PA: Stackpole Books, 2000.

Mc Intyre, James R. *The Development of the British Light Infantry, Continental and North American Influences, 1740-1765*. Point Pleasant, NJ: Winged Hussar Publishing, 2015.

_____ *Johann Ewald, Jäger Commander*. New York: Knox Press, 2020.

Middlekauff, Robert *The Glorious Cause: The American Revolution, 1763-1789*. New York: Oxford University Press, 1982.

_____ *Washington's Revolution: The Making of America's First Leader*. New York: Alfred A. Knopf, 2015.

Millett, Alan R. and Peter Maslowski *For the Common Defense: A Military History of the United States of America*. New York: The Free Press, 1994.

Mintz Max M. *The Generals of Saratoga*. New Haven, CT: Yale University Press, 1990.

Montross, Lynn *Rag, Tag and Bobtail The Story of the Continental Army, 1775-1783*. New York: Harper & Brothers Publishers, 1952.

Morrill, Dan L *The Southern Campaigns of the American Revolution*. Mount Pleasant, SC: Nautical Aviation Publishing Company,

1993.

Nagy, John A. *Rebellion in the Ranks Mutinies of the American Revolution*. Yardley, PA: Westholme Publishing, 2008.

Nelson, Paul David *General Horatio Gates: A Biography*. Baton Rouge: Louisiana State University, 1976.

Neimeyer, Charles P. *The Revolutionary War*. Westport, CT: Greenwood Press, 2007.

O'Shaughnessy, Andrew J. *The Men Who Lost America: British Leadership, the American Revolution and the Fate of Empire*. New Haven: Yale University Press, 2013.

Pancake, John S. *Samuel Smith and the Politics of Business: 1752-1839*. University, AL: University of Alabama Press, 1972.

_____*1777: The Year of the Hangman*. University, AL: University of Alabama Press, 1977.

Peterson, Charles E. *Robert Smith, Architect, Builder, Patriot (1722-1777)*. Philadelphia: The Athanaeum of Philadelphia, 2000.

Peterson, Harold L. *The Book of the Continental Soldier Being a Compleat Account of the Uniforms, Weapons, and Equipment with which he Lived and Fought*. Harrisburg, PA: Stackpole Books, 1968.

_____*Round Shot and Rammers: An Introduction to Muzzle-loading Land Artillery in the United States*. Mechanicsburg, PA: Stackpole Books, 1979.

Piecuchs, Jim *Cavalry of the American Revolution*. Yardley, PA: Westholme Press, 2014.

Popek, Daniel M. *They "...fought bravely, but were unfortunate:" The True Story of Rhode Island's "Black Regiment" and the Failure of Segregation in Rhode Island's Continental Line, 1777-1783*. Bloomington, IN: Authorhouse, 2015.

Puls, Mark *Henry Knox Visionary General of the American Revolution*. New York: Palgrave Macmillan, 2008.

Reed, John F. *Campaign to Valley Forge, July 1, 1777-December 19, 1777*. Philadelphia: University of Pennsylvania Press, 1965.

Royster, Charles Charles Royster, *Light Horse Harry Lee and the Legacy of the American Revolution*. Baton Rouge: Louisiana State University Press, 1981.

_____*A Revolutionary People at War The Continental*

Army and American   Character, 1775-1783. Chapel Hill: University of North Carolina Press, 1979.

Schneider, Elena A. *The Occupation of Havana: War, Trade, and Slavery in the Atlantic World.* Chapel Hill: UNC Press, 2018.

Seymour, Joseph *The Pennsylvania Associators, 1747-1777.* Yardley, PA: Westholme Publishing, 2012.

Seymour, William *The Price of Folly: British Blunders in the War of American Independence.* London: Brassey's, 1995.

Sharpe, Philip B. *The Rifle in America.* New York: William Morrow and Company, 1938.

Smith, David *William Howe and the American War of Independence.* London: Bloomsbury, 2015.

Smith, Robert F. *Manufacturing Independence: Industrial Innovation in the American Revolution.* Yardley, PA: Westholme Press, 2016.

Smith, Samuel S. *Fight for the Delaware, 1777.* Monmouth Beach, NJ: Philip Freneau Press, 1970.

Snow, Dean *1777: Tipping Point at Saratoga.* New York: Oxford University press, 2016.

Spring, Matthew H. *With Zeal and With Bayonets Only: The British Army in North America, 1775-1783.* Norman, OK: University of Oklahoma Press, 2008.

Stempel, Jim *Valley Forge to Monmouth: Six Transformative Months of the American Revolution.* Jefferson, N.C.: MacFarland& Company, Inc, 2021.

Stone, Edwin Martin *The Invasion of Canada in 1775 including the Journal of Captain Simeon Thayer describing the Perils and Sufferings of the Army under Benedict Arnold.* Providence, RI; Knowles, Anthony and Company, Printer, 1867.

Storozynski, Alex *The Peasant Prince: Thaddeus Kosciuszko and the Age of Revolution.* New York: St. Martin's Press, 2009.

Stryker, William S. *The Battles of Trenton and Princeton.* Trenton, NJ: The Old Barracks Association, 2001 reprint of 1898 orig.

Sullivan, Aaron *The Disaffected: Britain's Occupation of Philadelphia During the American Revolution.* Philadelphia: University of Pennsylvania Press, 2019.

Syrett, David *The Royal Navy in American Waters 1775-1783.* Aldershot, UK: Scolar Press, 1989.

_____ *Admiral Lord Howe: A Biography*. Annapolis: Naval Institute Press, 2006.

Taaffe, Stephen R. *The Philadelphia Campaign, 1777-1778*. Lawrence: University of Kansas Press, 2003.

Ward, Christopher *The War of the Revolution*. 2 vols. Old Saybrook, CT: Konecky & Konecky, 1952.

Webster, John C. *The Life of John Montresor*. Ottawa: Royal Society of Canada, 1928.

Weigley, Russell F. ed. *Philadelphia: A 300 Year History*. New York: W.W. Norton & Company, 1982.

_____ *The Age of Battles: The Quest for Decisive Warfare from Breitenfeld to Waterloo*. Bloomington: Indiana University Press, 1991.

Welch, Richard F. *General Washington's Commando: Benjamin Tallmadge in the Revolutionary War*. Jefferson, North Carolina: McFarland and Company, Inc., Publishers, 2014.

Williams, Catherine R. *Biography of Revolutionary Heroes: Containing the Life of Brigadier General William Barton, and also, of Captain Stephen Olney*. Providence, RI: Privately Printed, 1839.

Willis, Sam *The Struggle for Sea Power: A Naval History of the American Revolution*. New York: W.W. Norton and Company, 2015.

Wilson, David K. *The Southern Strategy: Britain's Conquest of South Carolina and Georgia, 1775-1780*. Columbia, SC: University of South Carolina Press, 2005.

Wilson, Peter H. *War, State and Society in Württemberg, 1677-1793*. Cambridge: Cambridge University Press, 1995.

Wright, Robert K. *The Continental Army*. Washington, DC: Center of Military History, United States Army, 1989.

Wood, W.J. *Battle of the Revolutionary War, 1775-1781*. New York: De Capo Press, 1995.

Articles:

Balderston, Marion "Lord Howe Clears the Delaware." in *PMHB* 96 (1972): 326-45.

Barker, Thomas M. and Thomas M. Huey, "Military Jägers, Their Civilian background and Weaponry." in *The Hessians: The Journal of the Johannes Schwalm Historical Association.* 15 (2012) 1-15.

Black, Jeremy "British Military Strategy." in Donald Stoker, Kenneth J. Hagen and Michael T. Mc Master, eds, *Strategy in the American War of Independence,* London, Routledge, 2010.

Brackenridge, Hugh M. ed. "The Siege of Fort Mifflin." in *PMHB* 11(1887): 82-88.

Bellas, Henry H. "The Defenses of the Delaware in the Revolution." *Wyoming Historical and Geological Society Proceedings and Collections.* Vol. 5 (1900): 47-73.

Fyers, Evan W.H. "General William Howe's Operations in Pennsylvania, 1777." in *Journal of the Society for Army Historical Research.* 8 (October 1929): 228-241, 9 (January 1930): 27-42.

Guttridge, George H. "Lord George Germain in Office, 1775-1782." in *American Historical Review.* 33, 1(October 1927): 23-43.

Goodrich, Francis L.D. "John Montresor, 1736-1799, Engineer and Cartographer." in *Michigan Alumnus Quarterly Review.* 64 (1988): 124-129.

Hall, John W. "'My Favorite Officer' George Washington's Apprentice, Nathanael Greene." in Robert M.S. McDonald, ed. *Sons of the Father: George Washington's and his Proteges.* Charlottesville, VA: University of Virginia Press, 2013, 149-68.

Hitchcock, Dan. "So Few the Brave (The Second Rhode Island 1777-1781)." in *Military Collector & Historian,* 30 (Spring, 1978): 18-22.

Jordan, John "Biographical Sketch of Colonel Thomas Hartley of the Pennsylvania Line." in *PMHB* 25 (1901): 303-6.

Kellogg, Louise Phelps "Journal of a British Officer during the American Revolution." in *The Mississippi Valley Historical Review.* 7, 1(June 1920): 51-58.

Larabee, Leonard W. "Benjamin Franklin and the Defense of Pennsylvania, 1754-1757." in *Pennsylvania History* 29 (1962); 7-23.

Leach, Josiah G. "Commodore John Hazelwood, Commander of the Pennsylvania Navy in the Revolution." in *PMHB,* 26, 1 (1902): 1-6.

Liggett, Barbara and Sandra Laumark "The Counterfort at Fort Mifflin" in *Bulletin of the Association for Preservation Technology.* 11, 1 (1979): 37-74.

Mc Intyre, James R. "On the Origins and Development of the Pennsylvania-American Longrifle, 1500-1700." in *Seven Years War Association Journal*. Vol. 14, no.1 Fall, 2005, 40-55.

Mervine, William M. "Excerpts from the Master's Log of His Majesty's ship eagle, Lord Howe's Flagship, 1776-1777." in *PMBH* 38 (1914): 211-226.

Moomaw W.H. "The Denouement of General Howe's Campaign of 1777." in *English Historical Review* 79 (1964).

Nead, Benjamin M. "A Sketch of General Thomas Proctor, with Some Account of the First Pennsylvania Artillery in the Revolution." in *PMHB* 4,4 (1880):454-470.

Oaks, Robert F. "Philadelphia Merchants and the First Continental Congress." in *Pennsylvania History: A Journal of Mid-Atlantic Studies*. 40, 2 (April 1973): 148-166.

Papenfuse, Edward C. and Gregory A. Stiverson, "General Smallwood's Recruits: The Peacetime Career of the Revolutionary War Private." in *WMQ* 1,1 (1973): 117-132.

Presser, Carl *Die Soldatenhandel in Hessen*. Marburg: R.G. Einwert, 1900.

Putman, Tyler Rudd "'Darkened by Tides and Time': The History and Material Culture of His Majesty's Ship *Augusta*." in *Military Collector and Historian* 66, 2 (Summer 2014): 110-124.

Rankin, Hugh F. "The Moore's Creek Bridge Campaign, 1776." in *North Carolina Historical Review*, 30 (1953): 23-60.

Raymond, Marcius S. "Colonel Christopher Greene." *Magazine of History, with Notes and Queries*. (September/October, 1916): 138-49.

Raudzens, George "War-Winning Weapons: The Measurement of Technological Determinism in Military History." in *The Journal of Military History* volume 54, number 4 (October 1990): 403-33.

Reichmann, Felix "The Pennsylvania Rifle: A Social Interpretation of Changing Military Techniques." In *The Pennsylvania Magazine of History and Biography*. Vol 69, no.1 (January 1945): 3-14.

Retzer, Henry, and Donald Landahl-Smidt "The Philadelphia Campaign 1777-78: Letters and Reports from the von Jungkenn Papers, Part I." in *Journal of the Johannes Schwalm Historical Association* 6, no.2 (1998)

Sellers, Nicholas "Lieutenant Colonel Samuel Smith: Defender of Fort Mifflin, 1777." *Cincinnati 14 Newsletter of the Society of the*

Cincinnati. 31,1 (October 1994): 17-23.

Smith, Samuel "The Papers of General Samuel Smith." in The Historical Magazine, 2nd Series, 7, 2 (February 1870):81-92

Stoker, Donald and Michael W. Jones "Colonial Military Strategy," in *Strategy in the American War of Independence.* Donald Stoker, Kenneth J. Hagan and Michael T. McMasters, eds. London: Routledge, 2010: 5-34.

Stone, Edwin M. "The Invasion of Canada in 1775: Including the Journal of Captain Simeon Thayer." in *Collections of the Rhode Island Historical Society,* IV (1867): 70-79.

Störkel, Arno "The Anspach Jägers." *The Hessians: Journal of the Johannes Schwalm Historical Association.* 14 (2011): 1-31.

Syrett, David "The British Landing at Havana: An Example of an Eighteenth Century Combined Operation." in *The Mariner's Mirror.* 55, (1969): 325-332.

_____ "The Methodology of British Amphibious Operations during the Seven Years' War" in *The Mariner's Mirror.* 58, (1972): 269-280.

_____ "H.M. Armed Ship Vigilant, 1777-1780." in *The Mariner's Mirror.* 64,1 (1978): 57-62.

Urwin, Gregory J.W. "The Continental Light Dragoons, 1776-1783." in Jim Piecuch ed. *Cavalry of the American Revolution.* Yardley, PA: Westholme Press, 2014

_____ "To Bring the American Army under strict Discipline': British Army Foraging Policy in the South, 1780-81." in *War in History* 26, 1 (January 2019): 4-26.

Vivian, Frances "A Defence of Sir William Howe with a new Interpretation of his Action in New Jersey, June 1777." in *JSAHR*, 44, 178 (June 1966): 69-83.

Wiener, Frederick Bernays "The Military Occupation of Philadelphia in 1777-1778." In *Proceedings of the American Philosophical Society.* 111, 5 (October 16, 1967): 310-313.

Wilson, Peter H. "The German "Soldier Trade' of the Seventeenth and Eighteenth Centuries: A Reassessment." *The International History Review.* 18, 4 (November 1996): 757-792.

Wright, Robert K. "A Crisis of Faith: Three Defeats that Cost a Reputation." in *The Hessians: Journal of the Johannes Schwalm Historical Association.* 21 (2018): 45-69.

_____ "British Employment of German Troops in the War of American Independence: Use or Misuse?" in *The Hessians: Journal of the Johannes Schwalm Historical Association.* 20 (2017): 19-43.

Pamphlets and Papers:

Unpublished:

Carpenter, Stanley D. M. "British Strategic Failure in the Southern Campaign, 1778-81." U. S. Naval War College Paper, 2008.

McLeod, Toby "British Amphibious Operations in the American War of Independence, 1775-1783." MA thesis, University of Birmingham, 2008.

Published:

Anonymous *How Fort Mifflin Saved America During the Revolutionary War*. Private Published, 2012.

Olton, Charles S. *The Perplexing Interlude" Washington's Defensive Strategy in 1777*. Schenectady, NY: Friends of the Union College Library, 1971.

Stewart, Frank H. *History of the Battle of Red Bank with Events Prior and Subsequent thereto*. Woodbury, NJ: Board of Freeholders of Gloucester County, 1927.

Strittmatter, Isidor Paul *The Importance of the Campaign in the Delaware*...Philadelphia: The Medical Club of Philadelphia, 1932.

Stryker, William S. *The Forts on the Delaware in the Revolutionary War*. Trenton, NJ: John L. Murphy Publishing Co., 1901.

Online Sources:

Witting, Nicole and Lawrence E. Babits "A Mnemonic Artifact: A 1777 Cheval de Frise from the Delaware River Battlefield." Online source: https://www.academia.edu/9354605/A_Mnemonic_Artifact A 1777 Cheval de Frise from the Delaware River Battlefield Last accessed, 4/20/15.

Unpublished Conference Papers:

Mc Intyre James R. "Oh, What a Tangled Web We Weave, When First We Practice to Recruit." Unpublished paper presented at 75th Annual Meeting of the Society for Military History, Ogden, Utah, April 19, 2008.

Palmer, Jason "Dutch" "For Cause and Family in the American Revolution." Unpublished paper presented at 75th Annual Meeting of the Society for Military History, Ogden, Utah, April 18, 2008.

Outten, Andrew "'Destruction & Wanton Waste': The Impact of War in a Peaceful Valley.

Unpublished paper presented at the Seventeenth Annual Fort Ticonderoga Seminar on the American Revolution. Fort Ticonderoga, New York: September 26, 2021.

INDEX

Adams, John 184, 193n.117, 172.

Adams, Samuel 275, 303n.61.

Alexander, Charles 67, 121.

André, Major John 123, 147n.17; 241, 249, 256n.52; 258n.91; 299.

Andrea Doria 292

Angell, Israel 133, 144, 147n.3, 169, 189n.56, 234, 255n.20, 281, 292, 295, 321.

Anson, Admiral George 88.

Anspach Jägers 107, 115 n. 80; 165, 281, 300, 307 n. 170.

Arendt, Baron d', Colonel 157-58, 197, 202-3, 207, 209, 223n.4, 225n.56, 230, 238, 245, 317, 321.

Army of Observation 239.

Arnold 68.

Artillery 35-8, 43, 45-6 n.8, 51, n.95-96; 56-58, 64, 65, 82, 96, 100, 109, 111 n.19, 114, n. 65-6, 120-1, 125, 132, 135-6, 138-40, 143, 150 n.89, 159, 163-5, 170, 175, 177-8, 181, 195-96, 198, 204, 214, 223, 234, 237, 241, 250, 253, 263, 272, 281, 293, 311, 322, 324, 327, 331, 334, 338

  Uses of 35, 45-6 n.8, 96

  Fourth Continental 36

Assunkpink Creek, battle of 81.

Augusta, HMS 177-85, 195-6, 198-9, 212, 214, 237, 311, 315, 338.

Ballard, Lt. Col. Robert 120, 179-80, 192 n. 98.

Ballard, Maj. 140, 263.

Barry, Captain John 62, 71, 79 n.82, 211, 226 n.74.

Bellew, Henry Capt.67, 206, 225, n.48-49, 226, n.87.

Belton, John 40, 52 n.123-24.

Bethlehem 244, 273.

Betsy 67, 70.

Biddle, Edward 47, n. 26.

Biddle, James 58

Biddle, Nicholas 33,

Biddle, Owen 24, 35, 40, 47 n.26, 58, 62-63, 66.

Big Timber Creek 127, 284, 289.

Billings Island 125, 208

Billingsport, Fort at 11-12, 28, 55, 57 59, 82-83, 85-86, 124-30, 132, 134, 143, 154, 170, 179, 199, 200, 206, 211-12, 214, 218, 220, 225 n.48, 57, 226 n. 82, 227 n.93, 97, 99, 103; 233, 255 n. 27, 257 n. 84, 267-8, 281, 284, 289, 291, 293, 297.

Blewer, John 144.

Board of War 82, 144, 279.

Bombay Hook 67.

Boston 15 n.2, 9, 20, 22-3, 43, 55, 74-75, 88, 90-91, 131, 133, 239, 263, 312.

Bradford, Colonel William 126-28, 130-32, 140-42, 148 n. 34, 39, 149 n. 55, 57, 59; 151 n. 97,99, 107, 112; 199, 223 n.11, 263, 301 n. 12,

Brandywine, Battle of 13, 45 n. 2, 50 n. 88, 81, 96-98, 108-9, 115, 117

n. 113, 114, 119, 120, 127, 145, 185, 192 n. 99, 270, 276-77, 288, 305 n.115, 310, 316, 325, 330.

Brig 30, 62, 67, 70, 104, 129, 132, 139, 218-19, 235, 241, 291-92, 293.

Bristol, PA 161, 280, 290, 292.

Britton, John 73.

Brown, Nicholas 238, 256 n.39, 40.

Bull, Colonel John 38, 82, 84.

Burgoyne, John 88, 90, 99, 117 n. 111, 124, 137, 154, 249, 279, 283 295, 309-10.

Burke, Thomas 275.

Burlington, New Jersey 156, 201, 292-94.

Bush Island 84, 125, 232.

Cadwalader, Jonathan 47 n. 26, 63, 244.

Caldwell, Andrew 56, 59, 61.

Cape Henlopen 39, 60, 74.

Cape May County, NJ, 163.

Cape May County Militia 160.

Carpenters Island 140, 143, 209, 211, 213, 217, 228 n. 122, 230, 240, 249.

Cavalry 25, 100, 213, 287, 298, 329, 334, 339.

   types and roles of 96-7 112-13 n.43; 114, n. 67-68; 116 n. 85.

Chamberlain, Edward 34.

Chandler, Col. 242, 295.

Cheltenham Township 163.

Chester, Pennsylvania 29, 39-40,

42, 48 n. 28, 67, 123, 125, 130, 132, 208-9, 225 n. 65, 228 n. 114, 272, 281-82, 297, 302 n. 33,

Chesapeake Bay 103, 106-7, 120.

Chevaux de Frise (also chevaux de fries, chevaux de freez) 11, 25-9, 34, 39-43, 48 n. 41, 47; 49 n. 51, 55, 59, 61-64, 68, 85, 85, 128, 130-31, 143, 155, 157, 159, 181, 183, 195, 209, 213, 220, 222, 237, 249, 253, 264, 269, 281, 284.

Christiana River (see also Wilmington Creek) 67.

Clark, Maj. John 172, 190 n. 74.

Clark, Joseph 183, 192 n. 113, 321.

Cleaveland, General Samuel, also given as Cleveland 121, 143, 154, 196, 223 n.3.

Clinton, George 173, 190 n. 77.

Clinton, Sir Henry 88, 147 n. 17; 256 n. 52; 309, 321.

Clymer, George 40-41, 43, 55, 59, 62-64.

Coburn, John 60.

Committee of Safety 24, 27-30, 32-43, 47 n. 26-27; 48 n. 29, 32, 38, 40; 49 n.47-49, 52-53, 56-9; 50 n. 70-74, 77-79, 90-1; 51 n. 94, 97, 103-6, 110; 52 n. 114, 118-19, 123-29, 132-34, 139; 55-57, 59, 61-64, 66-67, 71.

Concord, skirmish at 23, 88.

Continental Army 38, 41, 51 n. 111; 75, 87-88, 91, 93-94, 99-100, 102, 113 n.56; 114 n. 70; 116 n. 81; 131, 133-5, 144, 145, 157-8, 172, 183, 200, 207, 225 n. 62; 240, 273-74, 277-79,

283, 286, 289, 298-8, 309-10, 336.

Regiments:

Fourth Connecticut 238.

Second Rhode Island 133-4, 169, 171, 234, 238, 240, 337.

Seventh Massachusetts 252.

Continental Congress 22-24, 35, 41-3, 55-56, 74-75, 85, 87, 94, 99, 122, 144, 184-85, 192 n. 115; 214, 221, 227 n. 91; 267, 275, 277, 280, 296, 299, 300, 307 n.168; 309-11,

Continental Navy 34, 64, 94, 205, 211, 214, 218, 221, 226 n. 74; 228 n.116, 132; 290, 314, 333.

Conway Cabal 226 n.70; 271, 276, 280, 288.

Conway, Thomas 276-77.

Cooch's Bridge, skirmish at 108-9.

Cook, Captain 135-6.

Cornwallis, General Earl Charles 12, 100, 108, 110, 119, 120, 249, 281-2, 290-92, 294, 296-97, 299.

Cornwallis, Captain William, R.N. 182, 192 n. 110; 198-99, 206-7, 216, 218, 223 n. 9, 13; 225 n. 48-9, 57; 226 n.69; 227 n.93, 99, 103; 228 n. 113-14; 235, 255 n. 27; 268, 301 n.6; 302 n. 33.

Cornwallis, HMS 117, 214, 216, 237, 239, 243, 249.

Coudray, Philippe Charles Trouson du 46 n.19; 85-6; 11 n.19, 112 n. 21; 125, 145, 148 n. 25.

Craig, Captain Charles 249, 258 n. 89; 281-82, 284, 304 n. 83, 95.

Crooked Billet, PA 283.

Cuthbert, Thomas 73.

David, Ebenezer 238.

David, Thomas 24.

Davis, Lewis 282, 304 n. 85

Davis, Captain William 38,

Delaware Bay 11, 29, 31, 39, 41, 48 n.32; 49 n. 51; 60, 64-67, 69, 72, 103, 104-6; 11 n.8; 120, 122, 208, 331.

Delaware River 7, 9-14, 18-9, 24-6, 29, 32-4, 38, 42-43, 45 n. 7; 48 n. 43; 55-56, 62, 82, 85-6, 103, 110, 120-21, 123-24, 129, 131, 137, 155, 159, 160-1, 170, 183, 186, 196, 214, 226 n.69, 87; 236, 263, 276, 287, 299, 301 n. 12; 309-12, 313, 318, 326, 327,

Donaldson, Arthur R. 25, 48 n.38; 60.

Donop, Colonel Count Carl Emil von 12, 156, 158-59, 160-1, 162-3, 165, 168, 169-71, 173, 174-78, 183, 184, 185-6, 187 n.9; 188 n. 35; 189 n. 41, 315, 322, 326.

Dougherty, Captain Henry 33 56, 68, 70-2.

Downman, Captain-Lieutenant Francis 121-22, 139-41, 150 n. 89, 91, 94; 151 n. 100, 105, 111; 214-15, 217, 220, 227 n. 95, 101; 228 n. 124; 240, 243, 256 n. 48, 50; 257 n. 59, 62, 66; 262, 281, 283, 284, 289, 301 n.8; 304 n.81, 93; 305 n. 124; 322.

Duane, James 275, 303 n.57, 58.

Duncan, Captain Henry 132, 149 n. 60; 209.

Easton, PA 244, 273.

Elmer, Ebenezer 322.

Ewald, Captain Johann 81, 108, 111 n. 2,3; 117 n. 112; 160, 163, 166, 189 n. 43; 322, 333.

Experiment (Pennsylvania vessel) 33. (HMS) 240, 256, n. 46.

Eyres, Emmanuel 24.

Fabian Strategy 75, 85, 94, 113 n. 57; 286, 305 n. 105.

Falconer, Captain Nathaniel 60-1.

Feilitzsch, Chaplin, Anspach Jägers 165, 307 n. 170.

Fire rafts 31-2, 34, 43, 63, 65, 73, 104-5, 143-4, 180, 219, 263.

Fisher, Felix 134, 137, 160-1.

Fisher, Henry 39, 42, 52, n. 132; 67.

Floating batteries 43, 64, 86, 104-5, 125, 140, 142, 174, 195, 208, 211-12, 213, 218-9, 220, 222, 243, 249, 281, 292.

Fleury Major Francois 145-6, 151 n. 125; 155, 156-57, 161, 179, 187 n. 6, 12; 189 n. 37; 191 n. 97; 201, 202-3, 204, 208, 212, 221, 224 n. 21; 226 n. 79, 81; 230-31, 234, 236-37, 239-40, 244-7, 251, 253, 255 n. 22, 24; 256 n. 32, 45; 257 n. 67, 69, 73, 76; 261, 326.

Forman, General David 200, 223 n. 17268, 302 n. 32.

Fox, Joseph, Barracks Master 37.

Franklin, Benjamin 24, 27, 40, 44, 46 n. 22; 47 n. 26; 48-49 n. 47; 53 n. 145; 124, 147 n. 20; 179, 331, 337.

Franklin 33.

Gage General Thomas 19-20, 22, 23 88.

Galley 31-2, 36, 49 n. 62; 70, 71, 121, 157, 177, 205, 213-14, 216, 224 n.42; 225 n. 52; 249, 267.

Galloway, Joseph 23, 46-47 n. 22; 93, 110, 329.

Germain, George 90-3, 102, 112-13 n.43; 174, 191 n.83; 313, 323, 337.

Germantown 6, 179, 191 n. 79; 230.

Battle of 11, 13, 116 n. 93; 117 n. 115; 129, 130, 145, 147 n.6, 10, 11; 147 n. 28, 29, 31; 185, 192 n. 99; 203, 212, 263, 270, 277, 302 n. 52; 310, 315, 316, 331.

Gerry, Elbridge 184, 193 n. 118, 276, 303 n. 63, 315, 319 n. 19.

Gill, John 161.

Gloucester, New Jersey, See also Gloucester Point 121, 289, 292.

Glover, Brigadier General John 283, 298-304 n. 89; 328

Gray, George 37, 40, 47 n. 26;

Greene, Colonel Christopher 133-37, 144, 149 n. 66; 150 n. 71, 80-82; 151 n. 117; 160-2, 168, 171-3, 179, 184, 190 n. 73; 203, 214, 238, 244, 252, 258 n. 98; 263, 267, 269, 284, 289, 290, 291-92, 295, 302 n. 38-39, 41; 322, 330, 338.

Greene, Major General Nathanael 111-12 n. 119; 125, 130, 133, 148 n.

26; 244, 245247, 257 n. 82; 279, 283, 285, 292-9, 304 n. 96-97; 306 n. 141-43, 146-49, 157-59; 317, 325, 330, 337.

Govett, Joseph 24, 28.

Guard Boat 32, 128.

Haddonfield, NJ 283-4, 288, 294, 298, 304 n. 96-97; 305 n. 118-20, 129.

Hall, Col Josias Carvil 119.

Hamilton, Alexander 155, 179, 187 n. 6; 201, 202, 224 n. 21.

Hamilton, John 33.

Hamond, Captain Andrew Snape 62, 66-67, 69-71, 103-5, 116 n.96-7; 120, 129, 144, 178, 235, 255 n. 27; 323.

Harlem Heights, battle of 75, 119, 156.

Hartley, Colonel Thomas 180, 192 n. 99-100; 337.

Hartnett, Cornelius 275, 303 n. 59-60.

Harvie, John 184, 193 n. 116;

Hazelwood, John 32-3, 43, 49-50 n. 67; 65, 84, 121, 133, 138-40, 143-44, 151 n. 97-98; 156-58, 164-65, 174, 178-80, 183, 188 n.22; 192 n.114; 199, 202, 204-6, 208, 209, 211-19, 224 n. 42-3; 225 n. 52, 54, 56; 226 n. 71, 84-5; 323, 235, 237-9, 243, 247, 249, 257 n.64; 263-5, 267, 284, 290, 293, 299, 314, 315-16, 337.

Hessians, see also Subsidy Troops 79 n.96; 115 n. 77; 115-6 n.80; 116 n.93; 142-43, 156, 158, 160-65, 168-70, 172-73, 176, 184, 187 n. 9-10; 188 n.26, 29; 189 n.36, 44; 190 n.70,

76; 193 n. 121; 298, 317, 321, 323, 324, 327, 337, 339, 340.

Hillegas, Michael 55.

Hornet 65.

Howe, Admiral Richard 12, 88-89, 103-7, 112 n. 38; 113 n.44-53; 116 n.94; 120, 122-23, 132, 145, 147 n.4; 151 n.111; 158, 175, 182, 195, 198, 199, 205, 207, 208, 212-13, 218, 223 n.9; 225 n.57, 99; 258 n.113-14; 230, 240, 249, 281, 302, n. 33-34; 311, 323, 324, 327, 330, 336, 338.

Howe, Robert 183.

Howe, General William 9, 11-3, 46-6 n.22; 74, 85, 86-9, 90-3, 94, 95, 98, 101-7, 108-10, 112 n.31, 35, 39-42; 113 n.44-53; 116 n.92, 98, 100-4; 117 n. 111; 120, 122-24, 125, 131, 1238, 139, 147 n.4; 147 n.17; 154, 155, 158, 159, 174-7, 182, 185, 187 n.2; 191 n.83, 88-9; 192 n.110, 112, 115; 195, 198, 200, 216, 220, 240, 242, 246, 249, 268, 273-74, 280-1, 287-88, 299, 300, 305 n.115; 309-10, 311-13, 319 n.9-11; 321, 323, 324, 325, 327, 330, 335, 337, 338, 339.

Howell, Samuel 41, 43, 62-4.

Hulk 33, 73, 133, 204, 212, 249, 264.

Independence Hall 23.

Iron Hill, skirmish at 108.

Isis, HMS 198-99, 206, 207, 214, 215, 216-17, 218, 223 n. 9-10, 13; 225 n. 49, 57; 227 n. 93, 96, 99; 235, 239, 243, 249, 255 n.27; 261,

268, 301 n.6.

Jefferson, Thomas 184, 193 n. 116.

Joy, Captain 57.

Knox, Major General Henry 111 n.19, 135, 254, 259 n. 112; 263-4, 274, 282, 285, 334.

Ladd's Cove 284, 289, 290, 292.

Lafayette, Marquis de 298.

Lamb, Colonel John 254, 259 n.112.

Lancaster, PA 192 n. 114; 274.

Laurens, Henry 192 n. 115; 221, 270, 272, 274, 296, 302 42, 45-6, 53; 306 n. 153.

Laurens, John 183, 252, 253 n.101, 104; 323.

Lee, Capt. James 214, 245

Lee, Colonel Henry "Light Horse Harry" 202, 209, 213, 220, 224 n. 31; 225 n. 65 226 n.88; 228 n. 122; 233, 255 n.11, 14, 16; 256 n.44; 275, 295, 303 n.61; 313, 314, 319 n.7, 14; 323, 328, 334.

Lengerke, Regiment von 159, 165,

Lewes, DE 39, 67.

Lexington, skirmish at 23, 88, 131, 133, 239, 328.

Lexington brig, 62, 65, 71.

Liberty Island 43, 57.

Linsing, Regiment von 159, 165, 170.

Linzee, Captain John 129, 148 n.43, 46; 216, 226 n.69, 82; 227 n. 97, 103

Liverpool HMS 65, 66,67-68, 70-71, 143, 157, 177, 184, 198, 206, 213,

225 n.48; 226 n.87; 243.

Long Island 109, 196

battle of 75, 119, 156, 304 n.89.

Lovell, James 275, 303 n. 62.

Loyalists 19, 31, 74-5, 91, 93, 110, 161, 163, 327, 329.

Manto Creek, NJ 214, 215, 216, 220, 265-66, 289, 291.

Marcus Hook, PA 40, 42, 67, 127.

Marsh, Joseph 24.

Massey, Capt. Samuel 126, 149 n.59.

Maxwell, William 108.

McNeal, John; 192 n.111

Mease, James 63, 64.

Mercer, Fort 7, 12, 26, 45 n.3, 7; 46 n.16; 48 n.32, 46-7; 49 n. 50-51, 61, 63, 66; 50 n. 68, 81, 84. 51 n. 102; 52 n. 115-16, 76 n.2; 78 n.56, 66, 68, 70-1, 73; 79 n.83, 92, 82, 84, 86, 111 n.6; 116 n. 105; 117 n.110; 122, 125, 133, 135-8, 147 n.22; 148 n.23; 149 n.67; 150 n.69, 75, 77; 155-6, 158-9, 161-5, 167, 171-2, 175, 176-78, 182, 183-86; 188 n. 26, 28-9, 35; 189 n.36, 41, 48; 190 n. 63, 91; 193 n. 130; 195, 200, 202, 207, 215, 219, 224 n.33; 227 n.98; 234, 237, 238-9, 252, 253, 259 n.110; 264, 268, 269, 280-82, 284-85, 289, 291-93, 294, 297, 299, 301 n.14; 302 n.35, 38, 41; 303 n. 76-7; 304 n.79, 98; 305 n. 127; 306 n.134, 150; 307 n. 162, 165, 167; 315, 316, 319 n. 18; 323, 326, 327, 328, 331.

Mercer, General Hugh 84.

Merlin, HMS 12, 177, 179-80, 181-85,

195, 196, 198, 199, 209, 214, 311, 315.

Middle Ferry 272, 282.

Mifflin, Fort 6, 7, 12, 45 n. 7; 46 n. 16; 47 n. 25; 48 n. 32, 39, 46; 49 n. 50-1, 61, 63, 66; 50 n. 68, 81, 83-84, 89; 51 n. 98, 102, 109; 52 n. 115-16; 73, 76 n.2; 78 n.56, 66, 68, 70-1, 73; 79 n.83, 92; 86, 111 n.6; 116 n. 105; 117 n. 110; 119, 120, 122, 125, 128-9, 131-3, 137-8, 139-41, 143-5, 147 n. 1-2, 22; 148 n. 34, 41; 149 n. 47, 55, 57, 59, 64; 150 n.93; 151 n.97, 125; 155, 156-62, 168, 172, 177-86; 187 n.6, 12; 189 n. 41, 48; 191 n.91, 97; 192 n.101; 193 n.130; 195-6, 198-204, 207-9, 211-13, 215-21, 223 n. 4; 224 n.20-1, 32-3, 40; 226 n. 78-9, 81, 83; 230-34; 236-49, 251-4, 255 n. 10, 24; 256 n. 45; 259 n. 110; 261-76, 278-81, 283, 287, 289, 296, 299, 301 n.5; 302 n. 43; 303 n. 71, 76-77; 304 n. 79, 98; 305 n. 127; 306 n. 134; 306 n.150; 307 n.162, 165, 167; 311, 313-14, 316, 317-18, 319 n. 14, 18; 321, 326, 329, 331, 337-8, 340.

Mifflin, Thomas 85, 276, 278, 279.

Miles, Samuel 62, 63, 67.

Miller, Jacob 24.

Militia 35, 38, 67, 82-4, 99, 102, 108, 119, 120, 125-7, 129, 130, 134, 135-7, 140, 144, 160, 161, 163, 172, 199, 200-201, 219, 239, 252, 261, 263, 268, 279, 281, 293-95, 297-98.

Mingo Creek 198.

Minnigerode, Remiment von 159, 175.

Molyneux, Thomas Moore 15 n.7; 50 n. 82; 147 n.18; 323.

Moncrief, Captain James 141.

Montgomery, Richard 55

Montgomery 64, 65, 68, 121, 128, 213, 281, 292.

Morgan, Colonel Daniel 279, 283, 295, 297, 298.

Moore, Allen 33.

Moorestown, NJ 161.

Morris, Robert 24, 40, 47 n. 26; 62.

Morris, Samuel 25, 33, 36, 37, 42, 47 n. 26; 57, 64.

Morristown encampment 100.

Morton, Robert 235, 239, 255 n.28-9; 256 n. 42; 323.

Mud Island 20-2, 25, 29, 35-37, 40-41, 104, 130, 132, 138-9, 154, 157, 161, 180, 196, 198, 203, 210, 211, 213, 230, 234-35, 262, 266, 269, 283, 289, 314.

Munchhausen, Friedrich Ernst von 160, 188 n. 29; 324.

Myers, Jacob 58.

Navy Board 144, 205, 211, 221, 226 n.74, 228 n. 132; 295, 306 n.151.

Newcastle, DE, 29, 72, 103, 105, 208.

Newcomb, General Silas 126-27, 130, 134, 148 n.29, 31; 149 n. 67; 268.

Newton Creek 57.

Nesbitt, John Maxwell 34.

Nevil, Thomas 37.

Nicola, Lewis 47-48 n.28; 48 n.29; 119, 324, 24.

Nixon, John 41 62, 63, 65.

Northern Liberties 18.

Orde, Cdr. John 157, 258, n.85.

Ourrey, Capt. 218.

Paine, Thomas 179, 191 n.95-96; 244, 324.

Pakenham, Lt. Edward 161, 189 n.38

Parker, Capt. James 132, 149 n.63; 154, 187 n.3; 249, 253, 258 n.92, 108.

Pearl, HMS 128-9, 148 n. 38, 43, 48; 157, 177, 198, 212, 214-17, 226 n.82; 227 n.97, 100, 103; 249.

Peebles, John 148 n.37; 174, 191 n.81; 198, 200; 223 n.8, 19; 324.

Pennington, Miles 67.

Pennsylvania State Marines 60, 67.

Pest House 37, 39, 58, 66, 132.

Philadelphia 6, 7, 9-13, 15 n.3; 18-20, 22-5, 27-30, 32-3, 35-6, 39, 41-44, 45 n.2-4, 7; 46 n.19; 46-7 n. 22; 47 n. 25, 28; 48 n. 32-3; 49 n. 62; 50 n.88; 52 n.131; 53 n.144; 55-6, 58, 60-2, 64, 65-7, 72, 73, 81, 83, 87, 90-4, 96, 97, 101-6, 110, 113 n.58 115 n.74; 116 n.86, 93; 117 n.113, 115; 119, 120-25, 128-29, 131-2, 137-9, 144, 145, 147 n. 5, 10, 16, 19; 148 n. 25; 154-5, 159-60, 170, 172-3, 181, 185, 187 n.3, 7; 188 n.21; 191 n.83, 89; 195, 199, 200, 104-6, 208-9, 211-12, 214, 216, 218-20, 225 n. 62; 235-6, 241-4, 246, 248, 252, 264, 266, 268-9, 272, 275, 279-84, 286-7, 289-96, 299-300, 302 n.34; 309-13, 315-17, 321, 323, 325, 326, 327, 331, 335, 336.

Philadelphia Associators 19, 33.

Point of the Island 86.

Potter, Brigadier General James 211-12, 226 n.77; 252, 258 n.98-100; 259 n.114; 261.

Princeton 101, 102.

  battle of 79, n 98; 81, 84, 92, 100, 111 n.1;

  119, 124, 329, 335.

Proctor, Francis 38, 51, n. 109.

Proctor, Thomas 36-38, 43, 51 n. 95, 109; 56-8, 338.

Proud, Robert 324.

Providence Island 201, 204, 230, 264, 268.

Province Island 37, 39, 58, 66, 131-2, 138-9, 141, 143, 154, 177, 179, 184, 201, 210, 212, 217, 230, 233, 235, 238, 240-1, 247, 252-53, 268-70, 272.

Rancocas Creek 290, 294-5.

Rage militaire 38, 51 n. 108; 288, 305 n.117.

Read, Thomas 33, 50 n. 69; 78 n.79

Reading, PA 244.

Reed, Joseph 282, 304 n. 85; 314-15, 319 n.17.

Reed, Captain Thomas 60.

Red Bank 6, 12, 57, 60, 82-4, 130, 133-34, 139, 150 n.71-2; 154-5, 157-59, 161-3, 166-7, 169-70, 172-

4, 176, 184-5, 192 n. 98; 195, 200-1, 227 n98; 246, 253, 266, 268-9, 272-4, 276, 282-5, 289, 295-6, 302 n.32; 311, 317, 328.

Reedy Island 56, 60, 67-8, 72, 106.

Reynolds, Capt. Francis 178, 180, 182.

Richards, Capt. William 60-1.

Riflemen 81, 95, 99, 108, 114 n.64; 187 n.9; 231, 283, 295, 298, 328, 331.

Riley, Richard 40, 52 n.120.

Rittenhouse, David 40, 57, 62-3.

Roberdeau, Daniel 25, 33, 47 n.26; 50 n.75; 63

Robertson, Archibald 180, 192 n.103; 324.

Robinson, Ebeneezer 25.

Robinson, Capt. Isaiah 218, 228 n.116; 290.

Roebuck, HMS 61-2, 64-72, 74, 103, 116 n. 96; 125, 129, 142-3, 148 n. 27, 45; 151 n.108, 114, 116; 157, 177-8, 198, 215-6, 227 n.100; 228 n.129; 249.

Rogers, Robert (ranger) 30, 49 n. 57.

Rogers, Lieut, Robert 134, 136, 149 n. 68.

Ross, John 34, 49 n.57, 57.

Royal Navy 11-12 88, 92, 103, 120, 124, 129, 155, 157, 161, 175, 177-8, 195, 214, 235, 239, 264, 284, 309, 311, 315-16, 332, 335.

Russell, Lt. Col. Giles 233, 238-39.

Salem County, NJ 163.

Saratoga Campaign 258 n.90; 273, 304 n.89; 329.

Saunders, John 39.

Shallops 292.

Simmons, Captain Leeson 61.

Simms, Lt. Col. Charles 161-62, 233.

Smallwood, Colonel William 119, 225 n.51, 338.

Smith, Robert 27-8, 48 n.33, 45 48-49 n. 47; 49 n. 49; 57, 59, 82, 334.

Somerset HMS 216, 218, 220, 222, 235, 249, 255 n.27.

Springfield, PA 282.

Stirling, Lt. Col. Thomas 125, 127-30, 148 n. 37.

Supreme Executive Council 180, 206, 225 n. 47.

Thayer, Maj. Simeon 120, 147 n.3; 239, 241-2, 244-5, 247, 251-4, 256 n.44; 257 n.79; 259 n. 112; 261, 264-65, 269, 318, 325, 335, 339.

Ticonderoga, Fort, NY 88

Big Timber Creek, NJ 163, 170, 218, 269, 284, 289, 293, 298.

Bridge over 127, 163, 170-1.

Little Timber Creek 294, 298.

Tinicum Island 84, 143, 182, 243, 258 n.85.

Towers, Robert 33, 36, 41, 50, n.75; 59.

Treat, Captain Samuel 120.

Trenton 156

battle of 79, n.98; 81, 92, 100, 119, 124,

176, 185, 187 n. 11; 304 n. 89; 329, 335.

Valley Forge, PA 6.

Varnum, General James Mitchell 130-1, 133, 149 n. 51; 201-2, 209, 211-13, 215, 216-22, 224 n.23; 225 n.67; 227 n.89, 102, 111-12; 228 n. 115, 117; 233, 235, 238, 241-5, 247, 251, 253, 256 n.36, 39, 57, 257 n.79; 258, n.103, 106; 259 n.111; 261, 263-7, 281-6, 288-94, 301 n. 4, 20-24, 26-7; 304 n.86-88, 99-100; 305 n. 106, 118, 129-30; 306 n.145; 314, 317.

Vigilant, HMS 139, 143-44,150 n.87; 151 n.115; 154, 157, 177-8, 182, 187 n.4, 16, 190 n. 90, 92-3; 201, 240-41, 243-45, 247-49, 251, 257 n. 84; 258 n. 94; 261-63, 265, 267, 271, 301 n.7; 311,313, 339.

Waldo, Dr. Albigence 232, 255 n.7; 289, 298, 305 n.122-23; 307 n. 163, 171; 309, 311, 325.

Wallace, Capt. Sir James 240.

Warren, James 184, 193 n. 118.

Warren Mercy Otis, 276.

Washington, Fort, NY 75, 305 n.101

Washington, George 75, 84-5, 87-8, 90, 93-4, 97, 99-102 106-10, 111-12 n.19; 113 n.56-57; 119, 120, 122, 124-6, 128, 130-35, 137, 138, 140, 144-45, 147 n. 21; 148 n. 26-7; 149 n. 47-8, 52, 93; 151 n.96, 104, 117; 156-58, 161, 172-73, 179, 184, 187 n.3; 188 n. 22-24; 190 n. 73, 74, 77;

192 n. 98, 115; 197, 200-209, 211-22, 223 n.4-6, 17-18; 224 n.23-5, 32, 40-43; 225 n.54-56, 65, 67-8, 226 n.70-73, 77-78, 83-85, 88; 227 n.89, 102, 109, 111; 228 n. 115, 117-22, 128, 131-32; 232-3, 238, 240, 242-47, 249, 252-53, 255 n. 10, 12; 256 n.36,45, 57; 257 n. 64, 82-83; 258 n. 89, 100, 103, 106; 259 n. 111, 114; 261-4, 266-90, 292-3, 295, 299, 301 n. 1-3, 11, 18-24, 26, 27; 302 n. 29-30, 32, 35, 38, 41-2, 45, 46-51, 53-55 303 n. 56; 304 n. 83-89, 95-97, 99; 305 n. 100, 106, 118, 129; 306 n. 138-43, 145-49, 151-59; 309, 310, 314-18, 319 n. 23-4; 321, 328, 330, 332.

Wasp 64, 67, 69-70.

Wayne, Anthony 24, 47 n.26;109, 202, 244, 318.

Westville, NJ 163.

Wharton, Joseph 24.

Wharton, Thomas, Jr. 47 n.26; 128, 131, 140, 142, 148 n.34-36; 149, n.55-59; 151 n.96-99; 180, 183, 192 n.100, 114-15; 206, 263, 301 n.12-13; 315, 319 n.17.

Whitall, Jacob 83, 136, 170-1, 202.

Whitemarsh 173, 178, 219, 242, 29, 263, 289, 299, 331.

Whitpain Township 180, 183, 200, 211.

White Planes, battle of 75, 119.

Whyte, Captain Robert 24, 35-36, 40, 42-3, 58, 62-4, 75.

Wilkinson, William 275, 303 n.59.

Wilmington Creek 70, 78 n.71.

Wilson, Lt. George 121.

Wilson, Sir Thomas 281.

Windmill Island 121-2.

Woodbury, NJ 127.

Woodbury Island 84.

Würmb, Lieutenant Colonel Ludwig Johann Adolph von 159, 165, 176, 191 n.86.

Würmb, Regiment 189 n.51.

York, PA 214, 275, 299.

ABOUT THE AUTHOR

Jim Mc Intyre received his Bachelors in History from Temple University in 1996 and his Masters from the University of Illinois in 1999. His main interest is the American War of Independence, on which he has written numerous articles and papers. He is the author of *The Development of the British Light Infantry, Continental and North American Influences 1740-1765* and *Johann Ewald: Partisan Commander,* as well as editing several other works and articles. He teaches History at Moraine Valley Community College near Chicago, Illinois and serves as a Fleet Professor in the United States Naval War College's College of Distance Education, Strategy and War Department as well.

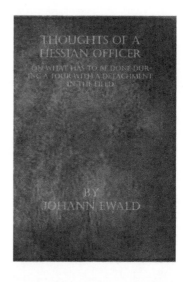

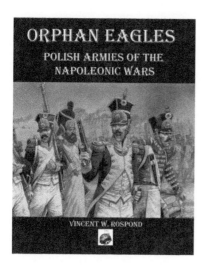

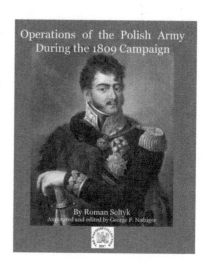

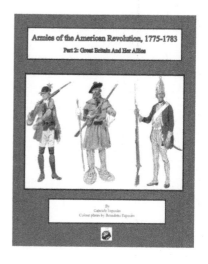